Pynchon's Sound of Music

Christian Hänggi

Pynchon's Sound of Music

DIAPHANES

PUBLISHED WITH SUPPORT BY THE
SWISS NATIONAL SCIENCE FOUNDATION

1ST EDITION

ISBN 978-3-0358-0232-0

LAYOUT AND PREPRESS: 2EDIT, ZURICH
PRINTED IN GERMANY

WWW.DIAPHANES.NET

Contents

Preface

When I first read *Gravity's Rainbow*, back in the days before I started to study literature more systematically, I noticed the novel's many references to saxophones. Having played the instrument for, then, almost two decades, I thought that a novelist would not, could not, feature specialty instruments such as the C-melody sax if he did not play the horn himself. Once the saxophone had caught my attention, I noticed all sorts of uncommon references that seemed to confirm my hunch that Thomas Pynchon himself played the instrument: McClintic Sphere's 4½ reed, the contrabass sax of *Against the Day*, *Gravity's Rainbow*'s Charlie Parker passage. I wondered if there was a way, based solely on the text itself, to prove that Pynchon was or was not a sax player—even an amateur one such as myself. That quest soon faded into the background and became less than interesting to me. However, it did spark my interest in a broader study of music in Pynchon's work. Unable to find a monograph on the topic, I enrolled in the Doctoral Program in Literary Studies at the University of Basel, Switzerland, to write it myself.

In my little world it is hard to imagine anything more fulfilling than to work on music and literature. Without a background in literary studies, I deemed it appropriate to first make myself familiar with the discipline's theories, methods, and styles. Some four or five years later, the work was accomplished. The result is a book that spells out many of the stories that music tells in its various forms and appearances in Pynchon's work, a story that inevitably also includes media and technology, warfare and social struggles, literature and other arts. In a way, what follows is a nonlinear history of music as seen through the lens of Pynchon's writing, a history that radiates outward rather than being streamlined into a central thesis or argument. Thankfully, the topic is not exhausted.

Writing about Pynchon and music broadened my musical horizon immensely. Still, I am unable to play much more than "Hail to the Chief" on the harmonica, occasionally mixing up sucking and blowing, or "Rocky Raccoon" on the ukulele, sometimes taking a short break to rearrange my fingering. I did become a member of the Association of American Kazoologists though and I still try to play the Charlie Parker solos transcribed by Jamie Aebersold.

By the time this book is published, the dissertation as I initially submitted it has produced a number of spin-offs: a commented list of bands, musicians, and record labels inspired by Pynchon's work, currently encompassing about 120 items, published at thomaspynchon.com; a book chapter about Pynchon's harmonica and kazoo published in a volume entitled *America and the Musical Unconscious*; an abbreviated version of the last chapter—a quantitative analysis of Pynchon's 925+ historical musical references including the database—published by *Orbit*; and, most excitingly, an album with interpretations of some of the many songs Pynchon wrote. Having invited my friend, the musician, poet, and high school teacher Tyler Burba, to accompany many of my talks on the East Coast, and after flying him in for a celebration of Pynchon's eightieth birthday at Cabaret Voltaire in Zurich, it was a logical consequence that, once my academic work was accomplished, we should let the music speak for itself. Masterminded by Tyler and produced by me, the album was recorded by Tyler's band Visit and is entitled *"Now Everybody—" Visit Interprets Songs by Thomas Pynchon*. It should be released any moment now.

So it goes. Keep your ears and eyes open for our album. But for now, sit back, relax, and have, as the makers of *South Park* would say, a rootin' tootin' good time with *Pynchon's Sound of Music*!

Introduction

When Penguin announced the upcoming release of Thomas Pynchon's *Inherent Vice* in 2009, they heightened the suspense with two marketing gimmicks. One was a series of short movie trailers with Pynchon providing Doc Sportello's slurred voice. The other one was a playlist of songs that would be mentioned in the novel. The choice of media was fitting since film and music, as readers of Pynchon have long noticed, provide the two most consistently important cultural reference systems for his characters. Music and movie references—much more accessible to the average Pynchon reader than, say, mathematical concepts or the fine points of rocket engineering—have long invited fans and scholars alike to chip in with their insights and interpretations, some of it wild and fascinating speculation, some of it carefully constructed criticism.

Kathryn Hume and Thomas J. Knight, for instance, find significance in "the fact that the two art forms he refers to most frequently are music and cinema, the two that order and manipulate our relationship with the flow of time" ("Orchestration" 381). So does literature, one might add, but literature works with a different conception of time, one that allows the reader to apprehend the work of art at his or her own pace. In 1980, David Cowart noted that a first wave of reception and interpretation of Pynchon's work focused on scientific allusions and references, most notably the concept of entropy, rather than references to the arts. He corrected this bias with his book *Thomas Pynchon: The Art of Allusion* in which he dedicated a chapter each to painting, film, music, and literature. The underlying message of the pictorial and film allusions, according to Cowart, was that "beyond life lies nothing more substantial than a blank white screen, a Void" (9). He observed a similarly bleak picture for the early reception that focused on entropy. He contrasted this with the musical (and literary) allusions: "The musical references seem always to hint at the extra dimensions of experience that we miss because of the narrow range of frequencies—physical or spiritual—to which we are attuned" (9). This pronouncement appears valid, particularly for the first three novels and for Cowart's focus on more erudite, that is, classical and new classical music.

Since the early 1980s, excellent contributions have been made on various aspects of music in Pynchon's work but none of them exceeded the length of an article or a book chapter. John Joseph Hess voices a common sentiment when he writes: "[I]n spite of these important critical accounts of what music Pynchon has used and how he used it, music has remained strangely undertheorized in Pynchon criticism" (2). This study aims to fill this gap and present the first book-length monograph dedicated to cataloging, exploring, and interpreting the musical dimension of Pynchon's work. My argument is that music is the most consistent and most central cultural reference point throughout the author's career of more than fifty years; he writes, to speak with *Mason & Dixon*, "Novels in Musick" (263). Music is of symbolic and structural importance and it helps set the historical frame. It permeates the writing, from basic structural metaphors to its style. And, finally, throughout Pynchon's work there is a strong moral undercurrent, an allegiance to the underdog, a solidarity with the preterite, which makes reactionary readings of his works almost impossible.[1] This moral undercurrent is particularly strong with the way he treats music.

The present study reads some of the most salient passages concerning music and organizes them along different but intertwined trajectories—or pre-texts. Chapter 1 is dedicated to sorting it all out. I follow the convention of many monographs on Pynchon's work by starting with a biography of the author. However, in contrast to the others, I do not provide a general overview based on what little material is out there but limit myself to one aspect of his life, namely music. His *vita* is followed by an inventory of the most important ways in which Pynchon weaves music into his narratives. This catalog may not be exhaustive but it gives a good

1 Pynchon borrows the terms Preterite and Elect—key terms of his *Weltanschauung*—from Calvinist doctrine. When Doomsday comes, so it goes, the Elect—the virtuous and God-fearing—will be saved while the Preterite will be passed over and left behind. Robert J. Lacey writes, "Pynchon celebrates preterition, the act of being disinherited or passed over. In a clever inversion of Calvinist theology, Pynchon suggests that preterites, the forgotten refuse of society, are the fortunate few who have received a kind of grace. They are the blessedly forsaken. Embracing the apolitical, preterites enjoy an invisibility that Pynchon believes is necessary to attain a modicum of freedom in late modernity." Although the Elect can be specific people, the concept of the Elect is perhaps better understood as an impersonal force of corruption by power. In line with Pynchon's frequent spelling, the Elect and the Preterite will be capitalized throughout when used as nouns. For William Slothrop's take on preterition, which seems to coincide with Pynchon's, see *Gravity's Rainbow* 565.

picture of various musical techniques, strategies, and references employed in the service of literature, and it may be a helpful resource for future scholarship.

Chapter 2 takes as a starting point the physical fact that every musical instrument produces sound only because it resists its player. By analogy, one could say that music is born out of resistance, and this is played out in the way a handful of instruments enter Pynchon's stories, in particular the ukulele, the kazoo, the harmonica, and the saxophone. Their respective histories have endowed them with specific material attributes and social uses. They have developed something like personalities that are remarkably consistent throughout Pynchon's work. The kazoo, for instance, is the ultimate Preterite of musicology, neglected, passed over, and so stubbornly subversive that it unsettles the ruling order of the Elect. The harmonica, the blues instrument *par excellence*, can bend the established frequencies but it is not altogether immune to co-optation by forces whose intent is at best shrouded in ambiguity. Still, like the ukulele, which also has a prominent place in Pynchon's heart, these instruments are cheap, relatively easy to learn, and they were mostly seen as instruments for amateur playing, which is why they and their players were not taken seriously by the music establishment. They enjoy the same respect and appreciation that Pynchon gives amateur musicians in general. The saxophone—the instrument of Charlie Parker and Ornette Coleman—also appears to be one of Pynchon's favorites but it has an altogether different history of being alternately promoted and condemned by the ruling classes. Its sexual connotations are widely played upon, as is its struggle against co-optation, the history of drug addicted players, and racial issues connected to black jazz men. A supplement to the second chapter is an index of musical instruments mentioned in Pynchon's work (see Appendix).

Chapter 3 takes its cue from Jacques Attali's widely discussed thesis that the development of music prefigures the organization of society and the distribution of power. There are a number of passages in Pynchon's work, mainly in the novels released after the publication of Attali's essay (1977, English translation 1985), that treat the thesis he adopted and adapted from Plato. Attali provides the framework for the close readings but, as in Chapter 2, the framework mainly serves as an organizing principle from which to branch out into musicological, historical, technological, and even psychological readings. A passage from *Mason & Dixon* serves to elucidate Attali's age of representation in which musicians are employed by the nobility and sing their praises; *Inherent Vice* provides the backdrop for the age of repetition in a mass-producing music industry; and *Bleeding Edge* inspires readings of the age of composition, a hypothetical future of music consumption and production freed from the previous constraints, an age of anarchistic musicianship, so to speak.

While much of Chapters 2 and 3 is dedicated to the detective's (or paranoid's) work of speculating on origins and derivations, listening for resonances and consonances, and discovering patterns, Chapter 4 approaches the subject from a quantitative angle. Based on every reference and allusion to existing musicians and works of music I was able to identify, well over 900 in number, I analyze what I call the Pynchon Playlist in relation to frequency, genres, temporal distribution, gender, and media. Partly as a homage to Pynchon's delectation in itemized lists—shared by many of his readers—I was curious to find out what those statistics would yield and if they confirm or contradict a more general impression the reader receives when working his or her way through the novels. It is an excursion into quantitative methods for literary studies to gauge what they can bring to light that would otherwise remain obscure. As was expected for a relatively low number of items (I do not analyze a corpus of, say, ten thousand or a million books), the interpretation of the results cannot be properly accomplished without having recourse to the singular items and putting them in context with what the perceptive reader already knows. The analysis yielded some expected results. It demonstrates, for instance, that Pynchon's novels can be divided into two groups: the 'maximalist' novels and the 'pop' (or California) novels. Some unexpected results did, however, surface too: as the number of historical music references grows, for instance, the characters become less interested in music as evidenced by a decline in references to live music, musical instruments, and songs penned by Pynchon. This may well be an implicit pronouncement on the effects of a mass-mediated music and consumer industry, namely that it revolves around the consumption and not the production or, better yet, generation of meaning.

Interpreting Pynchon's novels is no easy task. His plots meander and digress. They explore the seemingly most insignificant detail as much as the larger state of the world. They allow for connecting the dots in many different ways and for filling in the missing ones. The readers of his books, not unlike his characters, are hurled into a paranoid quest where ambiguity is the order of the day, where chance does not exist (or does it?), and where every sentence is an invitation to perceive multiple links and layers. Readers may always ask themselves with Oedipa Maas in the closing pages of *The Crying of Lot 49* if they have stumbled onto a secret richness and concealed density of dream—or if the secret is not at all secret and the dream not at all a dream—if something has been placed for them to find, if it is pure happenstance, if it is all an elaborate plot mounted against them to discombobulate the interpreters of signs, or if such a plot is only fantasized—in which case the reader may likely be insane. Or not. While the underlying message is mostly clear, and some of the puns entirely unambiguous, there is a movement of either/or/perhaps/however, a rejection of binaries, an impossibility of decision or, framed perhaps more positively, an aporetic opening. This in itself invites just the kind of readings that Pynchon aficionados do, the kind of work that literary scholars do. And it carries the risk of overinterpretation.

In *Interpretation and Overinterpretation*, Umberto Eco remarked that, "Once the mechanism of analogy has been set in motion there is no guarantee that it will stop. [...] Every time one thinks to have discovered a similarity, it will point to another similarity, in an endless progress" (47). This is precisely the mechanism—for it has something mechanical about it—that fascinates and fazes many readers of Pynchon (or of Jacques Derrida for that matter). While speculation has its place in literary interpretation, it is sometimes a fine line between interpretation—the work of a detective—and overinterpretation—the workings of a paranoiac. Although I have at times knowingly and willingly submitted to the irresistible beauty of what may be only "Kute Korrespondences" (*Gravity* 600), the guidelines I tried to follow were those of St. Augustine, in Eco's words, that "any interpretation given of a certain portion of a text can be accepted if it is confirmed by, and must be rejected if it is challenged by, another portion of the same text" (65). Although many of Pynchon's texts are byzantine and present multiple viewpoints and focalizations, they are never self-contradictory. Instead, they often reveal a fractal quality where minute details are images of the larger picture, and vice versa, and apparent contradictions are only two sides of the same coin. Hence, Eco's or St. Augustine's admonitions are for the most part applicable and may bring some grounding to the work of the literary interpreter irrespective of whether Pynchon placed the allusions, links, and references consciously or whether they were written by the text itself. This is not to say that Pynchon's texts have only one meaning to which everything will conform and fall into place if inspected with due care. Neither does Pynchon's postmodern rejection—for the most part—of binaries mean that anything and everything is plausible.

The range and eclecticism of Pynchon's musical allusions, references, and structural underpinnings can hardly be met with any one interpretive framework, any one literary or philosophical theory if one is to tease out everything they have to offer. The present study therefore employs a range of disciplines to contemplate the musical passages in Pynchon's work: music theory and history; social, political, and media history; philosophy; and literary theory, to name the most important ones. Naturally, the three approaches that were chosen—musical instruments, Attali's thesis, and an analysis of the catalog of musicians and works of music—do not allow everything on the topic to be said, which is why Chapter 1 will consider some aspects that do not easily fit into these approaches and foreshadow what will be treated in more detail later on. In other words, this book does not concern itself much with the question *whether* Pynchon's novels and other assorted writings are cases of musicalized fiction, to use a term Werner Wolf borrowed from Aldous Huxley's *Point Counter Point.* The musical dimension is so evident that I instead intend to show *how* and *to what ends* Pynchon stages music.

My three main approaches all reinforce certain observations. Even when music 'only' serves as a backdrop—the noise of culture, so to speak—and thus introduces an element of realism or verisimilitude, it has much more than just an ornamental function. Pynchon is very careful in his choice of music; there is hardly a name of a musician or a title of a song without good reason for being there. The references always seem to indicate something beyond their immediate signifieds and become parts of a great web of concerns about how the human individual and communities of human beings are to deal with the overbearing power of the military-industrial-technological complex. Music is one of the privileged sites where Pynchon locates pockets of resistance to dehumanized and dehumanizing forces without falling into the trap of a facile instrumentalization of music as an act of counterforce. Music itself—in Pynchon's work in any case—resists such instrumentalization precisely because it is something joyful and playful. He acknowledges this when he refuses to ridicule or denigrate even the most commercially conceived and produced works of music. Like certain drugs, like a certain type of humor, he treats them as means to momentarily escape the darker aspects of the human condition. The exceptions—the "Horst Wessel Lied" or the music of Andrew Lloyd Webber, for instance—do not depart from this stance but illustrate how Pynchon is aware of music's history being co-opted by the forces of the Elect.

Although the goal of this study is to close a significant gap in Pynchon scholarship, I believe it may also be of use for studying the interplays and interfaces between music and literature as such. While each writer of musicalized fiction has different musical and literary interests and deals with the topic in different ways, writers of Pynchon's stature set benchmarks, the study of which will shed new light on writings by other authors.

1

The Job of Sorting It All Out

In the opening lines of *The Crying of Lot 49*, Oedipa Maas famously returns home to find out that she has been named executrix of the estate of Pierce Inverarity with "assets numerous and tangled enough to make the job of sorting it all out more than honorary" (1). By the end of the novel, she is still trying to make sense of it all.

By analogy, the topic of music in Pynchon's work is also tangled enough to make the job of sorting it out more than honorary. To produce an exhaustive list of music's various intersections, interpretations, and interpenetrations of Pynchon's *œuvre* and *vita* can never be exhaustive, but, like Oedipa, one just has to give it a try.

A Brief Biography in Music

In his study of what makes literary fiction musical, Werner Wolf lists different indicators which, if aggregated, make it likely that the reader is dealing with a piece of "musicalized fiction." Somewhat against the grain of what is customary in literary studies these days,[1] he places emphasis on the author's intention to write a piece of musicalized fiction. He also names biographical evidence of music as a circumstantial or contextual indicator (*Musicalization* 73). In this spirit, it seems fitting to offer a brief sketch of Pynchon's life.

Biographical accounts of Pynchon are relatively scarce. Most of them center on the second half of the 1950s and rarely go beyond the marijuana haze of the late 1960s, but it is curious that almost every one hints at the importance music played for the writer. Useful sources for an overview of Pynchon's life are the chronology compiled by Paul Royster and the more detailed *vita* in Cowart's *Thomas Pynchon & The Dark Passages of History*. I will limit myself mainly to the aspects pertaining to music.

---

1 Consider, for instance, Michel Foucault's "What Is an Author?", Roland Barthes's "The Death of the Author," or W.K. Wimsatt and Monroe C. Beardsley's "The Intentional Fallacy."

Thomas Ruggles Pynchon, Jr., was born on May 8, 1937 in Glen Cove, NY. When he was around age four, the family moved to Oyster Bay, NY, where Pynchon graduated from high school in 1953. The first evidence of music dates back to those years: in his "Voice of the Hamster" series of contributions to the high school paper *Purple and Gold* from late 1952 and early 1953, the central character is the trigonometry teacher Mr. Faggiaducci who "used to be a bop drummer" and was "always telling be-bop jokes in class" (157; page number refers to the reproduction in Mead). His name will later resonate with *The Crying of Lot 49*'s Duke of Faggio.

After high school, Pynchon went on to Cornell University to study physics and engineering. At Cornell, he met fellow student Richard Fariña who would later become a folk musician. This appears to be the time when Pynchon was exposed to the Beat Generation and their heroes of the jazz idiom. In the "Introduction" to *Slow Learner,* he writes that he spent a lot of time in jazz clubs such as the Five Spot in New York "nursing the two-beer minimum" (8) and attending some of the trailblazing performances by Ornette Coleman (Witzling, *Everybody's America* 28; Hajdu 47) and the already established Thelonius Monk.

In 1955, he left Cornell to enlist in the U.S. Navy. During his time there he "knew people who would sit in circles on the deck and sing perfectly, in parts, all those early rock'n'roll songs, who played bongos and saxophones, who had felt honest grief when Bird and later Clifford Brown died" (*Learner* 8).

While most memories about Pynchon are written by fellow stoners and only refer to modern jazz and 1960s pop and rock music, literary evidence of Pynchon's exposure to more 'high-brow' music dates back to 1959's "Mortality and Mercy in Vienna" where he mentions the "Trio-Finale" from Charles Gounod's *Faust,* the "Catalogue Aria" from Mozart's *Don Giovanni,* and Béla Bartók's *Concerto for Orchestra,* Sz. 116, BB 123. According to Cowart, much of the exposure to classical music is owed to Pynchon's 1956 romance with Anne Cotton: "Both loved music. A jazz enthusiast, Pynchon took her to various Washington nightclubs for her education. She reciprocated by introducing him to opera on her hi-fi" (*Allusion* 63). The operas Cowart mentions are Puccini's *Madama Butterfly,* Massenet's *Manon*, and Mozart's *Don Giovanni.* While there is no mention of Massenet in Pynchon's work, *Don Giovanni,* Puccini's *Manon Lescaut* and *Madama Butterfly* are among Pynchon's most frequently mentioned works of music. Apparently, Cotton did not like Wagner, but "the author eventually came to know his music intimately" (64). Cowart does not say when this may have been, but Wagner (first mentioned in *V.*), Puccini, and Mozart are also among the most frequently referenced musicians in his work.

In 1957, Pynchon returned to Cornell to major in English. Although rock'n'roll had been around by then, "the formulation Dope/Sex/Rock'n'Roll hadn't yet been made by too many of us," Pynchon writes about 1958 Cornell in his introduction to Fariña's *Been Down So Long It Looks Like Up to Me* (vi). In a largely self-centered account of his times with Pynchon, fellow Cornell student Jules Siegel, in part namesake of the Cleanth Siegel character in "Mortality and Mercy in Vienna," remembers that Pynchon "could carry a tune well and made up ribald parodies of popular songs, which I seem to remember—surely I am imagining this—were accompanied on a ukulele. From the musical notations in the back of T.S. Eliot's *The Cocktail Party,* he puzzled out for me the tune of 'One-Eyed Reilly,' which we sang together one beer-soaked night in joyous disharmony [...]" (85). These memories—possibly somewhat unreliable due in no small part to the use of certain substances—were first published in a *Playboy* article in 1977, entitled "Who Is Thomas Pynchon... And Why Is He Taking Off With My Wife?", later reproduced in *Lineland.* Siegel, too, has memories of the New York City jazz clubs:

> Once he took me down to Greenwich Village to the Cafe Bohemia, where Max Roach was playing. It was the only band I ever heard in which the drums carried the melody. The Modern Jazz Quartet and the Kent Micronite Filter commercial were about as much modern music as I could handle. Pynchon, however, was deeply into the mysteries of Thelonius Monk. On religious grounds, I excused myself from attending chapel with him at the Five Spot to hear "God" play. I was an atheist. (88)

Evidently not much of an admirer of modern jazz, Siegel later writes that this Thelonius Monk anecdote is about as much as he has to say on the topic of Pynchon and jazz (141). He also remembers that Pynchon helped him move when the former was living in Queens, "playing a wastepaper basket as a conga drum in the back of the rented step van" (89).

During his English studies at Cornell, Pynchon and his friend Kirkpatrick Sale started to write a musical called *Minstrel Island.* The notes, outlines, and fragments of this unfinished work were acquired by the Harry Ransom Center at the University of Texas in 2002. The musical is set in the year 1998. The world is dominated by IBM (one of the songs is "Think," the IBM slogan) and artists are to be realigned to a world of machines. Although largely a work of male juvenilia, in subject matter it is reminiscent of Kurt Vonnegut's 1952 debut novel *Player Piano* and it features junkie jazzmen ("I can't con a monkey off a back, man"), sailmakers, prostitutes and a bomb maker, among others, as well as a reference to baritone saxophone player Gerry Mulligan.

After graduating with a B.A. in June 1959, Pynchon applied for a Ford Foundation grant to write opera librettos, intending to turn science fiction stories into a libretto, but the application was turned down. Explaining what he had learned at Cornell in terms of writing, "[Pynchon] compares this writing technique to the line of notes which provides a basis for the chord changes in jazz" (Weisenburger, "Sketch" 695). He admitted to getting goose bumps from cymbal crashes and harp glissandos, and he mentions Mozart, Bizet, Puccini's *Manon Lescaut*, Orff's *Der Mond*, and Stravinsky's *The Rake's Progress*. Two sci-fi novels Pynchon contemplated adapting were Alfred Bester's *The Demolished Man* and Ray Bradbury's *The Martian Chronicles*. After giving evidence of doubting his own lyrical talents, Pynchon wrote, "I have this guitar on which I occasionally kill time by making up rock 'n' roll lyrics" (Kachka, n.pag.) to be played over "one of the two standard chord progressions (i.e., the blues or tonic/related minors/dominant)."

Mathew Winston claims that Pynchon, after graduating from Cornell, "thought about becoming a disc jockey, an interest which emerges in the character of Mucho Maas in *The Crying of Lot 49*" (259–60). Although Winston does not divulge his source, looking at the evidence of Pynchon's love for music, this appears plausible.

By the late 1950s, the times had proceeded into a 'post-Beat' era. Pynchon and his peers were "already getting everything secondhand," and they had to adopt "Beat postures and props" (*Learner* 9). For many poets of the Beat Generation, jazz, and particularly bebop, was, apart from literature and poetry, their single most important cultural reference point. There are well-known passages in *On the Road* and *The Subterraneans*, for instance, where Jack Kerouac describes attending jazz concerts, the most famous one of those passages condensing the history of jazz up to that point into a few lines of prose (*On the Road* 225–26). Although that aspect of their prose, at least when compared to Pynchon's achievements, was less substantial and had more to do with admiration of their favorite jazz players and their own self-indulgence, they likened their writing to the fast-paced music of Bird, Miles, Dizzy. "As bop and rock'n'roll were to swing music and postwar pop," Pynchon writes about Beat literature, "so was this new writing to the more established modernist tradition we were being exposed to then in college" (*Learner* 9). In the field of music, the modernist tradition would find its way into Pynchon's writing with reflections on the works of composers like Stravinsky, Schoenberg, Webern, and, in a different vein, Stockhausen. Pynchon's own writing has been compared to the Beats' by Andrew Gordon: "Kerouac was the cool fifties; he wrote jazz fiction. But Pynchon was of the apocalyptic sixties; he wrote rock and roll" (169).

In 1960, Pynchon moved to Seattle to work for Boeing as a technical writer in nuclear missile programs. Little is known about this time in which he presumably wrote parts of *V.*

A book that offers some insight into Pynchon's affiliation with the music of the 1960s is David Hajdu's *Positively 4th Street: The Lives and Times of Joan Baez, Bob Dylan, Mimi Baez Fariña and Richard Fariña*, for which he was able to 'converse' with Pynchon through the interface of a fax machine. Pynchon was Richard Fariña's best man when he married Mimi Baez, Joan Baez's sister, and he acted as a pallbearer when Fariña died. Hajdu's book also answers the question of whether Pynchon himself is or was an amateur musician: "While he was known to have a few Red Cap ales at Johnny's or pick up a guitar at a party and strum a standard such as Rodgers and Hart's 'I Wish I Were in Love Again,' Pynchon, in contrast to Fariña, was clearly most comfortable in the smallest groups" (45). Their "tastes in music appeared irreconcilable. Pynchon was a fan of jazz, bebop in particular. Fariña, while attracted to the tragic romance he saw in the jazz life, listened to pop radio in the apartment and frequently accompanied his younger schoolmate Peter Yarrow [later of Peter, Paul and Mary] to the Sunday-evening 'sings' at Cornell's Folk Song Society" (46). Pynchon's introduction to Fariña's novel *Been Down So Long It Looks Like Up to Me* may not necessarily reflect his own musical predilections, but he drops a few names he must have been aware of in his college years: Peter Yarrow, Buddy Holly's "Peggy Sue," Mose Allison's "Back Country Suite," and Kurt Weill and Bertold Brecht's *Threepenny Opera.* When Fariña died in 1966, Pynchon first heard about it over an AM rock'n'roll station (xiv).

In 1965, Pynchon suggested to Siegel that he write an article on The Beach Boys. A year later, Pynchon had apparently lost interest in the surf band but that interest was revived when he first listened to *Pet Sounds* (Siegel 90). In 1966 or so, the two went to see Brian Wilson in his house in Bel-Air but Pynchon and Wilson did not exchange any words. Pynchon's interest in surf music and his references to Charles Manson in *Vineland* and *Inherent Vice* hail back to that time when he was living in California.[2]

In another article that says more about its author than about Pynchon, Gordon remembers meeting him in June of 1967 (172). One thing he remembers is that Pynchon caught a reference to Leonard Cohen's novel *Beautiful Losers*, published in 1966, a year before Cohen's debut album. Later that night, when "for some inexplicable reason, everyone had the hungry munchies" (173), Pynchon, Gordon, and two unnamed mutual friends went to a burger place in Berkeley: "The place featured a colorful old baroque Wurlitzer jukebox. We fed the machine streams of quarters: the Beatles' 'Strawberry Fields' and Country Joe's 'Sweet Lorraine.' Pynchon chose Procol Harum's 'Whiter Shade of Pale' and the Stones' 'Ruby Tuesday'" (173). Gordon then proceeded to introduce him to an acquaintance of his who was the manager of a local rock band: "[T]hey became engrossed in a technical conversation about music, and I was lost" (174). During the time he lived in California, Pynchon appears to have "maintained a quiet connection to the East Coast and to New York City, returning regularly to visit friends and check out the music scene," Nancy Jo Sales notes.

In 1972, six years after the publication of *The Crying of Lot 49* with its memorable Stockhausen electronic music passage, Pynchon is said to have played around with a primitive music synthesizer (Kachka, n.pag.). *Gravity's Rainbow* was published in 1973, and the subsequent two decades or so marked another period in which little is known about the writer except for his 1984 "Introduction" to *Slow Learner*. Only in the 1990s, after the publication of *Vineland*, do accounts of Pynchon's interest in music resurface

2 About two years after the above episode, Charles Manson and his following became frequent guests at Dennis Wilson's villa, and the two also wrote songs together. Brian and Carl Wilson produced some demo tapes for Manson. A contributor on the *Gravity's Rainbow* PynchonWiki argues that the minor character Murray Smile (*Gravity* 258–59) is a portmanteau of the Wilsons' father Murry and the Beach Boys' album *Smile*.

but they remain spotty at best and do not cover anything beyond a TV script and the liner notes of two albums.

On the John Larroquette Show of December 7, 1993, Dexter, a young waiter, quotes from Pynchon's song "Superhighways of July" and claims that "the author is a good friend of mine." He then tells an incredulous Larroquette that Pynchon had been in the joint the night before, wearing a t-shirt depicting Roky Erickson of the 13th Floor Elevators, a Texan psychedelic rock band. According to Sales, the script initially called for a Willy DeVille t-shirt but Pynchon requested that it be replaced with a Roky Erickson one—"although he likes Willy DeVille." The partly factual memoirs of Clarence Clemons, Bruce Springsteen's late saxophone player, belong in a similar category. In a chapter entitled "The Legend of Clarence and Thomas (A Screaming Comes Across the Bar), 2008," he claims to have hung out and had dinner with Pynchon, though the 'Legend' label given in the title indicates that this chapter contains "some fact and a lot of fiction," as the authors write in the book.

Pynchon's miscellaneous writings have appeared here and there over the years and do not refer to music as frequently as his novels and short stories. Two notable exceptions are the liner notes to *Spiked! The Music of Spike Jones* (1994) and Lotion's *Nobody's Cool* (1995).[3] The style of the—much shorter—Lotion liner notes is similar to that of his longer book endorsements but there is little to be learned about the actual music on the album. Apparently, Pynchon knew the mother of one of the band members and agreed to write the liner notes. Later, he was to do an interview with the band for *Esquire* magazine: "The Q&A ran beneath text so strange that Pynchon must have written it: 'The reclusive novelist loves rock and roll, and its name is, well, Lotion. He wanted to play ukulele, so the band gave him an interview'" (Kachka). In 2009, Christopher Glazek revealed in *The New Yorker* that a 1996 article in *The New Yorker* referring to the interview had been a hoax to which Pynchon *post factum* did not raise objection. The band had tried to make it sound "as Pynchonesque as possible" with references to drug use, a toilet once used by Elvis Presley, and 'Pynchon' wearing a Godzilla t-shirt. They have Pynchon say that, "I've been trying for forty years to learn to play the ukulele. All

3 For a joint review of those two albums, see David Ocker's "Spike Jones and Lotion: Connected by a Fragile Pynchon Thread."

my wanna-be instincts kicked in." The *New Yorker* article does not make it clear whether only their own 1996 article had been a prank or the *Esquire* interview too, but if the liner notes were in fact written by Pynchon, as seems agreed upon, he did not put much of his heart and craft into it.

The sleeve notes of *Spiked! The Music of Spike Jones* are a whole different story. They span more than eleven pages of the CD booklet and are Pynchon's longest piece on music. The Spike Jones rendition of "Der Fuehrer's Face" (not on the album) appears in *Gravity's Rainbow* (691), and when Pynchon explains a lesson he had to learn for writing, he offers an analogy with Jones's music: "Spike Jones, Jr., whose father's orchestral recordings had a deep and indelible effect on me as a child, said once in an interview: 'One of the things that people don't realize about Dad's kind of music is, when you replace a C-sharp with a gunshot, it has to be a C-sharp gunshot or it sounds awful'" (*Learner* 20). I would imagine that Pynchon's *Slow Learner* intro induced the Catalyst record label to inquire if he would be willing to write the liner notes. Pynchon clearly did a lot of research and, importantly, starting with the second—unmistakably Pynchonian—sentence, he writes about Jones's *music* and lyrics and not just his biography and times:

> Welcome, music lovers, to the cheerfully deranged world of Spike Jones and his City Slickers. There's gunshots and cowbells aplenty, not to mention class hostility, first-rate musicianship, subverted expectations, hair-trigger timing, and more than enough material for that interesting subset of folks actively looking to be offended, who might like to begin, actually, with the lyrics to the recitative or lead-in to the "Chinese Dance" in Spike's *Nutcracker Suite*—although mild compared to, oh say your average Chinese celebrity roast, this will require the sort of listener who either wants to wince with embarrassment or can find in vintage bigotry quaint refuge from the more virulent forms encountered in our own era. (6)

And on it goes with his peculiar mix of humor and musical erudition. Perhaps Pynchon did, figuratively speaking, learn to write C-sharp gunshots from Jones. More broadly speaking, however, the latter's high-precision music, with all kinds of quotes and cuts, a mixture of 'high' and 'low' cultural references, irreverent lyrics, and at times juvenile jokes can also be seen as a model, or at the very least a musical analogy, for Pynchon's writing, perhaps even for postmodern literature as such.

It is unclear if Pynchon himself played any instrument other than the guitar and the waste basket congas. However, he seems to have encouraged—or not discouraged—his own offspring: according to an *Adweek/GalleyCat* article from 2006, entitled "Jackson Pynchon's Rock 'n Roll Dreams," his son Jackson—at the time fifteen years old—played in "various rock bands, usually as a drummer and vocalist." In 2008, Jackson Pynchon published a short portrait of electro-pop artist Sam Sparro in *Rolling Stone.*

From the evidence presented above, it seems that Pynchon started publishing in earnest when his formative years of music education had been concluded, that is to say, around age twenty. The bits and pieces strung together here confirm a lifelong interest in many different musics of the Western canon—from classical to modernist and early electronic music; from jazz combos to rock bands. The music that was important to him in his youth appears again and again throughout his work, although the jazz and classical references seem to give way to pop music references over time, a fact that will be discussed in more detail in the final chapter.

If Wolf is right when he writes that biographical evidence of a writer's interest in music is one of the many indicators of musicalized fiction—albeit only as "circumstantial evidence" (*Musicalization* 73)—then Pynchon, even though little is known about his life, has passed this part of the test. Wolf does not argue in great detail why this should be so, but despite all good arguments around the death of the author and the fallacies of tracing a writer's intention, "[e]verybody gets told to write about what they know" (*Learner* 15). In criticizing his early short stories, Pynchon acknowledges that "Somewhere I had come up with the notion that one's personal life had nothing to do with fiction, when the truth, as everyone knows, is nearly the direct opposite" (21). As the next section—this entire study, in fact—will show, biographical evidence is hardly needed as a proof of Pynchon's interest in music, and the above sketch does not suffice to explain the high frequency of music in his work. Still, it can corroborate uncertain allusions the reader may spot, and, most importantly, it helps us take seriously what Pynchon writes about music.

An Inventory of Pynchon's Musical Techniques and Strategies

In the past decade or two, the study of sound and music in literature has enjoyed growing popularity, oftentimes under labels such as intermediality studies, sound studies, literary studies, or comparative literature. In my view, most of the exciting interplays between literature and music took place in twentieth-century North America. Experimentation with intermedial relationships of all sorts was taken to a new and different level. Leaving political catalysts aside—such as the role World War I played in bringing about Dadaism or World War II for the postmodern era—this had much to do with the emergence of new technologies that brought new possibilities for expression and experimentation, and it had to do with the emergence of new musical idioms, most importantly jazz, atonal, and electronic music.

Listing the techniques and strategies Pynchon employs to bring music into his prose, it becomes evident how wide a range of the canonical treatments of music in literature he brings to fruition. John Joseph Hess summarizes some of the musical elements:

> Pynchon's fifty year career as a novelist involves a sustained engagement with a range of musical effects. Music is a formal feature with thematic significance. [...] In addition to Pynchon's 'songs,' Pynchon's novels reference and emphasize a variety of historical and imagined musical styles, forms, instruments, keys, performers, and cultures. Pynchon deploys these musical elements to narrative ends that range from exposition and description to sustained thematic development. (1)

Although far from exhaustive, Hess gives a good idea of the means employed and the ends served. A similar undertaking is offered by Justin St. Clair in the chapter "Music and Sound" of the Cambridge volume *Pynchon in Context*. And finally, there is an excellent essay by Samuel Thomas on music in *Bleeding Edge* in which he also discusses music in Pynchon's work in general ("Blood on the Tracks"). Expanding their work, I hope to present an even more encompassing inventory of techniques, strategies, references, allusions, or effects of music, some of which overlap, but my undertaking will also have to forfeit any claim to completeness.

Setting the Tone: Dedications and Epigraphs

It does not take the reader long to intuit the importance of music in Pynchon's work. *Vineland, The Crying of Lot 49,* and *Inherent Vice* reference instruments, musicians, or works of music on their very first page, as do "The Small Rain," "Low-lands," "Entropy," and "Voice of the Hamster."[4] *Mason & Dixon's* opening also has sonic qualities, with its quasi-musical backdrop of "ringing Lids of various Boilers and Stewing-Pots" and "rhythmic slaps of Batter and Spoon."

Apart from the main body of the novel, Pynchon also uses paratext to set a mood for a musical reception of his work. *Gravity's Rainbow* is dedicated to his friend Richard Fariña. The dedication may be no more than a homage to a deceased friend and his novel *Been Down So Long It Looks Like Up to Me,* published just a day before his death in a motorcycle accident, for which Pynchon later wrote a preface and an endorsement. However, as will be argued in more detail later on, Fariña could be one of the real-life characters on which Tyrone Slothrop is modeled. Part 4 of *Gravity's Rainbow* initially had a quote from Joni Mitchell's song "Cactus Tree" as an epigraph. After the galleys were printed, it was replaced by a supposed quote of Richard Nixon: "What?"

While the dedication of *Gravity's Rainbow* resonates on a number of levels with its protagonist, *Vineland*'s epigraph does this too, but through the characters it serves simultaneously as a bracket for the entire novel. The epigraph is an excerpt from a blues by Johnny Copeland: "Every dog has his day, / and a good dog / just might have two days," a modification of a line popularized by *Hamlet:* "The cat will mew and dog will have his day" (Act 5, Scene 1). While it most immediately links to the family dog Desmond who appears on the second and last pages (see the section on character names below), it could also refer to Weed Atman's second coming and the reunion of the extended Wheeler/Traverse family in the closing pages. When the wheels of history have turned, Pynchon and Copeland seem to say, those who have karmically stayed on the right side will get a second chance.

More obscure is the epigraph of *Against the Day.* It does not appear to have much to do with any of the characters but its

4 When quoting the collected short stories, the page number always refers to *Slow Learner.*

enigmatic, or at least ambiguous, diction relates to the theme of the novel: "It's always night, or we wouldn't need light" is an aphorism attributed to Thelonius Monk.[5] Night/day or darkness/light resonates throughout Pynchon's work but particularly *Against the Day*. While the meaning of Monk's aphorism remains a puzzle, it may be significant that the quote belongs to a time not covered in the novel. It hails from the narrative's future, but then again, it may be prophetic in Jacques Attali's sense because *Against the Day* is the novel that witnesses the birth of jazz, introduces time travel, and has a number of chronological inconsistencies in the musical references as will be shown in Chapter 4.

The only novel that does not have musical references in the paratext or on its first page is *Bleeding Edge,* although two musical references—songs by Britney Spears and The Beach Boys—appear toward the end of the first chapter. However, *Bleeding Edge* is the novel with the most references to musicians and works of music in relative terms (adjusted to the number of words). In absolute terms, it is surpassed only by *Gravity's Rainbow*. The lack of musical references in the opening pages is in line with its low number of references to musical instruments and with its smallest number of Pynchon's own songs (except for *Slow Learner*). An interpretation of the meaning of this lessening will be offered in the last chapter. Suffice it here to say that it appears to imply that the time of the narrative, that is, the turn of the 20th/21st century, is a time when the music industry with its prerecorded music has rendered much of communal and individual music-making obsolete.

Paying close attention to the first pages of Pynchon's books and short stories reveals something about the musical qualities of the text. If Cowart is right in arguing that musical references "hint at the extra dimensions of experience that we miss," (*Allusion* 9) we may interpret this as setting the tone for the way the reader is supposed to make his or her way through Pynchon's intricate and complex networks of meaning. These paratexts also set a tone for a more hopeful reading that lets the reader discover the fictional worlds, and by extension the World As It Is, as something rich and meaningful as opposed to something devoid of meaning or hope.

---

5 A slightly different wording is found in a reproduction of a list by Thelonius Monk in Usher.

Musical Forms as a Structuring Device

Certain musical and literary forms appear to have a similar structure—although some fundamental differences between the two media reduce those similarities to analogies. Music is a time-based medium that presupposes a tempo that is more or less to be adhered to. Music unfolds in chronological time. Leaving aside the case of a remix DJ, the musician cannot replay passages at will the way a reader can reread passages or simply put away the score and start again from any point as is done with books. The skilled musician may read a musical score similarly to how a reader reads a literary text, but for most people, a work of music can be actualized only through performance. Yet even with the musical score there is a fundamental difference: music allows for the vertical simultaneity of different voices while literature is unable to stack voices polyphonically on top of each other for them to be perceived simultaneously.

Nevertheless, some musical forms have been taken as a model for writing literary texts. *Finnegans Wake,* according to James Joyce, is pure music and meant to be listened to as much as it is read. Wolf, and later Michelle Witen, for instance, have shown that the Sirens episode of Joyce's *Ulysses* is structured like a double fugue. The fugue seems to be of particular interest to literary scholars, possibly because it is a structurally specific and interesting enough model for writers to build their literary analogs on. Wolf has identified a good number of other literary fugues—and at times questioned the validity of some of their authors' assumptions.

Some of the most perceptive writing around music and Pynchon concerns the fugue in the short story "Entropy," Pynchon's densest piece of writing apart from the Spike Jones liner notes in terms of musical references and allusions. In 1977, Robert Redfield and Peter L. Hays published an article that takes up Pynchon's clues—key words like "fugue," "counterpoint," "canon," or "modulations"—and argued convincingly that "Entropy" is structured like a fugue. This concerns not only the names of some of the characters, the distribution of voices, and the architecture of the apartment building—"it would be very much as if we were looking at the upper two staves of a fourpart musical score" (51). Most importantly, the thematic motifs develop and contrast each other contrapuntally, the main division being between Meatball Mulligan's party (a reference to baritone saxophonist Gerry Mulligan) on the second floor and Callisto's hothouse on the third floor: "It is the general exchange between the two voices of essentially similar material which points up the fugal nature of Pynchon's structural underpinnings" (54). When the story mentions Modest Mussorgsky's "The Great Gate of Kiev" from *Pictures at an Exhibition* in the first paragraph (*Learner* 81), exhibition can be read as signaling its synonym exposition, the first part of a fugue. The story concludes with the words "and the hovering, curious *dominant* of their separate lives should resolve into a *tonic* of darkness and the final absence of all motion" (98, emphasis added). Carmen Pérez-Llantada Auría may not have been aware of Redfield and Hays' work when she published her own reading of the fugue structure of "Entropy" as she never mentions them in her 1991 article. She identifies many more details for which she finds musical analogs (arpeggio, affrentando, slur, trill, among others) and goes as far as to actually notate the literary passages on music staves and label them: anacrusis (the Henry Miller epigraph), subject (Mulligan's party) and countersubject (Callisto's hothouse), variations, the return to the tonic, and the final rest. Her notations are replete with themes, counterthemes, expositions, modulating bridges, codas, developments, reexpositions, and canons. In her reading, music "acts out as a perfect link of fragments and images, of ideas and voices otherwise impossible to connect and understand. [...] Music helps to counterbalance the meaningless void of signifiers without signifieds by means of its factual pattern-based order" (129).

While "Entropy" is Pynchon's work that can most convincingly be read as based on a musical structure, Bénédicte Chorier-Fryd has interpreted the overall structure of *Mason & Dixon* as that of a minuet, taking her cue from the minuet Ethelmer is playing on the piano. She writes:

> [T]he minuet is composed of three parts, of which the middle one is generally an expansion of the first minuet in more complex forms [...]. The first part of *Mason & Dixon* exposes the motifs of departure and exploration, taken up and developed in the second part, entitled "America." The third part distinguishes itself from the other two, not only by its brevity but also by its less flamboyant character: no more adventures, nothing extraordinary anymore, but attention to the sentiments and a restriction to a sphere of intimacy—an ending in *mezzo-voce* that contrasts the grandiloquent effects of the rest of the novel: no need even to play loud at the end. ("A Novel in Music;" my translation 206–07)

I would argue that this tripartite structure is a very common musical form that is also, for instance, found in the standard sonata form. But most importantly, the departure from exposition in the tonic, development in a number of keys (often in the dominant), and then the return to the tonic (the 'home key') is also a common structure for a novel: the hero or heroine sets out, lives through his or her adventures, and then returns home changed to come to rest: "a Novel in Musick, whose Hero instead of proceeding down the road having one adventure after another, with no end in view, comes rather through some Catastrophe and back to where she set out from" (*Mason* 263). The closing pages of *Mason & Dixon* make this even more explicit:

> Mason had married again, and become the father of five more boys and a girl, yet he never put Rebekah to Earth…tho' she herself, to appearance, might at last sigh, relax, and move on,—one would think,—with Old Mopery come to rest where he'd started out from. It is the way journeymen became masters, and the ingenuous wise,—it is a musickal piece returning to its Tonick Home. Nothing more would be expected of him now, than some quiet Coda. (762)

Although Pynchon's other novels do not follow this tripartite structure as clearly as *Mason & Dixon*, many have elements that correspond to this, what some may call cyclical, structure. 'Cyclical' fits the bill nicely—as opposed to 'circular'—especially if one has something like a Nietzschean model of history in mind where the eternal return never returns to the same coordinates but poses a similar challenge under different circumstances, a difference in repetition, to speak with Gilles Deleuze. Perhaps the inadequacy of the circle metaphor is why Pynchon is content with half of a circle, a slightly squished one, namely a parabola. The parabolic trajectory comes to rest at the end of its arc and is, in Pynchon's work, intimately tied in with the idea of starting from the tonic, rising to the dominant, and returning to the tonic again, a "simple-minded German symphonic arc, tonic to dominant, back again to tonic" (*Gravity* 450).

Such an arc is also, almost needless to say, inscribed by rainbows, the V-2 rocket, and any other object that flies through the air and is pulled back to earth by gravity. *Gravity's Rainbow* starts with "A screaming comes across the sky" (3) and ends with a missile descending on a movie theater. Similarly, *Mason & Dixon* starts with "Snow-Balls have flown their Arcs […]" (5).

In *Vineland*, after only a page, "the blue jays [...] came screaming down out of the redwoods" (4) to eat Desmond the family dog's food, and the novel ends with Desmond, "face full of bluejay feathers, smiling out of his eyes, wagging his tail, thinking he must be home" (385).

While Pynchon has a reference to the return to the tonic in "Entropy," it is only in *Gravity's Rainbow* that he takes up this metaphor again.[6] *Gravity's Rainbow*, *Mason & Dixon*, and *Against the Day* are the three novels that treat the topic most explicitly, although mainly in passing, and where Pynchon also makes frequent reference to the tonic as an invigorating or restorative medicine ("Tonick Salesman," "brain tonic," "nerve tonic," "hair tonic"). In line with his disregard of that metaphor in *V.* and *The Crying of Lot 49*, it would require some effort to see this overall structure present in those two novels. However, after Pynchon has begun to develop this trope in *Gravity's Rainbow*, it can be made out in the arc of suspense in all his later novels, most easily—if somewhat paradoxically—in the three novels where he mentions the tonic sparingly or not at all. These are the more family-centered—and, by extension, home-oriented—novels: *Vineland, Inherent Vice, Bleeding Edge*. These three, possibly more nostalgic, novels start and end in the tonic with a sense of returning home, being enveloped in the safety of a family or a community. *Against the Day*, partly because of the large number of characters, partly because its locations are scattered all over the known world and beyond, makes the return to the tonic more difficult to spot. Still, the novel starts out with "Now single up all lines!", a nautical term—and as such applicable to skyships too—that recurs in all but two of Pynchon's novels, designating hauling in all multiple lines or ropes to get ready for departure. The Chums of Chance skyfarers form something like an *ersatz*-family and their skyship is their home. At the end of the novel, they have founded a commune of families and "fly toward grace" (1220). Although the last part of *Against the Day* is entitled "Rue du Départ," this departure has many qualities of a homecoming: Dally (re)connects with her father Merle by means of a long-range radio transmitter and likely gets back together with her husband Kit. We learn

6 John M. Krafft told me that "Pynchon referred to tonic in the sense of a restorative ('Rachel, eyes cleared by loves tonic' [552]) in the typescript of *V.* but took it out" (personal communication, August 18, 2019).

that La Jarretière whom the reader remembers from *V.* did not die on the opening night of *L'Enlèvement des Vierges Chinoises* but was 'reborn' as someone else. Cowart, who calls *Against the Day* as a whole "a kind of fugal recapitulation" (*History* 166), rightly observes that the "Rue du Départ" section "functions only as a coda to the more elaborate conclusion of the long preceding section, which shares a title with the novel itself" (186). The last chapter of *Against the Day*, set in 1923, thus has a function similar, at least in musical terms, to that of the "Epilogue" of *V.*, set in 1919.

Although the narrative model of departure–adventure–return with its musical analogs of exposition–development–recapitulation (sonata form), exposition–development–final entry (fugue), or simply tonic–dominant–tonic (much of Western tonal music) can be found in the majority of novels, Pynchon makes this dominant structure in literature and music explicit. Discussions of the return to the tonic will come up a number of times in the course of this study.

Works of Music as a Plot Device

At times, Pynchon uses works of music as inspiration or plot devices. This appears to be particularly true for *V.* and *Gravity's Rainbow* but is less prominent—or wholly absent—in later works, except at a micro level. Cowart observed that "the really important [musical] allusions—those which examined all together reveal the most coherent and finely-wrought pattern, those which in other words reveal Pynchon's artistry most impressively—are in fact the classical ones" (*Allusion* 65). Although Pynchon has since published five more novels, there is little to contradict, and Cowart remains one of the most attentive observers of classical music references in Pynchon's work, particularly when it comes to plot structure informed by music. He has also pointed out that Pynchon does not choose his references haphazardly. He does not "decorate his fiction with the first opera title that comes to mind. He selects the one that resonates with his own theme and characterization and foreshadows subsequent developments in the novel" (69). This also seems to be true of many of the music references from other musical genres including those from film, but opera with its extended dramatic structure and its many characters is uniquely suited as a blueprint for parts of Pynchon's earlier narratives, much more so than a three-minute pop tune that might better work as a comment on a character's situation or state of mind.

Liebestod, or love-death, in various variations ranks high among Pynchon's operatic themes. Cowart notes allusions to *Madama Butterfly, Tannhäuser, Tristan und Isolde,* and *Manon Lescaut* in *V.* and observes that all operas in *V.*, except for *Don Giovanni*—Pynchon's most frequently referenced opera—are variations on the love-death theme (*Allusion* 77). In *V.* and *Gravity's Rainbow*, Pynchon provides numerous latter-day variations of this topos: the assassination of Porpentine (more clearly recognizable in "Under the Rose"); Mélanie's (or La Jarretière's) perishing by impalement on the opening night of *L'Enlèvement des Vierges Chinoises;* Brigadier Pudding's death from E. coli contracted during an act of coprophagy; Bianca's death under unclear circumstances, likely as the victim of child abuse; or Gottfried's sacrifice in the V-2 rocket (at one point, Slothrop intimates that "the two children, Gottfried and Bianca, *are the same...*" [685]). As will be shown below, Bianca's death—or at least her abuse—does not come as a surprise to readers who are attentive to Shirley Temple references where Pynchon likely had in mind Graham Greene, who saw a pedophile undercurrent in Temple's early movies. The fact that V-2 rockets strike in London where Slothrop previously had an erection, thereby jeopardizing the lives of his lovers, is yet another variant of the love-death nexus. As is also, more perversely perhaps, the death of V., in the guise of the Bad Priest in an air raid on Malta, as a result of her love (or perhaps rather fetish) for violence. When Cowart writes that "in Mélanie's death [...] the act of love and the act of death *are* one" (*Allusion* 77), this can be expanded to encompass other deaths too, particularly in *V.* and *Gravity's Rainbow*. Although one could argue that the close connection of love and death—consider the French *la petite mort* or much of Georges Bataille's work—is hardly exclusive to the domain of opera, Pynchon provides all the pointers for readers to connect his love-death themes to opera, mostly that of Wagner and Puccini.

Unlike Cowart (77), I have not been able to detect a *Tannhäuser* reference in *V.*, *Tannhäuser* being the opera by Wagner that Pynchon alludes to most frequently (by my reckoning, however, only in *Gravity's Rainbow*). As the full title *Tannhäuser und der Sängerkrieg auf Wartburg* suggests, Wagner brought together the old German ballad "Tannhauser" and the legendary medieval minstrel contest at the Wartburg castle in Thuringia. Like Wagner's operas, *Gravity's Rainbow* works with Germanic myths, and like Wagner, Pynchon takes the liberty he needs to rework them. Although many of the allusions to *Tannhäuser* and other Wagner operas could theoretically be based on the original myths, that is, on the 'primary' texts, it is evident that it was Wagner who brought those myths to Pynchon's attention as Pynchon alludes to no less than eight operas of Wagner's, which helped make the German composer the musician most frequently alluded to in his work (see Chapter 4 for details).

As will be seen, Tyrone Slothrop can be read as a number of string-plucking musicians. One is Orpheus, another one is Richard Fariña. There are also resonances with the British singer, comedian, and ukulele and banjolele player George Formby ("sort of an American George Formby" [18]), not only because Slothrop plays the ukulele but also because of Formby's delightful innuendo or outright 'obscenity' in songs such as "When I'm Cleaning Windows" or "I'm a Wanker," and his irreverence for military authority figures in "Our Sergeant Major." Before putting on pieces from "Wagnerian opera costumes" (371) reminiscent of Moondog's Viking attire, Tyrone Slothrop realizes that he is also Tannhäuser:

> The best you can compare with is Tannhäuser, the Singing Nincompoop—you've been under one mountain at Nordhausen, been known to sing a song or two with uke accompaniment, and don'tcha feel you're in a sucking marshland of sin out here, Slothrop? [...] And where is the Pope whose staff's gonna bloom for you? (370)

David Cowart notes that Tannhäuser's quest "helps to structure *Gravity's Rainbow*" (*History* 62). Like Formby at a couple hundred years' remove, Tannhäuser "to the outrage of all assembled, sings of [divine love's] carnal counterfeit" (63). Cowart continues:

> Like the minnesinger, [Slothrop] spends a season in the arms of the Zone's debauched Venus, Katje Borgesius [...]. But he does not go 'under the mountain' until he gets to Nordhausen—located, like the Wartburg, in Thuringia. *Stollen,* the word for the great galleries of the underground rocket factory there, happens also to be the musicological term designating the sections—bars—of a minnesinger's song. (63)

While the above examples take a work of music as inspiration for themes or to structure the plot, Pynchon also fictionalized a number of events in the history of Western music. The most salient ones are the birth of free jazz and the premiere of Igor Stravinsky's *The Rite of Spring* in *V.* and the birth of bebop in *Gravity's Rainbow*. These have all received some attention from scholars whose insights will be discussed and added to in Chapters 2 and 3. The birth of free jazz is not presented as one unique event but rather an evolution of discoveries—both on the side of the artist and on the side of the listener. The most sustained arguments have been made on the McClintic Sphere/free jazz passages although most scholars have focused on the racial dimensions of Sphere and his environment. Another musical event that has received less attention so far but can be read side by side with McClintic Sphere/Ornette Coleman's inauguration of free jazz is the early days of New Orleans jazz in *Against the Day*, a genre that also builds on collective improvisation. I consider these events in the sense that Alain Badiou might attribute to the term: something new and liberatory happens that changes the configuration of the world; an event is "rupturing with the presentative logic of the [world]" ("Musical Variant" 29). To be sure, Badiou is somewhat ambiguous about declaring *The Rite of Spring* an event and he does not say anything about the different subgenres of jazz that Pynchon is interested in. Still, one cannot pretend these events never took place, except as a reactionary gesture.

An event in the trajectory of Western music that would likely not figure in Badiou's understanding of an event is the premiere of Ralph Vaughan Williams' 1910 *Fantasia on a Theme by Thomas Tallis*, which Pynchon reimagines in *Against the Day*. While it may not have been of much consequence to the unfolding of the history of twentieth century music, Ruperta Chirpingdon-Groin experiences it as an epiphany that lifts her off the ground and completely changes her life to the point that she feels the need to atone for her misconduct in the past: "At the last long diminuendo, she returned calmly to earth and reoccupied herself, never again to pursue her old career of a determined pest" (1006). Pynchon does not explain what happened to her, although he insinuates that "flattened seventh sonorities" may have had something to do with it. What she experiences is akin to St. Paul's conversion and largely follows Badiou's requirements of a truth procedure as outlined, for instance, in *Saint Paul* (14–15). The original theme by Thomas Tallis from 1567 was written to the first verses of Psalm 2 and mirrors Ruperta's situation before the premiere: "Why fumeth in fight: The Gentils spite / In fury raging stout? / Why taketh in hond: The people fond, / Vayne thinges to bring about?" Verses 10 and 11 probably most resemble the advice Ruperta heeds although not necessarily in religious consequence: "Be wise now therefore, O ye kings: be instructed, ye judges of the earth. / Serve the LORD with fear, and rejoice with trembling" (King James Bible). The *Tallis Fantasia* has been read as bridging the world of romanticism and the world of modernism—and thus it is a fitting work of music for a novel that starts in 1893 and ends in 1923. Steve Schwartz writes: "Unlike Stravinsky [...] who creates artistic tension between two eras by keeping past procedures and present distinct, Vaughan Williams, like many good Romantics, essentially incorporates the past to reinvigorate the present." Similar things could be said about Pynchon's historiographic metafiction. Although Ruperta leaves the ground and returns to it changed, the change is so profound that it may be a misreading to say that this is a variant of the tonic–dominant–tonic theme—the parabolic trajectory—as the 'home' she returns to is not the one she left. However, her conversion shortly before she disappears from the narrative contributes to a sense of a return to the tonic of the entire novel.

Pynchon tends to stay on the sidelines of history: political events, for instance, shape the world of the characters—but the characters are rarely present at those events. Even when the towers of the World Trade Center collapse, none of the characters of *Bleeding Edge* are present even though the novel is set almost entirely in New York City. The closest a character may get to a political event of lasting consequence is Tyrone Slothrop's sneaking up to the Potsdam Conference in Rocketman garb to fetch a package of Nepalese hashish (where else but *Pot*sdam?), yet he stays outside and is not witness to the decision-making. Not so with those musical events where the characters—or at the very least the readers—are eyewitnesses. Pynchon seems to imply that the political sphere is inaccessible to everyone who is not in the inner circle of power brokerage whereas the arts are open to everyone with a mind open enough to be receptive. While we cannot, as a general rule, shape the course of political history, we can participate in the opening of the world through the arts. Considering an *œuvre* approaching 5,000 pages, these instances of the fictionalization of events in the history of Western music are few and far between; yet they are developed with great attention to detail and have rightly received much attention from scholars.

Geeking Out: Musicological Discussions

Presumably like Pynchon himself, his musically inclined characters revel in discussions—or outright bickering—about the history and theory of music. A selection of unrelated scenes will demonstrate the breadth of these musicological discussions: On the occasion of a 'mute' rehearsal, the members of the Duke di Angelis quartet in "Entropy" discuss what it means to play without root chords: "Nothing to listen to while you blow a horizontal line" (95). Another pianoless quartet appears in *V.* where McClintic Sphere reflects on the significance of electricity in reaching a wider audience.

In *The Crying of Lot 49*, Mucho Maas tries to impart his LSD-induced epiphany on frequencies musical and otherwise to his increasingly estranged wife: "Everybody who says the same words is the same person if the spectra are the same only they happen differently in time, you dig? But the time is arbitrary. You pick your zero point anywhere you want, that way you can shuffle each person's time line sideways till they all coincide" (116–17).

In *Gravity's Rainbow*, Gustav Omnopon ('all bridge') and Säure Bummer have what Cowart calls a "theological argument" (*Allusion* 87) about German vs. Italian and dodecaphonic vs. tonal music, echoing the positions of Nietzsche in various works (*Nietzsche Contra Wagner, The Case of Wagner*, or *Gay Science*) before his breakdown in Turin: "Tonality is a game," Gustav maintains, and Säure counters: "The row is a game too [...]. *Sound* is a game. [...] I'm choosing *my* game, one full of light and kindness" (*Gravity* 634). In the end, the discussion is not resolved, probably cannot be resolved, but it echoes the struggle between more traditional and more progressive stances that continues to influence many of today's musicians and music lovers.

In *Mason & Dixon*, there is a long passage where the Wicks/LeSpark family discusses Plato's view on musical innovation and the music that is emerging in their days, notably the forerunner to the "Star-Spangled Banner" (see Chapter 3). Again, there is no resolution but it is made clear that this is not an argument just about musical tastes but about world views.

In *Against the Day*, a Chopin nocturne induces the ukulele player Miles to ruminate on chords vs. melody. Sean Carswell, following remarks Cowart made about Pynchon's early novels (*Allusion* 77), thinks that, "This melody would be a violation of the timelessness and multitude apparent in Miles's meditation on chords" ("Ukulele" 213).

Vineland, Inherent Vice, and *Bleeding Edge* are less rich in music-related discussions but by no means devoid of them. In *Bleeding Edge,* for instance, Ziggy and Otis discuss with their grandparents who sings the best "Nessun dorma." Otis has the last word, fittingly for a novel where 'serious' music has largely disappeared: "[I]t's Aretha Franklin, the time she filled in for Pavarotti at the Grammys back in '98" (98).

These discussions and many more are among the most impressive displays of Pynchon's musical erudition and can be considered the true gems of his engagement with literature and music. They are scattered throughout his work and cover a wide range of musics and viewpoints, but if Pynchon himself has a preference or takes a side in the respective arguments, he carefully avoids making his own opinion transparent. Most likely, he would opt for a non-judgmental both/and. If there is one thing that unites these diverse discussions, granting the odd exception, it is that the aesthetic judgment is never purely aesthetic. Through these scenes, Pynchon seems to say that the aesthetic—the philosophical as such—is always in some way political, while the *argumentum e contrario* cannot be made so clearly if at all. Pynchon is an eminently political writer but he approaches the political dimension aesthetically through his art—literature—and within his writing, oftentimes through alluding to other arts. What Philipp Schweighauser has said about literature in general seems true of Pynchon in particular: "[A]esthetic considerations have not led us away from politics. Instead, they have helped us understand that any consideration of a literary work's politics of representation that is worthy of the name must take a detour through considerations of literary forms and the impact of those forms on readers' perceptions of themselves and of the world" ("Some Reflections" 52).

The context and the interpretation of Pynchon's discussions of the history and theory of music are an essential part of this study and will resurface throughout it.

Grace Notes: Musical Terms as Tropes

Musical terms like 'harmony,' 'dissonance,' or 'rhythm' have made their way into everyday language to describe extra-musical objects and occurrences, and they naturally appear in Pynchon's writing too. Yet Pynchon goes beyond such naturalized terminology and turns musical concepts and terms into figures of thought, much as he does for other specialized fields of knowledge. These may be metonymies, metaphors, allegories, similes, and almost any number of other tropes. The many examples of the return to the tonic are perhaps the most prominent but far from the only ones.

In "Entropy," Aubade's perceptions "came to her reduced inevitably to the terms of sound: of music which emerged as intervals from a howling darkness of discordancy" (*Learner* 84). "[W]hen Callisto made love to her, soaring above the bowing of taut nerves in haphazard double-stops would be the one singing string of her determination" (88). Aubade's name denotes a morning love song and her synesthetic sensibility adds to the overall musical theme of "Entropy." It is also an invitation for the reader to perceive and decode the short story through the filter of music.

In the very last section of the 'coda' of *Against the Day,* "Heartsease discovers that she's expecting a baby, and then, like a canonical part-song, the other girls one by one announce that they are, too" (1218). Here, Pynchon chooses a metaphor that alludes to the role of every singular voice to make up a harmonic whole as it unfolds in time. He does not choose the first musical form that may have come to his mind. Instead, he picks one that was popular in the time frame of the novel and was championed by three composers referenced in *Against the Day*: Hubert Parry, Edward Elgar, and Ralph Vaughan Williams. These were, of course, not the only composers of part-song but all three appear in this novel and no other. The secular part-song in the short section entitled "Rue du Départ" is not only a song of different vocal parts but also a song of parting and departure. Heartsease's name, in turn, may well be taken from Act IV of *Romeo and Juliet* where Peter asks the musicians to play "Heart's Ease," "some merry dump to comfort me," after the discovery that Juliet has departed this life.

Musical terminology is sometimes employed to describe the closely related register of noise: "Outside glass has been breaking, long, dissonant cymbals up the street" (*Gravity* 122) or, "He turns back to draw the cork from a wine bottle, and its pop arrives as a grace note for a scream from one of the dancers" (188). Here, the "dissonant cymbals" and the "grace note" appear to introduce an element of negentropy into what is threatening to fall apart.

There does not appear to be a particular pattern of meaning in Pynchon's music-inspired tropes. He employs them to great effect on a variety of occasions. While they can be overlooked without consequences for understanding the novel, close readings reveal the extraordinary care with which they were chosen and allow for unveiling many layers of meaning that can be scaled up to entire paragraphs, sections, or novels.

On Rhythmical and Melodic Qualities of Prose

William Wordsworth famously claimed that "some of the most interesting parts of the best poems will be bound to be strictly in the language of prose, when the prose is well written" (676). One could turn this around by saying that some of the best prose will be bound to be strictly in the language of poetry. And, by extension, in the melody and rhythm of poetry and, by further extension, in the melody and rhythm of song. Although this risks leveling the differences between prose, poetry, and song and returning to a kind of Greek unity of the genres, some of Pynchon's finest passages are examples of carefully wrought prosody. Of course, finding the right words is the mark of every distinguished novelist. What is more, the English language may be a particularly bountiful medium to work with as Pynchon supposes in a December 2006 fax to *The Daily Telegraph* in which he came to the defense of Ian McEwan in a seemingly rather silly controversy about "who owns the right to describe using gentian violet for ringworm." He stated that, "Writers are naturally drawn, chimpanzee-like, to the color and the music of this English idiom we are blessed to have inherited. When given the choice we will usually try to use the more vivid and tuneful among its words."

As I will argue further below, parts of *Gravity's Rainbow*'s famous Charlie Parker passage (64–66) have a rhythmic pattern that emulates bebop; the trade-off of opinions in the discussions around the new "jass" music in New Orleans in *Against the Day* imitates collective improvisation; and there are anachronistic echoes of hip-hop in *Mason & Dixon*, both in rhythm and in rhyme. There are also odd passages with song qualities woven into the fabric of the prose such as this one: "And the crowds they swarm in Knightsbridge, and the wireless carols drone, and the

Underground's a mob-scene, but Pointsman's all alone. But he's got his Xmas present, fa la la [...]" (*Gravity* 170). It does not take the "fa la la" to recognize that these could be the lyrics to a song. In this case, a contributor to the PynchonWiki believes the lines to be modeled on (or sung to) The Kinks' "A Well-Respected Man," which seems a reasonable deduction. It is unclear whether the "fa" and "la" refer to F and A, or more generally the subdominant and the submediant, or whether they are just syllables indicating a melody. If the Kinks connection is valid, they would be the latter.

Bénédicte Chorier-Fryd has written about the notion of 'beat' in *Mason & Dixon* as it relates to speech ("A Beat Late"). The characters speak a beat late (or are a bit late), they are quite upon their beat, or there is a beat of silence; in other novels they take or wait a beat, half a beat, a perfect beat and a half, or a brief beat: "Though this is narrative prose, it evinces a number of identifiable poetic schemes which come into play with plainly linguistic prosody—the rhythm of ordinary language." (259) By hinting at beats, which could be "the heart's ticking (metronome's music)" (*V.* 46) or a song in the back of one's mind, Pynchon makes the reader aware that she or he may read his prose, or parts thereof, through a more rhythmically structured pattern.

Unreliable Homages: Characters and Their Names

Pynchon's densely populated worlds are filled with characters whose fanciful names do not follow a distribution approximating any natural language or region and invite speculation as to their origin. In 2008, Patrick Hurley published *Pynchon Character Names: A Dictionary* including every character in all of Pynchon's novels up to and including *Against the Day*. For each name there is a brief explanation of its likely origin or etymology. Hurley focuses mainly on last names, particularly where he considers a first name to be quite common. Many of the characters' names appear to be inspired by—or remixed and mashed up from—the names of actual musicians and works of music, some of which reoccur in different books. The largest number of those names seem to be inspired by names of musicians (Miles, Otis, Ditters), followed by works of music (Andrea Tancredi, Jessica Swanlake, Eddie Pensiero), and, finally, musical terms or instruments

(Margaret Quartertone, Maurice "Saxophone" Reed, Wolfe Tone O'Rooney).

Some of the names Pynchon openly reveals as having been inspired by music. Such is the case with Frenesi Gates, named for Artie Shaw's 1940 recording "Frenesí" (*Vineland* 75) and Toplady Oust, "[c]onceived in a choir loft during a rendition of 'Rock of Ages,'" (*Against* 422), the most famous hymn penned by eighteenth-century cleric Augustus Montague Toplady. Sometimes, a name may be based on misunderstood lyrics, such as Capt. Geoffrey "Pirate" Prentice (from Gilbert and Sullivan's *The Pirates of Penzance*), Geli Tripping (the song "Sir Joseph's Barge is Seen" from the same duo's *H.M.S. Pinafore*: "Gaily tripping, lightly-skipping"), or Eddie Pensiero (Giuseppe Verdi's "La donna è mobile / Qual piuma al vento / Muta d'accento / E di pensiero"). Desmond the dog may be a nod to alto saxophonist Paul Desmond[7] or to The Beatles' "Ob-la-di, ob-la-da," an idyllic vignette of family life where, at the end, "Desmond stays at *home* and *does his pretty face*," which is echoed in the last sentence of *Vineland:* "It was Desmond, none other, the spit and image of his grandmother Chloe [...], *smiling out of his eyes,* wagging his tail, thinking he must be *home*" (385, emphases mine).

Ultimately, however, the meaning of these musical character names has to be relativized. One, Pynchon invented many more characters whose names do not recall anything musical. Two, some of the deductions require a bit of a stretch and it is uncertain if another researcher would come up with the same connections. Three, in a number of cases, the immediate link to music may be just one of several valid deductions or interpretations. Such is the case, for instance, with *Against the Day*'s anarchist Wolf Tone O'Rooney, whose name may derive from the wolf tone, an effect that occurs when the note played on a bowed instrument has the same resonant frequencies as the instrument's body and produces an amplification of overtones. He may also be named for Theobald Wolf Tone, the leader of the 1798 Irish Rebellion. Four, perhaps most frustratingly for those who seek to establish a pattern of meaning, the majority of those names do not seem to offer a connection between the character and the biographical figure or the musical term by which they were inspired. As Terry P. Caesar

7 Paul Desmond is mentioned in the typescript of *V.* alongside Earl Bostic (389) when patrons ask Sphere "what he thought about other altos" (*V.* 280).

writes, Pynchon's "characters are often discontinuous with their names" (6). I believe they can largely be considered more or less well-disguised homages that Pynchon chose because he liked the sound or the comic connotations.

There are also a number of characters of various importance who play musical instruments. For *Gravity's Rainbow*, Bénédicte Chorier-Fryd noted that all the badasses ("les personnages 'badassiens'") are musicians (*Le Badass* 130). Among the professional musicians in Pynchon's novels are the sax players McClintic Sphere and Coy Harlingen, the composers Gustav Schlabone and Vladimir Porcépic, the former bebop drummer Mr. Faggiaducci, the bass player Mr. McAfee, the band leader Dope Breedlove, the DJ and later producer Wendell "Mucho" Maas. Among the many amateur musicians are Tyrone Slothrop, Zoyd Wheeler, Takeshi Fumimoto, Frank Traverse, Miles Blundell, Dewey Gland, Misha and Grisha, and Darren the intern. Here, too, it seems too much of a stretch to connect their names to their instruments or preferred styles of music. Of the musicians, only the alto sax player McClintic Sphere has inspired a significant number of scholarly contributions, for instance by David Witzling, and by Luc Herman and John Krafft. Apart from addressing racial issues, their studies trace the sources of the fictionalized passage to the historic Ornette Coleman and his performances. Even though much has been said, I will add my own in Chapter 2, arguing not only that Sphere is caught up in racial tensions of black vs. white, but that many of the binary opposites that organize the novel can be brought to bear on this character.

Very few historical musicians appear as characters in Pynchon's novels, and they are never given speaking roles, unlike the historical figures of Benjamin Franklin—inventor of the glass armonica—and Nikola Tesla. In fact, Ralph Vaughan Williams seems to be the only musician who appears when the characters are present, conducting the 1910 premiere of his *Fantasia on a Theme by Thomas Tallis*. Among the musicians that characters have met or intend to see but that are not present are Charlie Parker, Rick Wright of Pink Floyd, and the Karakaş Efendi.

Pynchon also delights in the creation of fictional bands that tend to play lesser roles in his novels. Unlike his character names, the band names often pick up and ironize the genre conventions: The Lederhoseners, the Lübeck Hitler Youth Glee Club, The Fool, Billy Barf and the Vomitones (a.k.a. Gino Baglione and the Paisans), Septic Tank, Fascist Toejam, The Corvairs, Eddie Enrico and his Hong Kong Hotshots, The Surfadelics, The Paranoids, Dope Breedlove and the Merry Coons, Holocaust Pixels, Nazi Vegetable, the Boards, and the Kugelblitz Bebop Ensemble. One of the most multi-layered of Pynchon's band names is perhaps *The Crying of Lot 49*'s Sick Dick and the Volkswagens, who might appear to have an album out on Roony Winsome's label Outlandish Records in *V.* (124). As J. Kerry Grant, among others, noted, the name riffs on the conventions of band names of the British invasion such as Gerry and the Pacemakers (32–33). Sick Dick and the Volkswagens recorded "I Want to Kiss Your Feet," a pun on the Beatles' "I Want to Hold Your Hand" and simultaneously a hint at *The Courier's Tragedy* and other instances of foot fetishism in Pynchon's work. What appears to have eluded commentators is that the Beatles connection goes even further. A name the Beatles briefly had around 1960 was Long John and the Silver Beetles (*The Beatles Anthology* 41). Thus, Long John becomes Sick Dick, and the Beetles—the Beetle being VW's most successful car model—turn into the Volkswagens, which also resonates with the Nazi/California connections in *The Crying of Lot 49*.

Active Ingredients: Musical Instruments

Up to and including *Bleeding Edge,* Pynchon makes frequent references to musical instruments and all sorts of ensembles. There are a total of 720 references to more than 130 different musical instruments (such as the alto saxophone and the tambourine) in 74 different categories (such as 'saxophone' and 'percussion') and uncounted references to musical ensembles, some of which are comically mixed bags of instruments. Many of these instruments, particularly the ones the author appears to cherish the most, stand for something specific that can often be traced in the history of the respective instrument. Not only is the medium the message in those cases; the instruments also tend to endow their players with some of their own characteristics. Such is the case particularly with the ukulele, the harmonica, the kazoo, and the saxophone. Sean Carswell has focused on Pynchon's ukulele and done insightful readings that include the genealogy and history of the instrument, musico-philosophical considerations, and most importantly, the political dimension of it all, mainly relating it to Michael Hardt and Antonio Negri's notion of Empire. As Carswell demonstrates, there is a wealth to be discovered in historical and close readings around a select number of instruments, which is why Chapter 2 will focus on the harmonica, the kazoo, and the saxophone and offer readings along similar lines.

Indented Interludes: Pynchon's Own Songs

Throughout his work, Pynchon has consistently, albeit not with equal weight in all his novels, written lyrics for songs, made up musicals, operettas, or albums, and hinted at fictional song titles. As Joshua Rothkopf has it in a *Rolling Stone* article: "Commit to Pynchon, and you will discover an unapologetically silly lover of pop songs. His text frequently breaks off into indented lyrics for completely fictional hits, spinning in a jukebox of his imagination." His 210 songs and 19 larger works of music amount to a total of 2642 lines of lyrics. 173 songs have more than four lines and 123 have more than ten lines of lyrics, the latter being about the minimal length one could turn into a song that follows one of the established forms. The first one of Pynchon's songs appears on the first page of his first novel and thus sets the tone that will be of importance for the rest of his writing career. In addition to his lyrics, there are a number of instrumental works of music he made up, such as McClintic Sphere's "Fugue Your Buddy," *Mason & Dixon*'s "Scamozzetta" from *I gluttoni*, the Vivaldi Kazoo Concerto in *The Crying of Lot 49* and *V.*, or songs of which only the title is known such as the above-mentioned "I Want to Kiss Your Feet."

Although most of Pynchon's songs are decidedly poetic, not all of them work as poems. Many require an inner voice that hums along a melody in order to stretch a syllable, a word, or a line in a way that spoken language would find difficult without turning absurd. This is particularly true for the novels set in the twentieth century. By contrast, most of the lyrics in *Mason & Dixon* follow conventional meter and rhyme schemes that can be read more easily independent of a melody.

Scholars have puzzled over the meaning of Pynchon's songs that are sometimes inserted without prior notice, sometimes contrasting with and at other times reinforcing the plot. While Joshua Rothkopf opines in *Rolling Stone*, "Do these tunes mean anything? Nope, wonderfully not," Kathryn Hume and Thomas J. Knight argue with reference to *Gravity's Rainbow*:

> The greatest number of lyrics and allusions might be said to concern the 'plane' of everyday reality, two-dimensional in the sense of being dull, material, and limited. Here music reinforces values within the social system and deals synchronically with contradictions and antinomies within that planar system. Add another dimension, however—somehow above and beyond the quotidian plane—and we find the second musical function, that of bridging the abyss between such levels. Finally, add the dimension of time, and we discover music's third function: projecting diachronically into the future, and thus serving as the vehicle of prophecy. ("Orchestration" 367)

In the first category are the fictive popular songs that "manage the fantasies of the masses, so that they are able to survive unpleasant realities and carry on their work" (368); "[S]inging makes possible their continuing to slave away. Song is the traditional opiate that so insulates them from the misery inflicted on them by The System that they do not revolt" (369). It appears that the first category makes up the largest number of Pynchon's own songs and it also appears that this is the function most often attributed to the interludes by other critics and commentators. The second category concerns supranatural realities—whether with metaphysical qualities, drug-induced, or otherwise fantastic. Its function is to bridge "the gap between everyday reality and other realities" (371). "The immediate bizarre stimuli [...] are transformed by means of the popular music clichés from elements of chaos to units of cosmos" (373). Into the third, prophetic, category fall the Charlie Parker passage from *Gravity's Rainbow* and the song "With a Peppermint Face in the Sky" (177–78) which in words and imagery appears to be a mash-up of any number of possibly LSD-induced Beatles songs such as "Magical Mystery Tour," "Strawberry Fields Forever," "Lucy in the Sky with Diamonds," and "Polythene Pam." It would take a systematic investigation of all of Pynchon's song lyrics to verify whether Hume and Knight's systematization is valid for all of Pynchon's work, but it appears plausible to me. This does not mean that Rothkopf is entirely wrong. In other words, the songs do not fulfill a central function without which the books would not be understandable, and it is perfectly admissible to read them, or hum along, in a carefree, good-natured spirit.

Anahita Rouyan reads the songs of *Gravity's Rainbow* as emphasizing "the disparity between the oral and written variants of language, suggesting that vocal performances hold potential for undermining the rational order behind the systematic conventions of written language" (119). She offers two classification schemes, referring to content and form. On the level of content, she divides the songs into three groups: "(1) real songs with original lyrics [...], (2) songs based on real melodies or lyrics, which have been significantly altered, (3) songs which belong to the realm of Pynchon's fiction" (123). She observes that formal experimentation with lyrics started only in *Gravity's Rainbow* and writes:

> In *Gravity's Rainbow* there can be found at least four different strategies of graphic experimentation: (1) transcription of songs as lyric poems following the conventions of written language, (2) indications of a song's rhythm or melody in stage directions located in brackets or outside the text, (3) selective phonetic transcription employed to mimic the sound of speech and singing, and (4) use of graphic symbols, such as long dashes, ellipses, or hyphens to mark the rhythm or prosody during vocal performances. (124)

Rouyan attributes the formal structure more significance in *Gravity's Rainbow* than the content because she focuses on questions of order and domination and on the disparity between oral and written language. Taking a detour through the "Aqyn's Song" and Tchitcherine's mission to alphabetize rural culture, she sees orality escape the domination of the written precisely through such musical outbursts that defy the orderliness and ordering power of justified, linear prose in standardized spelling.

The fact that the frequent silliness of the songs appears side by side with poetically and philosophically dense prose, in other words, that there is a juxtaposition of 'high' and 'low,' is a distinguishing mark of literary postmodernism (Jameson 165). But merely to leave it at that would amount to reiteration of a commonplace.

Sally E. Parry focuses on the songs of the Gilded Age that appear in *Gravity's Rainbow*. She links the "Vulgar Song" (*Gravity* 216) to the tune of "The Man Who Broke the Bank at Monte Carlo" (*Gravity* 206 and *Against* 1094) and concludes her short piece with these words: "The [Gilded Age songs'] rhythmic structures and, presumably, melodies are used in the *Gravity's Rainbow* songs, but the lyrics are full of vulgar words and implications. By juxtaposing a romanticized and contained past with a stark and frightening present and future, Pynchon deconstructs the conceit that there was ever a past better than (or worse than) the present" (178).

Not everyone thinks highly of the poetic merits of Pynchon's songs. William Logan, for instance, writes, "when Pynchon tries to write poetry, as opposed to embodying the methods of poetry, he shows a wooden and unschooled ear. [...] But they're masterful compared to his music-hall frolics, like this Jesuit recruiting song [from *Mason* 224–25]" (435). Logan does not explain why these would be particularly bad lyrics. Popular tunes do not have to obey the rules of poetry, nor exhibit poetic craftsmanship, and there is much greater freedom to stretch or condense words or syllables. Pynchon does not provide sheet music for his songs, so perhaps Logan "ain't hearing it aright" (*Mason* 263).

William Vesterman approaches the topic from a different angle. He does not focus so much on the function Pynchon's songs have in advancing or commenting on the plot but relates them to the author. To Vesterman, the fact that many songs appear comical and pop up almost out of nowhere, musical- or operetta-style, to punctuate the narrative, is a sign that they should not be dismissed: "[W]e can be sure song is a very serious issue precisely because of the frivolity with which it is treated. Be that as it may, songs do act like a magic cape in Pynchon's books by concealing not the characters but their author: they protect the author's ability to acknowledge, display and enjoy complexity without being dominated by it" (103). In other words, the respite the comical songs offer allows Pynchon to treat the very same topics with seriousness. The "Rocket Limericks" in *Gravity's Rainbow* and "Glee" in *The Crying of Lot 49*—a long enumeration of manufacturers of airborne military equipment—come to mind. In the case of the latter, the song lyrics do not in and of themselves appear comical or frivolous but they give that impression *because* they have been turned into song.

To be sure, not every one of Pynchon's songs is comical or frivolous. The masochistic "Love's a Lash" from *V.* (238), for instance, fails to convey any sense of comedy because the "sjambok," "the slave," the "cankered tissue" are very real in the context of the narrative. There is no ironic or humorous twist as there is with the "Rocket Limericks." The atrocities going on in colonial South West Africa are not as distanced as those in "Glee" sung by the shareholders of a fictional armaments manufacturer and hence the lyrics do not appear funny just by virtue of being turned into song.

Similarly, not every frivolous song treats a serious or painful subject or appears in such a context. *Bleeding Edge*'s "In the

Toilet" (307–08), for instance, resonating with toilet passages in other novels, or *Vineland*'s "Wacky Coconuts" (66) should be read (or listened to) primarily as funny songs. Although the performance of "Wacky Coconuts" also has the function of distracting the passengers of the hijacked airplane and expelling the intruders, the situation is altogether too surreal to be taken very seriously. The same may be said for Nazi Vegetable's "In the Toilet," which follows an elaborate description of the restroom area "with three dozen stalls, its own bar, television lounge, sound system, and deejay" (*Bleeding* 306) and ends with the lines "Toilet! flush all those / Troubles and dance!" The latter song may still be read in line with Vesterman as a meta-commentary on *Bleeding Edge*, which is decidedly less complex than Pynchon's longer novels, and with Hume and Knight's category of the opiate of the people, but, I believe, many of Pynchon's songs should be taken first and foremost in a good-natured spirit that does not pretend to depth, wisdom, or complex commentary. Perhaps Charles Clerc hits the target in his characterization of the function of songs in *Mason & Dixon* because he is the least specific:

> As in *Gravity's Rainbow*, they both interrupt and bolster the action; they change mood and focus; they comment or expand upon an incident; they render protests or pay tribute; they show the lighter side of a sad or tragic event; they show rifts between illusion and reality; by making fun, they affirm the necessity of laughter and joy. (116)

In the end, the fact that Pynchon has written so many song lyrics is significant. Although I find little reason to disagree with the different approaches of Rouyan, Vesterman, Clerc, or Hume and Knight, in order to get to the core of it, one has to look at every song individually and in its context, a feat this study will not be able to perform. If Rouyan is right in claiming that the oral nature of Pynchon's songs deterritorializes or at least comments on the form and function of writing (which territorialized orality in the first place), then Pynchon scholarship, including this book, is haunted by the irony that academic criticism and classification schemes intellectualize and reterritorialize this displacement.

Pynchon on Record, Vol. 4

In the "Introduction" to four short stories by Joseph Conrad, Cedric Watts writes, "One test of literary merit is fecundity, the ability to generate offspring" (xix). While Pynchon's literary offspring include many contemporary writers, among them Nobel laureate Elfriede Jelinek, who co-authored the German translation of *Gravity's Rainbow*, they may be difficult to spot unless they have referenced Pynchon or have acknowledged his influence in interviews. Perhaps more than many other novelists, Pynchon's work has also generated musical offspring. In 1982, Steven Moore made a first attempt to collect such songs and inspirations in *Pynchon Notes* under the title "Pynchon on Record," to which Laurence Daw added "More on Pynchon on Record" in 1983. Sixteen years later, Juan García and Oscar de Jódar published an article that added more names to the previous lists. Since then, the search algorithms on the internet have vastly improved—and so have increased the amount of available information and the possibilities of uploading one's own material. While a discussion of Pynchon-inspired music goes beyond his writing as such, I believe no large-scale study on music in his work would be complete without acknowledging his musical offspring. My entire list is published on www.thomaspynchon.com and, at the time this book goes to print, encompasses more than 120 items.

The Crying of Lot 49 and *Gravity's Rainbow* proved to be the most fruitful novels for musical adaptations: the former likely because its length made it more accessible to readers and because it has been around longer than any other Pynchon novel except for *V.*; the latter probably because of the position the novel holds in the canon of postmodern literature. The range of genres covered by these recordings spans jazz (remarkably little), new classical music, world music, and all sorts of pop/rock subgenres such as rock'n'roll, indie, punk, new wave, and metal. The references range from homages to quotations and from inspirations to adaptations.

Some were recorded by well-known or influential bands and musicians such as Laurie Anderson, Radiohead, John Zorn, Mark Knopfler, and Soft Machine, others by amateur bands. Finally, there must also have been unsuccessful attempts at recording Pynchon, most of which will never be known. According to a radio interview with Laurie Anderson, for instance, she once contacted Pynchon to ask for his permission to turn *Gravity's Rainbow* into an opera. He replied that he would give his permission only if she used banjos exclusively ("Transcript of the Laurie Anderson Interview"). I cannot recall where but I heard the same story—perhaps also involving Laurie Anderson, perhaps another artist—with Pynchon naming the kazoo as the only admissible instrument for an operatic adaptation of *Gravity's Rainbow.*

The fact that most of the works of music cataloged are from recent years can likely be explained by the better visibility lesser-known bands enjoy on the internet nowadays. I doubt that it took about fifty years after a novel was released for it to catch on in the music world. Most artists mentioned are based in Western Europe or North America. Although this may have to do with Pynchon's popularity in these regions, it is more sensible to assume that I simply did not find artists whose references are in languages other than English. The reason that the adaptations of songs penned by Pynchon are recorded predominantly by lesser known artists may have to do with legal considerations. If little or no money is involved and the visibility of the artist is not so great, the author or the legal departments of the publishing houses may not care to intervene. Furthermore, well-known bands tend to write all their own lyrics and not reproduce someone else's, partly as their own artistic endeavor, partly due to legal considerations or because of the royalties they receive for their own lyrics.

On the occasion of some of my New York and Philadelphia talks on the subject in 2015 and 2016, musician and poet Tyler Burba interpreted eight songs from four different novels, mainly from *Gravity's Rainbow*. Over time, he expanded his catalog of Pynchon's songs according to my wishes, and eventually, it all culminated in the collaboration on an entire album entitled *"Now Everybody—" Visit Interprets Songs by Thomas Pynchon*. When I presented my work on Pynchon's saxophone and kazoo in Atlanta, local musicians Reese Burgan and Caleb Herron accompanied the talk on the respective instruments, as did Peter Price (kazoos and electronics) in Philadelphia. There is no telling how many other artists have referenced Pynchon or recorded songs from his books or were simply inspired by his work, but if progeny is a mark of literary accomplishment, these albums, songs, and bands are testament to Pynchon's wide-ranging appeal as a writer of musicalized fiction.

Let us see why.

2

Lessons in Organology

Starting with the appearance of a guitar on the first page of *V.*, Pynchon's novels display an interest in musical instruments that only appears to fade with a marked decrease in *Bleeding Edge.* In total, Pynchon references 130 different musical instruments 720 times throughout his work—excluding signal instruments played for signal purposes (see Appendix). These 130 uniquely named instruments sometimes include members of instrument families such as the alto, the C-melody, the tenor, the baritone, and the contrabass saxophone and can be merged into roughly 70 instrument categories. By far the largest category is that of percussion instruments with a total of 115 references to 28 different instruments. Adding up the most frequently mentioned instruments, the following picture emerges:

Instrument family	*Different members*[1]	*References*	*Books*
Percussion	28	115	10
Keyboard	8	81	8
Guitar	5	71	9
Saxophone	5	59	9
Accordion	3	36	6
Bass	3	35	6
Harmonica	1	34	3
Ukulele	2	31	6
Trumpet	2	23	7
Kazoo	1	20	6

Table 1: Most frequent instrument references.

1 The percussion family here excludes tuned percussive instruments mainly used to play melodies or chords: the xylophone, the glockenspiel, the marimba, and the carillon. All harmonicas and kazoos were included in one respective family since many of Pynchon's different harmonicas and kazoos are fictional. The accordion category comprises the accordion, the bandoneón, and the concertina. The keyboard category comprises the upright piano, the grand piano, the player piano, synthesizers, harmoniums, claviers, harpsichords, and keyboards (71 of those references are upright and grand pianos). The trumpet category includes the cornet. Uncollected writings that did not appear in book form were grouped as one hypothetical book.

The bulk of these instruments fits into two groups: the first group is the jazz combo (sax, trumpet, bass, piano, percussion) which overlaps with the rock band (guitar, bass, piano, percussion; sax in earlier rock'n'roll bands). This is in line with Pynchon's preferred styles of music as evidenced in the scattered biographical accounts. The other group encompasses instruments that seem dear to Pynchon but are not part of the Western canon of orchestration: the ukulele, the kazoo, and the harmonica. While Pynchon stages all instruments of the second group with affection, insight, and a good deal of humor, in the first group only the saxophone and its players are developed with comparable care. The prominence of the accordion (whose sound-producing principle is the same as the harmonica's) is more easily overlooked, the reason being that Pynchon, it appears, stages it only as an instrument that is played to make music and not as one that has a set of historical, political, or socioeconomic characteristics useful to comment on or further the plot. The trumpet may figure high on this list, but Pynchon, having come of age when the trumpet as the central jazz instrument was already being replaced by the saxophone (by 1949, it was bordering on the anachronistic to call a book *Shining Trumpets: A History of Jazz*, as Rudi Blesh did), does not bestow any particular and consistent qualities on it. Pynchon does name or allude to a few trumpet players—Chet Baker, Miles Davis, Dizzy Gillespie, Clifford Brown—but they belong to the era of bebop, hard bop, and cool jazz, and there is no indication of a particular trumpet tradition that he refers to, leaving out entirely some of their predecessors, such as Louis Armstrong or his mentor King Oliver.

Musical instruments are extensions of humans. They, too, are media, and Pynchon makes it clear that for them, too, the medium is the message if "the 'message' of any medium or technology is the change of scale or pace or pattern it introduces into human affairs" (McLuhan 8). This becomes evident when Pynchon repeatedly refers to the Bösendorfer *Imperial*, one of the most expensive grand pianos, a full eight octave range, and brings the imperial quality of that instrument to our attention. This is not an instrument that is casually played or purchased, but its dimensions (almost three meters in length) and its sheer weight (552 kg) make it one of the most imposing musical instruments with the possible exception of the church organ, whose uses, however, are usually limited to sacred music.

It would be a misconception to see musical instruments as mere tools, as bodily extensions that execute the will and intention of their users. Every innovation of consequence has come about because the user discovered what else the medium could do apart from its intended use. There is always an interplay of resistance and discovery between the user and the instrument.

As Aden Evens has theorized, music arises only from this mutual resistance of the player and her instrument: "There must be a friction between musician and instrument, specific points of contact where the hard surfaces of the instrument meet the soft flesh of the musician" (160). This mutual resistance can be understood as forming something like the core of an ontology of organology. The mutuality also resonates with the notion that we shape the media and then the media shape us.

One of the instruments where the topos of resistance is historically evident is the ukulele. Sean Carswell has done a thorough reading of this little instrument in Pynchon's work, inspecting every instance of its occurrence. Its history is fascinating enough: In 1865, the Kingdom of Hawaii faced a shortage of laborers and commissioned one William Hillebrand, a German physician, entrepreneur, and botanist, to find contract workers abroad (Tranquada & King 34). In 1876, he landed on Madeira, an island of similar climatic but devastating economic conditions, and recruited a great number of Madeirans. The second ship of laborers to arrive in Honolulu in 1879, the Ravenscrag, carried the cabinet makers Manuel Nunes, Jose do Espirito Santo, and Augusto Dias, as well as a traditional small Madeiran guitar, the machete (38). After the expiration of their work contracts, they stayed on Hawaii and, although likely not trained instrument makers, began repairing and manufacturing stringed instruments, among them a small guitar which came to be called the ukulele. Before long, the ukulele was nearly ubiquitous and members of the royal family received music lessons on the instrument. Less than a decade after the Ravenscrag's arrival, the ukulele was considered Hawaii's national instrument (37). Carswell writes:

> Hawaiians were faced with the violent overthrow of their islands by a network of corporate and government interests from within the United States. They could not combat this network's overpowering military presence, so they sought resistance in other ways. Specifically, they sought to maintain and validate their culture. The 'ukulele became the symbol for this Hawaiian culture. ("Ukulele" 206)

By the beginning of the twentieth century, "the 'ukulele began to make appearances up and down the West Coast in the hands of young ladies" (Tranquada & King 67). Through its presence in a number of expositions, most notably the 1915 Panama-Pacific International Exposition in San Francisco, it quickly gained wide popularity in the U.S. In 1949, Mario Maccaferri, an Italian instrument maker, introduced the first plastic ukulele at $5.95. He soon had 50,000 orders for plastic ukes and then moved on to sell millions more (Beloff 106). Thanks to plastic, the instrument was now produced on a grand and mechanized scale.

Carswell writes that the ukulele "is born of colonialism, global markets, and militarization [...], but it is also born of celebration, community, and cultural identity" ("Ukulele" 207). The same can be said of the harmonica, the kazoo, and the saxophone. While the saxophone was at all times an instrument for professionals, the ukulele, the harmonica, and the kazoo were persistently derided as toys and given attention mainly for their comical effect. Their worthiness of being labeled musical instruments was much disputed, or outright negated, throughout the twentieth century. Nevertheless, due to their inexpensive manufacturing and compact size, they have enjoyed considerable success not only in musical education and home entertainment but also in boosting morale in various wars where the USA was involved. While only the kazoo is an all-American invention, all three of those Preterites of organology needed the creative soil and the mass market of the USA to really take off.

Carswell's writing about the ukulele can be viewed as a blueprint of how I will develop the following sections on the harmonica, the kazoo, and the saxophone. I will briefly sketch the respective histories and highlight resonances in the way Pynchon stages the instruments and their players before doing select readings of how this all plays out.

The Harmonica

Pynchon's harmonica appears in a great variety of contexts. It is Tyrone Slothrop's beloved instrument accidentally dropped into a toilet bowl to resurface later thousands of miles away, bringing solace before the protagonist's scattering. While its blues characteristics comfort the Preterite, both in *Gravity's Rainbow* and in *Vineland*, they also unnerve the Elect. The harmonica ridicules power relationships in *Against the Day* but, in the same novel, appears in an extended episode with a darker and more twisted undercurrent, mirroring the various appropriations and reappropriations in the instrument's often turbulent history.

The first European harmonica appeared in Vienna around 1820. Kim Field writes that by "1830 most Europeans knew the mouth organ as the *mundharmonika* [...]" (25). Already in 1827, the mouth harmonica came to the German village of Trossingen where thirty years later, Matthias Hohner opened his own business and turned out 650 instruments that year (26). In 1862, Hohner began exporting instruments to the United States, which laid the foundation of a global musical instruments empire, overshadowing its early competitors with high-quality instruments, clever marketing, industrial espionage, diversification, and by buying up rivals.[2] Unexpectedly, it would be the USA where the harmonica enjoyed most success, starting in the regions with large German immigrant populations, such as Texas and the Carolinas (Wenzel and Häffner 58). The small and affordable instrument that allowed bending notes for less rigidly defined tonal systems than the European one soon came into the hands of African-Americans as "even the poorest cotton picker could scrape together the few cents needed to acquire one" (58–59).

By 1911, the company—renamed Matth. Hohner AG—shipped out around eight million instruments annually and had branches in New York, Toronto, London, Warsaw, and Vienna (21). The harmonica was already widely distributed during World War I. In 1930, musicologist Curt Sachs wrote: "Inexpensiveness and smallness have earned the harmonica the favor of the broad masses [...]. The role it played in the World War will be a glorious chapter in its history; on never-ending marches, the undemanding harmonica [...] replaced entire regimental bands" (Eickhoff 66; my translation). The harmonica in World War I was commemorated with the exhibition *Lebensretter und Seelentröster* ("Lifesaver and Soul Comforter") held at the Deutsches Harmonika Museum in Trossingen in 2014, where, among other things, harmonicas were on display that had caught bullets and saved

2 In the course of the company's history, Hohner also manufactured saxophones, recorders, and a number of other instruments. While most other Hohner instruments were not as highly regarded as the harmonicas and accordions, some instruments such as the Melodica and Clavinet acquired outright cult status among musicians in the 1960s and later.

their owners' lives. In order to be able to export to countries such as France and Great Britain during the war, Hohner opened a branch in neutral Switzerland (Wenzel and Häffner 24). By the 1930s, Matth. Hohner AG employed 4,000 workers and manufactured about 25 million harmonicas each year.[3]

During World War II, Hohner was faced with the draft of many of their skilled employees. The company was unable to export to the USA and had to dedicate two thirds of the factories to the war effort, producing armaments with the use of Russian and Eastern European forced labor. The remaining production was geared toward soldiers. A Hohner advertisement from the time of World War II shows two happy soldiers with harmonicas in their hands and reads: "Wer dem feldgrauen Mann eine wirkliche Freude bereiten will, schenke eine 'Hohner'" ("If you want to bring real joy to the field-gray man, give him a Hohner," reproduced in Häffner 43 and Eickhoff 62). More than any other musical instruments manufacturer, at least to my knowledge, Hohner was not only instrumentalized by a war-waging government but in turn also instrumentalized the war to achieve further sales. Hohner was quick to capitalize on the circumstances by producing a number of war-themed harmonicas—ranging from sentimental to martial—by targeting families of soldiers as a new market, and by cooperating with the Nazi government. The main reason, however, Hohner was able to capitalize on the war—within the limits afforded in times of crisis—was its well-oiled marketing machinery and the fact that the harmonica is a small, inexpensive, and easy-to-learn instrument which is well suited for distribution in great numbers.

Once established, the harmonica became a staple mainly in folk, blues, and country music. The miniature four-hole Little Lady (produced since 1924) was the first instrument in outer space when astronaut Walter Schirra sneaked it aboard his spacecraft and played "Jingle Bells" on Christmas 1965 (Wenzel and Häffner 24). To this day, Hohner is the world market leader in harmonicas and accordions.

Pynchon's perhaps most famous harmonica scene takes place in *Gravity's Rainbow*. During a hospital visit in 1944, when Tyrone

3 The sources differ slightly. Eickhoff writes that the first major shipment to the USA took place in 1868 (29) and that 25 million harmonicas were produced in 1939 (30).

Slothrop receives an injection of the truth serum sodium amytal, he has a vision of visiting Boston's Roseland State Ballroom where a young Malcolm X works as a shoeshine boy and Jack Kennedy is a regular, albeit absent that night. As Slothrop vomits in the men's room, he accidentally drops his harmonica into the toilet bowl, "the low reeds singing an instant on striking porcelain" (*Gravity* 64). While he is deciding whether he should go after it, the 1938 jazz standard "Cherokee" is resonating through the walls from downstairs. Slothrop recalls the sweet and sentimental lyrics of the song alternatively titled "Indian Love Song" and deems it "one more lie about white crimes" (*Gravity* 65). As he plunges into the toilet bowl in search of his beloved harmonica and disappears down the white ceramic rabbit hole into the collective unconscious of the shit-brown sewage system, he barely escapes being sodomized by Red Malcolm and his gang: "In Slothrop's fantasies of sodomy, he anticipates the change in racial relations, when Blacks will not settle for being shoeshines and musicians, but will want power and revenge" (Hume and Knight, "Orchestration" 376). Yet Slothrop escapes, and if his penis is not his own (*Gravity* 219), at least his anus is. His descent into the underworld in the hope of retrieving his instrument is a first intimation of his becoming Orpheus later on in the novel. Slothrop disappears, as will become his habit, but only when he is reunited with his harmonica will he be able to disappear for good.

As he is looking for the harmonica, that German-Austrian instrument which in its African-American idiom allows "tunes to be played, millions of possible blues lines, notes to be bent from the official frequencies," he vainly places his hopes in Kennedy to help him retrieve it: "If anybody could've saved that harp, betcha Jack could" (67). If anybody could have saved those lost, the Preterite—the African-Americans, the Native Americans, and anyone who would come under the scrutiny of Joseph McCarthy and later the Nixon administration—and acknowledged what is bent from the official frequencies of white Anglo-Saxon capitalism, Slothrop seems to say, John F. Kennedy could have. But before the story is finished or the novel is published, Kennedy—who ended up maneuvering the world closer to nuclear meltdown than anyone else before or since—will have gone the way of all flesh, and it is Richard M. Nixon/Zhlubb who survives until the very last page.

As Slothrop emerges from the sewer line into an eery underworld, he hears a "mouthsucking giant five-note chords" harmonica accompaniment to "Red River Valley" with altered lyrics informing him that "the toilet it ain't going nowhar" (69). "Red River Valley," a sentimental song about a girl who must leave the valley, comments on the fate of both the harmonica and Eurydice. While many other lyrics were set to this song during World War II, the original lyrics go: "From this valley they say you are going / We will miss your bright eyes and sweet smile / For they say you are taking the sunshine / Which has brightened our pathways a while," and in the sixth verse: "As you go to your home by the ocean / May you never forget those sweet hours."

N. Katherine Hayles and Mary B. Eiser argue that White-Red-Black is the basic triad in *Gravity's Rainbow,* and "red, the third term, is meant to open a space in which color can again appear. [...] [R]ed is the mediating third term that comes between black and white to signify a potential for transformation, a germ of passion [...]" (7). It is the color associated with the Preterite. Red and its washed-down, pale companion pink/rose are very much present in this scene: Red Malcolm, Cherokee, the Roseland Ballroom, Roosevelt, to name a few. Still, Pynchon does not simply use the three colors white, red, and black (which were also the colors of the flag of Nazi Germany) as symbols for, say, white Americans, Native Americans, and African-Americans. This triad would exclude everything and everyone that does not match these colors, such as the West Indian bartender (*Gravity* 64). Instead, Pynchon complicates matters and undermines the notion of authenticity along ethnic lines: "Cherokee" is a song about an Indian maiden written by a British composer after his emigration to the USA. Only by being performed by African-Americans, most notably Charlie Parker, was it able to lose its sentimental undertones and become something other than "one more lie about white crimes." Gerhard Westerath's interpretation is that "Pynchon plays with the idea that preterite peoples, Indian subjects evoked by the title and black musicians, come together in the medium of jazz to counteract white structures" (110).

Some 600 pages later, during his meanderings through post-war Germany, Slothrop eventually finds the harmonica he lost in his flashback to or vision of the Roseland Ballroom—or the harmonica finds him. He immediately recognizes it as his, as it must be if there is only "[o]ne of each of everything" (*Gravity* 69) in the world. The rediscovered instrument comes up after the tail end of the bickering between Gustav the composer and Emil "Säure" Bummer about whether tonality as exemplified by "Spohr, Rossini, Spontini" (634) or atonality as exemplified by Schoenberg is of higher musical value.[4] This is significant insofar as neither the tonality whose end was introduced by Richard Wagner (who is ever present in *Gravity's Rainbow*; see J. O. Tate) nor the dodecaphonic row invented by Schoenberg as a consequence is able to break out of the European twelve-tone scale. It takes an instrument as small as the harmonica in the hands and at the lips of Americans to bend notes "from the official frequencies, bends Slothrop hasn't really the breath to do . . . not yet but someday . . ." (*Gravity* 67), and to move into the microtonality of blue notes.[5]

After Slothrop finds his harmonica, he becomes a "crossroad [...], and his chest fills and he stands crying, not a thing in his head, just feeling natural . . . ." (638). This scene occurs sometime after the day of the Feast of the Transfiguration, which in 1945 ironically or perversely coincided with the bombing of Hiroshima. It also brings to mind Martin Heidegger's notion of the fourfold of the earth, the sky, the mortals, and the divinities, another crossroad—the place of dwelling in the mode of safeguarding where one of the terms always already implies the fourfold of Being (Heidegger 344–45).

Slothrop disappears or dies or is transfigured somewhere in Germany's Harz Mountains, and if he indeed did die on the "green wet valleyed Earth" (638), or if death is another word for his disappearance and scattering, then "They will bury [him] where you have wandered / Near the hills where the daffodils grow," as the lyrics to "Red River Valley" go. Though Pynchon does not make this link explicit by mentioning "Red River Valley" here, the scene harks back to the Roseland Ballroom and Slothrop's escape from the sewer. Once reunited with the harmonica, he is allowed to let go and become one with the earth.

---

4 Like Gustav and Säure's discussion, Spohr's *Symphony No. 6 in G ("Historical")* undertakes, albeit in compositional terms, a survey of the history of Western music. Werner Wolf notes: "Louis Spohr's symphony no. 6 (the "Historical", 1840) [...] attempted to compose in the styles of four consecutive periods (Bach [and Handel, my addition], Haydn/Mozart, Beethoven, and the present)" ("Literature and Music" 461).

5 Incidentally, Pynchon does not seem to move beyond the micro-tonalities of blue notes in Western music (though he does in "world musics" such as the Tuva throat-singing in *Against the Day*). The Theremin which thrives on microtonalities appears only briefly in *Bleeding Edge* (454). See the saxophone section for more on the Roseland Ballroom scene and Chapter 3 for more on the blue notes and Gustav and Säure's discussion.

Now it becomes clear why Pynchon, with one exception (635), did not choose the word "harmonica" to designate Slothrop's instrument, but "harp," short for "mouth harp" or Hohner's famed "blues harp."[6] It allows him to link Slothrop to Orpheus, as is announced first by his descent into the underworld of the sewer and then by the insertion of an excerpt from Rilke's *Sonnets to Orpheus*. Weisenburger notes: "With his harp he is Orpheus, the dismembered Greek god [sic!]. He embodies the acceptance of pain in Rilke's *Sonnets to Orpheus,* with their climactic expression of being and flux—'To the rushing water speak: I am'" (*Companion* 321). And a few pages later: "Slothrop's Hohner is a sign of his identity with Orpheus, the mythic harp player and dismembered holy Fool. The Hohner is thus also a sign of Slothrop's preterition" (324–25). I would maintain that the analogy holds even though Pynchon and Weisenburger are a little imprecise when it comes to Orpheus's instrument. Orpheus is reported to have played the lyre and not the harp.[7] Nevertheless, I agree with Weisenburger when he links Slothrop's instrument to preterition but would maintain that the harmonica—like the kazoo and the ukulele—is always already a sign of preterition in Pynchon's worlds. It is never an instrument played by the Elect but always by the Preterite.

After Slothrop's disappearance, there is a passage where harmonica blues-playing is philosophized: "Blues is a matter of lower sidebands—you suck a clear note, on pitch, and then bend it lower with the muscles of your face. Muscles of your face have been laughing, tight with pain, often trying not to betray any emotion, all your life. Where you send the pure note is partly a function of that" (*Gravity* 656). The transformation of pain into laughter resonates with Slothrop's transfiguration in a state of *Gelassenheit* or selflessness. This loss of self, painful as it may be, is also liberating, as Sascha Pöhlmann writes: "At the cost of his self, he

6 The blues harp product line, distributed under the name Marine Band in honor of John Philip Sousa, is Hohner's best-selling instrument and has been in production since 1896.

7 Although both instruments were played in ancient Greece, the main organological difference is that the lyre has strings of equal length that run parallel to the soundboard while the harp's strings are of different lengths and run vertically to the soundboard (Montagu 128). There were different types of lyre: the *lyra* was "the instrument of amateurs, especially for after-dinner songs," while the *khitara* "seems to have been the choice of the professional bards and musicians" (129).

manages to break out of all hegemonic narratives that constructed and fixed his identity" (*Postnational* 358). Slothrop—if that is still his name after the transformation—finally escapes control and conditioning and cannot be apprehended anymore. Some believe that fragments of his former self roam the earth and have "grown into consistent personae of their own" (*Gravity* 757). The novel mirrors this by falling apart into more or less disjointed scenes, episodes, and fragments with increasing frequency as it nears its end.

Some twenty pages before the end, we learn that "[t]here's supposed to be a last photograph of [Slothrop] on the only record album ever put out by The Fool, an English rock group. [...] There is no way to tell which of the faces is Slothrop's: the only printed credit that might apply to him is 'Harmonica, kazoo—a friend'" (757). Like the novel itself, which is bracketed between a dedication to folk musician Richard Fariña and the singing of a hymn composed by Slothrop's ancestor William, its main character Tyrone Slothrop is introduced as playing the ukulele, "an American George Formby" (18), and is bid farewell by being credited for playing the kazoo and the harmonica.[8] Slothrop has left a "busted corkscrewing ukulele string" (19) on his littered desk at the beginning of the novel, constraining the potential of the instrument. But as Slothrop gradually loses his identity and finally his self, his music-making moves in the opposite direction: from the impossibility of playing the full range due to the busted string clearly attributed to Slothrop to a historical—though fictional—record, leaving some doubt if Slothrop really is The Fool's harmonica and kazoo player. He is compared to a real ukulele and banjolele player at the beginning and to a member of a fictitious band at the end, mirroring *Gravity's Rainbow*'s opening with a dedication to a real musician and its ending with a fictitious hymn.

Slothrop's entering and leaving are marked by the "symmetrical opposites" (146) that pervade the novel. He may disappear but, taking a cue from the Wernher von Braun quotation at the beginning of the first section, "Beyond the Zero," his spiritual existence will continue: "Nature does not know extinction; all

8 In *Been Down So Long It Looks Like Up to Me,* Fariña's novel prefaced by Pynchon, protagonist Gnossos Pappadopoulis carries a Hohner F in his back-back. The novel also shares some of the features encountered in Pynchon's writing: a keen interest in food, long lists of assorted items, a wide variety of drugs and musical instruments, paranoia, conspiracy, and sex.

it knows is transformation" (1). "Nothing disappears without a trace," the quote would continue. One of the traces is *Gravity's Rainbow* itself, another one is The Fool's record, and another one, of course, is air set vibrating to carry a tune. What Pynchon seems to say here is that in order to liberate oneself from the imposed order and leave a trace in the world, one must move into the realm of the imagination: becoming requires letting go. Or in Sascha Pöhlmann's words: "Pynchon [...] postulates no necessity except the necessity to imagine these worlds in order to change this one" (*Postnational* 365).

Although this is the last time Slothrop is referred to more than in passing, there are more harmonicas coming up. Shortly before the end of *Gravity's Rainbow*, in a prolepsis playing out around 1970, Pynchon takes up the harmonica politics of the Third Reich to underline the instrument's preterite nature and draw parallels between Hitler and Nixon a.k.a. Richard M. Zhlubb in a mock newspaper article entitled "Orpheus Puts Down Harp." The double meaning here is that Steve Edelman, after the disappearance of Slothrop another incarnation of Orpheus, puts his harp down or that the Orpheus Theater puts Edelman and his harp down.

> Richard M. Zhlubb, night manager of the Orpheus Theatre on Melrose [on which the rocket will descend in the last lines of *Gravity's Rainbow*], has come out against what he calls 'irresponsible use of the harmonica.' [...] Zhlubb states that his queues, especially for midnight showings, have fallen into a state of near anarchy because of the musical instrument. [...] Steve Edelman, a Hollywood businessman, accused last year of an 11569 (Attempted Mopery with a Subversive Instrument), is currently in Atascadero under indefinite observation. It is alleged that Edelman, in an unauthorized state of mind, attempted to play a chord progression on the Department of Justice list, out in the street and in the presence of a whole movie-queue of witnesses. (769–70)

Edelman commits three crimes or misdemeanors: in an unauthorized state of mind he *allegedly* and in public plays a banned chord progression on a subversive instrument. Even the Nixon administration would have to recognize that these allegations are too flimsy to justify a conviction. Therefore, he can only be accused and placed under indefinite observation under a doubly vague allegation: mopery, and that not even carried out but only attempted. Mopery is a vague term whose exact legal ramifications are unclear. According to the OED, mopery is "[t]he action of committing a minor or petty offence, such as loitering, etc.; contravention of a trivial or hypothetical law, esp. when used as an excuse to harass or arrest a person against whom no more serious crime can be charged." In *Gravity's Rainbow*, which was published in 1973, as the Watergate investigations were unfolding but before Nixon was forced to step down, Pynchon makes accusations which, if read literally, would not be substantial. Allegorically, however, they amount to a clear political statement about the FBI's COINTELPRO and similar programs which were assumed to be in place. The two gravest accusations Pynchon makes are that under Nixon and McCarthy (and others holding totalitarian conceptions of society and nation state) thoughts were not free and that petty accusations were fabricated to put supposedly subversive subjects away.

The other meaning of mopery, according to the OED, is the behavior of a moper. To bring these two meanings together, it is illegal to mope, that is, to fail to display enthusiasm for what is economically and politically given. By playing his subversive chord progression, Edelman breaks up the orderly rows of moviegoers that will be fed into Hollywood's feel-good machinery of the Orpheus Theater, symbolic of the globalization of depoliticized commodity fetishism, which will be further examined in *Vineland*, a novel that accuses film and TV of lulling formerly subversive forces and making them complicit with capitalism's consumer culture.

What appears to be a humorous fancy is based on the conflicting ways the Third Reich dealt with harmonica instruments, that is, the accordion and the harmonica. Already in 1929, one Georg Götsch wrote a "Report on the Adequacy of the Harmonica as a Students', Orchestra's, and People's Instrument" in response to a harmonica advertising campaign and criticized it harshly: "The harmonica is a machine that offers not only a ready-made tone but also a ready-made tone sequence, even a ready-made sound sequence, and is thus suited for tonal dullness at the most, but does not educate toward intellectual or creative freedom" (qtd. in Eickhoff 38–39; my translation). In 1933, it was argued that the accordion was not a jazz instrument, apparently the biggest threat to the *Volksgeist,* and there was no reason to ban it—unlike the kazoo or the harmonica in Zhlubb's world (*Gravity* 771). Although the harmonica was already hugely popular—Eickhoff reports that in 1938, there were 6,000 harmonica orchestras in Germany with a total of 300,000 members (241)—Hohner's mass-produced instruments did not accord with the spirit of the music pedagogy at the time (Eickhoff 36–37). In February 1938, the *Reichsjugendführung* (The Reich's Youth Leadership) prohibited the establishment of harmonica and accordion orchestras in all formations of the Hitler Youth (75, 241).

Steve Edelman has a Jewish-sounding name (*Edelmann* means noble man), another comment on the implied similarity between the Third Reich's anti-semitism and the Nixon administration (and this also sheds light on the other meaning of 'putting down' as euthanizing). Zhlubb, on the other hand, is a slippery name with a slippery, comical sound reflecting perhaps the sound of a flushing toilet where the excretions that are part of life but too shameful to talk about are washed away never to be seen again.[9] The name Zhlubb cannot be placed in any one natural language but it rhymes with Krupp—visually, but also when pronounced in German—the German steel production dynasty, which manufactured tanks, guns, submarines, and other war technology. The key to understanding the name Zhlubb might, however, be provided by Allen Ginsberg and William S. Burroughs. Initially—that is, around 1953—a tender onomatopoeia to express the desire to merge with a loved one, Schlupp, Ginsberg later writes, means "to devour a soul parasitically" (Burroughs 6), which clearly resonates with much of the criticism directed at Hollywood's culture industry. By giving the Preterite a noble name and the Elect a disfigured, comical one at the end of the alphabet, Pynchon implies that respectability resides with the Preterite and not the Elect: "So the last shall be first, and the first last" (Matthew 20:16, *King James Bible*).

While this scene at first appears to be an allegory and critique of the Nixon administration drawing parallels to Hitler, Nixon's anti-communist predecessor Joseph McCarthy is also implied. In this reading, the Hollywood executive Steve Edelman stands for the mouth organ virtuoso Larry Adler, who was of Jewish descent and much present in Hollywood. While *Adler* in German means eagle, *adlig* is also a synonym for *edel,* noble. Larry Adler's father

9 In his comic book series *Sin City* (1991–1992), Frank Miller uses the name Burt Shlubb for an incompetent criminal charged with disposing of dead bodies. For a more detailed discussion of schlupp and schlupping, see Kahn 299–312.

changed their family name from Zelakovitch to Adler because he was tired of being the last one called upon in the immigration queues (see Michael Freedland). Larry Adler was a member of the Committee for the First Amendment protesting the blacklisting of Hollywood writers. Before long, McCarthy's House Committee on Un-American Activities blacklisted him as well, which resulted in the virtual impossibility for Adler to find work in the USA and led to his emigration to Britain (see Freedland). While Edelman plays a banned harmonica chord progression, so does Adler: he plays the tune of resistance to repression and the constraint of creativity in the film industry. If history repeats itself, then Adler/McCarthy was the tragedy and Edelman/Zhlubb the farce.

However, Pynchon's lineage of totalitarianisms criticized for their ways of dealing with the arts extends further. In his preface to *The Bass Saxophone*, Josef Škvorecký, who had lived in Czechoslovakia as an amateur musician and jazz lover during both the Hitler and the Stalin eras and emigrated to Canada after the Prague Spring, observed that "many titles on Senator Joe McCarthy's index of books to be removed from the shelves of US Information Libraries abroad are identical to many on the Index issued in Prague by the Communist Party early in the seventies" (8). He also observed that the propaganda machineries of the Third Reich and communist-era Czechoslovakia dealt in a very similar—and not always consistent—way with jazz music. When he published a decalogue of regulations issued during World War II by the local *Gauleiter* in Czechoslovakia's first jazz almanac in 1958, the censors promptly confiscated the entire edition (11). If it were not tragic, the list of regulations would appear almost comical from today's vantage point; still, it makes Edelman's alleged breaking of laws and regulations seem less far-fetched than at first glance.[10]

10 The list of regulations, republished from memory in *The Bass Saxophone*, prohibits "Jewishly gloomy lyrics"; "Negroid excesses in tempo"; "drum breaks longer than half a bar"; "plucking of string instruments"; and scat singing. Double basses must be bowed, saxophones replaced with the cello or the viola, and mutes "which turn the noble sound of wind and brass instruments into a Jewish-Freemasonic yowl" are prohibited. "Pieces in foxtrot rhythm (so-called swing) are not to exceed 20% of the repertoires" and "so-called jazz compositions may contain at most 10% syncopation." Finally, preference is given "to brisk compositions over slow ones (so-called blues); however, the pace must not exceed a certain

To come back to Pynchon: Pöhlmann makes a point that Pynchon's novels transcend the boundaries not only of nation-states but of nation-ness as well: "*Against the Day* leaves no doubt that a nationalized view of the world is simply too narrow, even dangerously restrictive in many regards; it emphatically demands a global approach from its readers" ("The Complex Text" 24). Indeed, anarchist dynamiter Veikko Rautavaara—possibly a nod to Finnish composer Einojuhani Rautavaara—had "never seen much difference between the Tsar's regime and American capitalism. To struggle against one, he figured, was to struggle against the other. Sort of this world-wide outlook" (*Against* 92). While the totalitarian conception of society starts from a conception of nation-ness, of us and them, inside and outside, and may attempt to transcend the boundaries of the nation-state to gain further influence, anarchism—like communism before its corruption by real politics, personal greed, and hunger for power—has always had a transnational outlook. This also allows Frank Traverse, Irishman Wolfe Tone O'Rooney, and the African-American musicians of the Merry Coons jass band to have a discussion about anarchist theory (416–17), and it is further illustrated by the fact that both the Chums of Chance and their Russian counterparts Tovarishchi Slutchainyi ("accidental comrades") eventually break all ties with their respective governments.

Strains of Subversive Music Day and Night

In *Vineland*, the harmonica serves as a prop for strengthening communal bonds against overwhelming military power. On the outskirts of an army base on the Trasero County coast,

> Against the somber military blankness at its back, here was a lively beachhead of drugs, sex, and rock and roll, the strains of subversive music day and night, accompanied by tambourines and harmonicas, [...] finding the ears of sentries attenuated but ominous, like hostile-native sounds in a movie about white men fighting savage tribes. (204)

---

degree of allegro, commensurate with the Aryan sense of discipline and moderation" (10–11).

The harmonica finds itself placed between warfare and subversion again. The instrument which had afforded soldiers consolation in the trenches and barracks of the European wars and the American Civil War is reappropriated by dope-smoking hippies for their Dionysiac frolicking, mocking the orderly procedures of chains of command before the sentries' very eyes and ears. The beachhead meant to be reserved for military forces is situated on the periphery, in line with Pynchon's preference for staying at the margins. The threshold between land and water, but also between occupied and occupiers, becomes an extraterritorial space wedged between the forces of subversion and the forces of repression, defying the dichotomy between the open beach related to drugs, sex, and rock'n'roll and the closed fortress related to discipline and hierarchy. From this dichotomy will arise a process of deterritorialization and reterritorialization as described by Gilles Deleuze and Félix Guattari: "Deterritorialization must be thought of as a perfectly positive power that has degrees and thresholds (epistrata), is always relative, and has reterritorialization as its flipside or complement. An organism that is deterritorialized in relation to the exterior necessarily reterritorializes on its interior milieus" (5). Thus, the space around the College of the Surf which was deterritorialized by usage later "secedes" from California and becomes the self-proclaimed People's Republic of Rock and Roll (or PR^3, in which one cannot fail to hear 'public relations to the third power,' or in Deleuze and Guattari's words the reterritorialization of the interior).[11] In other words, the informal deterritorialization becomes solidified, formalized, before it is again reterritorialized by the armed forces.

The tambourine accompaniment harks back to the percussive nature of African musics, reminding the guards of "hostile natives." The tambourine is also an inexpensive instrument that requires little skill, apart from a feeling for rhythm. Anyone can pick it up, and many did, not always to the great delight of the

11 *Vineland* also refers to the fictitious "*Italian Wedding Fake Book*, by Deleuze & Guattari" (97), to my knowledge Pynchon's only direct reference to French theory. I presented a paper on Italian music in Pynchon's work at the International Pynchon Week in Rome in 2019, after finishing the manuscript of this book, in which I offered a reading of the *Italian Wedding Fake Book* and further analyzed the discussion, in *Gravity's Rainbow*, between Gustav and Säure, on the value of Italian vs. German music. Inexplicably, I was not aware of Jeeshan Gazi's *Orbit* article on Deleuze and Guattari's *Italian Wedding Fake Book*.

classically trained listener such as Nixon/Zhlubb, as we learn in *Gravity's Rainbow:* "'At least it's not those tambourines,' Zhlubb mutters. 'There aren't as many tambourines as last year, thank God'" (772). What Zhlubb cannot bear is the democratic nature of the tambourine, the harmonica, and the kazoo, the fact that anyone can participate without the intervention of an authority and everyone's voice is heard without passing through the filters of censorship. Zhlubb's comments on the tambourine are uttered or muttered in the early 1970s, after the end of an era full of hope, the time when *Inherent Vice* sets in. As Zhlubb correctly remarks, by the 1970s, there were far fewer tambourines played in public than just a year or two before, a sure sign that the repressive forces were getting the upper hand again.

The "savage tribes" and the "hostile-native sounds" resonate loosely with Barbara Stewart's supposition about the initial use of the kazoo's sound-producing mechanism by African shamans as "weapons of intimidation" and to convey messages from the beyond (2). Significantly for *Vineland*, there is no 'authentic' image of savages; it has already passed through the filters of Hollywood and is mediated by film or television. Towards the end of the novel, Isaiah Two Four (whose name alludes to the verse to which the Nixon family Bibles were open when Nixon was sworn in to office in both 1969 and 1973 as well as to the 24-frames-per-second speed of celluloid film)[12] seems to voice Pynchon's critique of the former subversives' surrender to the establishment and sheds light on why Pynchon made Richard M. Zhlubb the owner of a movie theater in *Gravity's Rainbow:* "Whole problem 'th you folks's generation [...] is you believed in your Revolution, put your lives right out there for it—but you sure didn't understand much about the Tube. Minute the Tube got hold of you folks that was it, that whole alternative America, el deado meato" (*Vineland* 373). Or, as Thomas Hill Schaub observes, "In *Vineland*, primary among the mechanisms maintaining the status quo is the mediating power of television and film" (35). The soldiers' worldview relating the subversive strains of music to savages has already been co-opted by television and film but the hippies will

12 "And he shall judge among the nations, and shall rebuke many people: and they shall beat their swords into plowshares, and their spears into pruninghooks: nation shall not lift up sword against nation, neither shall they learn war any more" (Isaiah 2:4, *King James Bible*).

not be spared either as time progresses and an entire generation that promised change comes of age.

The fate that already hovers over *Vineland*'s first harmonica scene is spelled out in the second one. Zoyd Wheeler and his baby Prairie embark on a bus to Vineland, cross the Golden Gate Bridge, and head into the countryside towards Eureka:

> Aislemates struck up conversations, joints appeared and were lit, guitars came down from overhead racks and harmonicas out of fringe bags, and soon there was a concert that went on all night, a retrospective of the times they'd come through more or less as a generation, the singing of rock and roll, folk, Motown, fifties oldies, and at last, for about an hour just before the watery green sunrise, one guitar and one harmonica, playing the blues. (315)

The nostalgia of a youth outgrown is first celebrated in a festive retrospective in which everyone takes part, a reliving of the old and carefree times, then in the early morning hours reverts to a lone blues with minimal instrumentation, symbolic of a community split up into individuals by Nixon's state apparatus's strategy to divide and conquer. Blues lyrics, which are as integral a part of the blues as its musical form, are usually first-person accounts that focus on the human condition as it is experienced personally. LeRoi Jones (Amiri Baraka) writes: "Blues was a music that arose from the needs of a group, although it was assumed that each man had his *own* blues and that he would sing them. As such, the music was private and personal" (*Blues People* 82). The blues is a democratic form of music, and this is why the harmonica is so well suited to the needs of it—apart from the fact that it can bend notes. Jones believes that the blues is African-American not only in origin but also in spirit, that, unlike jazz, it is not an American form of expression but an African-American one. Still, it speaks to the musical form and its resonance that it can be performed and understood by people of other sociocultural and ethnic backgrounds as well. Pynchon does not specify the ethnic origin of the person playing the blues, which is why it can be assumed that he does not intend to limit its value to any one ethnicity.

Blues melody lines begin with a high note, usually the octave or the fifth, and descend from there all the way down to the tonic (Jahn 28), and blues scales are the only ones that are notated from the highest note to the lowest. The descending melody lines point towards a sense of helplessness, resignation, or decline, but the return to the tonic also expresses a return home. This return to the tonic is reflected not only in the melody line but also in the overall structure of the standard blues form where the last two bars are set to the tonic. One could say that the bus riders' return home is accompanied by the distinct feeling that the celebration is over and the state of affairs has not changed. The blues developed in the cotton fields as a more or less solitary pastime and later moved to the city where it became music performed for the entertainment of others. The bus ride reverses this chronology. As the bus pulls out of San Francisco, the passengers celebrate the Haight-Ashbury spirit where music could be played for its own sake but where concerts were also the order of the day. As the bus heads "for nothing but trees, fish, and fog" (*Vineland* 315), fatigue eventually sets in and the passengers doze off one by one. What remains is two people playing music for no one in particular other than for their own comfort. This music may be performed, it may be heard, but essentially, it reverts from public and collective to private and personal.

In the intricacies of greed as practiced under global capitalism

It is in *Against the Day* that Pynchon brings the full comic potential of the harmonica to bear. The novel also contains the only passage where the harmonica is played in praise of the (albeit imagined) upper echelons and immediately ridiculed for it:

> "Little Hellkite they're looking for an amalgamator, seein's how with the altitude and breathin in those fumes, the current one's got it into his head he's the President."
> "Oh. Of… ?"
> "Put it this way, he has this nipper with a harmonica foll'n him around everywhere playin 'Hail to the Chief.' Out of tune. Goes off into long speeches nobody can understand, declared war on the state of Colorado last week." (87–88)

In his fume-induced megalomaniac haze, the amalgamator sees himself as the President of the United States and has a harmonicist play "Hail to the Chief," the United States' Presidential Anthem, whenever he appears in public. The two characters appear little more than village idiots, and it is precisely this quality which allows Pynchon to comment on and reverse the role of music played for the Elect. Having an out-of-tune preterite instrument announce the 'President' is a way to reappropriate the meaning of this music in the service of the Elect and subvert it by ridicule. The harmonica in turn is shown as unfit to celebrate those in power; it adamantly refuses to be appropriated.

But this is just a glimpse of what is to come in the way of harmonicas. In a cartoon-like episode worthy of a Spike Jones soundtrack, Pynchon has the Chums of Chance, the young skyship explorers and heroes of a fictitious boys' adventure-book series, "drift into the brief aberration in their history known as the Marching Academy Harmonica Band" (471). They stay at a harmonica boarding school in Decatur for an unspecified period of time, hiding from Trespassers from another time or dimension (471–78).[13]

Like Slothrop's Roseland Ballroom episode, the Marching Academy Harmonica Band episode takes place in the excluded middle between consciousness and unconsciousness or between the "indicative world below" (1149) and a dream world, or "on the Counter-Earth, on it and of it, yet at the same time also on the Earth they had never, it seemed, left" (1148).[14] The Chums will remember it "as if in a dream" (471), not unlike Slothrop on sodium amytal, making it impossible for the reader to distinguish between fact and fiction, which is further complicated by the Chums' adventures already ambiguously being fiction within fiction while at times intersecting with the narrative and characters more clearly presented as historical. In both episodes, objects or persons from the dream suddenly appear in the protagonists' waking state, and in the later one Pynchon inserts mind-stretching allusions to the Roseland Ballroom episode in the Commandant's opiated lecturing on "odd latrine behavior, evoking in short flashes white porcelain fittings voluptuous in form," "a rapid

13 Pynchon does not specify which Decatur, other than in the school's advertisement which states it is located in "The Heart of the Mississippi Watershed" (472). There are cities, towns, and villages named Decatur in fifteen U.S. states. One of the Rocket Limericks in *Gravity's Rainbow* mentions "a young man from Decatur" (340), again not further specified, but perhaps Pynchon is referring to Decatur, Illinois, here as in *Against the Day* (21) and *V.* (101).

14 The formula "on it and of it," appropriately for the labor struggles throughout the novel, echoes Eugene Debs's famous statement: "I said then, and I say now, that while there is a lower class, I am in it, and while there is a criminal element, I am of it, and while there is a soul in prison, I am not free."

swoop down between the white fixtures," "everything reflected, headed for the Point at Infinity along a great curve," and so forth (475). In the Harmonica Marching Band Academy episode Pynchon furthermore invents a function that could well apply to Richard M. Zhlubb, namely the "Pitch Integrity Guard" whose acronym is much more likely to evoke the slang term for police than Pynchon's favorite animal.

The name of the institution where the Chums—or possibly their stand-ins—reside also keeps shifting. Pynchon variously uses the designations Marching Academy Harmonica Band, Harmonica Band Marching Academy, Marching Harmonica Band Academy, and Harmonica Academy Marching Band.[15] By assigning different names to the academy and its various subroutines, Pynchon plays on the boarding school's elusiveness, its u-topic position, and its resistance to identity formation. As an institution with several names and an ambiguous location, it cannot be apprehended and remains outside the grasp of external forces. It is a microcosm ruled by an ambiguous power—reterritorialized on the interior—and it remains such in the memories of the Chums.

Into this hypothetical space "not strictly speaking on the map at all" (*Against,* back-cover blurb), Pynchon infuses a number of novelty instruments like the D-flat Reverberating Harmonica, the I.G. Mundharfwerke "Little Giant," the "two-hole silver and pearl Microharmonica," and the "bell-metal bass harmonicas six feet long—great whopping *tubas* of harmonicas" (473). He shows knowledge of the various shapes and sizes of harmonicas that have been manufactured over time as well as the names of the models—and exaggerates them to comical effect.

Harmonicas are available in all tunings, but according to Martin Häffner, director of the Deutsches Harmonika Museum, most diatonic harmonicas produced are tuned to D-flat.[16] While in a classical, European musical setting, D-flat is not the most usual of keys, a number of compositions were written in this key, and if

15 Perhaps Pynchon had Brion Gysin's permutation poems in mind here, as he later refers to Morocco's "Gnaoua musicians [...] playing lutes and keeping time with metal hand percussion" while the "people were singing themselves into trances" (585), a scene right out of Gysin's time in Morocco with the Master Musicians of Jajouka. Another instance of permutation, albeit by shifting around the emphasis (and punctuation marks) rather than the words, is the Kenosha Kid sentence in *Gravity's Rainbow* (61–63; 72), which was recently turned into a piece of internet art by Darius Kazemi.

16 Personal e-mail (November 13, 2014).

Pynchon had one of them in mind, it might well have been the second movement ("Largo") of Antonin Dvořák's *Ninth Symphony*, better known as the *New World Symphony.* The mood of the second movement contrasts with the merry goings-on at the Academy and brings to the fore the darker undercurrents of the school. Although Pynchon does not mention Dvořák, a number of connections lend plausibility to this interpretation, literary and musical ones. Dvořák was present at the Chicago World's Fair where he conducted his *Symphony No. 8* in G major on August 12, 1893, and some of his *Slavonic Dances* (Downey 174; Tibbetts 17). In a *New York Herald* article from December 15, 1893, Dvořák, who by then had been in the United States for a little more than a year, is quoted: "Now, I found that the music of the negroes and of the Indians was practically identical" ("Dvorak on his New York" 11). In an article in the *Boston Herald* from May 28, 1893, he stated: "I am now satisfied that the future music of this country must be founded upon what are called the negro melodies" ("American Music"). Possibly, he based his judgment on the use of pentatonic scales or the rhythms and drones in some native American musics, but today, there seems to be agreement that he must have had a shallow understanding of Native American music, as opposed to African-American music (see the articles by John Clapham, Charles Hamm, and Michael Beckermann in *Dvořák in America* [Tibbetts, ed.]). According to Dennis B. Downey, his

> comments transgressed the boundaries between elite and folk culture. But his more cosmopolitan sensibilities also ran contrary to the *educational* philosophy of the fair's own music department, which traced America's musical heritage to West European antecedents. Furthermore, and most controversial, Dvorak's statement contradicted reigning racial stereotypes of the day, ones firmly embedded in the cultural symbolism of the 'White City' itself. (176)

Perhaps unaware of the controversy this might provoke, Dvořák created a community of the marginalized by conflating the diverse ethnicities of Americans as the foundation of a future American music.[17] His gesture is Pynchonian or postmodernist in stepping

17 In a piece for the *New York Times* about the centennial of the *New World Symphony*, Richard Taruskin, however, laments an inherent nationalism, both an American one and a German one: "Like other colonialisms, this one

across the boundaries of 'high' and 'low' art. His admiration for African-American music and his linking it to that of Native Americans takes us back to the Roseland Ballroom with its many references to both African-Americans and Native Americans. Thus, in the D-flat Reverberating Harmonica, Dvořák's appreciation reverberates into the past of 1893 as well as into the future of 1939.

With the remaining three instruments of Pynchon's imagination, he stakes out the extremes between which the other harmonicas find their place in a continuum of possible musical expressions. The largest harmonica currently offered by Hohner is a Chord 48 with an impressive 192 holes, but its length is 58.7 cm, a far cry from Pynchon's six-foot harmonica. The smallest harmonica manufactured is Hohner's four-hole "Little Lady," a mere 35 mm in length. Pynchon plays on the name of that model by opposing it to the I. G. Mundharfwerke's "Little Giant." It would hardly make sense to manufacture a two-hole harmonica as such an instrument would produce only four notes (two for drawing and two for blowing, or, as Pynchon prefers: sucking and blowing) and no chords or harmonies, as opposed to the "Little Lady" with four holes and the full range of an octave. Pynchon does not specify the range or size of the Little Giant but its name indicates that it must be somewhere between the two extremes. With these four instruments, Pynchon posits something funny against the somber background of the Harmonica Academy and implicitly argues for diversity, as no single instrument could cover the entire range of expression or the different musical sensibilities.

Hohner was and is not the only manufacturer of harmonicas, but there is little doubt that Pynchon has Hohner in mind when he writes about the harmonica. The I. G. Mundharfwerke is a portmanteau of Hohner, rendered as mouth harp works, and I. G. Farben, the chemical-industry conglomerate frequently referred to in *Gravity's Rainbow,* known for having collaborated with the Nazi leadership and for having produced Zyklon B, the gas used in the extermination camps. This unsavory amalgam between music and war is historically precise, since Hohner also produced

sought justification in the claim that it could develop local resources better than the natives unaided. Like other colonialisms, it maintained itself by manufacturing and administering ersatz 'national' traditions that reinforced dependence on the mother country" (26). While this may be the case, I still think that a more benevolent reading of Dvořák and his time in the United States is admissible.

munitions with the use of forced labor and collaborated with the Nazi government. Hohner's market dominance, then and now, is also reflected in *Against the Day:*

> [The Harmonica Marching Band Academy] had its origins [...] in the intricacies of greed as then being practiced under global capitalism. German harmonica manufacturers, who led the world in production of the instrument, had for some years been dumping their surplus inventory on the American market, with the result that soon every community in the land had some kind of harmonica-based marching society, often numbering in the hundreds. [...] It was only a matter of time before this unforeseen outcome of the Law of Supply and Demand was consecrated as the Harmonica Marching Band Academy [...]. (472)

This characterization early on in the Harmonica Academy episode casts its shadow over the boyish fun the Chums have. Pynchon draws readers in with his comically absurd sidesteps, the "spirited cakewalk allowing opportunities for brief novelty effects, locomotive noises, barnyard animals" (473), the lectures in "Chromatic Harp Safety, and the particular need to keep those nasal hairs closely trimmed" (474) and the harmonica routine centering around the vanished harpman Alonzo Meatman (472–73). At a second glance, however, it becomes evident that there is a dark undercurrent at the boarding school and that the respite it offers is but temporary.[18] What Pynchon seems to ask of the readers is to look behind the act and consider the strict disciplinary regime which lies beyond a well-rehearsed show pulled off as if it were completely natural. He also cautions against thoughtlessly accepting the notion of hospitality. Like every traditional (that is, conditional) form of hospitality,

---

18 It is not clear whether Pynchon modeled the school on any actual harmonicists, but if he did, it might well have been Borrah Minevitch and his Harmonica Rascals. Kim Field writes that Minevitch "molded a raw crew of players, most of whom were still in their teens when they joined him, into one of the most successful show business acts of his day. [...] But to the beardless prodigies he hired, life could be chilly in the Minevitch shadow. [...] Minevitch worked a perverse, lifelong con that could have been lifted straight off the pages of Dickens's sagas of urban lowlife" (44). Many of the Harmonica Rascals' players went on to become the country's best known harmonicists, very much like the graduates of the Harmonica Marching Band Academy "who more often than not would go on to eminence in the profession" (*Against* 472).

that of the Academy as a safe haven from the Trespassers has its flip-side. While the youngsters are promised careers, they need to undergo hardship and submit to the rules of the sovereign. Conditional hospitality is always ambiguous and violent because it must by necessity posit a dichotomy between outside and inside, where the liberation from the rules and conditions of one always entails submitting to those of the other.[19]

In line with the strict formations and hierarchies of a marching band, a large part of the repertoire studied at the Academy is patriotic. Besides "My Country 'Tis of Thee," which served as a national anthem until 1931—the melody is based on "God Save the King"—it includes the 1896 John Philip Sousa march "El Capitan," the Marines' Hymn "The Halls of Montezuma," and, on the brighter and less patriotic side, the two Kerry Mills compositions "At a Georgia Camp Meeting" and "Whistlin' Rufus." Sousa is fitting as he also endorsed Hohner instruments, was a celebrated presence at the 1893 World's Fair, later composed a march entitled "Harmonica Wizard," and conducted the Philadelphia Harmonica Band on several occasions. The operetta *El Capitan*, from which the march is taken, tells the story of a Spanish viceroy in sixteenth-century Peru who kills the rebel leader and then takes on his identity to lead the rebels to defeat against the Spanish forces. The march is on the lighter side, in line with the overall mood of an operetta. "The Halls of Montezuma" is based on Jacques Offenbach's operetta *Geneviève de Brabant*. Its title is a reference to the United States army's victory over the Mexican forces at the Battle of Chapultepec in 1847 and, accordingly, it is played while the "playingfield casualties" are carried back from their game of Combat-Inside-Ten-Meters. The sheet music of "At a Georgia Camp Meeting," published by F.A. Mills in 1899, advertises the song as "A Characteristic March which can be used effectively as a Two-Step, Polka or Cake Walk." The cakewalk initially made fun of the mannerisms of white plantation owners, comically exaggerating their gaits and gestures. It was an African-American form of entertainment, which was later taken over by minstrel shows, first white ones and then black ones. Jones notes that "the first Negro minstrels wore the 'traditional' blackface over their own" (*Blues People* 85) and muses: "If the cakewalk is a Negro dance caricaturing certain white customs, what is that

19 For a more detailed reading of the philosophy of hospitality, see my book *Hospitality in the Age of Media Representation*.

dance when, say, a white theater company attempts to satirize it as a Negro dance? I find the idea of white minstrels in blackface satirizing a dance satirizing themselves a remarkable kind of irony—which, I suppose, is the whole point of minstrel shows" (86). In all of the songs practiced at the Academy, the question of authenticity and make-believe arises, that is, the relationship between 'reality' and what appears on the surface (or on the stage) and the question whether such a reality even exists or must be framed again and again according to its context and social setting. Pynchon's choice of songs shows how music as a living form of expression can be appropriated and manipulated across borders of nationality and ethnicity, from "God Save the King" to "My Country 'Tis of Thee," from *Geneviève de Brabant* to "The Halls of Montezuma," from light operetta to patriotic march, from black to white to black entertainment. What becomes interesting is not so much the origin of a tune but its history of derivations. Especially the cakewalk with its ever-shifting disguises and "The Halls of Montezuma" lead the readers to question the position and intent of the Harmonica Marching Band Academy, the Trespassers, Alonzo Meatman, and the Authorities sending the Chums of Chance on their missions.

The Kazoo

Inherently more comical than the harmonica is the kazoo, "Pynchon's favorite preterite musical instrument" (Fowler 223). No treatise on Pynchon and music would be complete without honoring this little noise-maker that—in fictional terms—has inspired composers such as Vivaldi and Haydn to write pieces, has been employed to praise the literary work of Richard Fariña, and deeply unsettles the Elect.

To this day, the origins of the kazoo are obscure, and the only (semi-)authoritative source appears to be kazooist Barbara Stewart's primer *The Complete How To Kazoo*. Stewart displays the same type of mock-seriousness as Pynchon—with her puns and humor a worthy rival of Pynchon's in his most family-friendly moments.[20]

20 Stewart's own kazoo ensemble Kazoophony, dressed in black concert suits and white bow-ties, played such timeless favorites as the "William To Hell Overture," the "Beermeistersinger's Song" from *Tannheuser Busch* and "I'm Inclined to Kazoomusik" by Wolfgang Amadeus Mozartsky.

From the family of membranophones, and more specifically tube or vessel mirlitons, the kazoo is not a musical instrument in the ordinary sense. The distinct sound is produced by humming, speaking, or singing, and not by blowing, into the instrument. A membrane or resonator—Pynchon calls it a reed—made of a material such as plastic or tin foil is inserted between the main body and the turret, producing inner and outer air vibrations. Within the main body, the vibrations are detracted from a single stream of air and intermingle. A similar effect is produced by the saxophone when, while blowing into the instrument and causing the reed to vibrate, the player hums or sings at a slightly different pitch or in harmony. This technique called 'growling' produces a raspy sound and is described in *Inherent Vice* as humming "through the reed of a tenor or sometimes alto sax a harmony part alongside whatever melody he was playing, as if the instrument was some giant kazoo" (37).

According to Stewart, the sound-producing principle of the kazoo has been known to many African tribal cultures. Unfortunately, she is not more specific about which cultures and at what times. She writes that this voice distorter was used to "impersonate voices of the dead, to make terrifying sounds and bring messages from the spirit world" which "were interpreted by tribal officials to make sure the meaning was clear" (2–3). This resonates with Friedrich Kittler's claim that, "from the beginning, occult media presupposed technical media" ("Doppelgängergeschichte" 96; my translation).

It is thought that the American kazoo was invented in the 1840s in Macon, Georgia, by Alabama Vest, an African-American, and built to his specifications by Thaddeus Von Clegg, a German-American clockmaker (Stewart 3). First exhibited at the Georgia State Fair of 1852, it was then sold to a toy manufacturer (5). Thus, the kazoo's sound-producing principle in the service of the ruling class underwent a process of profanation and became one of a small number of genuinely American musical instruments.

Early kazoos appear to have been manufactured from wood, such as the one patented "as toy or musical instrument" by Warren Herbert Frost in 1883, and a musical toy it seems to have remained ever since, making it a perfect fit for a 'preterite' instrument.[21]

21 Of the 59 kazoo-related U.S. patents registered between 1877 and 2003, 31 carry a designation that combines the terms "music" and "toy" in some way.

Frost also appears to be the first one to have "propose[d] to give [it] the name 'kazoo'" (Patent No. 270,534). It was not until World War I that, according to Stewart, referring to Rudolph A. Clemen, Jr., of the American Red Cross Library, the kazoo was introduced in significant numbers to Europe. Clemen believes that the kazoo was the most likely musical instrument to be sent overseas and distributed for free to American soldiers and sailors in 1917 and 1918 "due to the higher cost of harmonicas and the difficulty of fitting anything much larger into Red Cross boxes" (8).

Pynchon's first mention of the kazoo occurs in Via Porta Rossa in Florence, where "[t]hree rambling musicians, guitar, violin and kazoo, stood on a corner, playing sentimental airs" (*V.* 201), a funny notion of sentimental airs considering the timbre of the kazoo. Later, at a party in Washington D. C., Profane and Pig Bodine meet

> an unemployed musicologist named Petard who had dedicated his life to finding the lost Vivaldi Kazoo Concerto, first brought to his attention by one Squasimodeo [...] who had heard not only of its theft from a monastery by certain fascist music lovers but also about twenty bars from the slow movement, which Petard would from time to time wander round the party blowing on a plastic kazoo. (*V.* 419)

To choose Vivaldi as a composer, the violinist and priest from Venice who died in poverty in Vienna, is certainly fitting for a novel entitled *V.* Pynchon leaves no pointers as to a real Vivaldi concerto on which the Kazoo Concerto might be modeled. The possibilities are endless as Vivaldi was a prolific composer of concertos and established the concerto form with three movements, fast–slow–fast (Werner-Jensen 132). While some of his lost works have subsequently been unearthed, around fifteen concertos or parts thereof are still considered lost.[22] Why the musicologist-kazooist is named Petard, French for joint, makes sense once we realize that the shape of the classical kazoo makes it the most suitable shape for use as a hash pipe (*Gravity* 759–60).

For a list of all patents, see http://kazoologist.org/patents.html (March 22, 2017). Apart from the patent, the earliest mention of the kazoo in writing that I have encountered is in an article from 1884 in the *Shenandoah Herald* on display at the Kazoo Museum in Beaufort, SC.

22 These are RV (Ryom-Verzeichnis) 174, 193, 200, 255, 290, 304, 305, 316, 337, 351, 573, 751, 752, 784, and 805.

Petard or someone else is successful in tracking down the lost Kazoo Concerto because at the beginning of *The Crying of Lot 49*, Oedipa Maas listens to the Muzak version of "the Fort Wayne Settecento Ensemble's variorum recording of the Vivaldi Kazoo Concerto" featuring Boyd Beaver as a soloist (2). It is fitting to mention Muzak, the epitome of industrialized, planned, and calculated music to increase the productivity of cows and humans, early on in a novel dealing, among other things, with entropy and the proliferation of potentially empty signifiers. "Muzak," Philipp Schweighauser writes, "is the supreme expression of Oedipa's world. This world of undifferentiated sameness and cultural inertia corresponds to a thermodynamic state of maximum entropy at which the system has reached its final destination and come to a standstill" (*Noises* 159). Moozak, as R. Murray Schafer prefers to call it, "reduces music to ground," and unless one pays attention to it, it should not be discernible but act on a subliminal level; it "is not to be listened to" (98). Significantly for *The Crying of Lot 49* and for Pynchon's general interest in the overlap of the military-industrial complex and consumer culture, Muzak Holdings was founded by Major General George Owen Squier shortly before his death in 1934. Squier also developed not only a camera to measure the speed of projectiles but also the process of telephone-carrier multiplexing, which later allowed many signals to be transmitted simultaneously over a single telephone line. Having served in the Spanish-American War, he was later promoted to Chief Signal Officer in the California district.[23]

Drawing a line from Vivaldi to Muzak is not as strange as it may seem at first. In *Repeating Ourselves*, Robert Fink writes about the postwar baroque concerto revival:

> One of the most popular types of recording to pile on the spindle [of a record changer] featured instrumental music of the eighteenth century. Baroque music had, until this time, been a rather esoteric taste, but the advent of the LP and the record changer ushered in a revival, not so much of the Baroque per se, but of the kind of brisk, impersonal, generally upbeat concerto movements produced in large numbers by composers like [...] Vivaldi—a style of music so perfect for

23 For a detailed biography, see the National Academy of Sciences' "Biographical Memoir of George Owen Squier" by Arthur E. Kennelly.

> repetitive listening that it was quickly disparaged by musicological critics with the generic label *barococo.* (11–12)

Similarly, music critic David Patrick Stearns writes: "If ever a composer was too amiable to be controversial, it was Antonio Vivaldi, or so it has seemed, given his current status as the prince of classical Muzak in elevators, dentist's offices and on FM radio." Like Muzak, postwar baroque is intimately tied to technology, be it the record changer, the radio, or the mall's P.A. system.

In this particular work and its recording, Pynchon condenses many contradictions and absurdities. The most obvious one is to attribute the designation "kazoo," which first appears in 1883, to an Italian composer who died some 140 years earlier. To elevate—or denigrate—Vivaldi's Kazoo Concerto to Muzak not only links it to telecommunications, consumer culture, and the military but brings forth a number of contradictions. Although Vivaldi, especially *The Four Seasons,* is a favorite of Muzak and background music in general, the kazoo's timbre is such that it would never go along with the smooth and carefully orchestrated arrangements that rely heavily on strings, woodwinds, and brass. Solos in Muzak are rare, and when they do occur, they are usually played by an unobtrusive instrument such as panpipes or a harp. What is more, Muzak is not recorded by orchestras that have a name. The recordings seem to pop out of nowhere and return to nowhere; they are not tracked back to a particular performer, orchestra, or arranger. While Muzak recordings are based on a canonized, familiar repertoire, they do not lend themselves to canonization. To imagine a variorum recording is difficult as it is, but to imagine a Muzak version of a variorum recording is simply nonsensical.[24] If the kazoo is a subversive instrument, here it is co-opted to serve the purpose of the anonymous consumer industry, perhaps unaware that introducing the kazoo undermines the purpose of Muzak. Schafer claims that in order to defeat Muzak and bring it back from ground to figure, one must listen to it (98). Oedipa is intuitively on the right track with the Kazoo Concerto. She not only listens to the music rather than simply hearing it; she is also able to identify the composition, the recording, the orchestra, and

24 The term 'variorum' originates in literary criticism and is, as far as I know, not applied to music. It designates an edition of a text containing variants, earlier versions and notes by various editors and commentators.

the soloist, as well as noting that "she came through the bead-curtained entrance around bar 4" (*Lot* 2).

While *The Crying of Lot 49* contains Pynchon's perhaps best-known occurrence of the kazoo, it is in *Gravity's Rainbow* that we find the most elaborate descriptions. Toward the end, Pynchon presents us with another obscure and anachronistic kazoo composition. Roger Mexico and Seaman Bodine walk in on a concert by Gustav Schlabone (second violin/treble kazoo), André Omnopon (viola/alto kazoo) and an unnamed first violinist and cellist. This time it is Joseph Haydn's "suppressed" 'Kazoo' Quartet in G-Flat Minor (Op. 76) whose "Inner Voices are called to play kazoos instead of their usual instruments," that is, alto and treble kazoos, "creating problems of dynamics for cello and first violin that are unique in the literature" (*Gravity* 725). To this background music, a culinary gross-out contest unravels with alliterative favorites such as "scum soufflé [...] with a side of menstrual marmalade" (729). Eventually, "Gustav and the rest of the quartet have abandoned Haydn and are all following Roger and Bodine out the door, kazoos and strings accompanying the Disgusting Duo [singing Acne à-la-mode]" (731). Cowart summarizes the performance as follows: "Performed at a dinner given by munitions magnates, the 'subversive' Haydn composition disrupts the unsavory proceedings, its mannered silences intimating knowledge suppressed by military-industrial entities busy changing their Nazi spots" (*History* 122). While this dinner party is given by exponents of the weapons industry in postwar Germany, the anarchic festivity is reminiscent of the frolicking and dancing in Cuxhaven and it is again a preterite instrument which brings disorder by speaking a language the elect cannot parse.

Haydn's actual Op. 76 consists of six string quartets with four movements each. Pynchon indicates that his kazoo quartet refers to the second movement of the fifth string quartet, that is, the "Largo, cantabile e mesto" in F-sharp major. Pynchon's own G-flat minor as a key signature is as absurd as a Haydn kazoo quartet as it would have as many as nine flats and cannot be said to have a real existence in music theory. Nevertheless, the kazoo might be the only musical instrument for whose players G-flat minor poses no serious problem, as kazoos are hummed into and their players therefore much less hung up on musical notation. Because the pitch of kazoo music depends on the range of the performer's voice and not on the length of the instrument's body, it makes only comical sense to introduce alto and treble kazoos as instruments instead of voices. Finally, giving these inner voices to two men would require them to sing falsetto—that is, in a false voice.

Another reason for Pynchon's choosing G-flat minor may very well be his well-documented love of blue notes, especially the flatted fifth (which appears only as a blue note in bebop), to which he dedicates ample space in *Mason & Dixon* and *Gravity's Rainbow.* G-flat, as the flatted fifth of C major, is, after all, the first note that comes to mind when thinking of flatted fifths, and blue notes are themselves something like Preterites, that is, microtones that are always outside not only of the established Western scales but also of standard musical notation.

One reason for the suppression of the Kazoo Quartet is the

> subversive use of sudden fff quieting to ppp. It's the touch of the wandering sound-shadow, the Brennschluss of the Sun. They don't want you listening to too much of that stuff—at least not the way Haydn presents it (a strange lapse in the revered composer's behavior): cello, violin, alto and treble kazoos all rollicking along in a tune sounds like a song from the movie *Dr. Jekyll and Mr. Hyde,* 'You Should See Me Dance the Polka,' when suddenly in the middle of an odd bar the kazoos *just stop completely*, and the Outer Voices fall to plucking a non-melody that tradition sez represents two 18th-century Village Idiots vibrating their lower lips. At each other. It goes on for 20, 40 bars, this feeb's pizzicato, middle-line Kruppsters creak in the bowlegged velvet chairs, bibuhbuhbibuhbuh this does not sound like *Haydn*, Mutti! (*Gravity* 726)

The slow movement of the actual Op. 76 No. 5, has many piano-to-forte crescendos, but also a number of diminuendos from sforzato to piano. There is one diminuendo going all the way down to pianissimo, from bar 29 to 32. At the end of the quartet, there is a sforzato to piano descrescendo in bar 86. From then on it stays in piano until the last two-and-a-half bars, which are in pianissimo. It appears a little exaggerated to talk about "ppp-to-fff blasts" or vice versa in this softly played quartet, and it is not unambiguous which diminuendo is "the one, the notorious One" (*Gravity* 726). Since Pynchon—in analogy to the V-2—refers to the *Brennschluss* of the Sun, that is, the moment when the fuel burns out and the rocket (or the sun) is left to external forces, it is likely that he is talking about the diminuendo in bar 86, shortly before the end. The *Brennschluss* of the Sun contrasts with Haydn's previous quartet, Opus 76, No. 4, which is nicknamed 'Sunrise.' The sound-shadow, as Pynchon explains in the "Listening to the Toilet" episode (708–711), is a pocket of no-sound, "enveloping you in sun-silence" (709). The effect is the same John Cage experienced in the anechoic chamber: "He is hearing, for the first time, the mighty river of his blood, the Titan's drum of his heart" (710; for Cage's account, see *Silence* 8).

The rest of the description of the Kazoo Quartet bears no recognizable likeness to the "Largo, cantabile e mesto." It may be that Pynchon inserts another Haydn quartet, such as the Quartet in E-flat major, Op. 33 No. 2, subtitled "Joke," which bears some faint resemblance to "You Should See Me Dance the Polka," the tune Dr. Jekyll hums before turning into Mr. Hyde in the 1941 movie directed by Victor Fleming. In the entire Op. 76 there is no instance where the outer voices would fall into plucking a non-melody, which, among other things, accounts for not sounding like Haydn, as the Krupp employees complain. Still, not sounding like Haydn does not mean abandoning all rules. In her dissertation, Bénédicte Chorier-Fryd writes: "This is anomalous music in that it does not really transgress the rules of composition but uses the structures to leave them open to intrusions (musics belonging to other genres), like Bodine's popular tunes" (127; my translation).

Bodine does not say who suppressed the quartet, "meant to express a type of unearthly radiance" (Weisenburger, *Companion* 360). The most likely candidates are the Authorities or the musicologists of the present or the past. The unspecified "They" (or "they"; the pronoun is at the beginning of the sentence) points toward the former, broadly understood as the Elect. Why exactly they—or They—do not want you to listen to too much of that stuff is not evident. It could be that they do not want the Preterite to be reminded of the end of the parabola (in the case of the V-2) or the end of life on earth (in the case of the sun) for fear that the masses would break into doomsday mayhem and get out of control. It could be that They Themselves in their power fantasies do not want to be reminded of the apocalypse and their own mortality. It could be that They deem it inappropriate to make fun of such serious matters. It could be that getting under the sound-shadow can interrupt keeping the subjects "on the Dream" (*Gravity* 711).

But the fff-to-ppp reversed blast is only one reason for the suppression of the work. There could be any number of other reasons. One would be the supposedly subversive nature of the instrument, especially in Nazi Germany, where an instrument of African origin, invented by an African-American, produced in America, popular in American musics and distributed to American troops cannot be held in high esteem. Other reasons could be that its sound is offensive to classically trained ears and that here, Haydn becomes a prankster, which does not conform to the publicly held image of the revered composer. But perhaps Pynchon simply wants to stage the instrument as subversive and suppressed, irrespective of historical evidence, because this allows him to attribute the small and cheap noise-maker to the Preterite.

But why attribute this kazoo quartet to Haydn and not another composer of renown? Arnold Werner-Jensen writes that "the string quartet owes its unique status in chamber music to Haydn and through him became the benchmark and challenge for all subsequent composers and musicians" (186, my translation). Thus, while Pynchon attributes the Kazoo Concerto to Vivaldi, the master and trailblazer of the concerto, he attributes the Kazoo Quartet to the master of the quartet. As opposed to Mozart and Beethoven who were both born into families of privileged musicians employed at the court of counts, Haydn was the son of a wagonmaker (a *Wagner*) and Vivaldi the son of a barber who later became a violinist. From an emancipatory or democratic viewpoint, the inclusion of kazoos—instruments for anyone and everyone—in this hypothetical quartet would also be in line with the 1790 publication, allegedly by Haydn, of a *Gioco Filarmonico*, subtitled "an easy method of composing an endless number of minuets and trios, *even for those unlearned in counterpoint*" (Maconie, *Musicologia* 393, my emphasis).[25] This could be considered a subversive move by trained composers employed at the courts, as, with the help of this method, even the unlearned would be able to break into their profession and undermine the separation between classes.

In *The Complete How To Kazoo*, Stewart names extra-musical uses for the kazoo, such as "splints for small animals with injured legs" (44), lightning rods (without kazooist) (71), and punches for making pasta (171). What eludes her or was deemed inappropriate but could not be missed by someone like Pynchon or any number

25 At the time, there were a number of similar initiatives for aleatory compositions within established musical forms. See Maconie, *Musicologia* 392–95. Robin Maconie assesses these inventions as "already a good fit with an eighteenth-century aristocracy obsessed with mechanical automata and devoted to the Cartesian doctrine of human beings as machines" (395).

of potheads is its use as a hash pipe. Harking back to Petard, the unemployed musicologist of *V.* who is named after the French slang word for a marijuana cigarette (or possibly for farting, *péter*), Pynchon explicates this particular use with great gusto:

> Gustav and André, back from Cuxhaven, have unscrewed the reed-holder and reed from André's kazoo and replaced them with tinfoil—punched holes in the tinfoil, and are now smoking hashish out of the kazoo, finger-valving the small end pa-pa-pah to carburete the smoke—turns out sly Säure has had ex-Peenemünde engineers, propulsion-group people, working on a long-term study of optimum hashpipe design, and guess what—in terms of flow rate, heat-transfer, control of air-to-smoke ratio, the perfect shape turns out to be that of the classical *kazoo!* (*Gravity* 759)

It is not reported if the hippies in *Vineland* or *Inherent Vice* were aware of this use, but it would certainly lend the kazoo an extra aura of subversion in the eyes of the Elect. Almost needless to say that this use would not only require the classical kazoo shape but also the classical kazoo material, that is, metal and not plastic. Although Cowart states that "[d]rugs, at once destructive and subversive, correlate to powerlessness" (*History* 99), he also concedes that "taking drugs (as opposed, perhaps, to dealing them) remains a powerful metaphor for the idea of an alternative to the rapacious capitalism and consumerism that afflict American society" (120). By smoking hashish (as well as taking the many other intoxicants of their choice), Gustav and André turn on, tune in, and drop out. The kazoo is complicit with their becoming unavailable for the dominant discourses and the grand narratives of progress and the protestant work ethic.

One of the many recurring topics in Pynchon's work is animated objects or objects with a consciousness. In *Gravity's Rainbow*, the most conspicuous one is Byron the Bulb, the immortal Osram light bulb, protagonist of a story that runs about nine pages (660–69). Byron, whose life span has long exceeded the 1,000 hours determined by the Phoebus light bulb cartel, miraculously escapes the cartel's enforcement squads. Toward the end of the novel, it turns out that not only light bulbs but kazoos too belong to the species of animate objects. Kittler's conviction that technologies lead a life of their own also sheds a different light on the interpretation of musical instruments. Kittler writes: "[S]ince 1973, when Thomas Pynchon's *Gravity's Rainbow* was published, it has become clear that real wars are not fought for people or fatherlands, but take place between different media, information technologies, data flows" (*Gramophone* xli). To be sure, Kittler here is not thinking about light bulbs, kazoos, and mechanical ducks but paints war and disciplinary technologies in much broader strokes. Nevertheless, his analysis may just as well be applied to other extensions of man and woman. Following the hash pipe manual and its scientific justification, Gustav notices another oddity about the kazoo: "the knuckle-thread above the reed there is exactly the same as a thread in a light-bulb socket. [...] You fools think the kazoo is a subversive instrument? [...] You see? Phoebus is even behind the kazoo. Ha! ha! Ha!" (759–60). Whether this close fit is materially verifiable is debatable. Over the years, many sizes of light bulb threads were available (and different kazoos too) and I have not been able to find out which ones were in common use around 1945 in Europe. However, the test on today's standard-size light bulbs turned out negative: the larger standard thread (E27) is slightly too large and the smaller one (E14) too small for a classical kazoo thread socket or turret. But the point here is not whether the kazoo and the light bulb actually fit together. The point is that if real wars are fought between technologies or media, then real solidarity may also take place between them. Therefore, before giving Gustav's counter-subversive conspiracy theory much consideration, Pynchon immediately defuses it and elevates the kazoo to an order of objects with a consciousness: "But what Gustav's light bulb—none other than our friend Byron—wants to say is no, it's not that way at all, it's a declaration of brotherhood by the Kazoo for all the captive and oppressed light bulbs..." (760). Technology's saving power is also its biggest threat to mankind, as Heidegger has it in "The Question Concerning Technology" (307–41), and the opposite is true as well. Musical instruments may pose a threat to a fascist organization of society, just as much as they can be instrumentalized by those in power to establish some shared but imaginary national or cultural heritage. Nevertheless, what escapes Gustav in his hash-induced paranoia is that the kazoo, much as it may be a bonding prop at a camp fire, is particularly resistant to appropriation by fascist causes due to its toy-like nature and its sometimes unnerving timbre.

After Pynchon firmly established the organological status of the kazoo in his first three novels, kazoo lovers will be disappointed to find that, after *Gravity's Rainbow*, it appears only in passing in *Against the Day* (43) and *Inherent Vice* (37). Yet there is one more instance in *Gravity's Rainbow* that deserves inspection, firstly because it is the only time in Pynchon's work that the harmonica, the kazoo, and the ukulele appear together, and secondly because the scene has a mirror image in the novel.

August 6, 1945 (or August 5 in German local time): While the atomic bomb is dropped on Hiroshima—or shortly before—"a crowd of Army personnel, American sailors, NAAFI girls, and German fräuleins" convene at a bar in Cuxhaven, test-launching site of captured V-2 rockets, to celebrate: "Ukuleles, kazoos, harmonicas, and any number of makeshift metal noisemakers accompany the song ['It's Mouthtripping Time'], which is an innocent salute to Postwar, a hope that the end of shortages, the end of Austerity, is near" (*Gravity* 603). The harmonica, the kazoo, and the ukulele are grouped together and staged as instruments of communal music-making by the common woman and man. These instruments were the ones most likely to be available in a postwar setting as they were shipped in large quantities to soldiers during the war and possibly distributed by organizations like the British Navy, Army and Air Force Institutes (NAAFI).

Although the setting is quite different from the one in *Vineland* discussed above—it takes place in an alcohol dump in postwar Germany and not on a beachhead in Southern California during the Vietnam war—they share some characteristics. Both scenes take place in a territory where sovereignty is either unclear or temporary. The Potsdam Conference ended on August 2, 1945. Cuxhaven became part of the British Zone as agreed at the earlier Yalta Conference, but the plan was to restore Germany to the German people once the demilitarization was completed and democracy reinstated. The British Zone is simultaneously a postnational and a prenational one. Consequently, the crowd celebrating in Cuxhaven is composed of British, Americans, and Germans—civilians, military personnel, and civilians in uniform. Pynchon shows that preterition is a condition that defies separation into military and civilian functions and is not restricted to any one nation state. While the Preterite are not sovereigns over a territory, what is required for them to convene in a joyful way is a territory where the Elect's sovereignty is also in dispute. Only in the absence of power can there be a community of like-minded people who play along with no clear objective other than making music together, not in a hierarchical entertainer/entertainee setting but with everyone sharing equally, participating in and enjoying, that is, the production and consumption of music.

According to Steven Weisenburger, "the circular dancing of the gathered preterite forms a symbolic counterpoint to the mushroom cloud that will form eight thousand miles to the east" (*Companion* 310). What Weisenburger sees here is the use of symbolism such as the circle ("the ensemble opening out into a rose-pattern" [*Gravity* 604]) as a representation of the mandala indicating the complex interweavings of cosmic forces. This interpretation is valuable insofar as it does not pass judgment and implicitly acknowledges that polar opposites such as good and evil are complementary forces. On the one hand, the meeting of the three instruments and other noisemakers could be read as initiating a kind of a rite which, though powerless, karmically stands in opposition to the atomic bomb that was unleashed for the first time in a war, the memory of which came to dominate much of the politics and collective consciousness of the second half of the twentieth century. There is reason to celebrate the end of the nightmare and to hope for a brighter future, or at least more affluence. While the Elect never suffer from material deprivation, even in times of crisis, it is peacetime that benefits the Preterite. On the other hand, the atom bomb could be said to have inaugurated and sustained the Cold War, a very different kind of war that divided the world into polar opposites and gave the paranoid world leaders justification for wide-spread surveillance of citizens and sowing of dissent. The end of shortages in this reading also means the rise of unbridled consumer capitalism and, in the long run, the establishment of capitalism as, to many, the only conceivable socioeconomic system. The optimism at the end of the war, the hope for change, is celebrated—but history will show that it has been disappointed.

And if history did not bring evidence, the story itself would. In an analogous scene that takes place earlier in the novel, Webley Silvernail's lab rats at the White Visitation perform a dance and sing "Pavlovia":

> Who hears the small animals in the cages as they mate, or nurse, or communicate through the gray quadrilles, or, as now, begin to sing . . . come out of their enclosures, in fact, grown to Webley Silvernail–size (though none of the lab people seem to be noticing) to dance him down the long aisles and metal apparatus, with conga drums and a peppy tropical orchestra taking up the very popular beat and melody of: PAVLOVIA (BEGUINE) [...]

> They dance in flowing skeins. The rats and mice form circles, curl their tails in and out to make chrysanthemum and sunburst patterns, eventually all form into the shape of a single giant mouse, at whose eye Silvernail poses with a smile, arms up in a V, sustaining the last note of the song, along with the giant rodent-chorus and orchestra. (232–33)

Reading the Cuxhaven and the White Visitation scenes side by side, it becomes evident that one is a mirror image of the other. The dancing and singing, the circular patterns, and the end of the war ("arms up in a V") are only the outward manifestations of the singers' preterition. Like "Pavlovia," the Cuxhaven song "It's Mouthtripping Time," punning on mouth-dripping, obviously refers to Pavlov's experiments, a variant of which the infant Slothrop had been subjected to. The caged rats are a symbol of the caged Preterite, and although Webley Silvernail contemplates liberating the rodents, he decides against it because it appears futile to him:

> I would set you free, if I knew how. But it isn't free out here. All the animals, the plants, the minerals, even other kinds of men, are being broken and reassembled every day, to preserve an elite few, who are the loudest to theorize on freedom, but the least free of all. I can't even give you hope that it will be different someday—that They'll come out, and forget death, and lose Their technology's elaborate terror, and stop using every other form of life without mercy to keep what haunts men down to a tolerable level—and be like you instead, simply here, simply alive . . . . (233)

Robert J. Lacey writes that "Pynchon the allegorist is proposing that we are all just rats in a cage. Even outside the cages all life forms, including human beings, 'are being broken and reassembled,' subjected to a conditioning that makes freedom impossible" (n.pag.). In the end, what this illustrates is that the Elect are rarely human beings pure and simple, because they too are cogs in the wheels of the Great Machine, be it technology, the market, or the nation state, each system having its internal logic that privileges its own survival over that of the parts that make it up. Therefore, Pynchon's unambiguous villains are few while the inhuman forces in whose service they act pervade much of his work. When Lacey writes that "the program of conditioning eschews attacks on the body and goes straight for the soul," he paints a bleak picture. In the context of the two scenes here, however, a different reading is possible because music, at least in a somewhat simplified humanistic understanding, also goes straight for the soul. Perhaps music will be able to undo at least parts of the behavioral conditioning.

The Saxophone

While it is evident that the saxophone is one of Pynchon's favorite instruments—it appears in every novel save *Mason & Dixon* (which historically predates its invention) and in a number of short stories—it is very different from the preterite harmonica, kazoo, and ukulele. Pynchon makes few allusions to the history of the saxophone, even though the biography of the Belgian instrument maker Adolphe Sax and the resistance the instrument met could be straight out of one of his novels.

Born in 1814, Sax was one of eleven children of Charles Joseph Sax, who had been appointed Instrument Maker to the Court of the Netherlands (Liley 2). *Le petit Sax* studied the clarinet and the flute at the Brussels conservatory and worked in his father's shop, significantly improving the clarinet and the bass clarinet. By 1842, he was "widely recognized as one of the world's top acoustical craftsmen" (Segell 12). Around 1841, or 1838 by other accounts, he began developing the saxophone by giving the ophicleide, a brass instrument with a bassoon-like shape, a clarinet-type mouthpiece. He envisioned two families of seven instruments each, ranging from contrabass to sopranino (13), to improve military bands and symphony orchestras. Five of these instruments are explicitly mentioned in Pynchon's work.[26]

Like Pynchon, Sax was "[i]ntrigued by the parabola—the parabolic shape of the saxophone bore was the most distinctive feature of Sax's patent application [...]" (27). Much like a V-2 rocket, the missile from one of Sax's later inventions would also follow

26 The family that is in use today alternates E-flat and B-flat tuning (sopranino in E-flat, soprano in B-flat, alto in E-flat, and so forth). The gigantic subcontrabass saxophone was more mythical than playable, and only in 1999 did a playable subcontrabass sax appear as part of the Tubax family. The other family of saxophones Sax envisioned was one tone higher, alternating F and C tuning, and its notation better suited to symphony orchestras. The only saxophone of that family that enjoyed moderate success in the early twentieth century was the C-Melody (a second above the B-flat tenor).

a parabolic trajectory: his remotely triggered Saxocannon, conceived in 1855, was a "monster mortar capable of propelling bombs of 500 kilograms and 10 meters in diameter," which, at the time, would have been enough to devastate Sebastopol (Rorive 199; my translation).[27]

After his saxophone prototype was damaged by a jealous competitor (or an unknown person, depending on the account), Sax left for Paris where, in 1843, he presented his B-flat bass saxophone, still looking very much like an ophicleide (15), now named the saxophone, in line with other inventions mostly prefixed by his own name. Hector Berlioz was immediately taken with the new instrument. He arranged a number of compositions for the saxophone and wrote enthusiastically about it. In 1844, Lieutenant General de Rumigny wrote a letter to the French war minister pointing out the weaknesses of clarinets, oboes, bassoons, and ophicleides for military bands and proposed instead the introduction of saxhorns and the bass saxophone (17). When the Belgian instrument maker met resistance from the French music industry, a commission decided to organize a battle of the bands and let the public decide. Twenty thousand Parisians gathered on the Champ de Mars and gave overwhelming approval to Sax's innovations (18): "The final report, submitted to the Minister of War on August 9, 1845, was a distinct victory for the Belgian—the government had declared a near monopoly mandating the use of his instruments" (Liley 5). Soon, the saxophone was also adopted by Italian, Spanish, and Hungarian military bands, and made its way into 'civilian' music-making. Michael Segell claims that "Everywhere it landed, it was recognized as the sound of modernity and independence—an instrument that gave voice to the common man, whose creative spirit was being stifled by the depersonalizing forces of the industrial revolution" (20).

That was not the end of the instrument's struggle for recognition, however. Competitors formed the *Association générale des ouvriers en instruments de musique* and persistently launched attacks against Sax, which included manufacturing false evidence used to sue Sax for patent infringements. During the lat-

27 Michael Segell writes that it would have been able to propel bombs of 550 tons. I have not been able to obtain more information on the saxocannon, but if the bombs were ten meters in diameter (which already seems exaggerated), 500 kilograms appears too light and 550 tons too heavy.

ter part of his life, Sax was faced with "threats, thefts and legal battles" (Liley 4), suspicious fires, bankruptcies, slander, and a likely attempt on his life (Segell 12)—more often than not executed or commissioned by his competitors. When the 1848 revolution deposed King Louis Philippe, "one of the first orders of the new republic was to remove saxophones, as well as all other Sax-built instruments, from military bands" (Segell 21–22). Four years later, "when Napoleon III overthrew the Second Republic and seized dictatorial powers, the first law he passed, two days after he took power, restored saxophones to the army's ensembles" (22). After the saxophone had become a popular instrument in jazz, it was at various times banned or condemned by the Vatican (87), the Third Reich, czarist and Communist Russia, Japan, and Hollywood (39).

In Segell's *The Devil's Horn,* the classical saxophonist Jean-Marie Londeix claims:

> Everything we talk [sic!] about the saxophone, [...] it's always about being on the margin, working its way in from the outside. It's on the margin of the orchestra, on the edge of polite society, on the fringe of serious music. It's a troublemaker and a nonconformist, which is why it represents opportunity and freedom to so many people and why it is the soul of nontraditional music. It stands opposed to the institution, just like the man who invented it. (39)

We see in this pronouncement and in the early history of the saxophone parallels to the harmonica, the kazoo, and the ukulele in the way they were—or were not—accepted. Like many other instances of music in Pynchon's work, the saxophone's history was also intimately tied to warfare. The intrigues, assassination attempts, and mysterious fires are material for any good novel, and the Saxocannon and Sax's fascination with the parabola give everything a Pynchonian twist. Still, Londeix takes a bit of a one-sided view here, emphasizing the outsider position of the saxophone much the way Pynchon does with the kazoo, but eclipsing the support Sax and his inventions enjoyed at times. The saxophone did not come out of thin air but was essentially based on many derivations and previous improvements, yet Sax is considered the genius-inventor who reaps the sole credit for its invention. Although he was fiercely opposed by his competitors, and sometimes by fate, he had the support of the public, of important composers, of King Louis Philippe and Napoleon III. The saxophone was never considered a toy-instrument, and playable saxophones—perhaps until the Grafton plastic sax—were not affordable for strictly low-income households. Eventually, the saxophone was established as a serious and respectable instrument, something which, to this day, cannot be said of the other preterite instruments discussed in this chapter.

Just as the saxophone has an inventor attributed to it, its players have made names for themselves and achieved renown, most notably in jazz, but a select few also in classical music. Playing the saxophone is not just a recreational activity but an actual profession. Pynchon names two historical ukulelists, Tiny Tim and George Formby, but no historical harmonicists or kazooists. He does, however, mention seven historical sax players (Charlie Parker, Earl Bostic, Lester Young, Stan Getz, Gerry Mulligan, Lee Allen, and multi-instrumentalist Bud Shank), representing not only a specific period in jazz history but also the three most common sizes of the saxophone: the alto, the tenor, and the baritone. This is less than one would expect, but Pynchon makes up for it by dedicating ample space to ruminations on Charlie "Yardbird" Parker and by having two minor characters reappear throughout their respective novels: McClintic Sphere in *V.* and Coy Harlingen in *Inherent Vice.*

Crazy and cool in the same molecule

Much has been written about McClintic Sphere, perhaps more than on any other musical aspect of Pynchon's writing. Most of it has been dedicated to tracing the parallels between Sphere and Ornette Coleman and to highlighting issues of racial tension, both as manifested in the novel and as attributed to the author, a mere 24 years old at the time of writing. Particularly careful contributions are those by David Witzling and by Luc Herman and John M. Krafft. Herman and Krafft inspected the typescript of *V.* at the Harry Ransom Center in Austin, TX, and compared it to the published novel. They reveal that "Pynchon reduced and toned down the role of the African-American saxophone player character McClintic Sphere" at the request of the editor Corlies Smith, who advised that Sphere, the only significant African-American character in *V.*, "may be expendable" ("Race" 18).[28] Pynchon thought

28 The other African-American character, Dahoud, is much less prominent but he too is a sometime jazz musician: a singer.

differently but wrote that, "I will try to make it a little less doctrinaire liberal than it was actually meant to be," to which Smith in turn replied, "the best course will be simply to keep an eye on Sphere's tendency to represent Protest. It's tricky" (19). Pynchon also deleted a scene in Harlem in which a "tall, full-bearded [...] patriarch" preached that, "White is the color of sin. White is the color of evil. [...] The color of the Antichrist will be black. The Antichrist is anti-sin and anti-evil.[...] Prepare for the night when down Broadway will march a million black faces to bring good where evil has fallen; to erase white from the face of this fallen city, from the face of this fallen earth" (26). Herman and Krafft conclude that "Many Sphere passages were cut or rewritten so as not to foreground race and thus activate the idea of a protest novel, but Pynchon may also have been glad to eliminate others because, as a fast learner, he realized they were not so clever" (28). Still, the issues addressed in the Sphere character connect to the Southwest Africa chapter in which Pynchon "dramatically intensified his depiction of the consequences of racism—perhaps regaining some moral ground, even if at the safer-seeming remove of a historical episode" (27). Particularly the militant aspects (and those appearing too "doctrinaire liberal") were toned down, but Pynchon would take another opportunity in *Gravity's Rainbow*'s Charlie Parker episode to revisit his previous writing and again intensify it.

Jazz, and particularly the saxophone, are important sites for Pynchon to negotiate issues of racism and white (Pynchon, Roony Winsome) and black (Sphere) masculinity. He does so in the passages around McClintic Sphere, Charlie Parker, and the anarchist-musicians at Maman Tant Gras Hall in New Orleans in *Against the Day*. Since much has already been written on the topic, I will focus more on musical aspects. While the McClintic Sphere passages seem to have been read mainly along the lines of questions of racism, I will offer a reading that focuses not just on black and white but on many more polar opposites that organize the novel and are also brought to bear on Sphere. Sphere is set up to incorporate, and thus confuse, the binary distinctions of black and white, on and off, 1 and 0, organic and inorganic, animate and inanimate, life and death, soul and reason, nature and technology, much of which boils down to the flip-flop phrase he is fascinated by.

As many have noted, Sphere is an African-American alto player closely modeled on Ornette Coleman, about a month after the release of his ground-breaking pianoless album *The Shape of Jazz to Come* (1959) but, in the novel, set in 1956 ("the soul of Charlie Parker had dissolved away [...] nearly a year before" [60]). The historical Coleman materialized seemingly out of nowhere to open a new chapter in the history of jazz. His engagements at New York City's Five Spot Café with Don Cherry (cornet), Charlie Haden (bass), and Billy Higgins (drums) became legendary. Coleman, as Pynchon writes, "was coming on new, revolutionary, for some messianic," and he and Fariña attended many of those performances (Hajdu 46).

Some detective fun can be had by tracing the hints Pynchon left and comparing them to the Coleman quartet of c. 1959. Sphere's first name, McClintic, curiously has a Gaelic prefix, which may indicate that one of his ancestors in the male lineage was of Gaelic origin, but more likely embodies a black/white con/fusion, much as Pynchon does with Charles Mingus (who described himself as "kind of a mongrel, lighter than some but not light enough to belong to the almost-white elite and not dark enough to belong with the beautiful elegant blacks" [65]) in the law firm of Warpe, Wistfull, Kubitschek and McMingus (*Lot* 2, 121). As Hurley points out, McClintic may also be "a reference to Broadway and theatre producer Guthrie McClintic, who died the year *V.* was published" (149). Clintic also sounds like clinic, a term used for jazz workshops, and it has the same number of letters as Ornette (which contains two E's and two T's, as opposed to two I's and two C's in Clintic). While these interpretations need not exclude each other, it seems that Pynchon implicitly sets up an alliance by associating African-Americans and Scots—both minorities in their respective countries. As *Mason & Dixon* suggests, the bagpipes, Scotland's national instrument, were considered sheer acoustic terror by the English, and this is what many thought of Coleman's opening of the free jazz chapter in music history (and of Stravinsky, for that matter). What is more, the bagpipes can be played without interruptions for breathing, an effect similar to circular breathing, a technique mastered not only by Coleman but also by *Mason & Dixon*'s aunt Euphrenia who likens it to being an "Automaton Oboe player" (669). Sphere's last name coincides with the middle name of pianist Thelonius Sphere Monk, thus at least nominally making up for the missing piano in the performance at the V-Note. Pynchon, however, seems to have been unaware of this fact. He learned about Monk's middle name only in the fall of 1962 and wondered "whether legal trouble might result from his use of the name Sphere" (Herman and Krafft, "Race" 20). He was ready to change the character's name if necessary, even though Sphere "blows alto not piano, and his name was chosen because a sphere is a non-square in 3 dimensions" (20), as he wrote to his new editor Faith Sale at Lippincott. The round volume as opposed to a mere surface makes Sphere the opposite of square or unhip.

The V-Note is Pynchon's name for the famous New York City jazz club Five Spot Café where the Ornette Coleman Quartet debuted in 1959 (V being the Roman numeral for 5).[29] When Pynchon writes that Sphere's solos were "something else" (*V.* 59), he alludes to Coleman's 1958 debut album *Something Else!!!! The Music of Ornette Coleman.* Both combos, the real one and the fictional one, do without the customary piano to lay down chords and add rhythmic flourishes, the historical precedent in a different idiom being Gerry Mulligan's quartet, referenced in "Entropy." The second wind player in McClintic's quartet blows a natural horn in F, that is, a horn without valves, not unlike the post horn. Don Cherry played the cornet, which has a warmer, one could say more natural, sound than the trumpet due to its conical rather than cylindrical bore. In May 1959, after recording *Change of the Century,* Cherry picked up a "curiosity in the history of jazz, a trumpet hardly 10 inches long," which he called an "Indian pocket trumpet" although it had nothing to do with India or Native Americans (Jost, *Free Jazz* 138). Coleman, too, used to play curious instruments. At the time of *V.*'s narrative, he blew a white Grafton plastic alto, purchased in 1954, and later switched to a white lacquered Henri Selmer (with a low A, extending the normal range of the alto by a semitone), retaining some of the look of the Grafton. The other famous Grafton player was Charlie Parker, on the occasion of the Massey Hall concert in Toronto in 1953, after he had pawned his usual horn. Sphere, on the other hand, "blew a hand-carved ivory alto saxophone with a 4½ reed" (*V.* 59), not very different-looking from Coleman's horns. There has been some speculation about the origin of this ivory sax, but as far as I am aware, no one has noticed that Pynchon must have picked up the reference in Adolphe Sax's biography. An ivory saxophone never existed but the Belgian, at the age of fifteen, made a clarinet

29 As a contributor points out on the PynchonWiki, both V-Note and Five-Spot are also slang for a five-dollar bill or a five-pound note. There was also a New York jazz club named The Half Note, and two other equally famous jazz joints had a V in their name: the Village Vanguard and the Village Gate.

and two flutes from ivory and exhibited them at the 1830 Brussels International Exposition (Segell 12). With the ivory horn, Pynchon sets up the binary opposition of the European classical musician playing an ebony clarinet (with a cylindrical bore) and the African-American jazz musician playing an ivory saxophone (with a conical, parabolic bore). Both ebony and ivory were tied to colonial exploitation—some of it in the service of European classical music—and have now become scarce.

The ebony/ivory opposition (which also recalls the black and white keys on a piano) can be connected as well to Igor Stravinsky, which is justified insofar as Pynchon reimagines the scandalous first performance in 1913 of *Le Sacre du Printemps* toward the end of the novel.[30] In 1945, Stravinsky wrote the *Ebony Concerto* for Woody Herman, like Benny Goodman a European-American playing what Kurt Vonnegut called the licorice stick (*Interview* 91). It sounds nothing like what would be expected of a swing band. Robin Maconie explains that the *Ebony Concerto* is one of a group of works of Stravinsky's in which "the sounds of mechanical instruments are deliberately imitated and blurred for dramatic effect, including false intonations and incidental noises." For some, it "may evoke a monster computer, a Colossus of exotic design, winking lights and enormous power, delivering a ticker tape of chattering distortion from a speaker system in overdrive" (*Experiencing Stravinsky* 140).[31] This theme can be connected to the test dummy SHROUD and to the Bad Priest who turns out to be a kind of mechanical organism with artificial feet, false teeth, a glass eye, and a wig in which the children find, of all things, an ivory comb, when dismantling him and discovering that he may be a woman (*V.* 342–43). The question of animate and inanimate objects—or in this case more precisely organic and inorganic—haunts much of *V.* While a saxophone is usually made of inorganic material—brass—both plastic and ivory were at one point part of the animate, organic world, which puts into question the easily made distinction between organic and inorganic, between life and non-life. After all, many jazz fans in the novel are still in denial of Charlie Parker's death and scribble on subway station walls and

30 In "Entropy," he also refers to Stravinsky's *L'Histoire du Soldat* played by a small orchestra of violin, double-bass, clarinet, bassoon, cornet, trombone, and tympany, again doing without a polyphonic instrument like the piano.

31 Coincidentally, the tenor saxophone player on the recording (Everest, EVC 9049) was Flip Phillips, a further link to the flip/flops that fascinate Sphere.

urinals "Bird Lives" (60). Ivory connects not only to elephants, "chessmen, backscratchers, hollow open-work Chinese spheres" (40), Godolphin's nose bridge (100), V.'s comb and to colonial exploitation ("Make friends with them, feed them wine, kill them, steal their ivory" [321]) but also to Pynchon's dentistry theme, particularly in *V.* and in *Inherent Vice.*

Saxophone players often change their mouthpieces and make of reeds many times during their careers in a never-ending quest for the perfect sound and feel. A 4½ is an unusually hard reed (or was until recently, when many manufacturers have shifted designations to higher numbers). Charlie Parker—who was seen by many as Coleman's predecessor (*V.* 60)—used to play the hardest reeds available, Rico 5, and sometimes cut or burnt his reeds to make them harder, and only around 1947 switched to 2 and 2½ reeds (Russell 8, 247), possibly because of dental problems due to his heroin use. Thus, Sphere's 4½ reed at the beginning of his career is in line materially with this legacy. David Wild claims on his website that Coleman played a 4½ reed in Los Angeles and writes that this was "described by Don Cherry in a famous passage in an interview with Joe Goldberg." Unfortunately, he does not provide a proper reference for that interview.[32]

Many of these binary opposites are inherent in the flip/flop notion that fascinates Sphere:

> This word flip was weird. Every recording date of McClintic's, he'd got into the habit of talking electricity with the audio men and technicians in the studio. McClintic once couldn't have cared less about electricity, but now it seemed if that was helping him reach a bigger audience, some digging, some who would never dig, but all paying and those royalties keeping the Triumph in gas and McClintic in J. Press suits, then McClintic ought to be grateful to electricity, ought maybe to learn a little more about it. So he'd picked up some here and there, and one day last summer he got around to talking stochastic music and digital computers with one technician. Out of the conversation had come Set/Reset, which was getting to be a signature for the group. He had found out from this sound man about a two-triode circuit called a flip-flop, which when it was turned on could be one of two ways, depending on which tube was conducting and which was cut off: set or reset, flip or flop. (292–93)

32 See http://wildmusic-jazz.com/oc_pynchon.htm (retr. September 13, 2016).

Lee De Forest's invention of the triode in 1906 brought significant changes to amplification and long-distance transmission of signals and is said to be the beginning of the electronics age. It made possible or significantly improved telephony, radio, television, P.A. systems, and electric gramophones. According to Friedrich Kittler, "A world war, the first of its kind, had to break out to facilitate the switch from Poulsen's arc transmission to Lieben or De Forest's tube-type technology and the mass production of Fessenden's experimental procedure. […] Fighter planes and submarines, the two new weapons systems, required wireless communications, just as military command required vacuum tube technology for the control of high and low frequencies" (*Gramophone* 95). Elsewhere, Kittler writes that even today's CPUs are made largely of flip-flops, the English name given to the German *bistabiler Multivibrator* ("Wenn das Bit Fleisch wird" 153). From military applications, the technology spilled over to the entertainment industry, as is summed up in Kittler's notion of the "abuse of army equipment" (*Gramophone* 97) exemplified by Karlheinz Stockhausen's *Kontakte* (1958/59). The mass distribution of recorded music and thus Sphere's possibility to earn a livelihood beyond the limits of the pay for live gigs trickled down from technologies of mass destruction. What Stockhausen and Coleman have in common is that in 1959 they were both the avant-garde—another military term—in their respective musical fields (much as Stravinsky was around 1913), creating unheard-of sounds and blazing trails for those who were to come. While in *V.* Pynchon has a jazz musician learn about electronics and use engineering jargon in his composition, his next novel turns this around. In *The Crying of Lot 49*, the "cats" at The Scope—a bar with a "strictly electronic music policy" that plays Stockhausen to its disciples—hold "Sinewave Sessions" where "fellas come in just to jam from all over the state," to "really swing," and if one didn't bring one's own "ax" there is always something available in the way of flip-flop devices: audio oscillators, gunshot machines, and contact mikes, again, essentially army equipment (34).[33]

33 Seen in the flickering light of the "green neon sign" (34) of The Scope, Oedipa's lover Metzger ("butcher") might then be a reference not only to the German psychologist Wolfgang Metzger or to the *Metzgerpost*, an early form of the postal system from which the post horn emerged and which was later taken over by Thurn und Taxis, but also to the German music critic

The "nonsense words" Sphere makes up "to go along with Set/Reset" (*V.* 293) are grounded in the negro spiritual but change register to contemporary hipster language as well as that of science and engineering:

> Gwine cross de Jordan
> Ecclesiastically:
> Flop, flip, once I was hip,
> Flip, flop, now you're on top,
> Set-REset, why are we BEset
> With crazy and cool in the same molecule . . . (293)

"Gwine cross de Jordan" is to die or to flip and enter an afterlife; death is the flipside of life but inextricably linked with it like the black-and-white symbol of yin and yang, crazy and cool in the same molecule. However, as Eileen Southern writes, "the religious songs, more than any others, often had double meanings and were used as code songs" (195). One such code, in the American context, is that crossing the Jordan also meant crossing the Ohio River into the North to escape slavery. The Book of Ecclesiastes is a meditation on the theme that "all is vanity" (King James Bible) or that "everything is meaningless" (New International Version). A large part of it is dedicated to opposites: pleasure/toil, wisdom/folly, love/hatred and many more. Its Chapter 3 in particular is a long list of opposites subsumed under the idea that "There is a time for everything": "a time to be born and a time to die / a time to plant and a time to uproot / […] / a time to love and a time to hate / a time for war and a time for peace" (NIV).[34] This, again, resonates with the notion of yin and yang, opposite forces that refer to, embrace, and even penetrate each other.

When Norman Mailer writes about the hipster in "The White Negro" (which Pynchon refers to in the introduction to *Slow Learner*), he also employs polar opposites, although he does not unite them in an Eastern philosophical way: Square vs. Hip, rebel

---

and theorist Heinz-Klaus Metzger who promoted Stockhausen's music in his early career (see bibliography for two texts by Metzger).

34 In the late 1950s, around the time that Coleman made his debut, Pete Seeger used those passages for the song "Turn! Turn! Turn! (To Everything There Is a Season)", first published in 1962. It is possible that, at the time of his typescript revisions, Pynchon knew of the song. The better known version by The Byrds (Bird again!) was released only in 1965.

vs. conformist, and he states that "the hipster [is] the man who knows that [our] collective condition is to live with instant death by atomic war" (584) and that "it is no accident that the source of Hip is the Negro for he has been living on the margin between totalitarianism and democracy for two centuries" (585). With the backdrop of nuclear warfare, "Ecclesiastically" may or may not be a reference to Mingus's *Oh Yeah* album of 1962. There, the tune "Ecclusiastics," which "takes as its refrain the moans and groans of an ecumenical church, using the duality of 'the saints and the devils'" (Burba 99), is followed by "Oh Lord Don't Let Them Drop That Atomic Bomb on Me," the apostrophe of which also signals the classic beginning of a spiritual. To insert atom bombs and flip-flop devices into a spiritual-inspired postwar tune is by no means uncharacteristic of the spirituals of the antebellum period: "While the original inspiration for a spiritual may have been a Biblical story or a Protestant hymn [...], the poetic material was reshaped to the slaves' own immediate concerns" (Southern 194–95). Those concerns have shifted from living conditions, without leaving them entirely behind, to technology.

Another example of ambiguity is Sphere's African-American-seeming lover, the prostitute Ruby (possibly a reference to Monk's 1947 ballad "Ruby, My Dear," which was dedicated to his first love Rubie Richardson[35]). Ruby, however, is the Maltese Paola Maijstral. At one point, she asks Sphere: "What are you thinking about"?

> "Flipping," said McClintic.
> "You'll never flip."
> "Not me," McClintic said, "whole lot of people."
> After a while he said, not really to her, "Ruby, what happened after the war? That war, the world flipped. But come '45, and they flopped. Here in Harlem they flopped. Everything got cool—no love, no hate, no worries, no excitement. Every once in a while, though, somebody flips back. Back to where he can love . . ."
> "Maybe that's it," the girl said, after a while. "Maybe you have to be crazy to love somebody."

35 The tune was first recorded in 1947 but was possibly composed much earlier (Ira Gitler's liner notes from *Thelonius Monk with John Coltrane*). Monk also performed it during his engagement at the Five Spot Café with John Coltrane in the summer of 1957.

> "But you take a whole bunch of people flip at the same time and you've got a war. Now war is not loving, is it?"
>
> "Flip, flop," she said, "get the mop." (293–94)

The saxophone, too, flips and flops in accordance with the tastes of the current regimes, but as the above passage shows, it becomes impossible to take sides on the readings. The facile distinction between "cool" and "crazy" is complicated to the degree that it is not clear anymore if either can easily be labeled as a positive or negative term. Everyone flipped and became crazy, which ended in mass slaughter, but when someone switched the lever back, everyone flopped and became cool, all the life and excitement, the sensual dimension, gone. The mop—or mob?—will brush away the real, historical dead or the living dead. Or it will brush away the entire argument, clean the slate on which to reevaluate the situation and renounce any clear-cut distinctions in the old vocabulary.

Apart from Monk's middle name Sphere, there are also resonances between Pynchon's alto player and the historical pianist, not the least in the crafting of new languages. In the liner notes to Monk's *Criss-Cross,* "bebop baroness" Nica de Koenigswarter (whom Charles Hollander believes was a partial model for the ever-elusive V. as well as for Paola/Ruby[36]) writes: "[Monk's] greatness lies in the very fact that he transcends all formulae, all well-worn adjectives and clichés; only a new vocabulary, perhaps, could suffice."[37] The same can be said of Sphere/Coleman, of Bird, and of any art that is considered groundbreaking in its time.

36 Hollander's essay "Does McClintic Sphere in *V.* stand for Thelonius Monk?" has been available on the internet for much of my writing period but has now vanished. In an article about Monk, Steve Dollar also makes such a connection: "But just to certify Monk's underground cachet—he also turned up, after a fashion, in Thomas Pynchon's first novel, *V.*, which featured a cameo by an avant-garde saxophonist named McClintic Sphere" (42). Nica de Koenigswarter's life could be straight out of a Pynchon novel: a Rothschild turned decoder, driver, and radio host during World War II, friend and patron of Charlie Parker and Thelonius Monk, among others, charged with possession of marijuana etc.

37 *Criss-Cross,* echoing "flip, flop," was recorded in 1962 and released in 1963, so it is unlikely that Pynchon alluded to it unless Monk had played it live before.

As for the artist himself, "there came to McClintic something it was time he got around to seeing: that the only way clear of the cool/crazy flipflop was obviously slow, frustrating and hard work. Love with your mouth shut, help without breaking your ass or publicizing it: keep cool, but care" (365–66). Stephen Hock reads McClintic Sphere's creed as "a foundational statement of post-modern irony, an irony characterized not merely by the detachment signified by 'keep cool' but also by a genuine investment signified in the imperative 'but care'" (63–64). In other words: *Gelassenheit* and empathy, the latter of which is considered a distinguishing feature of humans and other animals.

However, as some of Philip K. Dick's novels show, empathy can also be simulated the way other aspects of nature can be simulated, which takes us to the stochastic music that interests Sphere. According to Maconie, "In serial, stochastic, or computer music […], the selection process is usually assigned to some other intelligence [i. e. other than chance music where 'the ostensible source of inspiration is the performer's subconscious'], so what is being revealed is a translation into musical terms of a mathematical selection process" (*Musicologia* 341), inspired by or even modeled on the probability found in nature. Such a fusion of the nature/technology dichotomy is *V.*'s test dummy SHROUD, which stands for Synthetic Human, Radiation Output Determined. A shroud is not only a veil or a screen but also a cloth in which a dead body is wrapped. SHROUD's flesh and skin are made of vinyl compounds—the material of Sphere's records that allows him to "reach a bigger audience"—and its technological make-up may contain some flip-flop latches (or maybe the flip-flops are in the meters the technicians use). Before Benny Profane leaves for Malta, SHROUD calls to him and bids him goodbye with Sphere's very words: "Keep cool. Keep cool but care" (*V.* 369). Ironically, it is a test dummy, possibly with flip-flop latches, that feeds Profane the formula to stay clear of the flip-flop. SHROUD's words are not contained within quotation marks, as opposed to Profane's answers. Its voice seems to come from nowhere, disembodied with no displacement of particles in the air. Perhaps it is Charlie Parker, covered by a shroud, who is speaking from the beyond, tapping Profane's head and miking his brain, as the line from the song "Snap to, Slothrop" goes that Kittler chose as an epigraph for *Gramophone Film Typewriter*.

Say it very (demisemiquaver) fast

By 1956, however, Charlie "Yardbird" Parker, trailblazer and innovator, is dead, irrevocably, despite the denials that "Bird Lives" which have become a buzz word:

> Since the soul of Charlie Parker had dissolved away into a hostile March wind nearly a year before [Sphere's performance at the V-Note], a great deal of nonsense had been spoken and written about him. Much more was to come, some is still being written today. He was the greatest alto on the postwar scene and when he left it some curious negative will—a reluctance and refusal to believe in the final, cold fact—possessed the lunatic fringe to scrawl in every subway station, on sidewalks, in pissoirs, the denial: Bird Lives. So that among the people in the V-Note that night were, at a conservative estimate, a dreamy 10 per cent who had not got the word, and saw in McClintic Sphere a kind of reincarnation. (*V.* 60)

The 34-year-old died in Nica de Koenigswarter's suite at the Stanhope Hotel in New York on March 12, 1955. At Boston's Roseland Ballroom though, in 1939, Bird's death will not be coming as a surprise. In a flashback that may be only a hallucination, but a historically precise one, Parker drifts into *Gravity's Rainbow*. This remarkable episode can and should be read alongside *V.*'s Sphere episodes as Pynchon radicalizes some themes he had begun to develop in his first novel but, on the advice of his editor, decided to leave out. Appropriate to the theme of Pavlovian conditioning, it is not only the injection of sodium amytal but the trigger words "sho nuf" that ring Pavlov's bell:

> [Y]owzah gwine smoke a little ob dis hyah sheeit gib de wrinkels in mah *brain* a process! straighten 'em all raht out, sho nuf!
> PISCES: That was "sho nuf," Slothrop?
> Slothrop: Come on you guys . . . don't make it too . . .
> White college boys, hollering requests to the "combo" up on the stand.

Anachronistically—or in reversal of cause and effect—Slothrop is reminded of the Parker and Gillespie composition "Shawnuff" (c. 1945). There is a cluster of Bird references and allusions, similar to the cluster of Glenn Miller references and allusions Jonathan R. Eller and William E. McCarron noticed in the orgy boat

Anubis episode. In Slothrop's flashback, before he loses his harp down the Roseland Ballroom toilet, he vomits "a pound of salted peanuts" (64), an allusion to the 1941 Gillespie/Kenny Clarke tune "Salt Peanuts" that was recorded by Parker, Gillespie, and others on May 11, 1945, three days after the end of the war, and issued in 1946 on Gillespie's album *Shaw 'Nuff*. Its perhaps most famous recording was at the Toronto Massey Hall concert in 1953 when Parker blew a Grafton plastic sax.

While "Cherokee" is playing in Boston, Slothrop contemplates going to New York to see Parker at Dan Wall's Chili House, already knowing (or channeling) on this night in 1939 that bebop will be invented with a new version of "Cherokee" that Parker will later turn into other compositions such as "Ko-Ko," "Warming Up a Riff," and "Homecooking." Pynchon draws from *Down Beat*'s 1949 interview with Parker and adds rhythmic flourish and biographical background. The interviewers Michael Levin and John S. Wilson write: "Working over 'Cherokee' with [guitarist Biddy] Fleet, Charlie suddenly found that by using higher intervals of a chord as a melody line and backing them with appropriately related changes, he could play this thing he had been hearing. Fleet picked it up behind him and bop was born." In *Gravity's Rainbow*, this interview material turns into:

> Down in New York, drive fast maybe get there for the last set—on 7th Ave., between 139th and 140th, tonight, "Yardbird" Parker is finding out how he can use the notes at the higher ends of these very chords to break up the melody into *have* mercy what is it a fucking machine gun or something man he must be out of his *mind* 32nd notes demisemiquavers say it very (demisemiquaver) fast in a Munchkin voice if you can dig *that* coming out of Dan Wall's Chili House and down the street—shit, out in all kinds of streets (his trip, by '39, well begun: down inside his most affirmative solos honks already the idle, amused dum-de-dumming of old Mister fucking Death he self) out over the airwaves, into the society gigs, someday as far as what seeps out hidden speakers in the city elevators and in all the markets, his bird's singing, to gainsay the Man's lullabies, to subvert the groggy wash of the endlessly, gutlessly overdubbed strings . . . . So that prophecy, even up here on rainy Massachusetts Avenue, is beginning these days to work itself out in "Cherokee," the saxes downstairs getting now into some, oh really weird shit . . . . (65)

Just like Charlie Parker's improvisation, this free indirect discourse appears to be an effortless pouring forth of words (or notes). The first, extraordinarily long sentence requires a lungful of air worthy of a professional horn player, and bebop syncopation becomes evident. The sentence is more than twice as long as the longest line in "Howl," if we think of Allen Ginsberg's extending "the line out to the length of his own long breath, thinking of himself—as Kerouac was doing in the poems he was writing in *Mexico City Blues*—as a jazz musician" (Charters 61).[38] Parker is said to have played 64 bars of "Cherokee" without breathing (which would be about fifty seconds of uninterrupted playing, more or less the time it takes to read the first of the two sentences. As an amateur saxophone player I take about three lungfuls of air to read the first sentence at a fast speed. When I recorded the passage with as few breaths as I could muster and sped it up digitally to forty-five seconds, the length for which one intake of breath would suffice, my voice was more than an octave higher, sounding like the Munchkins' speeded-up voices in the movie *The Wizard of Oz*, which came out in 1939, the year of the Ballroom episode and of the discovery of bebop.[39]

Parker could not be bothered much with writing down his compositions, let alone his recorded solos, and the way they are transcribed by Jamie Aebersold in the *Charlie Parker Omnibook*, a standard source for many of his transcriptions, is in 4/4 with eighth notes and tempo indications varying between, say, 236 ("Warming Up a Riff") and 302 ("Ko-Ko") beats per minute, both of which are breakneck speeds and could also be notated as

38 The 239th, 240th, and 241st choruses of *Mexico City Blues* are about Charlie Parker.

39 Another instance reminiscent of the Munchkins' speeded-up voices occurs in *Against the Day* when Lew Basnight, under the influence of Cyclomite, observes in his steak "the hivelike activities of a race of very small though perfectly visible inhabitants who [...] sang miniature though harmonically complex little choruses in tiny, speeded-up voices," i.e. the song "Beavers of the Brain" (204–03). As for *The Wizard of Oz*, there is another mention of the Munchkins in *Gravity's Rainbow* (274) and Albert Krypton hums "Follow the yellow-brick road" (607). Part 3, "In the Zone," opens with an epigraph quoting Dorothy: "Toto, I have a feeling we're not in Kansas any more . . . ." (283). To my knowledge, Pynchon's *Wizard of Oz* references have not been fully interpreted yet. Coincidentally, Pink Floyd's masterpiece *The Dark Side of the Moon*, of which pop lore has it that it was composed to be played over a muted version of *The Wizard of Oz*, was released in 1973, the same year as *Gravity's Rainbow*.

demisemiquavers at a slower tempo (or with a different time signature), although that would render the score less readable.[40] My speeded-up version of Pynchon's passage above revealed rhythmic patterns and a tempo similar to bebop improvisation with long lines of notes of equal length (quavers), sometimes broken up with rhythmic figures such as triplets leading up to a beat ("out of his mind") or four semiquavers followed by two quavers, with an accent on the first quaver ("demisemiquaver"). "These endlessly gutlessly overdubbed strings" is a pickup followed by a series of three quaver triplets (accent on the first note of every triplet) and ending on a quarter note, an example of which can be heard after the head of "Ornithology," in the trade-off between trumpet, alto, tenor, and guitar. The passage ends like Parker's solo on "Confirmation" with a quarter triplet and a quarter note, giving the impression of a *rallentando* ("really weird shit"). The parenthetical remark about Mister Death can also be likened to Parker's insertion of fragments of a different theme into a solo, an idea he picked up from Art Tatum. Such formal imitation of music in literature can also be found in the Sphere passage. In the case of Sphere, Witzling notes: "The lengthy first sentence of the passage follows a loose iambic rhythm suggestive of bop syncopations [...]" ("Sensibility" 397). Gerhard Westerath, in what may have been the first scholarly contribution on the Parker passage, writes:

> It is a major concern of Pynchon's not only to transport his ideas on the level of meaning and content but to transcend the limitations of his medium and speak to our senses directly. He does so not only by alluding to musical or, more generally, acoustic phenomena but by playing with words as if with acoustic objects in a manner that charges his language with sound even on a formal level. (113)

Westerath sees Parker (and, by extension, Sphere/Coleman) as representing life: "Charlie Parker and with him all real musicians

40 "Billie's Bounce," the tune played by the Kugelblitz Bebop Ensemble in *Bleeding Edge*, is notated at 165 BPM in the *Omnibook*, quite a bit slower than many other Parker tunes (Kugelblitz is an intertextual reference to the benevolent ball lightning in *Against the Day*). The slowest tempo indicated in the *Omnibook* is 70 BPM for "Ballade," but this requires long lines of nearly unreadable demisemiquavers (and sometimes demisemiquaver triplets).

form a counterforce against the white plastic world of the establishment. Their function is to 'gainsay the Man's lullabies,' 'the Man' being the generic name for white society as seen from a black, preterite perspective" (112). And although "Parker's music is an affirmation of life under the shadow of destruction" (112), he will not have lived forever either. He is believed to have started to do heroin at age fifteen, around 1935/36, a habit he was unable to kick for good and which was—along with excessive eating and drinking—responsible for his early demise in an aged body. Therefore, by 1939, his drug trip as well as his trip into the underworld had well begun and Mister fucking Death was already dum-de-dumming along in every note he played (still, he outlived Slothrop's scattering by ten years). An intimation of this can perhaps already be made out in the song "Snap to, Slothrop," a few pages before the Parker episode. The lyrics go perfectly with the tune of the 1926 jazz standard "Bye Bye Blackbird," which in this context can also be read as "Bye bye, black Bird."[41]

Bird with Strings was recorded in 1949 and 1950 and turned out to be the commercially most successful recordings during Parker's lifetime, addressing a mainly white, mainly middle-brow audience. While some critics praised the recordings, others did not think highly of this new, smooth sound. Slothrop must belong to the latter if he is anticipating these recordings and not referring to the potted palm music popular in broadcasting at the time. To me, Bird's string orchestra recordings sound very much like Muzak, music to be played in the city elevators and in all the markets, except for the alto parts. The recordings do not contain a single Bird composition and the orchestral arrangements have no resemblance to the music of Stravinsky, Varèse, Schoenberg, and other contemporary composers Parker admired at the time, all of which are referenced in Pynchon's work. Contrary to what some critics claimed, this was, in my opinion and possibly in Pynchon's, not 'classical music meets jazz' but pop music with a great master playing the lead. As far as I know, the recordings were

41 The song—written by two white men—was popularized and made into a standard by African-American musicians. However, as its Wikipedia article claims, it "was copied by Charlie and His Orchestra during World War II as part of Joseph Goebbels' propaganda campaign." It was also sung by segregationists in Selma, as Renata Adler writes. Paul McCartney's "Blackbird" alludes to the race riots in the late 1960s (what is more, both Paul McCartney and Ringo Starr have also recorded "Bye Bye Blackbird").

not overdubbed, but they might as well have been as no interaction was required between the soloist and the orchestra. Joe Goldberg writes in the liner notes to *Charlie Parker with Strings: The Master Takes*: "No matter how many times he went on to perform these arrangements, the strings played exactly the same thing." Contrary to Slothrop's and many bebop lovers' opinions, however, Parker did not experience this as a sell-out. Goldberg writes that he was in awe of the string players and that he was most proud of his best-selling single "Just Friends" from that album.

In the end, the Sphere and the Parker passages develop the same themes: segregation (or social inclusion/exclusion), white male anxiety and well-meant liberalism, the creation and reception of a musical avant-garde (a term which will never be able to rid itself of its military origin). Once stripped of poetic license, particularly in *V.* (ebony vs. plastic horn; 1956 vs. 1959 etc.), Pynchon's most famous saxophonist passages are striking for their historical accuracy. Coleman is often considered the successor of Charlie Parker and both are seen as major innovators in jazz, equaled by few and surpassed by none. Like Pynchon in his own art, they crafted new idioms, new openings. Pynchon cut a radical black preacher (see Herman and Krafft, "Race," 26) and an instance of "sho nuf" (23) from *V.*, but kept the reference to discussions about "the rising rhythms of African nationalism" (*V.* 60). In *Gravity's Rainbow,* he made up for it by inserting Malcolm X. In both passages, the white college boys request songs. The whitewashed *Bird with Strings* recordings (initiated by Norman Granz) can be read alongside "Night Train," the jazz standard—a simple twelve-bar blues—the college boys in *V.* request. "Cherokee" is denounced as "one more lie about white crimes" (*Gravity* 65). Similarly, in *V.*, Sphere's producer Roony Winsome deplores the "Ballad of Davy Crockett" for falsely offering its namesake as a "towering and cleanlimbed example of Anglo-Saxon superiority" (*V.* 220). Westerath writes: "In musical terms, the white lie is in covering up the truth [of life] with a 'groggy wash of the endlessly, gutlessly overdubbed strings,' thus turning the immediate reality of black, improvised, creative music into white, artificial, sterile 'Muzak'" (112). And while Sphere fantasizes about shoving his alto up the ivy-leaguer's "white ass" (*V.* 281), ivy-leaguer Slothrop also has a white male anxiety about being sodomized by a black person. The Sphere passages are organized around the inadequacy of polar oppositions, but Pynchon introduces some of the excluded middles that are "bad shit" (*Lot* 150) in his Parker passage.

Apart from alcohol and marijuana, heroin was the drug of choice for many jazz men and sometimes women: Charlie Parker, Miles Davis, Gerry Mulligan, Chet Baker, Thelonius Monk, Stan Getz, Billie Holiday, to name a few Pynchon refers to. Whereas Pynchon's harmonicists and kazooists are for the most part presented as recreational players and recreational drug users, perhaps addicted to a high but not a particular one, his saxophonists, at least the addicted ones, are professional players and appear to be addicted to heroin. In fact, in Pynchon's world, the only musicians addicted to heroin are the saxophone players. The heroin theme, however, is less intricately developed than what else has been said about the saxophone so far; it recurs throughout his work but more as a way to provide his tales with a historical backdrop and to reflect the image of the saxophone and saxophonists.

It is widely believed that Parker pawned his horn before his 1953 Toronto gig in order to buy heroin. Pynchon replays a variation of this story with his baritone saxophonist Krinkles Porcino, a minor character in both "Mortality and Mercy in Vienna" and "Entropy." In "Mortality and Mercy in Vienna," Krinkles is a junkie whose girlfriend pawns his horn to buy food for her new lover or room mate Sam Fleischmann.[42] In "Entropy," Krinkles reappears although no mention is made of his habit. *Vineland* mentions two unnamed saxophone players who, "both fond of heroin, often dematerialized someplace, perhaps to inject their drug of choice, though perhaps not [...]" (284).

Only in the case of Coy Harlingen, the saxophone player in *Inherent Vice*, does the heroin habit have consequences for the plot. His desire to get clean and do something for his country propels him into the hands of the CIA. He feigns an overdose and goes undercover turning agent provocateur. "Inside the surf-sax category," he "passed for a towering figure, because he actually improvised once in a while, instead of the way second and even third choruses usually get repeated note for note?" his wife explains with that peculiar inflection that turns statements into

42 *Against the Day*'s saxophonist and band leader Gastón Villa was also "[o]bliged more than once to leave his instruments in soak to pay hotel bills, bar tabs, and gambling debts" (355).

questions (37).[43] At the end of the novel, thanks to Doc's intervention, Harlingen has kicked his addiction, is let off the hook by the CIA and is reunited with his lady and his daughter, returning to the tonic after the turmoil in the dominant and sub-dominant, so to speak, and all comes to a happy ending. It is hardly strange that, of all instrumentalists, it is a saxophone player who makes a pact with the repressive forces since the saxophone's origin and history in the nineteenth century are intimately entwined with the military. At the same time, it is hardly strange that Pynchon eventually gets the CIA off Harlingen's back and returns him to his family as Pynchon never has musicians fall in permanently with the bad guys. In Harlingen's case, it may be significant that he does not play the tenor at the end but the baritone. Throughout the novel, his main instrument is the B-flat tenor, a fifth above the E-flat baritone. Although tuning is not the same as functional harmony, the analogy here is that during the development phase, Harlingen plays in the dominant, that is, in the fifth degree with respect to the E-flat instrument, only to return to the tonic, the first degree of the scale (as well as tonic in its meaning of giving strength or repose, or of restoring well-being), when he is again reunited with his family.

A curious thread that runs through many of Pynchon's sax players, especially the tenor players, is the fact that they tend to take off, escape, hide, or go undercover. In the case of Harlingen and the two anonymous sax players of *Vineland,* this tendency is linked to their use of an illegal substance that is not usually consumed in broad daylight, but other sax players have other reasons, oftentimes amorous ones. In *Against the Day,* an entire subplot of the novel is set off because Zombini's assistant Roxana runs off "with the tenor sax player from the pit band at the local opera house" (75). Erlys Rideout helps Zombini out for that evening's performance and ends up falling in love and running away with him to found a new family lineage.

Later on in the novel, we learn the back story of the band leader and saxophonist Gastón Villa: he "ran into an audience whose ideas of rejection proved fatal, his wife packed up all his old

43 While Pynchon treats the reader to a few performances of Coy Harlingen, practicing "Donna Lee" or playing "Desafinado," for instance, Harlingen's character in Paul Thomas Anderson's movie rendition of *Inherent Vice* (2014) is never heard or seen playing and only occasionally carries a sax case.

costumes and gear for Gastón, kissed him adios at the depot, and sent him off to become a saxophone player for the band of a Wild West show" (*Against* 355). He later founds his own band, which Frank Traverse joins expressly to go undercover. The instrument Frank is given, however, is not a saxophone but a galandronome. Pynchon describes it as a "towering contraption of tarnished and beat-up brass covered with valves and keys, whose upper end flared open like something in a marching band," "a military bassoon, once standard issue in French army bands" (355). This description poses a bit of a challenge, organologically speaking, as it resembles more that of a valved ophicleide. According to the literature and the images of the only known surviving galandronome at the Metropolitan Museum of Art, its main body is not made of brass, like the saxophone, but of maple wood. Only its bell (and the keys) are made of brass and it has no valves.[44] Furthermore, since the first name of its inventor, a Parisian instrument maker by the name of Galander, is lost, and there is only one known instrument left, it is unlikely that it was ever a standard military issue. Perhaps Pynchon saw a valved ophicleide on display at the Metropolitan Museum of Art and mistook it for a galandronome. The parallels with the tenor saxophone are, however, notable. Both were created for military bands—Will Jansen appears to be the only one who challenges this view—; both instrument makers were based in Paris, invented their instruments within a decade of each other (1840s for the saxophone family, around 1853 for the galandronome), and lent them their last names. Both instruments are tuned to B-flat, are made of brass (at least in Pynchon's version), and have keys. Both are reed instruments: the saxophone a single-reed and the galandronome a double-reed. Since Pynchon's description appears imprecise, perhaps the key to understanding it is the double reed. While *Gravity's Rainbow* proposes that there is only one of everything in the world, *Against the Day* introduces doublings: there are at least two of everything in the world, mirror images as in Iceland Spar calcite, frequently—though not exclusively—opposites intimately tied to one another. In this reading,

44 Until I wrote the Wikipedia article for the Galandronome, there was virtually no information available about it on the internet. Images and a brief description can be found in the collection of the Metropolitan Museum of Art (http://www.metmuseum.org/art/collection/search/502238, retr. September 1, 2016). More detailed descriptions are found in Augustin Tiffou (49; 53; 132–34), Will Jansen (130–31), and Lyndesay G. Langwill (23).

the galandronome is the mirror image of the tenor sax, and the reference to the standard army issue points to a doubled universe or a doubled Earth where different choices have been made and an alternative history allowed to unfold, a history that, from time to time, may break into our indicative world.

There is a precedent that can be read as the blueprint of the theme of going undercover and that Pynchon likely alludes to, particularly in, but not limited to, the passages involving Gastón Villa and His Bughouse Bandoleros, and that is Billy Wilder's *Some Like It Hot* (1959). When the speak-easy in which Joe (Tony Curtis) and Jerry (Jack Lemmon) work is busted, they put on women's attire and go into hiding in an all-female band as a tenor saxophonist (Curtis as "Josephine") and a double-bass player (Lemmon as "Daphne"). They both fall in love with the band's vocalist and ukulelist (!) Sugar (Marilyn Monroe, whose death Pynchon grieved heavily [Siegel 90]). She confesses that she is through with saxophone players because time and again they have stolen her heart only to run away.[45] Unlike Pynchon's precision elsewhere with respect to the history of the saxophone—allowing for occasional poetic license—here he does not rely on the history but on a filmic representation of the instrument to inspire parts of his plot.

But running away is not the exclusive domain of male saxophone players. In line with the sax's historical reception and historiography, female instrumentalists are somewhat rare in Pynchon's work. Still, women were some of the saxophone's earliest pioneers in the USA. The first saxophone recording was made by Bessie Mecklem in 1892 at the Edison factory (Segell 60–61), which is why it seems fitting that Pynchon also creates a female sax player, albeit only in passing. She appears in his 1964 short story "The Secret Integration." Mr. McAfee, the alcoholic jazz bass player, remembers meeting a girl on a bus "who played tenor and had just left a white musician she'd been with" (*Learner* 180), which in turn triggers the memory of his leaving his wife or lover Jill. As Chapter 4 will show, Pynchon's underrepresentation of female musicians is the case not only for the fictional ones but for the references to historical musicians and works of music as well.

---

45 The movie's most memorable tune, the tango "La Cumparsita," is referred to in *Vineland* (78); however, the reference there is to Orson Welles's 1938 radio drama *The War of the Worlds*.

The major accusation brought against the saxophone by the Elect of the twentieth century was that its sound was 'negroid' (Third Reich) or 'carnal' (Hollywood). In the nineteenth century, Berlioz and some of his contemporaries praised the instrument for its "trueness and beauty of sound" (Liley 13) but later, it became a sex symbol, and not just because it is enough to change one vowel to move from sax to sex or because it may look like a phallus.[46] With its conical, parabolic shape, it can produce a great bandwidth of different sounds and is theorized to approach very closely the range of expression of the human voice, which is likely why it has often been linked to sex and sensuality—Earl Bostic's raucous sound an example of the former, Stan Getz's lyricism of the latter. Even in the 1950s, it came under the scrutiny of Hollywood censors and had to be cut out of some movie scores because it was too arousing (Segell 39). Conn, the Indiana instrument maker, picked up the saxophone's sex symbolism: from 1935 through 1971, they manufactured an influential model nicknamed 'Naked Lady' for its engraved image of a naked lady on the bell, reminiscent of the images painted on missiles and military airplanes. Of the saxophonists Pynchon refers to, Charlie Parker, Lester Young, and Gerry Mulligan played the 'Naked Lady.' Perhaps it is no coincidence then that the President of the United States who secured a large number of votes by putting on shades and playing the tenor sax on TV was also the one who was very nearly impeached for sexual misconduct, an ordeal Pynchon makes fun of in *Bleeding Edge* (302, 369).

Apart from runaway lovers, the saxophone and its players appear a number of times in a sexually more explicit context. McClintic Sphere meets his lover Ruby in "a friendly rooming (and in a sense cat) house" (*V.* 281), and after Oedipa and Metzger's love-making, the movie they had been watching ends "with that strange 30's movie music with the massive sax section" (*Lot* 30). The most explicit saxophone sex scene is at the orgy on the Anubis in which Slothrop participates:

> A C-melody saxophone player has the bell of his instrument snuggled between the widespread thighs of a pretty matron in sunglasses, yes

46 Perhaps the main reason the saxophone lost popularity to the electric guitar in the 1960s is that the electric guitar is even more phallic in shape and more versatile in handling.

> sunglasses at night, this is some degenerate company Slothrop has fallen in with all right—the saxman is playing "Chattanooga Choo Choo," and those vibrations are just driving her wild. (*Gravity* 475)

The Anubis scene has two music clusters: a Glenn Miller and a Shirley Temple. The Glenn Miller one comprises the reference to "Chattanooga Choo Choo," a tune which, by 1944, was synonymous with Glenn Miller, and discreet allusions to "A String of Pearls" and "Tuxedo Junction" (Eller and McCarron 193) and, I may add, to "One Dozen Roses." The Shirley Temple cluster comprises "On the Good Ship Lollipop," "Animal Crackers in My Soup," and, later, "Oh My Goodness." The Temple tunes, as will be argued below, are there to set up the theme of child abuse and pedophilia. The Glenn Miller ones, on the other hand, appear to point to him as another musical innovator who perished in the war. Eller and McCarron write:

> In *Gravity's Rainbow*'s constant parade of composers and performers, Miller remains the great shadow figure, the innovator who is barely heard through the subtle, almost subliminal allusions. Miller's reed-dominated arrangements (he carried four saxophones and a clarinet) and the highly choreographed visual showmanship of his band place him in the company of other musical innovators mentioned in the novel—Hugo Wolf, Anton Webern, Charlie Parker—who were also, like Miller, cut down in their prime. Thus Miller is yet another exemplar of one of the major motifs of *Gravity's Rainbow*: the innovative artist who seems destined for Election but suffers a Preterite death instead. (193–94)

What is degenerate about the company on the Anubis, one might argue, is not so much the lady's sunglasses as the fact that they take two artists with impeccable public images and turn those images into fore- and background music for their various forms of copulation and masturbation. The humor here is not very sophisticated: the saxman's C-Melody (a variant between the E-flat alto and B-flat tenor, tuned in C, and discontinued when the Great Depression hit) acts as a vibrator. He plays a song about a train driven by pistons, letting off steam, where the 'choo choo' could be an onomatopoeic groaning or orgasm. While the Glenn Miller references can be taken lightly, the Temple ones bring in a dark undercurrent that foreshadows Bianca's death (see footnote 11 in Chapter 4).

As always with Pynchon, looking closely at his novels reveals a multiplicity of connections both among them and between those works and military, social and economic history as well as the musical tradition. As with Oedipa Maas's continuing quest for clues, it is difficult to determine where something was placed for the reader to discover and where those links and references are coincidental. What is evident, however, is that Pynchon has intimate knowledge of his subject matter. Even in *Vineland*, where the harmonica appears mainly as a prop, he places it in a history of struggle between the Preterite and the Elect, between music-making and war-making. He portrays the harmonica, the kazoo, and the saxophone as American instruments. While he stages them as subversive and played by the Preterite—with the exception of the ambiguity of the Harmonica Marching Band Academy—he makes clear that the instrument per se is innocent but its history is not. In that history we can find the struggles between de- and reterritorialization, appropriation and reappropriation, a continuous game of who has the upper hand. In all of this, however, Pynchon stays true to his belief that music offers respite and that making art—popular, lowbrow, participatory art in particular—may be the only way to put up resistance to top-down hierarchies of power, be they economic or otherwise political. Much of what Carswell writes about the ukulele is also true for the other instruments, indeed for most of the amateur music-making in Pynchon's work, and, in this spirit, it seems fitting to quote the end of Carswell's article on the ukulele:

> The counternarrative that tells us to have fun, sing goofy songs, join together in whatever family or communities work as long as they work for the mutual benefit of everyone, understand the context of contemporary society with all its flaws and all our flawed complicities, never sacrifice social relations for accumulation, and use any moments of respite to provide a counterbalance to the power of Empire. ("Ukulele" 216)

The greatest power of 'subversive' music-making then comes from refusing to speak the language of the Elect and choosing instead a means of expression which, as some believe, cannot lie. At the same time, Pynchon shows that such resistance can be only temporary—and this is perhaps why it is so important. He seems to say that while music can be appropriated by political and economic forces, a living, continuously changing music based on practice among the like-minded cannot turn fascist but will remain dialogic, to use Vilém Flusser's distinction between broadcast and network media (172–74).

3

The Sounds of Societies to Come

Music can be a political force in the present. With respect to a number of musical instruments, Pynchon stages this as a force of bottom-up politics that resides and operates outside of capitalism's and its institutions' necessities and constraints. It is a political force that finds its aim and expression within itself and refuses the hierarchies, compartmentalizations, and scope of action offered or imposed by institutions and their legal frameworks. In other words, it acts outside—or at the very least on the margins—of *Realpolitik* and the markets while maintaining the emancipatory momentum and hope that democracy in a non-institutionalized, non-capitalist sense—a democracy that is closer to the utopias of socialism, communism, or anarchism—promises. Such a conception of democracy is founded on "the equality of citizens" and "extends equality to the level of the economy and then into other social relations, such as sexual, racial, generational, and regional" (Mouffe 52). Chantal Mouffe may be right when she claims that, "Democracy is our most subversive idea because it interrupts all existing discourses and practices of subordination" (52). This ideal of equality continues to haunt contemporary political thinkers—sometimes under the label of communism, socialism, or democracy (and for Pynchon's characters more than once under the label of anarchism)—who attempt to strip these notions of their real-political histories, oftentimes corrupted by individual greed and lust for power, and to restore their idealistic and ideological foundations.[1]

However, music on the margins in the present time, much as it may be unnerving for listeners like Nixon/Zhlubb or the Krupp employees at the industrial magnates' dinner party, would not elicit fear and anxiety in the ruling classes if it were not believed to be a harbinger of political change. Since as early as Plato, there has been a persistent belief in the West that "the modes of music

1 See, for instance, *Democracy in What State?* with contributions by Giorgio Agamben, Alain Badiou, Jean-Luc Nancy et al., *The Truth of Democracy* by Nancy, *The Meaning of Sarkozy* by Badiou, or *Hatred of Democracy* and *Chronicles of Consensual Times* by Jacques Rancière.

are never disturbed without unsettling of the most fundamental political and social conventions" (Plato 1930, 333).[2] Plato—evincing a conservative view that has survived into present times—appears to believe that such innovation ("not new songs but a new way of song") is undesirable and that changes in music are not just early warning signs but the *cause* of changes in political and social conventions: "For a change to a new type of music is something to beware of as a hazard of all our fortunes" (Plato 1930, 333), which is why the guardians must "be watchful against innovations in music […] counter to the established order" (331). This trope is already familiar from *Gravity's Rainbow*: John Joseph Hess observes that "Socrates is essentially the classical precursor to […] Richard M. Zhlubb" (14) and that "For Socrates and for Richard M. Zhlubb, music can inspire the potentially transformative passions outlawed in *The Republic*" (15). In a more liberal view of artistic innovation and the social order, the passage from Book IV of *The Republic* has been taken up both by Pynchon and by the French economist Jacques Attali who in his influential 1977 *Noise: The Political Economy of Music* claims that the development of music prefigures the political and economic order of society. This is also in line with one of the functions Kathryn Hume and Thomas J. Knight attribute to music in Pynchon's work: "projecting diachronically into the future, and thus serving as a vehicle of prophecy" ("Orchestration" 367).

Before outlining Attali's argument, it is worth looking at the wordings that Attali and Pynchon chose from a plenitude of available translations. The translation from Greek by Robert Baccou, which Attali chose for the original edition of his book, reads: "Nulle part, on ne modifie les lois de la musique sans modifier en même temps les dispositions civiles les plus importantes," which I translate as "Nowhere are the laws of music changed without simultaneously changing the most important civil dispositions" (*Bruits* 68; this is the only time I refer to the French original). In his English translation of *Noise*, Brian Massumi chose the 1930 Plato translation by Paul Shorey quoted above. Other translations of *The Republic* read "For the forms of music are nowhere altered without affecting the greatest political laws (Trans. Chris Emlyn-

2 This belief has made it into popular culture with songs such as The Fugs' 1968 "When the Mode of the Music Changes" that continues with "the walls of the city shake," a wording frequently employed by Allen Ginsberg too.

Jones and William Preddy, 359) and "For one can never change the ways of training people in music without affecting the greatest political laws" (Trans. C.D.C. Reeve, 108). Finally, in Alain Badiou's contemporary rewrite of *The Republic,* Socrates says, "any huge change in the styles of music that are in fashion signals a change in the most fundamental laws of the state" (118). The differences among the translations—every one by a scholar of Greek or Plato—are striking. Baccou speaks of the laws of music and the civil dispositions, Shorey of the modes of music and the civil and political conventions, Emlyn-Jones and Preddy of the forms of music and the political laws, Reeve of the training of musicians and the political laws, and Badiou of the styles of music in fashion and the laws of the state. Most noticeable, however, is that Badiou's Plato is the only one who unambiguously states that changes in music *signal*—not cause—changes in society. Society is changing—and music reflects this more quickly than other indicators of change.[3] Another noticeable difference among the translations is that Shorey's "musical modes" could designate the musical modes as the term is used today, that is, scales such as Dorian, Lydian, and Mixolydian, which each have their own characteristics and may elicit a certain mood in the listener. An early theory of those scales and how they are suited or unsuited to underline and convey certain content and moods is found in Book III of *The Republic*. However, since other translations distinguish between "musical scales" (in the case of Plato's moral theory of scales) and "musical modes" (in the case of Plato's warning against innovation), "modes" can also be read as the forms of music in general, that is, harmonic, melodic, and rhythmic conventions. The value of working with Baccou's and Shorey's translations (as do Attali and Massumi) is that they avoid the notion of political laws that could be misconstrued to mean the legal framework and instead choose the broader notions of political *and* civil/social dispositions/conventions. It is changes in the established order of society, and not so much in the legal framework, that elicits the fears of the ruling classes. In the end, the ruling classes' reaction to musical changes—for instance with censorship, reappropriation,

3 Of course, other indicators could possibly serve Attali's claims too, but would need to be developed elsewhere in a different context: fashion, design, environmental change, stock market, etc.

or disregard—depends on their reading of Plato or Attali, that is, on whether they see music as an early sign or a driver of change.

In *Mason & Dixon*, Ethelmer paraphrases Plato, provoking his relatives by changing the notion of a threat to that of a promise: "When the Forms of Musick change, 'tis a Promise of civil Disorder" (261). In this more rebellious reading of Plato, there is, at first sight, a clash between the words "Promise," generally assumed to be something positive, and "Disorder," generally assumed to be something negative—unless the speaker has antipathies to the current order of society and desires revolt, revolution, anarchy, or just some excitement, as the youthful Ethelmer seems to display when he later says: "These late ten American Years were but Slaughter of this sort and that. Now begins the true Inversion of the World" (264). But even without Ethelmer's predispositions—likely insouciantly boyish rather than based on political convictions—the perceived positivity of promise and negativity of disorder may not necessarily clash if we follow Jacques Derrida: "Serious theorists of speech acts maintain that a promise must always promise something good. [...] [A] promise is not a threat. But I'd venture to claim that a promise must always be haunted by the threat, by its becoming-threat, without which it is not a promise" (458–59). I would add to this that a threat, a performative speech act as well, must also be haunted by the promise in the common sense, that is, by the possibility that something bad may turn out to be something good. Thus, in the undecidable valuation of the promise or threat of civil disorder, which may or may not materialize, fear and hope intersect, and only context can tell the listener/reader what moves the speaker. Whereas Plato—or Socrates—is moved by fear,[4] Ethelmer is not, although it is not quite clear whether he is moved by hope or just by adolescent disagreement with the elders.

Attali employs both the conservative, fearful futurologist Plato and the progressive, hopeful futurologist Marx to design a template that allows, firstly, for historical inspection of changes in musical forms and what they mean for changes in the social order and the distribution of power, and then, secondly, for a prediction or a forecast. Attali thus reads music as the medial apriori of the

4 Badiou's reworking of *The Republic* takes the liberty of changing the way Plato is usually read when Socrates says, "The emergence of new styles in music is no doubt something inevitable and desirable" (118).

organization of society. The starting point of his analysis is Pieter Brueghel the Elder's 1559 painting *Carnival's Quarrel with Lent.* In it, he sees two antagonistic forces at work: festival, "whose aim is to make everyone's misfortune tolerable," and austerity, "whose aim is to make the alienation of everyday life bearable through the promise of eternity" (Attali 21–22). Antagonistic as these forces of noise and silence, as he calls them, may be, both serve to keep the lower classes docile. "Brueghel," according to Attali, "cries out that music and all noises in general, are stakes in games of power" (24).

Attali draws up three consecutive yet overlapping periods of musical development in the West which he sees reflected in the social order a hundred or two hundred years later. The first era is that of Sacrifice. Music is seen as a channeler of violence. It "is used and produced in the ritual in an attempt to make people *forget* the general violence" (19). Its purpose is to "unify a people through the ritualization of the sacrificial violence that grounds the social order" (Price, *Resonance* 116). This era roughly corresponds to the time before 1750 AD, a time whose music is somewhat underrepresented in Pynchon's work.[5]

The second era, that of Representation, is characterized by the emergence of the musical spectacle and the consumption of music in enclosed spaces. Music tries to "make people *believe* in the harmony of the world" (Attali 19) under the current distribution of power. Nobles employ composers and musicians to sing their praises and that of the existing order. The orchestra becomes a status symbol, the musician a salaried employee, and the spectacle in the enclosed space makes it possible to charge entrance fees. Music starts being commodified (51). "The theory of political economy of the nineteenth century," Attali writes, "was present in its entirety in the concert hall of the eighteenth century, and foreshadowed the politics of the twentieth" (57).

Technological innovations at the end of the nineteenth century, most notably the phonograph and the gramophone, as well as Fordism, then give rise to the third era, the era of Repetition. In this period, "each spectator has a solitary relation with a material object; the consumption of music is individualized" (32). The stockpiling of essentially intangible information paves the way for

5 Only 29 of the 935 identified references to works of music date from 1751 or earlier and there is only a small number of musicians from that time. See Chapter 4.

a new organization of capitalism, "that of the repetitive mass production of all social relations" (32), which is an apolitical (110) or anti-political one. From today's vantage point, the "repetitive mass production of all social relations" brings to mind the so-called Social Media, that is, our lives mediated by capital.

The three eras of Sacrifice, Representation, and Repetition are not discrete but overlap to some degree. Attali also names a fourth era, the era of Composition, which he situates in the future. This period is marked by the consumer turning into a producer who "will derive at least as much of his satisfaction from the manufacturing process itself as from the object he produces" (144). Although Attali remains by necessity vague on this era, we cannot fail to hear in his call echoes of the enthusiasm present today not only in amateur, DIY, and DJ culture but also in the political realm, where interactive technology and the widespread means of media production such as cameras, sound-recording devices, and software are thought to promise democracy, participation, and creativity, but, as is my conviction as well as Attali's, also carry the danger of a falling back into the networks of representation and repetition. The heavy reliance on technology of this type of enthusiasm does not take into account technology's flipside as theorized by Heidegger. For one thing, it may just as well serve top-down surveillance and exploitation of the producer/consumer. Moreover, current software—even the promising forms—is always programmed as a set of rules and limitations which may allow for creative misappropriation or reinterpretation of its possibilities but never for transcending the mindset of the software's creator, generally that of a Western paradigm.[6,7]

---

6 For example, Peter Price told me that most commercially available music software is so wedded to Western musical paradigms that it is, for instance, not able to parse a tabla rhythm where odd numbers of beats, syncopations, and accents are played against each other. One would have to turn to a programming environment such as MaxMSP or Pd (Pure Data) to make it work. Perhaps, philosophically, the reason for the domination of Western paradigms in programming is the fact that computers are based on mutually exclusive binaries (0 and 1, off and on) and it remains to be seen whether the underlying paradigms will change with the advent of quantum computing.

7 I see no reason to hypothesize a different fourth era for today's situation (not repetition anymore nor composition yet) that may or may not lead to a fifth era of composition, as was suggested to me by Philipp Schweighauser. Firstly, there is every indication that we are still firmly rooted in an era of repetition of goods, services, and social relations, and that the category of the consumer is psychologically, sociologically, politically, and economically

Attali's claims prove fruitful for an interpretation of a number of musical passages in Pynchon's work. The most obvious one—because Plato is directly quoted—is in *Mason & Dixon*, but the same kind of gesture can also be observed elsewhere, for instance, in the discussion of jazz and anarchism in *Against the Day* and in the *Inherent Vice* scene where Doc, Denise, and Japonica drive past Wallach's Music City. The era of composition can be glimpsed in the scenes involving the kazoo, the ukulele, and the harmonica, as well as in Chandler Pratt's intern Darren, the young rap artist of *Bleeding Edge*, or in the many songs in Pynchon's work composed on the spot by amateur musicians.

The Age of Representation

At Christmastime in 1786, the Reverend Wicks Cherrycoke recounts, Sheherazade-like, his own version of Charles Mason and Jeremiah Dixon's lives and careers as astronomers and land surveyors. His tale is interrupted from time to time by oboe and clavier interludes performed by his host family, who, at one point, slip into a discussion that is possibly Pynchon's densest and most carefully crafted musical passage. The family evaluates Plato's views on the transformative power of music with reference to their own post-revolutionary days, their own songs and hymns, and the new music which, supposedly, is beginning to take shape in South Philadelphia. The passage that spans more than three pages (261–64) brings us back to Plato and allows for nearly endless unraveling. While it would be desirable to reprint the entire passage, I will forgo the sense of continuity and reading pleasure this would afford and instead highlight the important parts and discuss them

speaking, a more important category than that of the citizen or the homo generator, no matter the promises of and occasional inroads into the era of composition. Secondly, Attali's eras have never been entirely discrete but bleed into each other. And thirdly, such eras have a long duration and can be established only in retrospect. Nominating an era for our immediate present carries the danger of falling into a kind of hysteria about the most recent technological advances, seeing an ever-accelerating development of which the present is the apex, and, correspondingly, the current state of civilization as the natural point of convergence of history.

in depth, taking at times the liberty of musicological digressions to shed light on the density and coherence of Pynchon's writing.[8]

The passage is set at the tail end of Attali's era of sacrifice and in the first decades of the era of representation, both of which employ their specific strategies to keep the lower classes docile. In other words, it is set at the dusk of Christianity and the dawn of the scientific era. While there has been a major shift in perspective on the place of the human in the world, both of these eras build on dualities to subjugate the natural world. As Joseph Dewey writes, "Within the sciences—as within Christianity—the cosmos is simplified into a battlefield, hostilities inevitable as long as we are held to be separate from nature and as long as we resolve to dominate and direct" (121). A third way—for instance, that of Eastern mysticism to which the Reverend Cherrycoke feels drawn—has no place in either of these worldviews.

Musico-historically speaking, the scene takes place somewhere in the transition period between the Baroque and the Classical. By then the suite, a succession of dances first mentioned in dance books of the sixteenth century (*Der Brockhaus Musik* 769)—the time of Brueghel the Elder—had found its standard form of Allemande–Courante–Sarabande–Gigue but allowed for variation with other dances such as the minuet, the gavotte, the scherzo, and the bourée.[9] In Aunt Euphrenia's words:

> "— most of the new pieces us'd to be one Dance-Tune after another, or, for the Morning Next, a similar Enchainment of Hymns,—no connection, Gigue, Sarabande, Bourrée, la la la well a-trip thro' the Zinnias of Life, and how merry, of course,— but 'my' stuff, 'Thelmer,"—waving a Sheaf of Musick-Sheets,— "all is become Departure and sentimental Crisis,—the Sandwich-Filling it seems,— and at last, Return to the Tonick, safe at Home, no need to even play loud at the end." (263)

8 For an overall picture of music in the novel, refer to John Joseph Hess's excellent article "Music in *Mason & Dixon,*" which, perhaps more aptly, should have been titled "Harmony and Music in *Mason & Dixon.*" Hess also indicates a number of musical and literary texts of that time that treated the subject of the connection between musical and social orders (7–8).

9 In her discussion of the passage, Bénédicte Chorier-Fryd focuses on the minuet, taking her cue from the "tempo of the minuet" indicated when Ethelmer plays "To Anacreon in Heaven" ("A Novel in Musick"). While the 'minuet and trio' does share some characteristics of other musical forms, especially the sonata with its I–V–I structure, I believe that the sonata form is more pertinent to the present discussion.

From around 1690 on, the suite (a French word which could be translated as 'succession,' 'progression,' or 'onward journey') was also called the 'partita' (departure), which corresponds to "proceeding down the road having one adventure after another, with no end in view" (*Mason* 263). What Euphrenia indicates is the shift from the idea of Departure to the idea of Departure–Crisis–Return. As she correctly observes, the different tunes of a suite were intended to be dance music and usually merry—in any case not melancholy or mournful—and did not need a connection to each other except for the key signature, which usually stayed the same throughout the suite. While the dances of the suite correspond to the festival, the "Enchainment of Hymns" corresponds to Lent. Around 1750, the Late Baroque period gives way to the Classical period with its less highly calculated and more sentimental musical forms, a standard movement usually being based on four stanzas of eight bars each, to which Ethelmer refers: "Four Stanzas,— sentimentally speaking, a 'Sandwich,' with the third eight 'Bars' as the Filling" (262). At the same time, the standard sonata reaches its final formalization with exposition (first in the tonic, then in the dominant), development (dominant and other keys), and recapitulation (return to the tonic)—as well as possibly a coda. The reference to departure, crisis, and a safe return home is also reflected in the overall structure of the novel, as Bénédicte Chorier-Fryd notes. The three parts of the "Novel in Musick" (263) are entitled "Latitudes and Departures," "America" (from which the passage under discussion is excerpted), and "Last Transit," and Mason and Dixon's travels and internal turmoil correspond to this tripartition. At least since *Gravity's Rainbow* Pynchon has been interested in this "simple-minded German symphonic arc, tonic to dominant, back again to tonic" (*Gravity* 450). To tonic or "teutonic" (450).

To shift into a political reading: Whatever may be going on in the development part of the classical sonata, the "Departure and sentimental Crisis," the form safely returns to the tonic to promise eternal harmony and the reestablishment of the existing order.[10] A "dialectic resolution" has been reached "between

10 The textbook version of this social order goes as follows: first an elite of wealthy and educated white men—the only ones worthy, in their own view, of public office—then propertied white men, and then the rest of the population without electoral rights: nonpropertied white men, white women, freed slaves, slaves, and finally Native Americans (Boyer et al. 171–75).

the light and dark of major and minor" (Burba 104). The transgressive, ecstatic, Dionysiac forces are tamed and life goes on as before with the social order left unchanged. There is "no need to even play loud at the end" (*Mason* 263) because this harmony of the existing power structure appears to be a natural, universal harmony that every sensible human being must accept and that therefore does not need to be trumpeted aloud. This would be Uncle Ives' interpretation as "a good sermon aim'd at keeping the Country-People in their place" (263).

But if we could leave it at that, it would not be Pynchon at his best. The above reading—perhaps a reactionary one that still feeds on the promises of 'modern' music of the time—is one based on a sentiment of harmony, a notion that Hess has problematized with reference to music in *Mason & Dixon*. It corresponds to Attali's era of representation in which music "is employed to make people believe in the harmony of the world, that there is order in exchange and legitimacy in commercial power" (19). Enthusiasm for that type of 'modern' music was not shared by all contemporaries. One Ezra Baker, for instance, hailing from the era of sacrifice, complains in a letter of August 31, 1780, to Moses Stebbins, the descendant of a friend of Thomas Pynchon's ancestor William: "But they so Suddenly exchanged old Tunes for New ones and introduced them into the Publick Worship and the old ones being neglected it was but a few that could bear a part in the delightful part of Divine Worship" (qtd. in Smith 784). And later on: "Now Merry Tunes come in a pace, So full of Cords or Discords that Another Set of good Singers are Shut out of bearing a part in that Workshop unless they will be at the pains to learn, and in that case it is not so certain they will not soon be left behind if the Wheals continue to Trundle as they have of late" (785).[11] Although concerned in earnest, this complaint, as well as the call for reviving church discipline (787), resonates with the Reverend Wicks Cherrycoke's—likely ironic—complaint that nothing is sacred anymore. An age in which nothing is sacred anymore is also one in which sacrifice is not possible anymore.

11 Since this letter, reproduced in 1931 under the title "The American Revolution Hits Church Music," shares so many concerns of the *Mason & Dixon* passage (as well as its wording and spelling), and since the introduction to it mentions William Pynchon (and the second-to-last paragraph ends with "Here lys the pinch."), it is not improbable that Thomas Pynchon knew of it.

Like the LeSpark family discussion in 1786, the surveying of the dividing line between the Penn and Baltimore families, between Pennsylvania and Maryland, between the abolitionist states and the slave states takes place in this new scientific era, musico-historically corresponding to the Classical period with its new, modern paradigms:

> "Mason and Dixon's West Line," Aunt Euphrenia setting her Oboe carefully upon the arm of her Chair, "in fact, shares this modern Quality of Departure and Return, wherein, year upon Year, the *Ritornelli* are not merely the same notes again and again, but variant each time, as Clocks have tick'd onward, Chance has dealt fair and foul, Life, willy-nilly, has been liv'd through…." (*Mason* 263)

Mason and Dixon return year after year to the line they will become namesakes of. Each year, they live through a variant—a *ritornello,* a small return—of their previous years. When Euphrenia laments that, in the old music, "I seek in vain after madness, and Rapture" (263), she displays dissatisfaction with a lack of difference in the *ritornelli* and a desire for ecstasy. Hess observes that rapture such as she desires "would soon appear in the twin cults of nineteenth century nationalistic fervor and turbulent Romantic expression" (15). It is, in fact, also Euphrenia who entertains the family with tall, romanticized stories about being kidnapped by pirates and sold into a harem, a different but closely related meaning of 'rapture.' She too, by the time she regales the family with those stories, has safely returned home from her supposed journey.

Tyler Burba, with reference to Deleuze's *Difference and Repetition,* observes that mere repetition of the same does not bring about ecstasy; what it takes is a repetition that is a variant of the original statement: "Ecstatic music must start with the known, the refrain, and expand it, always moving outside of it, toeing the line between total destruction of the form and absolute allegiance to it. The listener through this process will be moved out of his or her egoic relation to the world because what is presented to the senses draws in as it alters" (138).[12] The topos of ecstasy through

12 It is worth noting here that Brian Massumi, who translated Attali's *Noise,* chose to translate *ritornelle* not as 'ritornello' but as 'refrain' in his 1987 translation of Deleuze and Guattari's *Mille Plateaux.* Paul Patton, in his 1994 translation of *Différence et Répétition,* follows Massumi.

difference in repetition will later in the novel also seize Dixon, by outward appearance a seizure not unlike Nietzsche's breakdown in Turin—Nietzsche being, after all, one of the most formative thinkers of both difference in repetition (albeit more in the form of large than of small returns) and the Dionysiac. After having returned to the line a few years in a row, each time being a variant of the former years, and having witnessed many variations on the theme of slavery, the Quaker witnesses a particularly appalling scene of abuse of slaves and finally loses his composure. He grabs the instrument of abuse, and threatens to whip the slave owner (698–700). After having built up his anger over the fact of slavery, a dominant of the New World, over many years, he submits to ecstasy and releases his pent-up anger, which restores him to the tonic. He understands "his Obligation, henceforward, to keep Silence upon the Topick" (700). In other words: no need even to play loud at the end.

Chorier-Fryd writes that in "America," the second part of *Mason & Dixon*, "American independence is rendered as a musical revolution" ("A Novel in Musick" 205). In Ethelmer's words:

> 'Tis ever the sign of Revolutionary times, that Street-Airs become Hymns, and Roist'ring-Songs Anthems,—just as Plato fear'd,—hast heard the Negroe Musick, the flatted Fifths, the vocal *portamenti*,—'tis there sings your Revolution. These late ten American Years were but Slaughter of this sort and that. Now begins the true Inversion of the World. (*Mason* 264)

At the close of the American Revolution and shortly before the signing of the United States Constitution, there is a clear feeling, at least as voiced by the character Ethelmer, that America has not seen the last of the revolution. To hark back to Mouffe: "As soon as the principle of equality is admitted in one domain [...], the eventual questioning of all possible forms of inequality is an ineluctable consequence" (94). What the LeSpark family has lived through is merely the prelude to the "true Inversion of the World," in other words, the liberation of the black slaves and the subsequent inclusion of the Preterite (that is, women and black and native people) as American citizens with full and equal rights. This emancipatory inversion is announced, the passage suggests, by the spread and rising popularity and acceptance of "Negroe Musick." What is slowly taking shape in music is the ascendency of 'low' black and street culture into 'high' white culture. The "Marches and Anthems, for Triumphs that have not yet been made real" (262) may be read as the precursors to the New Orleans marching-band music—the work songs and spirituals—or as the early forms of liberation anthems that were important for the American Civil Rights movement of the twentieth century.

That the "Roist'ring Songs" become anthems and the street-airs hymns is not so much a turning sacred of the profane. Both anthems and hymns are forms that emerged primarily from a religious context. However, with the death of God, the ascent of the Age of Reason, and the separation of church and state, both terms acquired a more worldly—although admittedly still metaphysical—meaning in the form of *national* anthems (in German, *Nationalhymnen;* in French, *hymnes nationales*). Of course, many national anthems (and hymns, for that matter) still have religious imagery or make appeals to God, such as in the fourth verse of "The Star-Spangled Banner"; but the lyrics turn mainly toward the patriotic and martial. The profanation of sacred terms—and not the turning sacred of the profane—is the sign of revolutionary times, be they American or French ones.[13] In this reading, "the true Inversion of the World" (*Mason* 264), of the Western world in any case, begins with the French Revolution, a mere three years after the frame narrative, then triggers the slave uprisings of the Haitian Revolution and has profound repercussions on the fears of slave owners in the USA.

When Ethelmer says "'Tis the Elder World, Turn'd Upside Down," he refers not only to what in his intuition is to become an emancipatory movement. "The World Turned Upside Down" was initially a ballad protesting Oliver Cromwell's prohibition of traditional—merry, or possibly even carnivalesque—English Christmas carols in 1645, and is thus in line with the season of the frame narrative. Essentially, its lyrics lament the newly imposed austerity and solemnity of Christmas, mourning that "Likewise then did die, rost beef and shred pie / Pig, Goose and Capon no quarter found," reflecting Pynchon's delectation in culinary feats. According to popular belief (shared by Ethelmer)—although Andrew Jackson O'Shaughnessy writes that there is no contemporary

13 "La Marseillaise," however, has a different history. It was composed only in 1792 and was declared the French national anthem on July 14, 1795. Although different variants have existed over time (such as "La Marseillaise pour le désarmément" or "La Marseillaise Bacchique"), it was from the beginning a worldly revolutionary song.

evidence for it (281)—the song was also sung by British troops upon surrendering after the battle of Yorktown in 1781, a surrender which paved the way for the independence of the formerly British colonies. If indeed it was played at Yorktown (the British troops were "only permitted to play their own marches," and they were "prohibited from playing *Yankee Doodle*," which initially made fun of the American citizen militia [281]), it may be the tune that Sarah Osborne, an army cook and washerwoman, heard when "the British officers rode right on before the army, who marched out beating and playing a melancholy tune, their drums covered with black handkerchiefs and their fifes with black ribbands tied around them" (Brown 205).

The other tune Ethelmer refers to is "To Anacreon in Heaven":

> "In C, if ye like,— here is something the fellows sing at University, when we are off being merry,— 'To Anacreon in Heaven' 's its Name,— [...]"
>
> The Air he plays to them would be martial but for its Tempo, being more that of a Minuet,— thirty-two Measures in all,— which by its end has feet tapping and necks a-sway. "Here, I say, is the New Form in its Essence,— Four Stanzas,— sentimentally speaking, a 'Sandwich,' with the third eight 'Bars' as the Filling,— that Phrase," playing it, "ascending like a Sky-Rocket, its appeal to the Emotions primitive as any experienced in the Act of— "
>
> "Cousin?"
>
> "— of, of Eating, that's all I was going to say..." (262)

Although musically quite different from "The World Turned Upside Down," "To Anacreon in Heaven" has its origin in the celebration of worldly pleasures too, each chorus ending with a variation of its last two lines "And long may the Sons of Anacreon intwine / The Myrtle of Venus with Bacchus's Vine." The British drinking song was most likely composed sometime in the 1770s, and it seems fitting that Ethelmer, in this context, speaks of the sandwich and its filling, and replaces the word 'fucking' with 'Eating' when caught off guard. In 1814, Francis Scott Key set his poem "Defense of Fort McHenry" to this tune which, with slight musical alterations, was eventually titled "The Star-Spangled Banner." In 1931, the former "Roist'ring-Song" finally became the official national anthem of the USA and thus officially received its seal of approval for having announced a social change.

Not unlike some of Pynchon's favorite musical instruments that have undergone changes in their public reception, these two musical pieces he highlights have undergone a series of appropriations and reappropriations. Perhaps this mixing of songs is what the Reverend Cherrycoke refers to when he says the context of the Plato quote was his "Quarrel [...] with the Dithyrambists" (262). This would place Plato, not surprisingly, on the side of Lent in Brueghel's *Carnival's Quarrel with Lent.* The reference to "quarrel" may also feed the suspicion that, perhaps, Pynchon's subtext here is not only Plato's *Republic* but also Attali's *Noise,* since the more common English translation of the title of the Brueghel painting is *The Fight Between Carnival and Lent.*

While "The World Turned Upside Down" (1646), hailing from the tail end of the Renaissance, briefly references the Roman Empire with Caesar and Herod in the second line, "To Anacreon in Heaven" is filled with references to Greek and, to a lesser degree, Roman deities, the initial publishers—the Anacreontic Society—having been named in honor of the Greek lyric poet who praised wine and love. Although there is only one instance in the Plato passage where eating is mentioned (when Ethelmer is reminded that there are children in the room), a novel food item, the sandwich, is mentioned twice in this passage when first Ethelmer and later Euphrenia refer to the "Sandwich-Filling" of the new music.[14] The inventor of the sandwich is thought to be John Montagu, 4th Earl of Sandwich, who held a number of military and political offices, among them First Lord of the Admiralty during the American War of Independence (Rodger 287) and—more intertextual Pynchon—Potsmaster General of the United Kingdom in 1768, an office the American counterpart of which was held by Benjamin Franklin a few years later. Montagu having been a strong supporter of James Cook, the latter named the Sandwich Islands—now Hawaii, the origin of the ukulele—in honor of his patron.[15] After his naval career, the 4th Earl of Sandwich

14 The sandwich, that "great modern Advance in Diet which bears [the Earl's] name" (*Mason* 367), is the most frequently mentioned food item in *Mason & Dixon*, also appearing on pages 73, 327, 338, 366–67, 404, 414, 585, and 720, usually in scare quotes indicating the not-yet fully established neologism. Only in the Plato passage and in the "percussive 'Sandwich' of hammer, anvil, and the Work between" (585) is the word used metaphorically.

15 *Mason & Dixon* contains the anachronistic mentions of "Surf Music" (264) and of a "Eukalely" (319) as well as of two instruments that may allude to the ukulele, namely a "modest Guitar upon which to strum this very

became a promoter of what he called "ancient music," with a particular interest in Handel (311–13).

The original sheet music of "Anacreon in Heaven" is set in C major, and "The Star-Spangled Banner" may be sung in any key. However, the official Department of Defense version is set in B-flat major for higher voices. This is the key in which—according to Shana L. Redmond—it is most often performed (49) and the key—according to Euphrenia—toward which everything gravitates. To understand why this key signature—a favorite of national anthems—would be disquieting or ominous, one has to look earlier in *Mason & Dixon* where a standard military issue fife is "tun'd in that most martial of Scales, B-flat major, stirring in all who heard it, even Philosophers, the desire to prevail over a detestable Enemy" (21). Throughout music history, particularly the Baroque, composers and music theorists have, often contradictorily, assigned different emotional characteristics to different modes and key signatures. This can be said to go back to the Greeks, particularly to Plato's explications in Book III of *The Republic.* It is, however, not clear where Pynchon gets his characterization of B-flat major as the most martial of scales. Christian Schubart's *Ideen zu einer Aesthetik der Tonkunst* from 1806, for instance, correlates B-flat major with cheerful love, clear conscience, hope, and longing for a better world; characteristics in line with a national anthem as well as with Haydn's fourth quartet of his Op. 76, "Sunrise," which is also in B-flat major. In *Das Neu-Eröffnete Orchestre* from 1713, Johann Mattheson considers the key signature very diverting, splendid, and modest (§18). The difficulty is that, unless one has a perfectly

[Surf] Musick" (264) and a "diminutive three-string'd Lute" (80), that is, a "Fiji Islander's Guitar, first introduc'd there two hundred years ago by Portuguese Jesuits" (81). When Pynchon shifts the spelling from ukulele to eukalely, he also shifts the meaning from the Hawaiian 'jumping flea' to a neologism with the Greek prefix eu-, indicating something good or sweet, as in the sweet-sounding euphonium.

James Cook was assigned to observe the 1769 transit of Venus on Tahiti, eight years after Mason and Dixon were sent to Sumatra by the Royal Society for a similar purpose (but ended up on the Cape of Good Hope). He was killed on Hawaii by natives in 1779. Even though Cook is not mentioned once (as opposed to the noun and verb 'cook' with about 45 mentions throughout the novel), with his naval career, his great skill in drawing maps, and the many inventions and discoveries made possible during his voyages, including the possibility of taking longitude measurements at sea, the spirit of Cook could be said to haunt much of *Mason & Dixon,* more so even than does that of his patron, the Earl of Sandwich.

equal-tempered tuning, such characterizations depend on the tuning system, and tuning systems were abundant and subject to personal preferences. In the absence of equal-tempered tuning, the intervals between adjacent notes are different and produce different sounds depending on the scale. Since interpretations, also known as *Affektenlehre*, the theory of affects, were as abundant as the tuning systems, it is to be assumed that Pynchon refers to a particular interpretation I have not been able to unearth or that he plainly refers to the official 1918 service version of the national anthem which is in B-flat major.[16,17]

When Ethelmer performs "Anacreon," he leaves out the chorus that would repeat the last eight bars, what could be called in baroque terminology a *ritornello*. The sheet music at the time was set in 6/4 meter, which would yield a total of 16 bars, but the way Ethelmer interprets it (and the way the national anthem was later notated) is in 3/4 yielding a total of 32 bars, which could be why Pynchon puts the word 'Bars' inside scare quotes (262). The repetition of the last eight bars as a chorus was eventually dropped from the national anthem.

There is "no need even to play loud at the end," Euphrenia says with reference to the form of 'her' music that returns to the tonic. As an oboist, she would find it difficult to play very loud anyway, which is the main reason Adolphe Sax set out to replace the double reeds of the military bands with his own inventions of the saxophone and the saxhorns. The original sheet music of "Anacreon" does not contain dynamics and thus leaves it up to the interpreter, but the 1918 service version contains dynamic markings and ends in fortissimo.

16 For a more in-depth discussion of the *Affektenlehre*, see Maho A. Ishiguro's master's thesis *The Affective Properties of Keys in Instrumental Music from the Late Nineteenth and Early Twentieth Centuries*.

17 Jimi Hendrix's performance of "The Star-Spangled Banner" at Woodstock, possibly the national anthem's most famous rendition, is played in E-flat major, as are all other versions of his that I was able to trace. Intended or not, there is probably no other version in which the rockets' red glare and the bombs bursting in air are more audibly present than in the one performed at Woodstock by the former paratrooper of the 101st Airborne Division.

In Pynchon's work, there are two more mentions of the national anthem, one an epitaph in a "bouncy Star Spangled Banner meter" (*Gravity* 27–28), the other Sasha Traverse's memory of singing it at the playoffs in her junior year (*Vineland* 78). Jimi Hendrix is mentioned in *Vineland* (18, 117, 279), in *Inherent Vice* (37), and in *Bleeding Edge* (174). For a variety of historical scores and commentaries, see http://starspangledmusic.org/free-scores.

The first arrangement to appear under the title "The Star-Spangled Banner" (in 1814) was set by Thomas Carr. He kept the original 6/4 measure (as opposed to 3/4 in later arrangements) and the original key signature of C major, however, raising the fourth in the second and sixth bars by a semitone.[18] Enharmonically (but not functionally) speaking, this is the same as a flatted (or diminished) fifth or a tritone and needs to be resolved.[19] This augmented fourth makes the move away from the tonic stronger because it is the leading tone to the dominant and it is the furthest note from the tonic. It amplifies the crisis, whose resolution then makes an even stronger point. In the context of *Mason & Dixon*, and of some other passages in Pynchon's work, two interpretations can be given of the tritone and/or the flatted fifth. They can be called 'European' and 'American' interpretations. The European one refers to the tritone as the devil in music, the note that must be avoided in medieval music and that becomes so important in functional harmony—as a function demanding directionality and resolution—to the point that Wagner uses it to disrupt the expectation of resolution. The American interpretation refers to the flatted fifth which with bebop became a blue note of the blues scale (along with the minor third and seventh), now easily recognizable by every person with even a little exposure to mainstream Western music. On the keyboard of a piano (which Ethelmer is playing), the flatted fifth or the augmented fourth corresponds to a tritone (again, enharmonically and not functionally speaking). Playing a blues scale with its minor characteristics over major chords, as is not uncommon, creates an even stronger friction.

The tritone itself posed a problem for functional harmony, as is made evident by the crisis that Richard Wagner's Tristan chord (1865) with its augmented fourth posed for contemporary ears and analysis.[20] Although the tritone is a strong component of the

18 I start counting bars after the introduction and pick-up. In 3/4 measure, not counting introduction and pick-up, the bars would be 3 and 11. Raising the fourth occurs only in these two bars and not in the entire piece.

19 I have a theory that many national anthems have such a moment of crisis, frequently toward the end, which is then resolved by the return to the tonic: the nation is born from a moment of crisis that is resolved to promise eternal harmony.

20 The Tristan chord has been read in many different—sometimes contradictory—ways by many different musicologists and has compelled some to write books on the subject. An overview of these interpretations is beyond the scope of this investigation.

Tristan chord, what is at issue is not so much the tritone itself as the way Wagner stages its preparation and resolution (or its lack thereof). Many interpret the Tristan chord as the inaugural moment of atonality, a major change of mode, to speak with Plato. It posed serious problems for analysis because it could no longer be explained in terms of functional harmony. Price says that it was "heard by many listeners of the time of its composition to be pure noise as it could not be parsed by existing harmonic conventions" (*Resonance* 94), which is why he calls it the "'God is dead' of tonality" (162)—Wagner's preceding Nietzsche's proclamation of the death of God by seventeen years (*The Gay Science* §108 and §125). Perhaps Wagner simply decided to go for sonority and not for function as Nietzsche, in an only slightly different context, said: "The color of sound is decisive here; *what* resounds is almost indifferent" ("The Case of Wagner" 21). This move, in the musico-historical context, was anarchistic but also inevitable in a situation of the equality of notes demanded by equal temperament starting with Bach, a demand that would eventually lead to Anton Webern—the composer who, more than anyone else of his time, demanded absolute equality for all twelve notes and abandoned functionality—as Gustav explains in *Gravity's Rainbow:* "The young barbarians coming in to murder the Last European, standing at the far end of what'd been going on since Bach, an expansion of music's polymorphous perversity till all notes were truly equal at last . . . . Where was there to go after Webern? It was the moment of maximum freedom. It all had to come down. Another Götterdämmerung—" (448). The Bach–Wagner–Webern sequence Pynchon constructs here starts with Bach's equal temperament (which allows for enharmonic substitutions), goes to the beginning of the end of tonality and ends with the absolute equality of all notes in the equal-tempered twelve-tone scale. Webern is the Last European because this is the end of European music. He is killed in Austria, the nation that brought forth both Adolf Hitler and Sigmund Freud, who coined the notion of polymorphous perversity. And after Webern, along the European trajectory, where was there to go? The answer to this question Pynchon already set up in his previous novel: Karlheinz Stockhausen, the composer whose parents, like Webern, became casualties of the Third Reich.

The 'American' reading of the flatted fifth goes back to the "Negroe Musick" (*Mason* 264) Ethelmer refers to. Relatively little is known about African or African-American music around the time of the narration. While slaves and former slaves did not write down their ever-changing songs, contemporary white American analysts did not possess the means to faithfully repeat or notate the songs.[21] Consequently, the little they wrote down were the lyrics of songs, descriptions of what the music sounded like, and approximations in the European notational system that was, however, unable to accommodate the profuse embellishments (such as the *portamenti* [264]) invented on the spot or the exact pitch of a melody, which eventually tended to be obscured by the improvisation and embellishments (Southern 16–17). The Englishman Thomas Edward Bowdich, who was born in 1791 and was sent on various missions in Africa, tried to record some African songs, but he observed: "To have attempted any thing like arrangement [...] would have altered [the melodies], and destroyed the intention of making them known in their original character. I have not even dared to insert a flat or a sharp" (qtd. in Southern 18). As for the African-American tradition, Eileen Southern writes that the "black man sang all kinds of songs at all times" and on different occasions: psalms, hymns, old African songs, ballads, and tribal songs, and "when he tired of singing those or he exhausted his repertory, the black man made up his own songs, stumbling a bit over the unfamiliar English or Dutch or Swedish or German or French words [...], but managing, nevertheless, to express his ideas in the alien tongues" (49).

Pynchon does not make clear precisely which "Negroe" musical tradition or occasion he is referring to. Perhaps he had contemporary records at hand to which I have no access; perhaps he, too, had to imagine the music of the time, extracting his knowledge from various sources and beliefs about African and early African-American music. There seems to be agreement that many African musics are based on a pentatonic scale.[22] There are not-so-slight shifts of pitch with respect to the European well-tempered scale. The blues scale—one of the modal changes Plato "did not foresee" (*Mason* 264)—is based on a minor pentatonic scale. The minor third, diminished fifth, and minor seventh of the equal-

21 Eileen Southern believes that "the earliest record of the influence of slave music on the white colonists" was written by one Nicholas Cresswell as late as 1774 (64).

22 There are also heptatonic and other kinds of scales as well as micro-intervals and regional and situational variations difficult to describe with the vocabulary and theory of Western music. However, with reference to African-American music, most authors focus on the pentatonic scale.

tempered scale are flatted or sharpened a little bit to become the blue notes. From the vantage point of equal temperament, they become microtones. They belong neither to the major nor to the minor scale (nor to any of the Greek scales or church modes) but are situated somewhere in between, and not always in the exact same place. Price told me that the major difference between the Greek and the African conception of scales and tuning is that the Greeks had a mathematical model to which the instruments needed to conform whereas for African forms of music-making, scales were local and based on material practice. And indeed, when discussing the new music with its flatted fifths, Ethelmer's "*mathematickal* cousin DePugh is disquieted" (264, emphasis added) by deviations from Plato's forms. Thus, in this reading of the passage quoted, the blue notes *avant la lettre* turn into, or at least anticipate, the crisis of Western classical music and the beginning of the end of functional harmony less than a hundred years later—and along with it the changes in society.

If we were to look for a *political* equivalent of or analogy to these blue notes, generally attributable to tones in the twelve-tone scale but always hovering on the edge in the area of micro-tones, it could perhaps be found in the refutation of the biological fiction of human 'races' and in the assertion that 'race' is a social construct with any number of positions between, say, black and white, like blue notes, whose materiality requires not notation but performance and context. This contingency is performed by *V.*'s Paola/Ruby, the Maltese who passes as a black prostitute without even putting on black-face (350), as if it were not enough that the Maltese as an overarching and perhaps likewise fictional category already have a complex genetic pool due to their history of appropriations.

The *literary* equivalent of blue notes, on the other hand, could be precisely the genre Pynchon helped inaugurate, that of postmodernism with its—albeit highly constructed—ways of appropriating and mixing forms, its references high and low, its enactment of undecidability, and, at times, its difficulty to place in the formerly established Western canon. But more than Pynchon's own work, that equivalent is perhaps the work of African-American writers such as Ishmael Reed and Xam Wilson Cartiér, to name only two, with their interest in the plight of African-Americans, their inclusion of idiolects, and their profoundly musical writing—musical poetically as well as in their choice of themes and references.

There is also a parallel here with the emancipation of noises in their double meaning as that which cannot be musically parsed and those who stand outside of society, the Preterite in Pynchon's terminology. John Cage writes: "We no longer discriminate against noises [...]. Sounds formerly considered out of tune are now called microtones" (Cage, *Empty Words* 177). The microtone-noises that were unable to attach themselves to an established semitone were finally liberated and allowed to express themselves in their own right. The emancipatory strategy connecting music and politics can be summarized in Cage's words: "By making musical situations which are analogies to desirable social circumstances which we do not yet have, we make music suggestive and relevant to the serious questions which face Mankind" (183). In essence, and in line with Attali, Pynchon's text here seems to suggest that the social and political development of the twentieth century was present in nascent form already in the American musics of the eighteenth century. However, Cage does not say that if we change the music we change the world; he says we make our choices in line with what we would like to see politically.

While I—and possibly Pynchon—favor an emancipatory reading of the Plato passage, one can also read the air that "would be martial but for its Tempo" (and, one might add, for its time signature in 3/4 or 6/4, better suited to dancing than to marching) in a more dystopian manner. The German national anthem ("Das Deutschlandlied"), composed by Joseph Haydn in 1797, also follows the AABA form with its sandwich-filling (if one leaves out the repetition of the last stanza as Ethelmer does for "Anacreon"), albeit in 4/4 meter and with each stanza being four rather than eight bars long. Here too, the music was composed first and the lyrics added later on.[23] The initial second verse that praised German women, wine, and song was dropped by the Third Reich leadership (Hanson 7). The "Deutschlandlied" underwent many different reinterpretations, for instance after World War I when the "imperialistic tone of Hoffmann's first stanza was [...] cast as a defiant harbinger of things to come" (7), and to this day, it plays a role in right-wing extremism, particularly the first stanza which

23 Its lyricist August Heinrich Hoffmann von Fallersleben's publisher Julius Campe apparently "hoped to find something that spoke to the German national identity while also avoiding the expensive payment of royalties to a living composer" (Hanson 4). Von Fallersleben "was a patriot and ardent nationalist, yet he championed the democratic principles that were so quickly discarded in the name of German pride during the dark years of the country's history" (11).

is not part of the official national anthem. The point of the dystopian reading is that the rise of national anthems in the eighteenth century, albeit in modern forms, was the harbinger of nationalisms later on in history that—in the case of Hitler's Germany—would reappropriate and reinterpret composers like Richard Wagner and denounce a wide range of contemporary avant-garde music as degenerate. And sadly, even the liberation and occupation by the Allies led to the inadvertent killing of Anton Webern by an American soldier in September 1945 (incorrectly dated May in *Gravity's Rainbow* [448]).

What to make of Ethelmer's reference to the "South Philadelphia Ballad-singers, [...] generally Tenors, who are said, in their Succession, to constitute a Chapter in the secret History of Musick yet to be, if not the Modal change Plato fear'd, then one he did not foresee" (264)? Most likely, this is another anachronistic intimation of music history (shortly after this passage, there is also a mention of surf music), alluding either to Italians or to African-Americans. Around 1786, there was no South Philadelphia as it is known today and there does not seem to be an actual musical group or a musical tradition called "South Philadelphia Ballad-singers." There is a significant gap in the historiography of that part of the town and its inhabitants. In a short essay on Italians in Philadelphia, Mary Rizzo writes that "When [William] Penn began planning Philadelphia, South Philadelphia was rural farmland outside the city center. It remained that way through the eighteenth century." One key to understanding this reference might be found earlier on in the novel, when Aunt Euphrenia with her oboe enters the narrative for the first time: "Do find a way," she jokingly says to the twins, "to wrangle with less Noise, or your old Uncle will have to sell you, as a Brace, to the *Italians* rumor'd to live South of this City, where you shall have to learn to sing their vulgar Airs [...]" (*Mason* 103). Rizzo also writes that, "Although Italian immigration to Philadelphia began in the eighteenth century, it was only in the 1880s that large numbers of Italians settled here." How large that population was is unclear to historians, as Richard N. Juliani asserts.[24] What seems to be clear, however, is that the image of the

24 According to Juliani, Philadelphia was connected to Italian seaports by 1760 (3). John Palma, a musician and composer, "is generally identified as the first Italian to arrive at Philadelphia. In an advertisement in the *Pennsylvania Gazette*, the newspaper published by Benjamin Franklin, Palma announced a concert under his direction at the Assembly Room in

Italians was associated with music and art from the very beginning (5). It was only with the start of the industrial revolution that South Philadelphia began to grow rapidly by an influx of immigrants from predominantly Catholic European nations and, later, of African-Americans. During the twentieth century, it became one of the most culturally diverse parts of Philadelphia with a rich musical history. Around the mid-twentieth century, it was "the mecca of the Teen Idol business" (Hoskyns 43), a role that would be challenged only by Los Angeles in the 1960s.

On the one hand, therefore, Pynchon may refer to a musical tradition coming out of South Philadelphia starting around the 1950s with Italian-background crooners such as Frankie Avalon, Fabian Forte, and Al Martino (who played Johnny Fontane in *The Godfather*[25]), or even the slightly older Eddie Fisher, the most successful pop star at the time (who is mentioned in *Vineland* [431]), though not of Italian origin.

On the other hand, since Ethelmer also mentions "Negroe Musick," flatted fifths, and "vocal *portamenti*," Pynchon could be referring to the doo-wop groups that appeared around the same time in the same neighborhoods, with Lee Andrews & The Hearts or Harold Melvin and the Bluenotes, and possibly also Fabian Forte's childhood friend Chubby Checker (mentioned in *The Crying of Lot 49* [114]).[26] Although coming from a different ethnic background, the doo-wop groups' socio-economic background was very similar to the crooners', and both the doo-wop groups and the teenage crooners can be said to have been ballad singers in new idioms—but certainly not the kinds of idioms that Plato would have to fear: both the doo-wop groups and the crooners

---

Lodge Alley at six o'clock on the evening of January 25, 1757" (5). I am also indebted to Philadelphians Peter Price and Arthur Sabatini for their thoughts on this passage.

25 Although Al Martino is never mentioned, *The Godfather* makes a few appearances in Pynchon's work, most notably (and not explicitly referenced) as the Italian wedding in *Vineland*. One of the songs the *Vineland* wedding party requests is "C'è la luna mezzo mare," also played at the wedding in the opening scene of *The Godfather*.

26 The list of well-known singers from that time coming out of South Philadelphia—a considerable number of whom went to South Philadelphia High School and had an Italian background—includes Buddy Greco, Fred Diodati and Al Alberts of The Four Aces, Bobby Rydell, Georgie Shaw, or the opera singers Mario Lanza and Frank Guarrara. The female singers included Gloria Mann, Kitty Kallen, Micki Marlo, Jodie Sands, as well as opera singer Marian Anderson.

sang very suave music and not the kind of rock'n'roll of an Elvis Presley or a Jerry Lee Lewis that still had some threat.

Additionally, it seems that Pynchon employs yet another musical idiom in this passage on modal changes, an idiom that is less melodic than modal—albeit not comparable to ballads. Extracting the direct speech, the following passage appears to adhere to the rhyming, rhythm, and conversational style of hip-hop music:

> "[T]he secret History of Musick yet to be,
> if not the Modal change Plato fear'd,
> then one he did not foresee."
> "Not even he." [...]
> "My point exactly!" (264, line breaks added)

The rhyming trade-off between Ethelmer and DePugh is yet another musical style somehow mixed into the Plato passage (where surf music, ukuleles, ballads, and the rhythm of engines, among other references, are mentioned). This takes us back to Wicks Cherrycoke's lesson on Plato's fear of mixing up one form of song with another, "or abandoning them altogether" (262): hip-hop does the former with its remixing of existing material, and the latter with the introduction of rap and the relinquishing of melody and harmony. Although I am unable to assign a particular rhythmic structure to the whole prose passage spanning three pages, it is conceivable that, at least in parts, it was constructed rhythmically, because towards the end, Brae makes a suggestion "quite upon her 'Beat'" (265), in contrast to Dixon who, earlier on in the novel, is "[s]tarting a beat late" (19). Chorier-Fryd writes that, "*Upon her beat* may be read here both in a temporal (taking her turn in the conversation) or in a spatial sense (she is on her beat like a hooker fending for her street corner, or a policewoman on duty)" ("A Beat Late" 263). Both the hooker and the cop are among the recurring tropes of Gangsta Rap, a subgenre whose origins are commonly credited to Philadelphia rapper Schoolly D.

While Pynchon, the former Boeing employee who wrote about the perils of loading and unloading IM-99A missiles ("Togetherness" [1960]) and made the V-2 rocket a central symbol of *Gravity's Rainbow,* has obviously studied the "rockets' red glare" as well as "bombs bursting in air," there may have been another lineage of anthems in his mind that extends beyond "The Star-Spangled Banner," whose liberatory symbolism became fragile at best during the Vietnam War if not before. This lineage led, in the early twentieth century, to another kind of anthem—that of African-Americans in their struggle for recognition. In her book *Anthem: Social Movements and the Sound of Solidarity in the African Diaspora*, Shana L. Redmond singles out and discusses in detail a number of anthems that have become important for Black social movements in the twentieth century, among them "Ethiopia (Thou Land of Our Fathers)," the anthem of the Universal Negro Improvement Association (UNIA); "Lift Ev'ry Voice and Sing," named "The Negro National Anthem" by the National Association for the Advancement of Colored People (NAACP); and "We Shall Overcome," another key anthem of the Civil Rights Movement. Besides asserting that "'The Star-Spangled Banner' was a frequent visitor to the Black nation" (49), Redmond sees a number of connections between the American national anthem and "Ethiopia":

> The sound of "Ethiopia" intimately connects it to the accessible and familiar icons of the majority society, namely "The Star-Spangled Banner." Measures 33 and 34 of "Ethiopia" use two chords in variation: measure 33 starts with an augmented I on a half note, transitions to a V dotted-quarter note, and ends on the I on the last eighth note of measure 33 and the three count hold in measure 34. This ending not only mirrors the chord progression of "The Star-Spangled Banner"—a song often performed in B-flat major—but also follows a very similar rhythm, despite the time signature difference. While "The Star-Spangled Banner" is performed in 3/4, its ending of a dotted-quarter, eighth, quarter, and dotted half note is very similar to the ending of Ford's composition. (48–49)

The analysis holds, except that there is no augmented I on the half note in measure 33 of "Ethiopia" but a I in its second inversion, that is, with a fifth as the bass note.[27] Although Redmond is right, I would maintain that the rhythmic figure and particularly the I^6_4–V^7–I chord progression is a common way in Western music—perhaps *the* most common way—of ending a piece of music, the latter producing a friction or micro-crisis with a tritone between the third and the seventh of the dominant and resolving it into the tonic. Perhaps the analogy is stronger when taking into con-

27 Shana Redmond confirmed this to me by email. This correction makes the comparison between the two anthems more plausible.

sideration the genesis of the material and its effects, as Redmond does when she observes that the American national anthem was also sung at UNIA meetings and that the "UNIA's use of the 'Star-Spangled Banner' [...] played to the sympathies and allegiances of an already embattled population" (52–53). Thus, the drinking song becomes a national anthem by a minor alteration of the third, which then inspires an anthem for the oppressed.

There seems to be little agreement over what constitutes an anthem and what constitutes a hymn. Both terms have been used for sacred as well as secular music and many times they have been used interchangeably to designate the same songs. Redmond, however, offers a useful distinction. She writes: "Hymns are sacred texts, written as praise or prayer, and are often religious in nature, offering adoration to deities or their personification. While often contained within the purview of the church or other religious organizations, hymns are not without political import; they are organizing tools that manage services [...]" and then goes on to designate anthems as "those songs that organize citizenship practices" (79). However the lineage of the American national anthem may be read or interpreted, Pynchon stages the "Anacreontic Song" as the "Anachronistic Song."

When Euphrenia observes that "ev'rything, suddenly, has begun to gravitate toward B-flat major," we can also focus not so much on the actual key signature as on the 'gravitating toward.' This reading points to Attali's era of repetition, the era in which music "serves to silence, by mass-producing a deafening, syncretic kind of music, and censoring all other human noises" (Attali 19). The gravitation toward one key is then not so much an egalitarian development where all would have the same conditions to begin with. Instead, it heralds a general flattening of musical or cultural expression and experience. A study by Joan Serrà, Álvaro Corral, Marián Boguñá and others, conducted by computerized analysis of pop song material covering more than 450,000 recordings from 1955 to 2010, revealed that pop music underwent a continuous leveling. The researchers measured loudness, pitch, and timbre. They found "three important trends in the evolution of musical discourse: the restriction of pitch sequences (with metrics showing less variety in pitch progressions), the homogenization of the timbral palette (with frequent timbres becoming more frequent), and growing average loudness levels (threatening a dynamic richness that has been conserved until today)" (Serrà et al.). We can understand the political repercussions of this development when we contemplate Attali's thesis. It also confirms Price's observation that "Increasingly, within the commodity music form, the temporal is redefined as the stringing together of identical units. This is time from which any eventful happening is being ruled out ahead of time" (*Resonance* 213). The keynote is the tonic of the major scale—metaphorically and often musically too. The stringing together of identical units is what Euphrenia is dissatisfied with. Observing the musical structure of much of today's popular music, which often does not even depart from the tonic, it appears that history is repeating itself. Or in another register: The citizen has been replaced by the consumer in capitalist 'democratic' societies, and what is catered to him or her must be apolitical, mass-tailored, and optimistic. It must gravitate towards its lowest common denominator to make possible mass targeting, interchangeability, economies of scale, and a smooth transition to the next element of mass culture. But perhaps this monotony is the end as well as the beginning of music, as Kittler hypothesized with reference to Syd Barrett's last performances with Pink Floyd ("Gott der Ohren" 62), that is, before starting from and returning to the tonic in a circular structure, one first has to establish the tonic.

Thus, to tie it up, this passage from *Mason & Dixon* points to different possible futures, but not to mutually exclusive ones. As different musics can coexist, different social orders and world views can too. Music can be read as a harbinger of emancipation but also as a force of political containment and a leveler of expression and experience. This is in line with Attali's analysis that, despite its prophetic tone, does not allow making reliable forecasts. Instead, Attali sketches a framework that retrospectively allows us to situate the present social order as the realization of past musical developments.

However, perhaps it is not so much the changes in music itself which may be a threat to the existing power structures as Plato feared, but the contemplation of these changes. In a possibly ironic voice, the Reverend Cherrycoke—who is not exactly averse to the pleasures of the secular world but is also troubled by both the Christian and the scientific programs and drawn to Eastern philosophies—laments the analysis of changes in the musical forms of drinking songs: "Anatomizing your own drinking songs!— is nothing sacred, and is there not but a small skipping Dance-step, till ye be questioning earthly, nay, Heavenly, Powers?" (263). 'If the magic of drinking songs isn't sacred anymore, what is?' he seems, at a first reading, to say. Another reading, however, shifts the focus: it is not the actual musical developments that endanger the pre-established earthly and heavenly order, one could argue along these lines, but their analysis and critical reflection in the age of reason's compulsion to mastery.

The Age of Repetition

The scene from *Mason & Dixon* at the turning point of the eras of sacrifice and representation leaves a lot of ambiguity. Fast-forwarding to the era of repetition with its scene from *Inherent Vice* where Doc, Japonica, and Denis drive past Wallach's Music City reveals a much clearer pronouncement on its day. It is set in California in 1970 as the marijuana fog of the peace and love generation is evaporating into thin air along with that generation's dreams and ideologies:

> They were crossing Vine and about to go past Wallach's Music City, where each of a long row of audition booths inside had its own lighted window facing the street. In every window, one by one as Japonica crept by, appeared a hippie freak or small party of hippie freaks, each listening on headphones to a different rock 'n' roll album and moving around at a different rhythm. Like Denis, Doc was used to outdoor concerts where thousands of people congregated to listen to music for free, and where it all got sort of blended together into a single public self, because everybody was having the same experience. But here, each person was listening in solitude, confinement and mutual silence, and some of them later at the register would actually be spending money to hear rock 'n' roll. It seemed to Doc like some strange kind of dues or payback. More and more lately he'd been brooding about this great collective dream that everybody was being encouraged to stay tripping around in. Only now and then would you get an unplanned glimpse at the other side.
>
> Denis waved, yelled and flashed peace signs, but nobody in any of the booths noticed. At last he slid back down into the Mercedes. "Far out. Maybe they're all stoned. Hey! That must be why they call those things *headphones!*" (175–76)

The context of the novel is summarized in one of the trailers for the *Inherent Vice* movie by Paul Thomas Anderson, either penned by Pynchon himself or excerpted and remixed from the novel:

> It's the tail end of the psychedelic sixties and paranoia is running the day. If it isn't Charlie Manson, it's the LAPD or the FBI or the mysterious body of something called the Golden Fang. Everything's gone from groovy and "where you at, man" suggesting a high level of fear or discomfort with the way things are headed.

Charles Manson and the government institutions were not the only indicators that things had gone haywire.[28] Something was up in the music industry as well. The passage takes place after the legendary festivals of the late 1960s (Monterey 1967; Atlanta Pop Festival 1969; Woodstock 1969) and before the second Atlanta Pop Festival in 1970, drawing estimated crowds of up to 600,000 "hippie freaks."[29] The untimely death and subsequent sanctification of Brian Jones (July 1969), the Altamont Free Concert-turned-nightmare (December 1969), the growing dissemination of hard drugs, and no end of the Vietnam war and Nixon's surveillance state in sight, all signaled the end of a collective dream, an era that had seemed full of promise.

Barney Hoskyns pinpoints the birth of the rock music industry to the Monterey Pop Festival, the "key sixties event in California's pop history" (142). For the first time on a large scale, it brought together the scenes of San Francisco and Los Angeles in June 1967: "Nothing was the same after Monterey. That 'international pop festival' signalled not only the birth of the rock industry as we know it today, but the onset of the decadence which characterized the music scene in general—and the Los Angeles scene in particular—through the late sixties and seventies. Monterey was the end of the innocence, the High Moment of the hippie dream which inadvertently opened up pop to every mogul in the record business" (149). Monterey is likely one of those events Doc has in mind when he muses, "Was it possible, that at every gathering—concert, peace rally, love-in, be-in, and freak-in, here, up north,

28 The proximity of Charles Manson's name to Charles Mason's as well as Nixon's to Dixon's invites paranoid interpretation worthy of William S. Burroughs. As many Pynchon scholars have observed, Pynchon employs the figure of the twin or the double throughout his work. Perhaps, then, Manson & Nixon are *Inherent Vice*'s evil twins of Mason & Dixon.

29 Depending on the focus, the Sixties can be said to have started as early as the Beat Generation (many of whose most prominent exponents did not think highly of the hippies) and their repercussions (feminism, anti-war protests, environmentalism, destigmatization of homosexuals, equal opportunity, etc.) to have lasted well into the seventies and even until today.

back East, wherever—those dark crews had been busy all along, reclaiming the music, the resistance to power, the sexual desire from epic to everyday, all they could sweep up, for the ancient forces of greed and fear?" (*Inherent* 130). At the same time, "[w]hat Monterey really represented was the transition from Pop to Rock—from toe-tapping teen discotheque music to FM Art for young adults" (Hoskyns 146). The ground-breaking *Sgt. Pepper's Lonely Hearts Club Band* had just come out and proved, for the Beatles, to be a turning point much as it influenced L.A.'s Phil Spector and Brian Wilson.[30] Psychedelic rock had come about, and highly produced music and Spector's Wall of Sound concept were nearly impossible to reproduce in spontaneous or live settings.

One of the actors of the L.A. music industry was Glenn Wallichs who had co-founded Capitol Records in 1942. He also owned Wallichs Music City on the corner of Sunset Boulevard and Vine Street in Los Angeles. The company was founded in 1930 and remained in operation until 1978. The Sunset/Vine location was the world's largest music store selling records, tapes, sheet music, musical instruments, and all sorts of equipment.[31] The 21 listening booths were not new at the time of the narrative; although I have not been able to determine the exact year they were added, I have found photographs of the booths dated 1956 and it appears that they had been there since 1940. The reference to the listening booths is one of the indications that the novel is set in the first half of 1970, as the December 18, 1971 issue of *Billboard* magazine reported that the booths had been done away with eighteen months prior and

30 Like Manson, Phil Spector was convicted of murder (although much later, in 2003). Manson also recorded at the studio of Brian Wilson whose brother Dennis had hosted the Manson Family in 1968, another connection between surf music and Aryan ideology as will be explained in more detail below. If there is a filmic equivalent to Pynchon's engagement with Aryan ideology in California, it is the work of Kenneth Anger, particularly *Lucifer Rising* (1972; music by Manson Family member Bobby Beausoleil).

31 A picture of a shopping bag indicates that Wallichs Music City as a company must have existed since 1930: "Since 1930 the World's largest and most complete store of music" (http://blogs.dailybreeze.com/history/files/2015/07/wallichsbag.jpg). I first became aware of Wallichs Music City as having been an actual record store as well as of the different spelling thanks to Justin St. Clair's paper "The *Inherent Vice* Soundtrack," delivered at the 2015 International Pynchon Week in Athens, Greece.

that the company had gone public in May 1970.[32] Nineteen seventy was, in fact, only the third year since 1939 that the company had incurred a financial loss, thus the year marked something of a turning point for Wallichs Music City as well.

It is unusual for Pynchon to get the spelling of a name wrong (the owner's name was Wallichs, and there was no apostrophe in the store's name), but even the former part-time Wallichs employee Frank Zappa misspelled it Wallich's (Zappa 61), a homophone of Wallach's and, Wallichs.[33] This misnomer and variations of it were not uncommon, and no matter if it was intentional, it is telling. *Wallach* is the German word for a gelding, a castrated equine. Not only is castration supposed to make a male horse calmer, more tractable, and easier to handle; in many cases only castration allows a horse to become an excellent racehorse (Bramlage n.p.). (Horse, of course, is also slang for heroin, the most important illegal substance in the novel besides marijuana but not very useful for making people productive.) Thus, the misspelling of Wallichs Music City already implies that the listening booths and the music industry (as well as hard drugs) have, figuratively speaking, cut the balls off of its unruly youth and turned them into sterile racehorses for the military-industrial complex. A generation has been deprived of its generative capacity, much like what happens in *Vineland* to the same generation under the influence of TV (Wallichs also sold televisions).

This is the second time that Pynchon has a group of Californians listen to different musics in their own heads and dance at their own pace and rhythm. When Oedipa Maas is swept into the dance

32 Another indication is that Pynchon does not reference the deaths of Janis Joplin and Jimi Hendrix in the fall of 1970. Although Joplin is never mentioned in Pynchon's work, some echoes of her reverberate through this scene: Japonica (whose first name references Japan but is also a near-anagram of Janis Joplin's name) drives a Mercedes, the car that Joplin asked the Lord to buy for her in the song "Mercedes Benz," inspired by a line from Michael McClure and recorded three days before her death on October 4th, 1970; like the Porsches her friends drive, it is a German car in California. As are, of course, Sick Dick and the Volkswagens in *The Crying of Lot 49*. Of course, there may be more conspicuous markers, as John M. Krafft pointed out to me, for instance the NBA playoffs (March 25–May 8, 1970) or the upcoming Manson trial (July 24, 1970).

33 Besides in the introduction to *Slow Learner* (23), Frank Zappa is mentioned in *Vineland* (39, 281) and in *Inherent Vice* (146, 223). One time, Zappa appears on a girl's t-shirt and one time on a girl's dress, so perhaps Zappa as an icon or a symbol was more important than his avant-garde rock music.

of the California Chapter of the American Deaf-Mute Assembly, "[e]ach couple on the floor danced whatever was in the fellow's head: tango, two-step, bossa nova, slop" (*Lot* 107). There are, however, crucial differences between the two scenes. The deaf-mute assembly is a community of sorts, a group that has gathered together in one room and is not part of a culturally dominant population but rather belongs to the vast population that is below the radar. They dance in couples, that is, in a constellation allowing for communication. Whatever the different rhythms going on in their heads, their bodies or minds have to come to some sort of agreement as to how they should dance as a couple. A dance is also an opportunity to meet potential mates, thus procreation becomes possible. Furthermore, the deaf-mute communicate by sign language (*Lot* 80), and although Oedipa does not understand or 'speak' it, she still becomes part of the community on the dance floor, as opposed to the hippies—the heads—in the booths at Wallach's who are oblivious to Denis's peace signs. And finally, since the deaf-mute listen to their own musics, and perhaps make them up on the spot, there is no need to buy into the commercial world of the music industry and its mass-produced records. Thus, what the brief juxtaposition of the two scenes reveals is that the issue at hand is not the music in one's head but the social, economic, and political context.

Kittler may be right with his thesis that rock music—the entertainment industry and civilly used media as such—is an abuse of army equipment (*Gramophone* 96–97), a phrase he borrowed from World War II's General von Wedel.[34] This is not the case just since Stockhausen's "Gesang der Jünglinge" of 1955–56 or

34 For a more subtle reading of this *bon mot*, see for instance Steve Goodman, 31–34, or Geoffrey Winthrop-Young, *Friedrich Kittler*, 115–131. Winthrop-Young cites a number of critiques of Kittler: (1) Kittler tends to mix facts and rhetoric; (2) It is not always clear whether Kittler talks about the invention or the dissemination of media; (3) There are a number of civilian technologies whose military uses have not been recognized right away; (4) The question remains whether the civil uses of military equipment have not advanced to such an extent that their military origin is only of antiquarian interest. However, as Winthrop-Young also notes, if we accept the thesis that there is always war, as Kittler does, that mobilization, both military and civilian, advances continuously, many of these points of critique become futile. Similarly, Goodman counters those arguments, explaining that "the concept of war becomes an attempt to describe a low-intensity warfare that reconstitutes the most mundane aspects of everyday existence through psychosocial torque and sensory overload" (33).

"Kontakte" of 1958–60; a large part of media technologies—although by no means all of them—originated in or were significantly improved or disseminated by military research and use in the field, from Pynchon's own instrument, the typewriter, to plastics, and Laurie Anderson's vocoder.[35] Kittler, of course, was much influenced by Pynchon, in particular *Gravity's Rainbow*, when he adapted the phrase for his media theory.[36] In Steve Goodman's words, "For Kittler, military research and development infects popular culture with a kind of technological contagion [...]. The contagion of military technology spreads through misuse, or reverse engineering, with knowledge acquired by espionage, accident, or experimentation" (32). Pynchon shows awareness of this lineage when he has music by Stockhausen play at the Scope. The "audio oscillators, gunshot machines, contact mikes" were likely appropriated by the employees of a defense contractor, the bar being a "haunt for electronics assembly people from Yoyodyne" (*Lot* 34). But Pynchon does not leave it at that. He also shows time and again not just how military equipment is appropriated—"abused"—by avant-garde art and the counterculture, but how technology which has trickled down into pop music and novel social uses is reappropriated by commercial and military interests. To quote Kittler again: "Every culture has its zones of preparation that fuse lust and power, optically, acoustically, and so on. Our discos are preparing our youths for a retaliatory strike" (*Gramophone* 140), or elsewhere: "Every discotheque, which of course intensifies tape effects and couples them in real time with the respective optics of stroboscopes and flashbulbs, advances war" ("Rock Musik" 211, my translation).

---

35 For a more elaborate take on Stockhausen and war, see my essay "Stockhausen at Ground Zero," published on September 11, 2011. For the history of the vocoder, which initially used gramophone records for the encryption and decryption of military communication, see Dave Tompkins' *How to Wreck a Nice Beach: The Vocoder from World War II to Hip-Hop.*

36 Not only is *Gramophone Film Typewriter* prefaced with an excerpt from *Gravity's Rainbow*; Kittler's article "Rock Musik – ein Mißbrauch von Heeresgerät" ("Rock music—an abuse of army equipment") is prefaced with a few lines from Richard Wharfinger's *The Courier's Tragedy* from *The Crying of Lot 49*. In turn, it appears not improbable that Pynchon alludes to *Gramophone Film Typewriter* when he describes Dally's use of a new radio transmitter in Paris to talk to her father Merle in California: "Clearly an unauthorized use of the equipment, but to tell the truth it was new, and some of it was army parts, and it all tended to drift a bit" (*Against* 1197).

Sound ecologist R. Murray Schafer coined the word 'schizophonia' for the "packaging and storing techniques for sound and the splitting of sounds from their original contexts" (88). Schizophonia belongs to the age of electroacoustic repetition, an era that had been a commercial one since the mass distribution of shellac records (and prior to that pre-pressed wax cylinders, and prior even to that, although not schizophonic or electric, the sale of music scores for home use). However, if we are to follow Kittler, it was the LP and stereophony that really turned music into a large-scale commercial operation. As of EMI's first stereo record in 1957, Kittler writes, "the two ears that humans happen to have were no longer freaks of nature but a source of revenue" ("Gott der Ohren" 65; my translation), and it is almost needless to say, as Kittler does in passing, that top sales in the music industry far surpass those in the realm of literature (61). Unlike cassette tapes or the phonograph, which also allowed for recording, the records customers buy at Wallach's are one-directional, top-down media. What follows from this can be summarized in McLuhan's words: "[E]ntertainment pushed to the extreme becomes the main form of business and politics" (277).

Schafer's criticism of this technological development is fierce but implicit. He does not make a clear statement about the kind of interpersonal relationships that individualized listening brings about, but his choice of the word schizophonia, deriving from schism, a split, clearly points to its near-homonym schizophrenia, thus pathologizing some forms of sound. One of the symptoms of schizophrenia is apathy. Clinically speaking, apathy is a mental state characterized by indifference, an absence of emotions, and a lack of activity and responsiveness (Fröhlich 64). Fittingly, Chuck Casell wrote in 1971 in the liner notes to *The First Great Rock Festivals of the Seventies: Isle of Wight and Atlanta Pop Festival* that, "the Age of the Rock Festival is dead. State governmental restrictions, local ordinances and a general sense of *apathy* have led to its demise" (my emphasis). Of course, when read against Doc's ruminations, these liner notes on a mass-produced and commercially distributed schizophonic recording become almost ironic. Perhaps it would be a bit far-fetched to diagnose the hippies in the recording booths with clinical apathy and a lack of emotion. Still, they experience the music in solitude. Their headphones interiorize the musical experience and make the listeners immune to outside stimuli and social relations. In the audition booths, no one "creates in common a code" (Attali 143), no one shares "the same brain" (*Against* 417). Instead, they are confined and muted, moving around to the different rhythms of the industry's commercial products only then to buy the records to be able to listen to them in the confinement of their homes. It is no coincidence that the last fragment of Slothrop appears on the cover of a record.

What is more, the hippies are possibly stoned and lingering in the "vast dimensions of their inner worlds" (Benjamin 39; my translation), which further exacerbates their solipsism. Not only gramophone records and weapons are media or technologies—drugs are too. For thousands of years, intoxicating substances were used in warfare, from Alexander the Great's crusades to the US-American wars of the twentieth century and the indigenous population's struggle against Peruvian gold-mining interests. All technologies are two-fold. Cowart has pointed out in his discussion of *Gravity's Rainbow*'s Gustav Schlabone and André Omnopon (and the same may be said of *Against the Day*'s Neville and Nigel) that drug use "remains a powerful metaphor for the idea of an alternative to the rapacious capitalism and consumerism that afflict American society" (120). Avital Ronell also writes that "Their usage seemed to belong to the socio-juridical precincts of civil disobedience" (*Crack Wars* 19). It is significant that Ronell uses the past tense because, in her interpretation, this all changed with the advent of crack, which can be situated historically around the time of *Inherent Vice:* "Ever since its inception as legal category, this all-American crime has earned its dose of moral defensibility from a link to anti-war activities. But crack, when it brought the War to drugs, brought war unto the law. Civil disobedience split away from constitutionally sanctioned habits: this war, unlike others, permits no dissent" (19). While allowing people to tune in and drop out, drugs can also be instrumentalized to make people pliable and productive in the service of others' master narratives. Fittingly, since 2012 (three years after the publication of *Inherent Vice*), the corner of Vine and Sunset, where Wallichs used to be, now houses a Wallgreens drug store where people can purchase the uppers and downers of the globalized pharmaceuticals industry, depending on whether they need to perform or to rest in order to be able to perform again.

Admittedly, using the word 'drugs' as an overarching category that comprises every illegal or controlled substance blends the characteristics of each particular drug and its use in the same way that the narrative of the 'war on drugs' does—and marijuana simply is not the same as heroin, crack, or cocaine, the last of which, by 1969, "would be the preferred rock'n'roll mood-alterer" (Hoskyns 150). Still, the use of marijuana, especially the solitary use, interiorizes the experience of the world in a not-so-different way from putting on headphones. While marijuana may be less suitable than other drugs in making youth obedient and productive, in the media link with the entertainment industry, at least in this scene, the listeners become inaccessible to the demands and promises of the rock'n'roll revolution: "What war and drugs and media do to bodies continues as music" (Kittler, "Medien und Drogen" 131; my translation).

Although this scene takes place ten years before the marketing of the Walkman in the USA, Pynchon seems to foreshadow the individualized, plugged-in music consumption of the 1980s to the present day. Now that so much music is listened to directly on mobile phones instead of portable single-use music devices with headphones, there is no need to be a 'head' anymore, one might add.

Of course, the portability of the devices makes only a qualitative difference from the first opera transmissions by telephone in Bellinzona, Warsaw, or Paris. Today, the military uses music to torture captives, and troops in combat are plugged into hip-hop or heavy metal. Anders Breivik, who in a first report was diagnosed with paranoid schizophrenia (later replaced by the diagnosis of a narcissistic personality disorder), was reportedly tuned into his iPod which drowned out his victims' screams and gave the assassinations the hyperreal qualities of a first-person shooter game. "The lunatic was in his brain," to quote Kittler quoting Pink Floyd, and "the history of the ear in the age of its technological explosiveness is always already a history of madness" ("Gott der Ohren" 67; my translation). Breivik's technologically overdriven apathy during the atrocities on Utøya brings this discussion full circle to World War I where apathy's modern use was first diagnosed as one of several forms of shell shock. Or to quote Goodman in his discussion of Kittler: "Media technologies discipline, mutate, and preempt the affective sensorium. Entertainment itself becomes part of the training" (34). In this vein, it is worth mentioning Lawrence Rickels' psychoanalytical reading of Attali in his study of California and observing the parallels with the *Inherent Vice* scene. Rickels writes:

> Taking music as primal mass medium, Jacques Attali recasts group formation, from classical music to jazz and rock and roll, in terms of socialization of melancholia. Headsets plug into a scene of sacrifice

> which doubles as primal past and repast of music. From the symphony concerts to the 'live' performances of jazz or rock (which are only replicas of already released recordings) Attali observes in musical culture beginning with the Enlightenment a sadomasochistic dialectic which shifts from representation of the work of mourning to mediatized models of repetition; primal aggression comes to be phantasmatized, internalized, and, at the same time, autoeroticized. (61)

Doc's reminiscence about the free concerts of the past, however, is not one that would put 'live' in quotation marks as Rickels does, mere replicas of recorded material that sometimes go as far as to reproduce a once-recorded solo note by note. Doc respects the ex-junkie Coy Harlingen because, unlike other surf sax players, he is capable of actually improvising solos. Harlingen does not submit to what Rickels calls the "mediatized models of repetition," which, in this context, replace the mourning of the dead in Vietnam but also the mourning of more auratic music performances. The consequence of the models of repetition is that the primal aggression formerly directed at the government-sanctioned or even sanctified war-machinery is sublimated and internalized. What is interesting is that Rickels later brings in the topic of childhood: "[I]t is not so much music that has become fetishized, canned, or commodified as childhood itself" (Rickels 62). L.A., after all, is "the capital of eternal youth" (*Inherent* 208) and "[c]irca 1970, 'adult' was no longer quite being defined as in times previous. Among those who could afford to, a strenuous mass denial of the passage of time itself was under way" (172). In the music context discussed here, "those who could afford to" can be read as "those who can afford to buy records." The denial of adulthood follows a logic by which music stars "are always the idealized age of their audience, an age that gets younger as the field of repetition expands. This channelization of childhood through music is a politically essential substitute for violence, which no longer finds ritual enactment" (Attali 110). The headsets plug in, the listeners celebrate their denial of adulthood and tune out of the revolt. They revert to the "solipsism of infancy," one of the phases of development according to *Bleeding Edge*'s psychoanalyst Otto Kugelblitz (2).

But we needn't even militarize and psychologize the use of headphones to this extent. What is important is that they introduce a fundamental change—or schism—in the social settings of music consumption, from collectivity to individuality and from exteriority to interiority. They split the individual away from his or her community and environment by inserting a sonic barrier in a way that mirrors commodity capitalism: "[E]ach spectator has a solitary relation with a material object; the consumption of music is individualized" (Attali 32). The age of repetition heralds "a new stage in the organization of capitalism, that of the repetitive mass production of all social relations" (32). Headphones, one could say, introduce a way of listening in "mutual silence." The listeners are kept in their cubicles like those in a large office space (or in a stable) so that each can be productive without disturbing the others. The phantasmatized group affiliation (like the idea of belonging to a work force of a certain company) comes from individualized experience, not from the experience of group *inter*action. Attali writes that "mass production compels silence. [...] An extraordinary spectacle: the double silence of men and commodities in the factory" (121). This double silence of mass-produced commodity music is the spectacle that makes Doc Sportello ask Japonica to drive slower outside Wallach's Music City: the silenced music listened to by silenced listeners in separate booths, unresponsive to Denis's yelling and flashing of peace signs.

This scene can also be read from an entirely different angle, though, one that Justin St. Clair began to develop in his paper "The *Inherent Vice* Soundtrack." Leading up to the publication of *Inherent Vice,* Penguin tried out new marketing strategies, among which were a video promotion trailer with Pynchon's own voice (ending with "*Inherent Vice.* Penguin Press. Twenty-seven ninety-fi—. Twenty-seven ninety-five? That used to be, like, three weeks of groceries, man. What year's this again?") and an Amazon playlist of forty-two songs from the novel, "courtesy of Thomas Pynchon."[37] Amazon did not provide any information about the individual songs or their context in the novel but claimed that Doc is "animated by the music of an era whose hallmarks were peace, love, and revolution" and directly linked the non-fictional songs—

37 One could say that *Inherent Vice* has three different soundtracks: Apart from the Amazon playlist and the novel's list of songs and musicians, there is also the soundtrack of Paul Thomas Anderson's movie. The only song in the movie adapted from the novel is The Marketts' "Here Comes the Ho-Dads" (also on the Amazon list). The movie poster, title, and credits also retained many elements of the novel's dust jacket design and thus turned the novel's design into something that more appropriately could be called corporate design.

many from a different era or musical tradition from the peace and love generation's—to the pages where prospective readers and anyone interested could "actually be spending money to hear rock 'n' roll" (*Inherent* 175).[38] The novel is musically more comprehensive than the Amazon playlist and contains more than 130 historical music references (some of which also populate *Vineland*), about half of which are references to tunes or songs.

St. Clair made a point that the songs in the playlist are almost all songs that are not associated with a particular subculture or counterculture but mainstream tunes, a nostalgic soundtrack with most songs from the 1950s and early 1960s.[39] This is true to a certain extent—and it always has been with Pynchon's eclectic choice of song material, from Italian opera to Broadway show tunes, themes from Hollywood blockbuster soundtracks, and any number of best-selling hits. This is music that was popular in Doc's (*1940) and Pynchon's (*1937) childhood and teenage years, an age, it seems, when music has the most profound impact. And in fact, when Doc listens to the Super Surfin' Marathon on his car radio, a number of songs are "souvenirs out of a childhood Doc had never much felt he wanted to escape from" (125). About half the actual songs and artists on the Amazon playlist can be counted as nostalgic, and about 60% of those in the novel. A number of psychedelic tunes are difficult to align with something like a middle-class 'mass culture' to which they could successfully be marketed: for instance, Pink Floyd's almost ten-minute-long "Interstellar Overdrive," released on their 1967 debut album *The Piper at the Gates of Dawn.* The novel's soundtrack also includes artists such as Frank Zappa, Elephant's Memory, The Electric Prunes, Fapardokly, and the instro-surf rocker Dick Dale. Of the 66 historical works of music mentioned or alluded to in *Inherent Vice*, 41 made it to the U.S. Billboard charts, 32 all the way to the top ten, and 15 peaked at #1.[40] Top-selling songs and albums are

38 Eight of those songs were invented by Pynchon or performed by bands of his creation, hence no purchase was possible. "Telstar" by The Tornados does not appear on the Amazon list; however, The Tornados' "Dreamin on a Cloud" is included in the film soundtrack.

39 A closer look reveals that there are 17 songs from the 1950s as opposed to 37 songs from the 1960s. Seven references are from 1966, followed by six from 1968, and four each from the years 1962, 1963, and 1965.

40 Sources for this were Wikipedia, billboard.com, and allmusic.com. When no billboard rank was available for a song, I instead chose the rank for the album containing the song or, in the case of a B-side single song, the A-side

rarely avant-garde or countercultural material but often cater to a middle class and the teenage sentiments of its youth. Although "the *Inherent Vice* soundtrack is entirely dependent on the mass distribution of popular music" (St. Clair), to a large extent anyway, Pynchon's choice of song material reflects a plausible picture of what was likely on the air at the time of the narrative and before, songs that had become part of American twentieth-century popular culture or found entry into the Great American Songbook. This also appears to be true for the *Vineland* soundtrack that has some overlap with the *Inherent Vice* one, both novels being set in California around the same time. What is more, L.A. was not necessarily the place for far-out music, as could be witnessed already in the 1950s' paring down of the East Coast be-bop into the West Coast cool jazz for which the young Pynchon seemed to have a liking.[41] This does not necessarily mean that the soundtrack features only Pynchon's or Doc's favorites. Doc, for one, "was not a great admirer of torch material, had in fact been known to discreetly withdraw to the nearest toilet if he even suspected some might be on the way" (*Inherent* 160).

The claim of verisimilitude or plausibility is further supported by the local flavor of the soundtrack that does not seem to leave out any surf, pop or rock band important in L.A. in the 1960s as well as by the ethnicity of the identified or likely performers: of the 65 identified songs and albums, only 7 were recorded or performed by African-American singers. This very much reflects the L.A. music and entertainment scene from which, by the end of the 1960s, black performers seemed to have all but disappeared and which was dominated by white singers, executives, and producers. There is some uncertainty about why there were so few

ranking. One of the references is an album, not a song (Blue Cheer's *Vincebus Eruptum*). The Byrds' "Eight Miles High" did not make it to the top ten, peaking at #14, possibly because it was subject to a radio ban due to its drug connotations. Thunderclap Newman's "Something in the Air" made it only to #37 in the U.S. but was a #1 hit in the UK. And, finally, while Frank Sinatra's recording of "Fly Me to the Moon" did not make it to the charts, it is still considered the definitive version of the jazz standard. Like Hohner's "Little Lady" that was played in outer space, the studio version of the Sinatra song was played on the Apollo 10 and radio-broadcast to Apollo 11.

41 See, for instance, the references to Gerry Mulligan and Chet Baker in "The Small Rain" (1959) and "Entropy" (1960) as well as the baritone sax in "Mortality and Mercy in Vienna" (1959), a likely nod to Gerry Mulligan. Mulligan also appears in the incomplete and unpublished script of *Minstrel Island*.

black performers at the time, Detroit's Motown being the most important major label to sign black artists. However, as Barney Hoskyns points out, the fascination with the idea of an all-white Californian culture had begun early on: "Joseph Widney, the University of Southern California president, [...] argued in *The Race Life of the Aryan Peoples* (1907) that Los Angeles would one day be 'the Aryan capital of the world'" (1).[42] Pynchon, whose "Journey into the Mind of Watts" Hoskyns considers "[p]erhaps the most astute white response to the Watts [Riot] events" of 1965 (105), was already very aware then that L.A. "is basically a white Scene, and illusion is everywhere in it" ("Journey"). By having all-white surf music (and nearly all-white top-placed Billboard chart tunes) dominate the *Inherent Vice* soundtrack and by frequently mentioning Charles Manson and the Aryan Brotherhood, Pynchon demonstrates he has not forgotten that part of the Southern Californian past.[43] Rock music itself is, in Rickels' words, "the careful filtering or vampirization of 'black despair' which fuels the commodification of (white) childhood" (63, see also Attali 105). As a gesture of retroactively correcting this white dominance in surf music, Pynchon created "one of the few known attempts at black surf music, 'Soul Gidget,' by Meatball Flag" (*Inherent* 155), the "seldom-heard oldie" that will also appear in *Bleeding Edge* (362).

Although it may be a bit of a stretch, the soundtrack of *Inherent Vice* can also be read in relation to the overall form of the novel. Pynchon here imitates a particular genre, that of the hard-boiled detective novel or noir fiction. However, he also deviates from the genre's conventions, which already depart from the rigid structures and assumptions of the detective genre solidified

42 The parallels between California and Germany or Nazi Germany are numerous. In *The Case of California*, Lawrence A. Rickels "locates 'the intersection between technology and the unconscious' and thus reconstructs the political front of psychoanalysis which arose to combat National Socialism. California and Germany, he contends, are two coasts of an era that 'lets roll' in the Enlightenment and continues to this day. [...] And the invention of the California teenager—the archetypical adolescent—begins with 'a certain central-European refusal of death" (blurb). In a not dissimilar aside, Kittler reads the theme of *Gravity's Rainbow* as "German-American friendship as technology transfer" ("Medien und Drogen" 114; my translation).

43 The only time Charles Manson is mentioned in *Vineland* is as a "fledgling musician" whom Mucho Maas was "one of the very first to audition, but not, he was later to add hastily, to call back" (309).

in the catalogs of dos and don'ts in its golden age of the 1920s and 1930s. By doing so, he partly follows Bigfoot's advice to Doc when he says, "Try to drag your consciousness out of that old-time hard-boiled dick era" (33). Something similar could be said of the soundtrack. Pynchon references conventional pop tunes, the type of music that one would associate with the readership of conventional detective novels, but also departs from this conventionality by including the occasional surprise listing more in line with a pop or rock avant-garde.

Starting with its blurb, *Inherent Vice* remains a melancholic and nostalgic novel about "how the Psychedelic Sixties, this little parenthesis of light, might close after all, and all be lost, taken back into darkness..." (254). The melancholy mood of the very last song mentioned, The Beach Boys' "God Only Knows," resonates with Doc's nostalgia driving past Wallach's Music City, but its title also reflects the last paragraph of the novel, when Doc has run out of gas and is waiting for whatever may happen, imagining all sorts of possibilities, the last one being "For the fog to burn away, and for something else this time, somehow, to be there instead" (369).

How is Pynchon's Amazon playlist significant in this discussion? There has been some speculation as to the author's motives for publishing the playlist with the world's most powerful online shop. Nick Levey, for instance, dismisses the ready idea that "Pynchon has finally given in to 'the man'" (42). His point is that novels like *Gravity's Rainbow*, *Mason & Dixon*, and *Against the Day* have proven great material upon which to build an academic career, which, in the end, is just another competitive market. While references in the earlier work were more obscure and meaning harder to get, the world of *Inherent Vice* is one that "anyone can know" (42). What is more, the Internet and the Great Search Engine make it seemingly much easier to decypher and decode those references, which threatens not only academics' employment but that of private investigators too: "Guess I better learn something about this or I'll be obsolete" (*Inherent* 365), as Doc observes toward the end of the novel. Levey argues that "the fact that Pynchon (or Amazon with his permission) has organized a lot of the novel's real-world referents for easy access, seems to suggest that the author is keen to derail or at least meddle with the sort of reading his novels have offered some professionals in the past" (45). And later: "Indeed, the Amazon playlist warns us against these habits of 'wised up' readers, and doesn't allow us to escape the novel by focusing on its facts and references" (53). He sees some evidence that the warning has been heeded in the fact that *Inherent Vice* has attracted much less scholarly attention than its predecessors. Ultimately, however, this original interpretation, much as it is appealing and well argued, is not wholly satisfactory, mainly for two reasons. One, although *Inherent Vice* is much easier to digest than the previous novels and it is plausible that it will not spawn as much scholarship as the others, it has also had much less time so far to be digested by readers and scholars. Two, the Amazon playlist contains only 34 historical music references and eight references to songs penned by Pynchon from a total of the novel's 132 historical references and twelve works of music written or imagined by Pynchon. Thus, the opposite conclusion could be drawn from these figures: namely, that Pynchon wanted to prompt academics and enthusiasts of lists to fill the gaps and read the novel through the filter of music. Perhaps he recognized that the novel would have less to offer in terms of finding clues and interpreting them and thus wanted to light the way for one possible approach. But whether the author simply needed money to send his child to college, whether the playlist was an ironic statement about the purchase of commodified music and buying into a near-global distribution empire of mass-produced and mass-distributed cultural artifacts, whether it was just another marketing idea by Penguin or Amazon, whether it was a gift for Pynchon's fans, whether it was a clever meta-comment on the novel, or whether it was an indication that the novel should be read through its music (or all or none of the above): God only knows.

Although *Inherent Vice* is clearly set in the age of repetition, its characters had also been given a glimpse into the age of composition in their immediate past, an age with public festivals and gatherings in parks that did not have the enclosed space to charge admission. Although Pynchon does not mention Haight/Ashbury's Grateful Dead, their spirit of free concerts in parks, of jamming at their flat with whoever showed up, and of insisting that the shows could be taped by anyone who brought recording equipment clearly shines through. All these points may be read as indications of an age of composition, and while recording a concert produces a schizophonic artifact, it remains auratic until its mass distribution insofar as the recording is unique and the person recording had been present at the singular event. Since Attali's periods can overlap, a critic may also read the short time span from, say, 1965 to 1969 as a prolonged festival in the age of sacrifice to serve as a channeler of violence and a sublimation of noise (Attali 23). Still, since no matter what time the narrative is set in Pynchon tends to make political statements about the present at the time of writing (and has the occasional eerie insight into the future[44]), what Doc Sportello is seeing is both his present day of the mass production of goods and individuals and possibly a future of further individualized consumption. And that future is now. Our present time appears to have elements of all four eras stacked on top of and pervading each other. To see the possible dawn of a truly egalitarian age of composition, an age that might be able to thwart the trends toward solitude and individualized consumption laid out in *Inherent Vice*, we have to look elsewhere in Pynchon's work.

The Age of Composition

What, then, characterizes this era of composition and the political and social organization it heralds? For Attali, composition can be equated with improvisation, but it does not end there: "Composition can only emerge from the destruction of the preceding codes" (136), that is, the codes of sacrifice, representation, and repetition. "It is the advent of a radically new form of the insertion of music into communication, one that is overturning all concepts of political economy and giving new meaning to the political project" (134). Essentially, what Attali is driving at is the musician, the human, or *bios* (to follow Agamben in his use of the Greek term for "the form or way of living proper to an individual or a group" as opposed to *zoē*, the fact of life as such [*Homo Sacer* 1]), as an entity that generates meaning and code in an open-ended, non-instrumentalized way intimately tied to his or her body. Production and consumption collapse into one. There are strong resonances with Wolfgang Schirmacher's concept of homo generator, which is useful to get a firmer grasp on what Attali envisions. Homo generator "concerns the whole person and embraces embodiment and communal action as well" ("Artificial Life" 87). "Homo generator is an open call [Bestimmung], a concept only now beginning to unfold that might well be interrupted, to begin anew, and then perhaps double back. There exists no Homo yet,

44 For instance, I have always read *The Crying of Lot 49's* Alameda County Death Cult (AC/DC) as a strange premonition of the Manson Family.

but rather s/he is a self-fulfilling prophecy. [...] There exists for us the force, the power, and the opportunity to generate—that alone is what is referred to by the concept 'Homo generator'" ("Media and Postmodern Technology"). As I have argued elsewhere, this homo generator (I chose to term it *generans* as a life force to avoid the gendered and anthropomorphic ring that, to my knowledge, Schirmacher did not intend in the first place) "has responsibility already built in [...] and the name of this responsibility is sustainability" (*Hospitality* 156).

Both for Attali and for Schirmacher, what is also essential is the intrinsic *pleasure* afforded by living a life of simultaneous generation and consumption of meaning and by the creation and sharing of new codes as well as the everyday character of this activity. It is, in Attali's case, "music for immediate enjoyment, for daily communication" (140), "a day-to-day and subversive practice" (141). The German term *Lebenskünstler*, life artist or artist of life, seems to capture much of what they both envision. The point is to do something not for an extrinsic aim or reason but "solely for the sake of doing" (134).

In this new era, Attali places great emphasis on instruments, as opposed to printing which he sees as the basis of representation and recording, that is, as the basis of repetition. With excitement he observes a renaissance of the creation of new musical instruments in the twentieth century. But while Attali speaks about tools and instruments, and not entirely inappropriately so in a discussion of music, he inevitably runs into a contradiction, at least on the surface, with his call for a non-instrumentalized use of instruments. The problem with instrumentalization is that "the moment labor has a goal, an aim, a program set out in advance in a code—even if this is by the producer's choice—the producer becomes a stranger to what he produces" (134–35). Another problem, of course, is that, having a pre-set goal or code, technology is not free to develop its own life and surprise us with something radically new that was inscribed into it from the start but needed open-endedness to express itself. This, as a side note, was the problem with the early uses of the theremin, a radically new instrument with unheard-of possibilities. However, near the hands of Clara Rockmore and at the advice of its inventor Léon Theremin (or Lev Sergeyevich Termen), it was deployed only to re-enact a Romantic repertoire: "what new (and more appropriate to its essence) the theremin could do was not discovered" (Price, *Reso-*

nance 204).[45] In Schirmacher's philosophy, as opposed to Attali's, the terms 'tool' and 'instrument' have been entirely abandoned in favor of the term 'life technique' to avoid just such problems and to broaden the horizon to include technology's life of its own as well as everyday, life-sustaining and life-affirming activities. This approach to life as well as to technology in the broad sense allows for bridging Attali's ruminations on music and those on the future organization of society.

Such an Attalian organization of society is no easy task, as is true of any egalitarian, post-organizational—one could term it anarchist—organization:

> One may wonder whether a model such as this, composed of liberated time and egoistic enjoyment, is possible. And in fact, on closer inspection, seemingly insoluble problems of coherence arise: first, others' noise can create a sound of cacophony, and each difference thus created, between units of composition, may be felt as a nuisance. Second, the complementarity of productions is no longer guaranteed, because compositional choices are not confronted by a pricing system (the market in representation) or ranking (planning in repetition). (Attali 145)

Attali's solution is easy to conceptualize and difficult to achieve. It presupposes "two conditions: tolerance and autonomy. The acceptance of other people, and the ability to do without them" (145). From a Derridean viewpoint, tolerance is, of course, already an impossibility because one can only be tolerant of that which is intolerable. Furthermore, to equate tolerance and acceptance is problematic at best as the former implies a dimension of suffering and hardship whereas the latter implies a good degree of ease and voluntariness. But perhaps at this point Attali's conceptualization is not meant to be deconstructed but meant to be read through the lens of everyday language. By necessity, the era of composition must do away with the economic and political networks of the present and the impositions a mass market places on musical products and the creation of demand for them. In the

45 Like the vocoder's history, the theremin's could be straight out of a Pynchon novel, yet it is only in *Bleeding Edge* that Pynchon briefly mentions "theremin music" (452). The documentary *Theremin: An Electronic Odyssey* (1994) gives fascinating insights into the lives of Clara Rockmore and Léon Theremin and the instrument's early days.

twentieth-century music of the West, Attali sees promising developments in free jazz and in John Cage's innovations, both of which have to this day resisted commodification.

Pynchon evidently shares many of Attali's aspirations for a future egalitarian society of composition. While Cage is not present in name in Pynchon's work, a number of ruminations on the sonic resonate strongly with or may even have been lifted from Cage. Perhaps the most striking one is *Gravity's Rainbow*'s episode "Listening to the Toilet" (708–11) that imagines the possibility of absolute silence, even from the roar of the sun, and the consequent discovery, like Cage's in the anechoic chamber, that one "is hearing, for the first time, the mighty river of his blood, the Titan's drum of his heart" (710). Pynchon may not share Cage's open, process-driven, environment-influenced, or chance-procedural compositional strategies. The open endings of some of Pynchon's novels are of an entirely different kind from Cage's open compositions, and Pynchon's permutation games with the Kenosha Kid and the Harmonica Marching Band Academy are closer to Brion Gysin's poems than to Cage. Still, Pynchon and Cage share a certain sensibility. While undeniably occupying an intellectual position, both are very much concerned with letting in the noises of the street, the everyday, the pedestrian; both forged new idioms that were not easily assimilable by the markets of their days (the exceptions for Pynchon being perhaps *Vineland*, *Inherent Vice*, and *Bleeding Edge*). Both share an anarchist sensibility while being acutely aware of the problems of a vulgar understanding of anarchism as 'anything goes' and 'each according to his or her own momentary desires.' And we can hear echoes of Doc Sportello when Cage says, as he does in Peter Greenaway's *Four American Composers* (1983), that a recording is not useful at all, that "it merely destroys one's need for real music. It substitutes artificial music for real music and it makes people think that they're engaging in a musical activity when they're actually not."

With Attali's emphasis on the musical instrument (the new instrument that has not yet revealed its essence and can still surprise us; novel ways of playing an established instrument, such as Ornette Coleman's; and instruments like some of Pynchon's favorites discussed above), it is perhaps no coincidence that many of the music scenes in Pynchon's work can be read as promising in Attali's terms: McClintic Sphere's appearances in *V.*, the beachhead or the bus ride out of San Francisco in *Vineland*, the post-war party at Cuxhaven in *Gravity's Rainbow*, to name some of the more striking ones. It would be difficult not to see the harmonica, the kazoo, and the ukulele in this emancipatory, egalitarian lineage when Attali writes: "No study is required to play this kind of music, which is orally transmitted and largely improvisational. It is thus accessible to everyone, breaking the barrier raised by an apprenticeship in the code and the instrument. It has developed among all social classes, but in particular among those most oppressed" (140). What Attali values, Pynchon fictionalizes.

The scene in Maman Tant Gras Hall around the birth of New Orleans jazz may be exemplary in a discussion of the future of music and the future of the organization of society.[46] Reef Traverse's telling band leader "Dope" Breedlove that he has noticed in their playing "the most amazing social coherence, as if you all shared the same brain," points to the kind of musical exchange Attali writes about, a back-and-forth or, simply, 'communication,' which, of course, also implies community. However, Breedlove is reluctant to call this musical exchange "organization" and calls it simply "jass," since to him the phrase "Anarchist organization" is self-contradictory (*Against* 417). What is important in this scene is that the musical performance itself, the improvisation, the communication among the performers, becomes a model for what shortly thereafter develops at the table when people from different ethnic backgrounds converse without hierarchical order, each listens to the others, picks up a cue or admits a moment of silence, then responds in kind or steps back to let someone else respond. The new and shared code is that of jazz during the performance and that of anarchism at the table. Still, the scene offers only a glimpse of what might eventually be. Very much like McClintic Sphere's experiences at the V-Note, the setting of the saloon and its clientele are so infused with racism and racial stereotypes that this conversation among like-minded can be only a model for the society to come, not the thing itself.

Another emblematic scene that deserves a reading is in *Bleeding Edge*. When Maxine Tarnow meets Chandler Platt in his office, she is briefly left alone with Darren, an intern of Asian extraction, who, besides apparently acting as something like a bodyguard for Platt, sees himself as an artist in the Gongsta Rap subgenre (an

46 For a brief social history of New Orleans as the birthplace of jazz and an account of the dynamics among various social strata and shades of skin color, see Ekkehard Jost (*Sozialgeschichte* 17–40).

invention of Pynchon's, an allusion to the gongs widely used in Asian musics and ceremonies[47]). Maxine immediately associates rap with Jay-Z, only to be informed that Darren is "more of a Nas person" (282), Nas being of lesser mainstream fame than Jay-Z. After Darren explains having taken a side in the feud between Jay-Z and Nas, or the "old Queens-versus-Brooklyn thing," he pulls out a Roland TB-303 clone, a bass synthesizer with built-in sequencer, and plays Maxine a song of his own full of references to African-American, Asian, and Scandinavian pop culture, mentioning or alluding to—in quick succession—Tupac, The Notorious B.I.G., "Piggie Bank" by 50 Cent, and "Hong Kong" by Screamin' Jay Hawkins, among a number of non-musical references. Every song mentioned, including Darren's own, contains either metalanguage, references to other rap artists (not always respectful ones), or self-deprecating—or preemptive, as Darren sees it—racial overtones: "They gonna give me all rice-nigga remarks and shit, this way I beat 'em to it" (283). His song is a remix of "nigga" and "rice" references, albeit all from a Western perspective. One could map the references, follow them to the next layer of references, map that one, and so forth and arrive at a highly intertextual rhizome with no clear center or hierarchy, the only possibly recognizable structure dictated by chronology. Darren, one could say, employs some of Pynchon's own postmodern narrative strategies and tactics: borrow, juxtapose, quote, remix, throw in meta- and intertextual references. Like Pynchon, Darren relies heavily on the references of a globalized Western culture as those perhaps most recognizable to his audience. The result hovers somewhere between critique and self-irony (or, at the very least, humor), between an awareness of racial stereotypes and a reliance on Western paradigms to express this awareness.

Darren's instrument, the TB-303 clone, has a highly interesting genealogy.[48] The original TB-303 was manufactured by the

47 Notice, for instance, the Chinese bronze dinner gongs (*Against* 163), the Chinese Gong Effect (401), the Vietnamese nipple gong (*Inherent* 327), and the "gong from a hitherto-unreleased Fu Manchu movie" (*Bleeding* 99), as well as a number of other gongs of mainly Chinese origin.

48 Unless otherwise noted, the information in this paragraph is taken from the Wikipedia entries "TB-303," "Acid House," and "Second Summer of Love" (retr. May 12, 2016), the Sonic Pi manual, and my conversation with Peter Price in November 2016. Sonic Pi was developed for the Raspberry Pi computer, highly affordable at a price of about USD 40. Its Linux operating systems ships with programming software such as Python; its reliance on

Roland corporation between 1982 and 1984 as a practice aid for guitarists. It was something of a bleeding-edge technology, which makes it emblematic of much of the technology that surfaces in the novel of that name. In the case of the synthesizer, early adopters, such as guitarists and stores that put it on their shelves, were disappointed. In the manual of the Sonic Pi live coding software, Sam Aaron explains:

> Unfortunately there were a number of problems: they were a little fiddly to program, didn't sound particularly good as a bass-guitar replacement and were pretty expensive to buy. Deciding to cut their losses, Roland stopped making them after 10,000 units were sold and [...] they soon could be found in the windows of second hand shops. These lonely discarded TB-303s were waiting to be discovered by a new generation of experimenters [...]. Acid House was born.

From today's point of view, the birth of Acid House circa 1985 is intimately wedded to the TB-303. The name of the genre riffs on Acid Rock, and the summers of 1988 and 1989, when Acid House first hit the U.K., became known as the Second Summer of Love, replete with tie-dye shirts and mind-expanding drugs. Since only 10,000 units of the TB-303 were built, few were available considering the great popularity the instrument had started to enjoy. By the mid-1990s, the demand sharply increased with electronic dance music, and in 1996, Fatboy Slim released his song "Everybody Needs a 303," already nostalgic about the instrument. His demand was met partly by the relatively inexpensive ReBirth software, and partly by a number of manufacturers who started to build hardware clones. Such reinvention, cloning, and imitation require a curiosity about the instruments, their circuits, and what novel sounds they can produce. It was mainly the practitioners, and not the industry, who pursued this interest. Such a do-it-yourself approach was important to the entire field of electronic instruments from the beginning. Stockhausen was one of the pioneers, but his disciples in *The Crying of Lot 49* also put together their own gear to jam. Even Friedrich Kittler, who wrote about

open source software, its versatility as a desktop computer, media center, TOR node or access point, household technology and robot controller, and the many sensors and motors that can be attached to it make it an ideal technological fit for the age of composition.

Pynchon, Stockhausen, synthesizers, and software, built his own synths with his brother Wolf. In 2004 (three years after Darren's impromptu performance), a do-it-yourself kit for a TB-303 clone came out, the x0xb0x, much more affordable at a price of USD 500 than an original synthesizer. Many electronic instruments are not, or not necessarily, finished or circumscribed products. They offer a great, near endless range of sounds for those who care to experiment and they can be plugged in to all kinds of other equipment to produce new sonic worlds. The point of the TB-303 clone in connection with Attali is that it is a new instrument that first had to be 'misappropriated' in order to help inaugurate a new code (that of acid house), which then influenced another one (that of rap) while being embedded in a community of professional and amateur musicians experimenting and learning from each other without formal instruction.

Some of the same can be said for the rap genre whose practitioners tend to have no formal training but grow from experimentation and imitation of their peers and predecessors, sometimes in solitude, sometimes as part of a community, often using inexpensive or not yet established instruments, turntables, records, samples, home computers—and their voices. The listener becomes the composer, as Attali has it, in a materially more evident way than when the reader becomes the author, as Roland Barthes has it. Rap is a genre in constant flux, borrowing, lending, juxtaposing, quoting, sharing, bleeding into other genres. Paul D. Miller a.k.a. DJ Spooky That Subliminal Kid (a reference to Burroughs's *Nova Express*), a practitioner and theorist of remix culture, writes in his *Rhythm Science*, a book that comes with a CD of audio snippets and samples:

> Sound. Think of it as a mirror held up to a culture that has learned to fly again, that has released itself from the constraints of the ground to drift through dataspace, continuously morphing its form in response to diverse streams of information [...]. Think of it as a dance of neologisms, an anemic cinema for the gene-splice generation where sign and symbol, word and meaning all drift into the sonic maelstrom. This is a world where all meaning has been untethered from the ground of its origins and all signposts point to a road that you make up as you travel through the text. Rotate, reconfigure, edit, render the form. (5)

Remix culture borrows from whatever source seems interesting and has become something of a global music, although some doubts must remain about how much this self-stylization as a global music accessible to and for everyone is just an easy way not to consider the unwanted byproducts of a Western musical imperialism. The heavy reliance on 4/4 meter, Western tuning systems, appropriation of exotic samples, and a sense of progression (except in modal music, which these days makes up much of pop music) indicates a dominance of Western paradigms.[49] This seems true of all the songs and artists referenced or implied in the *Bleeding Edge* passage as well as of Darren's own artistic production. The remix relies on the archive, hence it requires the stockpiling of music that, to Attali, is a relict of the age of repetition and not a product of the age of composition.

Still, with its sharing culture, that type of music practice operates outside or on the margins of economic circulation. Before Maxine leaves, Darren gives her a CD—at no cost, almost needless to say. This unnerves the capitalist Chandler Platt: "I made the mistake of asking him once how he expects to make money. He said that wasn't the point, but has never explained what is. To me, I'm appalled, it strikes at the heart of Exchange itself" (283). Of course, Platt is wrong. It does not strike at the heart of exchange; it emblematizes exchange as such. Platt does not understand this because the only currency of exchange he knows is money, Exchange with a capital E, or the Exchange of Capital. The *ideology* of remix culture has freed itself from monetary circulation to produce a circulation of ideas (as Attali envisions), although co-optation by the industry is always looming for a select few—and along with it, to speak with McClintic Sphere's personal take on electricity, the ability to keep oneself in J. Press suits and the Triumph in gas (*V.* 292). However, handing out mix tapes or CDs does not guarantee their circulation beyond the first act of gift-giving: Maxine is never reported to actually listen to the CD or to give it to someone else. It seems that the chain of exchange or circulation was broken.

While the 160-odd-item 'playlist' of *Bleeding Edge* does not contain any recognizable music that was copylefted or attributed with a Creative Commons license or that has passed into public

49 For a concise and thoughtful critique of DJ and remix culture, see Peter Price's "Sound as Art in the Age of Global Entertainment" 48–60.

domain (except for a few classical compositions), nor any musicians who have been known for fiercely defending less proprietary-oriented forms of copyright, the topic remains one of the subthemes of the novel.[50] An excellent discussion of all of this can be found in Samuel Thomas's article on music in *Bleeding Edge* in which he devotes ample space to the sharing platform Napster in the novel's context and to some of the most vocal opponents of sharing culture ("Blood on the Tracks" 12–15).

The thinking about a culture of sharing is not present only in music relying on samples but has strongly been influenced by the open-source software sector. *Bleeding Edge*'s Lucas and Justin could conceivably demand any price for their SecondLife®-like (notice the registered trademark), highly secure and anonymous DeepArcher, the main reason for the high demand for it being that it offers the best available anonymity and track-erasing through the employment of something like an anonymous remailer, an early form of onion-routing technology.[51] At first a haven for hackers, computer geeks, and nerds of all sorts who contribute their own visuals without payment or attribution, DeepArcher—a bleeding edge technology with its inherent vices and virtues—eventually becomes colonized by the old capitalist and commercial forces, not unlike what happened to SecondLife. In the end, Lucas and Justin decide to decline the offers made by Apple, Microsoft, the NSA, the Mossad, and hashslingrz and to go open source: "Anybody with the patience to get through it, they want it, they got it. There's already a Linux translation on

---

50 For more on Creative Commons (CC) and questions of copyright, see, for instance, Lawrence Lessig's *Free Culture: How Big Media Uses Technology and the Law to Lock Down Culture and Control Creativity* (in electronic form available free at www.free-culture.cc/freeculture.pdf) and www.creativecommons.org. Although there is a CC-licensed PDF of Lessig's book available, to publish it with Penguin Press, Lessig had to attribute an ordinary copyright license to the print version and there is, at least on the copyright page, no note of regret, unlike street artist Banksy's likewise copyrighted *Wall and Piece* that first states "Copyright is for losers©™" and then "Against his better judgment Banksy has asserted his right under the Copyright, Designs and Patents Act."

51 Onion routing was developed in the mid-1990s, in and for the 'defense' sector. Today, there are a number of open-source and free-of-charge ways of accessing this technology to erase tracks and access the dark web, mainly developed by the Tor Project as well as others such as Tails. However, it remains a two-edged sword as it still has not been able to shed its military- and government-related origins. See Yasha Levine's article "Almost Everyone Involved in Developing Tor was (or is) Funded by the US Government."

the way, which should bring the amateurs in droves" (*Bleeding* 356). In the case of DeepArcher, however, it is not only the conviction that such software should be open source; Lucas and Justin finally act because they believe that Gabriel Ice is plotting to take their source code away by means of a protective covenant. What is more, there is no guarantee that software (or music, for that matter) developed in the spirit of sharing will not also benefit the corporations for whom the hordes of contributing programmers, artists, and amateurs are a form of free labor.

As much as software can be appropriated by unwanted forces, music can too—by both prohibition and enforcement—and securing copyrights does not prevent misuse. After 9/11, the radio network corporation Clear Channel issued a memorandum listing songs that ought not to be played on air. It was roughly the same length as the *Bleeding Edge* playlist and contained all sorts of pop music, from heavy metal to folk. Pop songs were also played at high volume to torture prisoners at Guantanamo Bay. However, to this day, there is no complete playlist available; Internet searches reveal only 13 heavily played songs and a list of artists. This practice of sonic warfare for torture was a continuation of what appears to have started in December 1989 when U.S. troops bombarded opera-lover Manuel Noriega hiding out at the Vatican embassy in Panama City with loud popular music (of which a list of nearly a hundred titles is available).[52] Pynchon has his own hints at torture by music, albeit much more light-hearted. For instance, in *Vineland,* DL informs Takeshi that she won't be able to return to the Ninjette retreat before her year of penance for mistakenly administering the Vibrating Palm, or Ninja Death Touch, is over. The sanctions she could expect include, but are not limited to, "The Ordeal of the Thousand Broadway Show Tunes" or the "Andrew Lloyd Webber Chamber of—" (167), presumably "Torture," although "Commerce" would also fit the bill.

In *Bleeding Edge*, there are a few songs and artists that also appear on the Clear Channel playlist, although many of them by

52 For the Clear Channel list, see https://en.wikipedia.org/wiki/2001_Clear_Channel_memorandum, retr. 20 May 2016. For the Noriega list, see Goodman, 207–08, footnote 17, or http://nsarchive.gwu.edu/nsa/DOCUMENT/950206.htm, retr. May 20, 2016. For the Guantanamo Bay list, see https://theantimedia.com/playlist-used-by-the-cia-to-torture-detainees/ and https://www.mic.com/articles/87851/11-popular-songs-the-cia-used-to-torture-prisoners-in-the-war-on-terror, retr. October 10, 2019.

way of allusion and not explicit reference: Rage Against the Machine (all songs), "Dancing in the Street" and "Nowhere to Run" by Martha and the Vandellas, "Run Like Hell" by Pink Floyd,[53] "It's the End of the World as We Know It (And I Feel Fine)" by R.E.M. (mentioned twice), the "Theme from *New York, New York*," by Frank Sinatra. More Pynchoniana on the list, albeit not appearing in *Bleeding Edge*, was Elton John's "Rocket Man" (published a year before *Gravity's Rainbow*) and "Wipe Out" by The Surfaris (appearing in *Inherent Vice*). Of the artists on what little is known of the Guantanamo Bay playlist, the following also appear in *Bleeding Edge*: Britney Spears, Rage Against the Machine, Tupac Shakur, Meat Loaf, and, possibly, Christina Aguilera (it is not clear if "Love Will Find a Way" [*Bleeding* 464] refers to her song of that title or to another artist's). Finally, the Noriega playlist includes the following songs found in *Bleeding Edge*: "Dancing in the Street" (albeit in David Bowie's version), "Nowhere to Run" by Martha and the Vandellas, "Run Like Hell" by Pink Floyd, and "Time Is on My Side" by the Rolling Stones. (Black Sabbath's "Paranoid" expresses a recurring theme in Pynchon although the song itself is never mentioned.) According to Noam Chomsky, "in December 1989, the US celebrated the fall of the Berlin wall and the end of the Cold War by invading Panama outright" (52). It is somewhat ironic that "Run Like Hell" from *The Wall* was used against a Noriega trapped in the embassy with "Nowhere to Run," precisely as the wall was coming down and people were "Dancing in the Street." While it is up for debate whether Pynchon had the war-related playlists in mind when writing *Bleeding Edge*, it is curious that — barring oversights—the only three songs that are on both the Clear Channel and the Noriega lists should also appear in *Bleeding Edge*.

Another war connection is that *Bleeding Edge* is Pynchon's first novel to mention the genres of metal and hip-hop although they would have been present in their early forms already in the 1984 of *Vineland*. As Jonathan Pieslak argues in his book *Sound Targets: American Soldiers and Music in the Iraq War*, these two

53 Pynchon uses the phrase "run like hell" twice in *Gravity's Rainbow* (before Pink Floyd's *The Wall* [1979] was released) and once in *Bleeding Edge*. Although the phrase in the latter is not an explicit reference ("Maybe I should be telling him to run like hell" 59), I think it may have been an implicit reference to the Pink Floyd song because it occurs shortly after the first implicit reference to R.E.M.'s Clear Channel–blacklisted song "It's the End of the World as We Know It."

genres were the ones most often listened to by soldiers in the field of early twenty-first century American warfare.

Even if the cross-references between these sonic warfare playlists were unintended, Pynchon certainly picked up what was in and on the air at the time leading up to the wars in Afghanistan and Iraq. In the end, this all illustrates at the very least the interplay between progressive and repressive forces and between entertainment and war. If rock music is an abuse of army equipment, the army can also abuse rock music. If Maxine's father Ernie is right when he refers to DARPAnet and says that the Internet "was conceived in sin, the worst possible. As it kept growing, it never stopped carrying in its heart a bitter-cold death wish for the planet, and don't think anything has changed, kid" (420), the question remains whether something similar is also true of rock music, lending itself (and its techniques such as endless loops and high volume) to abuse for military ends.[54]

Pynchon's insertion of those three songs links the two Bush presidencies, that of George H. W. Bush (1989–1993) and George W. Bush (2001–2009), much more subtly than does Driscoll's comment, just before Maxine evokes Reagan's notion of the 'Evil Empire' (which is also the title of the second album by Rage Against the Machine): "Word around the cubes is there's 'ese huge U.S. government contracts, everybody's after em, big deal comin up in the Middle East, some people in the community sayin Gulf War Two. Figures Bush would want to do his daddy one better" (48). Noriega, Saddam Hussein, and, allegedly, Osama Bin Laden were all products of the CIA—bleeding edge too: high cost, high risk—that eventually backfired and, in the eyes of the respective Bush governments, had to be eliminated by military intervention. In between Bush Senior and Junior was the saxophone-wielding president Bill Clinton and his vice-president Al Gore, who made neoliberalism appealing to democrats and paved the information superhighway that would, again in Maxine's father's words that echo Deleuze's "Postscript on the Societies of Control," have dire consequences: "Call it freedom, it's based on control. Everybody connected together, impossible anybody should get lost, ever

54 In *Weird Scenes Inside The Canyon: Laurel Canyon, Covert Ops & The Dark Heart of the Hippie Dream,* an interesting but not entirely unproblematic book, David McGowan documents the close ties of the budding musicians of the late 1960s in Laurel Canyon with the military and intelligence complex.

again. Take the next step, connect it to these cell phones, you've got a total Web of surveillance, inescapable" (420).

During the Clinton administration, the telecommunications sector was deregulated by the Telecommunications Act of 1996, not only allowing cross-media ownership but also raising the number of radio stations a company could own. As a consequence, Clear Channel began its rise to the largest owner of radio stations in the U.S. and the world, and, in 1997, entered the outdoor-advertising business where it would eventually also rise to number 1 or 2 worldwide. Incidentally, Clear Channel Communications, now called iHeartMedia, is owned partly by Bain Capital, an investment firm founded by 2008 and 2012 Republican presidential candidate Mitt Romney. Cowart, referring to a *Rolling Stone* article by Matt Taibbi, argues:

> [Romney serves] as one of the models for Pynchon's villain, Gabriel Ice. […] During the period depicted in *Bleeding Edge*, Romney was disentangling himself from Bain Capital, headquartered in Boston. The novel ends a few months before the 2002 Massachusetts gubernatorial election, which Romney would win. Known for 'leveraged buyouts,' Romney preyed on economic vulnerability, taking over failing companies, stripping their assets, pink-slipping employees, and, before selling out, taking out massive loans with which to pay executive bonuses and investor dividends. Ditto Ice. ("Barroom Floor")

The ultimate dream of neoliberal ideology—although not its *Realpolitik*—is that by taking the state out of the economy, the economy will self-regulate. And indeed, by September 11th, 2001, Clear Channel did not need a government order to issue a list of undesirable songs. It acted preemptively, on its own, much like the Recording Industry Association of America (RIAA), when accused in 1985 by Al Gore's wife Tipper (not by a government body) "of exposing the youth of America to 'sex, violence, and the glorification of drugs and alcohol'" (Zappa 262). The RIAA too bowed to Plato's self-appointed guardians and put a Parental Advisory label on potentially youth-corrupting albums, many of which in the course of pop music history would turn out to be hip-hop albums.[55] Hence, it is perhaps no coincidence that Darren,

55 For Frank Zappa's account of Tipper Gore's Parents' Music Resource Center (PMRC) initiative, see Zappa 261–91. It is noteworthy that Rage Against

confronted with the allegation of racial overtones in his rap song, responds that they are preemptive.

There is also another point that *Bleeding Edge* appears to make between the lines. While its playlist is the longest one in any Pynchon novel in relative terms (i.e., per word) and is second only to *Gravity's Rainbow*'s in absolute terms, *Bleeding Edge* is also the novel that contains the fewest songs composed by Pynchon, the fewest Pynchon songs sung by the novels' characters, and the highest count of canned music playing. Furthermore, it has the smallest number of references to musical instruments and, except for *The Crying of Lot 49*, refers to the smallest variety of musical instruments. Possibly as a result, or as a symptom, it is the novel that has perhaps the least to offer in terms of music philosophy and history. There are no in-depth discussions or treatments of music comparable to those in other Pynchon novels. This fact may indicate that Pynchon's hopes for resistance by means of making music have been disappointed and that Doc's observations outside Wallach's have, in Pynchon's worlds, proven correct, at least for the time being.

Not all hope is lost, though. The liveliest genre in *Bleeding Edge* is that of rap/hip-hop, not just with Darren, but also with Misha and Grisha, a "sort of Russian hip-hop act" (386), rapping along every chance they get, and with Ziggy and Otis doing a "hip-hop version of the Peaches & Herb oldie 'Reunited and It Feels So Good'" (467). These are the instances where the performers seem to have the most innocent fun, unspoiled by cynicism or looming dark forces, and it is perhaps no coincidence that it is in a genre heavily influenced by amateur and DIY approaches. Reading the music in *Bleeding Edge* as a commentary on the music in *Inherent Vice* would amount to something like this: The role that rock'n'roll

---

the Machine, a political band whose music has no sexual overtones (their use of "fuck" has nothing to do with copulation) and no noteworthy allusions to drug use, was given the "Parental Advisory" sticker. It was also the only band that was banned wholesale in the Clear Channel memorandum. This hints at other motives behind the PMRC intervention. It remains ironic that Tipper Gore's husband would become the vice president to the first sex, drugs, and rock'n'roll president of the USA. See *Mason & Dixon* for an allusion to Clinton's marijuana use ("If you must do the latter, do not inhale" 10) and *Bleeding Edge* for a reference to Clinton and Monica Lewinsky: "Prabhnoor and Amrita are dressed as Bill Clinton and Monica. [...] Prabhnoor is handing out cigars. Amrita, in a blue dress of course, is holding a dead karaoke mike and sweetly singing 'I Did It My Way'" (369).

and folk music played for the 1968 generation before their large-scale industrialization is akin to the role rap and hip-hop music play for millennials. And, taking into account McClintic Sphere in *V.* (free jazz, around 1959), Charlie Parker in *Gravity's Rainbow* (be-bop, around 1939), and "Dope" Breedlove in *Against the Day* (New Orleans jazz, early twentieth century), one could add that different subgenres of jazz played that role for previous generations. As much as early rap music and rock'n'roll were commercialized by the music industry, so were New Orleans jazz in its Dixieland version and be-bop in its hard bop version. Only free jazz, it seems, akin to atonal music, has resisted the music industry, which may be why these two genres never appear after *Gravity's Rainbow*. The remix, being the most current of these musical practices, may be the harbinger of a more just, more creatively oriented future society not reliant on the imposed economic necessities of today; or it may just as easily be reterritorialized and instrumentalized by Global Capital. Only time will tell.

The question remains whether Pynchon can show us that future of composition. He is, among many things, a fiction writer of science—but he is not a science fiction writer. His works are firmly grounded in history and in the "outward and visible."[56] His understanding of science and its history is deeper and more knowledgeable than that of many a science-fiction writer's, which by no means precludes flights of fancy, elaborate inner worlds, or the creation of what is maybe "not the world, but with a minor adjustment or two [...] what the world might be," to quote the blurb of *Against the Day*. Pynchon's novels do not play out in strictly alternative universes that can be constructed from scratch following a manageable number of premises, nor do they play in the future or in outer space. Hence, we cannot expect from him the creation of a large-scale egalitarian future society as Attali envisions it, a society, moreover, that might not be very interesting to fiction writers since compelling fiction always demands friction. Yet, what Pynchon offers is much more than a neatly mapped-out hypothetical future. His slight deviations from the everyday and his—at times romanticized—pockets of resistance connect both to

---

56 Variations of the phrase "outward and visible" occur many times in Pynchon's novels, for instance, in *Inherent Vice*, *Gravity's Rainbow*, and *Mason & Dixon*, and in the Spike Jones liner notes, and deserve a study of their metaphysical or religious implications.

musical and to political discourse in a soft reading of Plato, that is, a reading that makes no causal claims linking music and society. They allow for hypotheses and uncertainties and therefore offer the reader considerable freedom in becoming, in Barthes's sense, the author of Pynchon's texts. Still, this creative reading does not amount to materially creating something that others can contemplate and participate in. With Barthes's idea of authorship being transferred to the reader and his notion of *musica practica* (142–54), we do not yet arrive at Attali's era of composition. However, pointers and sympathies in Pynchon's work resonate unmistakably with Attali. Pynchon's sympathy for the Preterite and his interest in the possibilities of an anarchist 'organization' of society, for instance, do not waver. Although his pronouncements on music for mass markets throughout his work are far less harsh than Attali's, the two authors share an appreciation for the "Novel in Musick" and for amateur music-making to the extent that they see in it the promise of a revolution leading to a more bottom-up, democratic, just, egalitarian society.

4

Analyzing the Pynchon Playlist

Starting as early as J.O. Tate's "*Gravity's Rainbow:* The Original Soundtrack" from 1983, scholars have compiled catalogs of musicians and works of music referenced or alluded to by Pynchon in particular novels. Since late 2006, playlists for some of Pynchon's novels have been available on Tim Ware's PynchonWiki.[1] However, to my knowledge, there has not been an effort to gather the 'playlists' or 'soundtracks' for all of Pynchon's work and analyze them in a statistical or otherwise empirically meaningful way.

Intending to fill this gap, I compiled such an all-encompassing playlist in the course of writing this book and published it in 2018 as an Excel file with *Orbit*.[2] It is an attempt to put together every identifiable reference to non-fictional musicians and works of music in Pynchon's eight novels, one short story collection, and uncollected articles, essays, endorsements, and liner notes published to date. It can be seen as a homage to Pynchon's own delectation in listing items, but, more importantly, the intention is to give an accurate picture of the characters' musical horizons and perhaps a glimpse into their creator's. The result is a catalog of 935 references, about 190 of which have multiple entries (see pp. 239–288). The most important sources for compiling the catalog were the PynchonWiki, a number of articles from *Pynchon Notes*, particularly the *Index Issue (Pynchon Notes* 36–39), and the *Companions* to Pynchon's novels by Steven Weisenburger and J. Kerry Grant. To these I added the references and allusions I spotted myself.

Such a substantial catalog cannot be analyzed based solely on intuition, which is why a series of analyses were made and graphs plotted. Some of the questions that were of interest included, but were not limited to: Which musicians or works of music does

1 See www.pynchonwiki.com to access the wikis for the respective novels. Some of the playlists on the PynchonWiki were added, expanded, or corrected by me. Unfortunately, I am unable to recall the exact additions I made over the years.

2 The *Orbit* list has 927 items. I since discovered more and the list now encompasses 935 items.

Pynchon reference most frequently? Which genres occur most often? Which novels contain most references? How often is music performed live, listened to on the radio, stereo system, or TV, or just talked about? Are there any notable anachronisms? Is there a correlation—possibly an inverse one—between the number of musical references and the number of Pynchon's own songs? Does the number of references increase or decrease over the course of Pynchon's career as a writer or are they dependent on the periods in which the novels take place? How inclusive is Pynchon of female musicians?

One of the merits of the resulting statistical analysis is that it is able to qualify or rectify some assumptions that may have been made intuitively. In Chapter 3, I already discussed that some of the assumptions Justin St. Clair made in the context of *Inherent Vice* do not hold up to this level of analysis. At the 2015 International Pynchon Week, he stated that the majority of songs in *Inherent Vice* are not associated with a particular subculture or counterculture but are mainstream tunes, a nostalgic soundtrack with most songs from the 1950s and early 1960s. While this is true to a certain extent, my playlist reveals that, firstly, a good number of tracks in *Inherent Vice* are clearly not nostalgic, and, secondly, Pynchon always tends towards something like a musical mainstream. Similarly, John Joseph Hess claims that "Pynchon's self-composed lyrics appear [...] with roughly the same frequency [in *Mason & Dixon*] as they do in his other works" (2). As will be shown, this does not hold true either.

Such a bird's eye view naturally has its limits, which is why it is designed to complement rather than replace the close readings and historical contextualizations. Even someone like Franco Moretti, who is credited as the founder of distant reading, cannot do without contextualizing and interpreting his quantitative findings. The Pynchon Playlist and its analysis will hopefully entice other researchers to investigate Pynchon's musical references in a similar manner with different research questions or to verify or falsify my own findings. In order to ensure intersubjectivity among other researchers, parts of this chapter are purely descriptive, explaining in detail what I did and the rationale for the decisions.

Within the catalog, each reference or allusion to a single work or musician on a book page comprises a unit. If the unit spans more than one page but is uninterrupted, it is considered one unit and hence one entry. If the unit spans more than one page but is interrupted, the entry is repeated. Most references (of which there are 766) are direct, unambiguous references made by the characters or the narrators. They include the name of the musician or the title of the work. For instance, when Puck says "everything's coming up roses, as Ethel always sez" (*Inherent* 247), it was coded as a direct reference because it contains the song title (as well as the artist's first name), in this case Ethel Merman's recording of "Everything's Coming Up Roses" from the Stephen Sondheim musical *Gypsy*. Some references (100) are only allusions. They are more easily overlooked and require more investigation to identify (many by simply entering the passage into a search engine). Such is the case, for instance, when Puck says, "overnight, forever, et cetera et cetera, and so forth as the King of Siam always sez" (*Inherent* 248), an allusion to the song "Puzzlement" from the Rodgers/Hammerstein musical *The King and I*. When it appears evident that Pynchon is referring to a specific artist or piece of music, the entry was coded as an 'indirect' reference. Finally, there are 69 entries that are likely musical references but that are seamlessly woven into the narrative, often without a musical context. When Jet says to Mason, "Don't forget to-night, Charles" (*Mason* 78) and a few lines later Dixon says "Tell me [...] what'd I say?" (79), I assume that these are allusions to Frank Sinatra's "Don't Forget Tonight, Tomorrow" and to Ray Charles's "What'd I Say." Linking the name of Charles Mason to that of Ray Charles may or may not validate this deduction.[3] Another example is Maxine's linking Gabriel Ice to the "Evil Empire" (*Bleeding* 48), a notion of Ronald Reagan's. I attribute the phrase to the 1996 Rage Against the Machine album of that title because two lines down, Driscoll says "fodder for the machine." Some of the deduced allusions can be contested, and I have undoubtedly

3 Similarly, when Doc is at the fictional Kismet casino in *Inherent Vice*'s Las Vegas he 'coincidentally' comes across FBI agents he has been acquainted with in Los Angeles. Kısmet is Turkish for 'fate' and there are a number of plays, films, songs, and albums that include this word. However, once we realize that the Elvis Presley song "Kismet," which is never directly referenced, includes the lines "When you meet by chance, it's not by chance / It's kismet" and "The wheel of fortune spins, round and around it goes," it becomes highly likely that Pynchon named the casino after the Elvis song. Further supporting this deduction is the fact that there are four other Elvis references in *Inherent Vice*, three within a few pages of the Kismet. Other deductions are possible, of course: in *Bleeding Edge*, there is a brief mention of Vincente Minnelli who directed the 1955 movie *Kismet*.

missed others because of their clever placement.[4] For brevity's sake, in what follows, direct references, allusions, and deductions are all termed (musical) references, except when explicitly referring to one particular category.

The only references I omitted from the catalog are those in the liner notes to *Spiked! The Music of Spike Jones* and Lotion's *Nobody's Cool* and the *Esquire* interview with Lotion that pertain directly to the musicians and the songs on the respective albums. It is to be expected that liner notes include information about the artists and tracks, and the inclusion of the many musicians and songs, particularly in the long Spike Jones liner notes, would have distorted the overall picture.

Each entry in the Playlist is complemented with additional information, such as the composer, year of publication, gender of the artist, or likely or referenced recording/performing artist, mainly thanks to the help of websites such as Wikipedia, Discogs.com, and AllMusic.com. The musicians' entries are complemented with brief biographical notes. If a reference is deemed too obscure for many readers to be able to make an immediate connection, the contextualizing passage from the novel is included.

Number and Frequency of References

Figure 1 shows the number of references in each book. All the uncollected published writings were grouped together in one hypothetical book:

4 Perhaps the most contestable allusion cataloged is the anachronistic "Chalk Outline" by Three Days Grace (2012), which came out about a year before *Bleeding Edge* and reached single-digit positions on a number of Billboard charts. Chalk marks are present at the scene where Lester was killed (206) and later, when Maxine is thinking about Lester, we read "the dead can't speak" (358), which corresponds to a line of the song. I decided to include this allusion since the album containing the song is entitled *Transit of Venus* and grace is a recurring theme, making it likely that Pynchon intended an allusion.

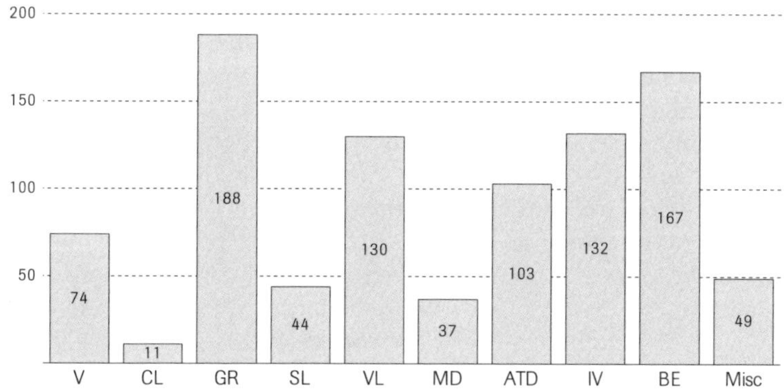

Fig. 1: Total number of musical references in each book, ordered by publication date. Henceforth: V: *V.;* CL: *The Crying of Lot 49*; GR: *Gravity's Rainbow;* SL: *Slow Learner*, VL: *Vineland;* MD: *Mason & Dixon*; ATD: *Against the Day;* IV: *Inherent Vice;* BE: *Bleeding Edge*; Misc: uncollected miscellaneous writings.

This general overview in itself does not say much as it does not take into account the length of each book. Since each novel has a different page layout and various editions with differing numbers of pages, it is more useful to relate the number of references to the number of words in each book. The following table shows the number of pages of the editions I worked with and the word count. To obtain the number of words, the texts were copied into a LibreOffice file and an InDesign file and then counted.

	V	CL	GR	SL	VL	MD	ATD	IV	BE	Misc.
Year	1963	1966	1973	(var.)	1990	1997	2006	2009	2013	var.
Edition	1975	1984	2006	1984	1990	1998	2007	2009	2013	var.
Pages	492	152	776	174	378	773	1220	369	477	158
Words	174,209	46,771	338,208	54,749	141,737	259,928	446,050	118,953	142,021	46,087

Table 2: Publication year, editions I worked with, and number of pages and words for each book.

Dividing the number of references by the number of words in each book and arranging them in ascending order, the above diagram looks as follows:

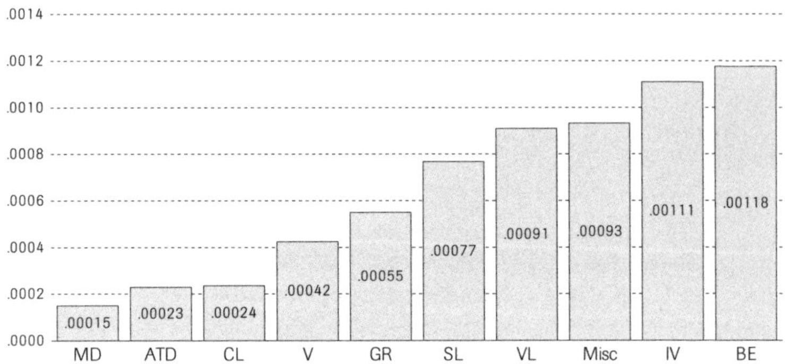

Fig. 2: Density of musical references, in ascending order.

Three periods are evident (see fig. 3): the first period comprises *Mason & Dixon* (set in the second half of the eighteenth century) and *Against the Day* (between 1893 and c. 1923); the second period comprises *V.* (between 1898 and 1956) and *Gravity's Rainbow* (mainly in 1945/46); the third period comprises *Vineland* (1968 and 1984), *Inherent Vice* (1970), and *Bleeding Edge* (2001–02). Figures 2 and 3 thus roughly confirm a hypothesis I had at the outset of this investigation: the density of references corresponds not to stages in Pynchon's writing career but to the eras in which the novels are set, with fewer references in novels set in the eras in which music was less present in everyday life, especially before the advent of mass-distributed recorded music. In his references to historical musicians and works of music, Pynchon therefore displays an element of realism or verisimilitude which is also noticeable in some of the following diagrams.

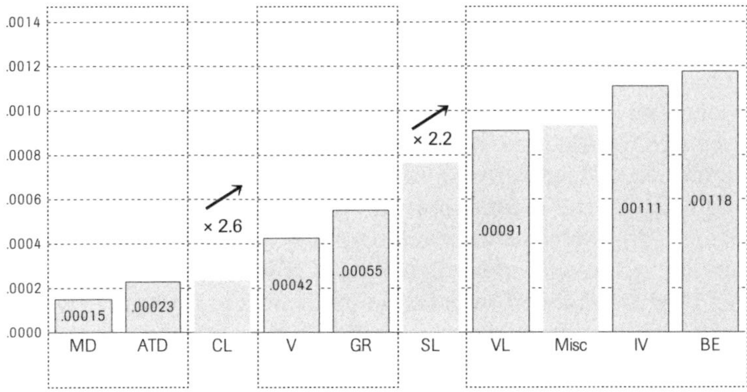

Fig. 3: Groups of novels according to density of musical references.

The Crying of Lot 49, *Slow Learner*, and the miscellaneous writings do not fit this picture, as will often be the case with other diagrams that follow. A number of explanations can be offered: the miscellaneous writings are made up of 52 texts of various literary and journalistic genres that appeared between 1952 and 2006. *Slow Learner* is made up of five short stories initially published between 1959 and 1964 and an introduction written in 1984. One of the short stories is set in the late nineteenth century (the one that later developed into chapter 3 of *V.*); the rest are set in the late 1950s and perhaps early 1960s. However, the short stories individually and together do not yield enough data to be comparable to the longer works. While "Entropy," constructed as a fugue (see Chapter 1), has the highest number of entries among the other short stories (21) and almost twice as many as all of *The Crying of Lot 49* (11), "The Secret Integration," in part revolving around a black jazz musician, has only one reference, "The Battle Hymn of the Republic." *The Crying of Lot 49* is by far the shortest novel, a little more than a third the length of *Vineland*, *Inherent Vice*, or *Bleeding Edge*. It might conceivably have included more musical references if it had somehow been developed into a novel the length of one of those three. *The Crying of Lot 49* contains one passage, that about Sinewave Sessions, that lends itself to more in-depth ruminations on music but even that passage is musicologically not quite as interesting as some of the passages in the other novels. For all these reasons, *Slow Learner*, *The Crying of*

Lot 49, and the miscellaneous writings are not much commented on in what follows.

In addition to the temporal pattern, the density of musical references also appears to be higher when large portions of the plot are set in or around major urban centers, Los Angeles in *Inherent Vice* and New York City in *Bleeding Edge*. *Vineland* may rank lower because the locations of the plot are geographically more scattered. In other words, while *Gravity's Rainbow* and parts of *V.* are set in a time of mass distribution of recorded music—albeit much less pronounced than in the other novels set in the twentieth century—the fact that much of the action takes place outside the U.S. and outside main urban centers may further explain their lower ranking.

When focusing solely on *Vineland*, *Inherent Vice*, and *Bleeding Edge*, the general trend of the correlation of chronology with density of references seems to be reversed. Without trying to explain this away, some explanations can be offered. *Vineland* may rank lower than the other two because the central medium of the novel is TV and, to a lesser degree, film. Pynchon was therefore probably more attuned to TV and film references than to musical ones. Harking back to *Inherent Vice*'s ruminations on headphones and communal music-reception, one can also observe that the proliferation of solitary-listening devices, first the Walkman (introduced in 1979) and then MiniDisc and MP3 players, has led to a different way of consuming music. The musical experience is less communal, hence the characters have fewer opportunities to talk about music or to sing along together.

What remains, then, are three groups: *Mason & Dixon* and *Against the Day* before the mass distribution of music and set in various parts of the world; *V.* and *Gravity's Rainbow*, in a transitional period and also set in many heterogeneous locations; and *Vineland*, *Inherent Vice*, and *Bleeding Edge*, after the advent of a full-scale music industry and set mainly in or around large urban centers. As we move chronologically from group to group, the average density of musical references rises about 2.2–2.6 times per step.

Types of References

The references can be divided into those to composers, to musicians, to larger musical works comprising multiple pieces, such as operas or albums, and to single musical pieces such as songs or arias. The category 'composer' includes both composers of music and librettists, and it is used for persons recognized mainly as composers and not as performers. The category 'musician' includes singers, instrumentalists, conductors, bands, and orchestras. A passage such as "Evan [...] began to sing Deh, vieni alla finestra from Don Giovanni" (*V.* 158) is a reference both to the aria and to the opera. For the purposes of this study, the more specific reference overrides the more general ones (single piece > larger work > composer/musician). Seven entries from *Against the Day* are categorized as 'other,' six of them because, in the context, the persons appear as ethno-musicologists even though some of them are recognized mainly as composers: Béla Bartók, Zoltán Kodály, Joseph Canteloube, Ralph Vaughan Williams, Eugénie Lineff, and Hjalmar Thuren (1057).

The total number of references for all of Pynchon's work is as follows:

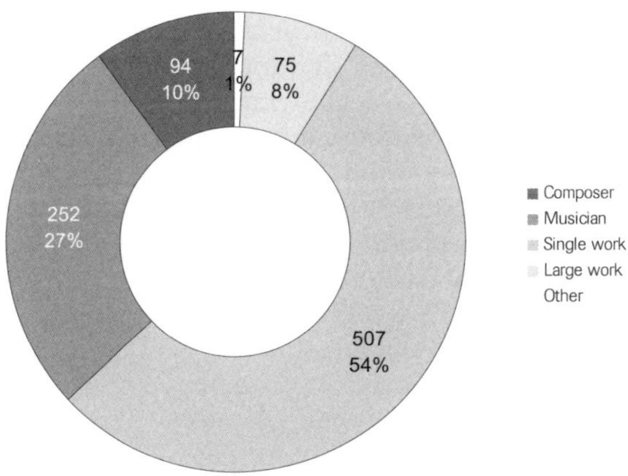

Fig. 4: Total number of references to composers, musicians, and works of music across all of Pynchon's work.

The large number of references to single musical pieces (mostly songs) relative to the other categories results partly from my decision that the most specific attribute of a unit determine the category of the entry. If this were changed to include multiple entries for the same unit, the absolute number of single-work references would remain the same but the number of composers, musicians, and larger works would rise, albeit not to the level of the song entries. The same is true if composers and musicians were grouped together. Only in *Inherent Vice* and *The Crying of Lot 49* do the musicians and composers taken together make up half or more than half of the references.

Fifty-two songs are not explicit references or allusions but more obscurely woven into the narrative. They have to be deduced from the context or certain key words, and it is possible that some of them are merely products of fancy or chance due to what I perceived as strong resonances. If every one of those references were contested as overinterpreted and inadmissible by another researcher, the number of songs would drop to 455. Nevertheless, even if my decision to have the most specific attribute override the others skewed the overall picture or if my deductions were too far-fetched, the single music piece remains the most important musical reference for Pynchon as it allows him to reference the lyrics or the title, explicitly or implicitly, and have them contribute to or comment on the scene or plot or foreshadow what is to happen. The high number of single works of music is also in line with the music industry's development after the 1940s when the 45 rpm single, the DJ, and the jukebox began to influence popular culture, up to today when songs can be purchased and downloaded from online stores or listened to on websites like YouTube. The single song also appears to be more important than the album for mass markets and radio airplay.

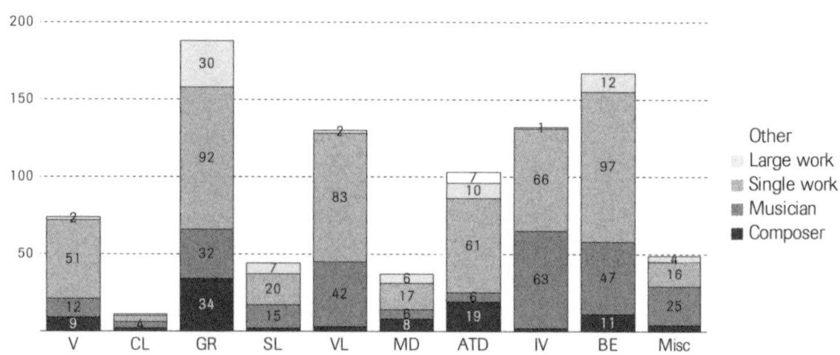

Fig. 5: Type of reference (absolute) per book.

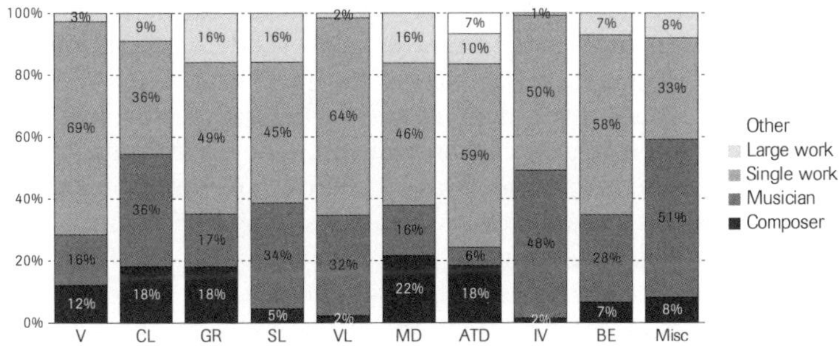

Fig. 6: Type of reference (relative) per book.

Relative to their length, the California novels *(Inherent Vice, The Crying of Lot 49, Vineland)* have the highest percentages of references to musicians, closely followed by *Bleeding Edge*, which may be considered an honorary California novel. Scott McClintock and John Miller (2014) have made a case for a distinct group of California novels and characterized the affinities among *The Crying of Lot 49*, *Vineland*, and *Inherent Vice* as follows: "In addition to their setting [...], [they] are the shortest of his novels; their plots, generally organized around a single protagonist, tend to be more linear [...]; they all invoke a genre often associated with Southern California, the detective story; and two of them center largely on female characters" (1). After the publication of *Bleeding Edge*, they added the following footnote: "If the qualities recited in that sentence are taken as criteria, *Bleeding Edge* would qualify as the most typically 'Californian' of Pynchon's work to date, putting aside the fact that it is set almost entirely in New York City and its immediate environs" (14).

Inherent Vice has almost as many musician references (63) as song references (66), and the musician references would be significantly more numerous if not for my decision to use the most specific attribute to determine the category. *Vineland*, *Inherent Vice*, and *Bleeding Edge* also have nearly negligible numbers of composer references. This may be due to the characters' musical preferences and to these three novels revolving around a small number of protagonists. In *Gravity's Rainbow*, for instance, the musical preferences are distributed among a much greater number of characters. The five novels set in eras before the music industry had grown to its current cultural significance have the highest relative percentages of composers and the lowest relative percentages of musicians. There are two ready explanations for this fact: On the one hand, composers have long had a medium to preserve their art—sheet music—whereas performers rely either on live performance or on recording media that can further their recognition beyond hearsay. We know only from books what admired singers and musicians of the past may have sounded like to contemporary listeners. On the other hand, much of the pop-music industry's money is made through the star system where recognition and fame are functions of the decision—backed with the necessary financial resources—to boost a musician (mostly a singer) who displays certain qualities, among them being photo- and telegenic, having a good stage presence, and having an appeal, mostly sexual, to the target audience.

Adjusted to the number of references per word, *Vineland*, *Inherent Vice*, and *Bleeding Edge* have by far the highest numbers of song references and the lowest numbers of composer references. *Inherent Vice*'s first composer entry is Charles-Louis Hanon (who was also a music pedagogue): "Spotted Dick's keyboard player Smedley [is] doing Hanon exercises on his Farfisa, a little Combo Compact model he had obtained on the advice of Rick Wright of Pink Floyd" (128–29). The second one is Vivaldi, possibly of the Muzak kind (like that in the opening lines of *The Crying of Lot 49* except for the kazoos), playing on the sound system of a restaurant (276). While the first composer entry is immediately linked to a fictional surf band and a real psychedelic rock band, the second one does not engage at all with the music. *Vineland* has one reference to Rossini, and one each to popular music composers Andrew Lloyd Webber (also mentioned twice in *Bleeding Edge*) and Bernard Herrmann. This further contributes to a sense of kinship among these three novels: they are about the same length and are set largely in an urban America after 1968; *Inherent Vice* and *Bleeding Edge* are both detective stories; and *Vineland* and *Inherent Vice* both comment on the decline of the late 1960s' counterculture.

Some findings countered my expectations. *V.* has only two references to larger works: the Puccini operas *Madama Butterfly* and *Manon Lescaut*. Intuitively, I expected more larger works, possibly because of the reimagination in chapter 14 of Igor Stravinsky's ballet *The Rite of Spring*. As it turns out, all the other classical references are either composers or arias/movements/themes/overtures and thus coded as 'single works.' The *Manon Lescaut* reference also appears twice in "Under the Rose." Reading both the short story and its reworking as chapter 3 of *V.* may have reinforced the false impression that there would be more opera references in the novel as their overlaps possibly fused the two texts into one in my memory. Finally, the reader experiences references to single works differently in *V.* than in the other novels because *V.* is the only novel where titles of songs are not set in quotation marks and so are more easily overlooked. The unexpectedly low number of opera references in *V.* (only six) will be corroborated further below when discussing genre.

Another interesting finding is that *Gravity's Rainbow* and *Mason & Dixon*, among Pynchon's most highly regarded works, have almost identical percentages and the most evenly distributed references among the different categories despite being very different in absolute terms.

Genre Distribution

One of the more challenging tasks was that of assigning every artist, composer, and work of music to a particular genre. Many attempts have been made to classify music according to genres or styles, but since music is constantly evolving and constantly being evaluated and reevaluated, and since one style develops out of another one or several others, no model is ultimately able to provide clear-cut demarcations. In the end, unless one works with countless nested subcategories, one will never succeed in creating an intersubjectively reliable model. For the purposes of this study, I distinguish broadly among the three most encompassing genres popular music, classical music, and jazz, and between the two compound categories military/patriotic and traditional/folk/world/religious.

'Classical music' here designates 'serious' or 'high' European music starting with Baroque (around 1600 A.D.), often orchestral or chamber music. It also includes music that is less 'serious,' such as *opera buffa*. Since opera is so important to Pynchon, I created a sub-genre for the opera-related references. The few instances of medieval music are classified either as 'religious' or, when the reference has become ubiquitous and the religious connotations no longer central (such as the fourteenth-century "In dulci jubilo"), as 'traditional,' even when the religious connotations might still be important for the interpretation. Initially, I considered modernist or high-modernist music, sometimes called atonal, post-tonal, avant-garde, or new classical (such as Berg, Schoenberg, Stravinsky, Varèse, Stockhausen, and Webern) to be a separate category. However, since there are only 15 such references (i.e. 1.6% of all references) and they all but disappear after *Gravity's Rainbow*, I decided to include them in the classical music category. Besides, this type of music often shares modes of composition, instrumentation, performance, and reception with classical (Baroque, Classical, and Romantic) music. Both seem philosophically and musically important to Pynchon's early work.[5]

Pop music and jazz turned out to be the most problematic categories. One reason is that popular music in its broadest sense has become a cultural force that is used as an identifier and self-identifier of tastes and lifestyles (to the extent of bleeding into fashion choices), which is why the subgenres proliferate profusely. Under the pop music umbrella can be found styles (not always with a mass appeal) as diverse as black metal, salsa, musicals, and funk. Another reason is that much of twentieth-century pop music would not have been thinkable without the influence of music of African-American origin, such as jazz and blues, hence pop bleeds into those styles or genres. Finally, there has not yet been an 'event' that would allow us to draw demarcation lines as with the turn to atonality. To identify 'pop' music, I used some positive criteria: 'low' or 'popular' Western (generally American or European) music, from the late nineteenth century (circa Tin Pan Alley) onward, which relies on easily identifiable repetitive structures, often eight or twelve bars, and which often has a chorus repeated several times. Pop mostly revolves around a vocal melody line. To a large extent, its popularity was enabled by technologies of mass reproduction, from sheet music to sound recording, and it often has a broad appeal. This description makes it clear that, musically speaking, an intuitively easy category such as pop music cannot always be distinguished from other genres such as jazz, blues, or some folk and world music. Generally, I made the distinction between pop and jazz intuitively, but when in doubt relied on these criteria: syncopation, phrasing, and, to a lesser degree, instrumentation specific to many forms of jazz. Since Pynchon often references show tunes

5 It could be argued that a number of Frank Zappa's albums are avant-garde (not least the orchestral ones); but since he mainly plays rock and pop music and since all five references depict him as a countercultural pop icon—not a single work of his is mentioned—he is classified as pop.

and Broadway musicals, I wanted to be able to designate this subcategory as well. Considering that opera is to classical music what musicals are to pop, I introduced a subcategory for popular music called 'musicals.'[6]

'Jazz' designates the trajectory of jazz music (which, like any historical trajectory, can be named and categorized only ex post and in relation to what followed), starting with ragtime and extending to modern and free jazz. I include blues and early soul music in the jazz category because they are musically related and grew out of an African-American socio-economic context. It could be argued that 'black music' would have been a better category, but I felt that 'jazz' is a more inclusive term and that, nowadays, 'black music' also includes genres such as R'n'B and hip-hop which more clearly belong in the pop category. While most jazz references are unambiguous, some could also be labeled pop. Some popular and showcase tunes have become jazz standards; some pop singers, for instance the oft-mentioned Frank Sinatra, also had careers as jazz singers, and some of Sinatra's interpretations have become part of the standard big-band repertoire.

The other prominent genres in Pynchon's work, although with far lower counts, are patriotic and military-related songs and marches (e.g. the "Horst-Wessel-Lied," John Philip Sousa's "The Stars and Stripes Forever," and national anthems); a few instances of 'world' music (e.g. the Karakaş Efendi, and the ethno-musicologists of *Against the Day*); some well-known 'traditional' material (e.g. "For He's a Jolly Good Fellow," "O Tempora, O Mores," and Stephen Foster) and some 'religious' or 'sacred' music (e.g. "Lead Me Lord," "Amazing Grace," and S. Cosma of Jerusalem).[7] In the analysis below, patriotic/military is a single category, and world, traditional, folk, and religious are grouped together.[8]

6 In a few instances, Pynchon mentions operettas or twentieth-century works for the stage such as those of Brecht and Weill, which do not seem to fit properly into the category of opera or musical. Since these instances are too few to have a noticeable impact on the overall statistics, I did not concern myself too much with the exact category but coded intuitively.

7 Bach is always categorized as 'classical' even though he wrote a lot of sacred music. Christmas tunes (eight in total) are categorized as 'religious' only if their subject matter is clearly religious: "Silent Night" is categorized as religious, "The Twelve Days of Christmas" as traditional, and "Rudolph the Red-Nosed Reindeer" as pop.

8 'Folk' in this context does not designate the 1960s-onward folk music of Bob Dylan, Richard Fariña, and others that became popular in an era of mass

I initially created subcategories such as surf, rap, folk music, labor songs, Christmas carols, tango, instrumental film music, and jingles/commercials. However, due to the relatively low numbers of entries, these categories did not yield much of interest and so were abandoned.

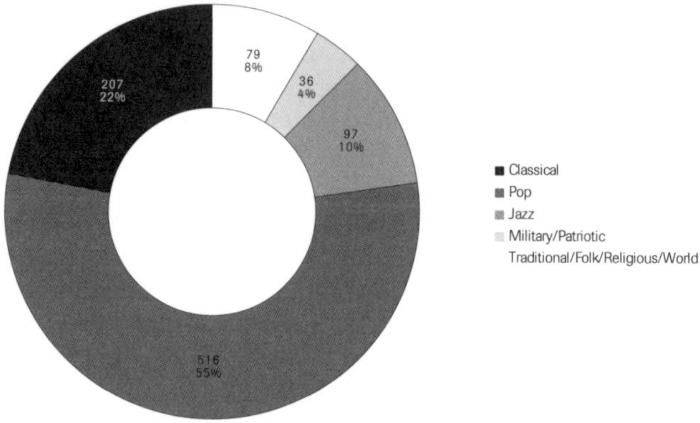

Fig. 7: Total references by genre (absolute and relative).

As figure 7 shows, pop music accounts for approximately 55%, classical music for 22%, jazz for 10%, traditional/folk/world/religious for 8%, and military/patriotic for 4%. Although the pop music category has the highest number of references, partly due to its inclusion of many sub-genres, many of Pynchon's more sustained ruminations on the form and history of music are found in the categories classical and jazz. Figure 8 shows that the average percentages across all of Pynchon's writings deviate greatly from the distribution in the individual books.

markets but socially conscious (or even socialist) folk music and labor songs from the nineteenth and early twentieth century, which I felt did not belong in the category 'pop' music. The most recent song designated 'folk' is Woody Guthrie's "This Land Is Your Land" from 1944.

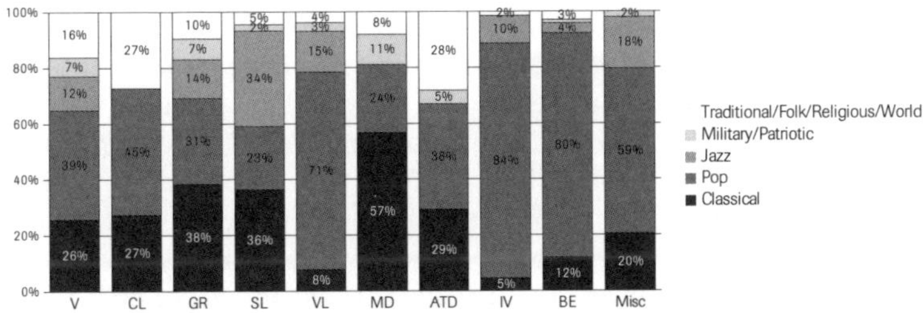

Fig. 8: Distribution of genres for each book.

Except for *Vineland, Inherent Vice,* and *Bleeding Edge,* which are in roughly the same range in their distribution of genres (and have by far the highest percentages of pop music), each book is quite distinct. Even *V.* and *Gravity's Rainbow* are different in that their shares of popular music and classical music are—very roughly speaking—inverted. Still, the pattern observed above also seems true here: the larger, more critically acclaimed and distant-historical works (*V., Gravity's Rainbow, Mason & Dixon,* and *Against the Day*) can be distinguished from the shorter, more recent-historical ones (*Vineland, Inherent Vice,* and *Bleeding Edge*) by the distribution of genres. The former have more classical and fewer pop music references, and the distribution among genres is more even.

After *Gravity's Rainbow* in 1973, Pynchon's narrators and characters seem to have lost interest in post-tonal or avant-garde music, and Stravinsky and Schoenberg are mentioned again only in the Spike Jones liner notes. Various explanations may be offered. Possibly Pynchon himself lost interest in this type of music after his early years or felt that the groundbreaking paradigms (the move to atonality of the early twentieth century and then the inclusion of all sounds and noises as musical material in a Cagean turn) were musically or philosophically exhausted. To quote Alain Badiou: "[T]owards the end of the 1970s, [serial music's] 'corporeal' capacities, those that could inscribe themselves in the dimension of the work, were more and more limited. One could no longer really find 'interesting' deployments, significant mutations, local completions. Thus an infinite subject comes to its *finishing [finition]*" ("Musical Variant" 30). In other words, until, say, the 1960s, an intellectually versed person might disregard pop culture but feel that post-tonal music's trajectory is something one had at least to be aware of; after the 1960s, these attitudes seem to have become reversed.

Other possible explanations are that two of the books published after *Gravity's Rainbow* are set well before or just around the time of the atonal turn, and that in the other three the predominance of pop music and the medium of TV (with its effect on viewers discussed in *Vineland*) makes it unlikely for characters to display an avid interest in avant-garde music. And again, the lower number of major characters in *Vineland*, *Inherent Vice*, and *Bleeding Edge* gave Pynchon fewer opportunities to distribute musical tastes among different people.

While the share of classical music is the lowest in *Vineland* and *Inherent Vice*, it rises somewhat in *Bleeding Edge*, partly thanks to Maxine Tarnow's parents' interest in opera, which they were able to convey to their grandchildren Ziggy and Otis. It is indicative of the high share of pop music, however, that in a discussion accounting for one third of the novel's classical references, Otis maintains that the greatest performance of "Nessun' dorma" from Puccini's *Turandot* is Aretha Franklin's while his grandmother Elaine opines that it is actress Deanna Durbin's in *His Butler's Sister* (1943) (97–98). *Against the Day* has such a high percentage of the compound category traditional/folk/world/religious partly because its settings are distributed around the world (often in rural areas) and partly because folk, labor and traditional songs are appropriate to its numerous anarchist and miner characters.[9] *Gravity's Rainbow* and *Mason & Dixon* have more patriotic/military songs than the other novels: the former novel because it is set during and just after World War II, the latter because military music was a more important part of the musical landscape in the eighteenth century. Although the absolute figure for *Mason & Dixon* is relatively low (only four), the discussion of bagpipes as a means of sonic warfare, the debate about the American national anthem, and the inclusion of military or patriotic songs written by Pynchon support this explanation.

Almost half of the 207 classical references are to opera (99), whereas only about an eighth of the 516 popular music references

9 In *Against the Day*, Pynchon slips in a pun on minor vs. miner: "Ellmore Disco did not appear to be of either Mexican or Finnish descent [...] —more like music-hall Chinese, maybe, the way his eyes retreated into protective pouches, leaving the observer with a ruinous C major ('or as they say in this town, "A miner"') octave on some abandoned upright [...]" (321).

are to musicals/Broadway (59, plus six Broadway references coded as 'jazz').

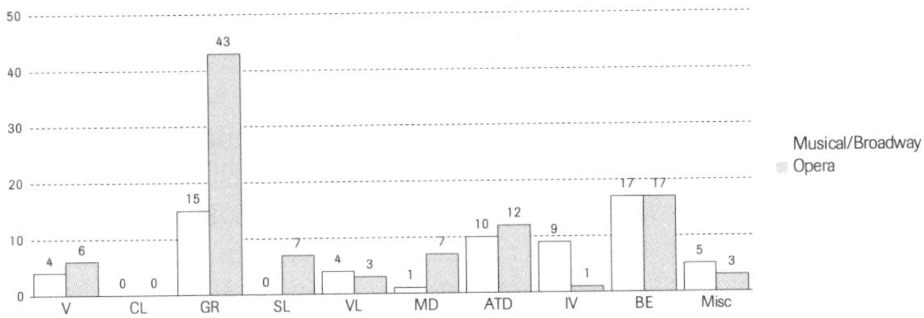

Fig. 9: Number of opera vs. musicals/Broadway references.

What is particularly interesting about these two sub-genres is that Pynchon has references to these two types of stage production in each of his novels except *The Crying of Lot 49*, in his short stories, and in his miscellaneous writings. Even in *Mason & Dixon* he sneaks in a brief allusion to "Singin' in the Rain," and in *Inherent Vice* Doc orders Eel Trovatore. The largest number of references to opera is in *Gravity's Rainbow*, with Wagner, Rossini, Verdi, Puccini, and others. The largest number of references to musicals is in *Bleeding Edge*, a novel set mainly in New York City. *Against the Day* has only five references to musicals but there are a number of fictional operettas or early forms of musical, particularly when the plot is set in New York City. Productions with a narrative—opera, operetta, musical, and also film—may be particularly useful as referring to them allows Pynchon also to allude to their plots, dramas, and conflicts, and to the light they cast on his own stories. Particularly in *V.* and *Gravity's Rainbow*, as David Cowart has demonstrated, many of the Puccini and Wagner references comment on or foreshadow the novel's plot (*Allusion*, see also Chapter 1 of this book).

If classical music and opera are part of the 'high' art discourse, then pop music and musicals are part of the 'low' art discourse. By continually referencing these two types of stage production that are nearly identical in their outward and visible form, Pynchon as a postmodern writer undermines this high/low distinction. With the exception of deriding Andrew Lloyd Webber, the occasional crooner, or muzak or new age as a genre, it is rare that a musician or a form of music is portrayed or referenced in a condescending manner, no matter how 'high' or 'low.' The undercurrent seems to be that it can all be appreciated for what it is and for the joy it brings its audience.

There are hardly any references to musicals that reached the stage after the mid-1970s when the genre enjoyed a revival following the early successes of Lloyd Webber. This is partly due to the fact that most of the novels are set before that time. However, the derisive treatment of Lloyd Webber allows for other explanations as well: one, Pynchon may think the newer musicals are less exciting and less subtle than the classic Broadway musicals; two, the classic Broadway musicals, for Pynchon, were a cultural force with many of the tunes becoming jazz standards, while the more current musicals, although widely popular, did not have a reach far beyond their stage performances and the occasional film adaptation.

Certain objects, characters, and themes recur as intratextual links among Pynchon's novels. Such is the case with toilets, light bulbs, ukuleles, and drugs, to name only a few. Sometimes, these links indicate a historical or social continuity among the novels in their themes and concerns, sometimes they allow Pynchon to give a new twist to something developed or hinted at before, and sometimes they appear to be mere tongue-in-cheek resonances for the delectation of readers who spot them. Many of these recurring objects, characters, and themes were already present in his first two novels, and perhaps part of the insistent referencing of both operas and musicals throughout his work—often with recurring composers and librettists—has to do simply with Pynchon's love of intratextual references among his novels. However, he also seems to imply that the great themes of literature in a broad sense—novels, operas, and musicals—the great themes of humanity perhaps, namely love and death, remain the same, from Orpheus to Broadway.

Temporal Distribution

Partially overlapping with genre considerations are the musical works' release years. I assigned years only to works, leaving it to future researchers to catalog the active years of composers and musicians. Where sources indicate only an approximate time of creation or release (such as '1890s'), I calculated a fictional average (1895).

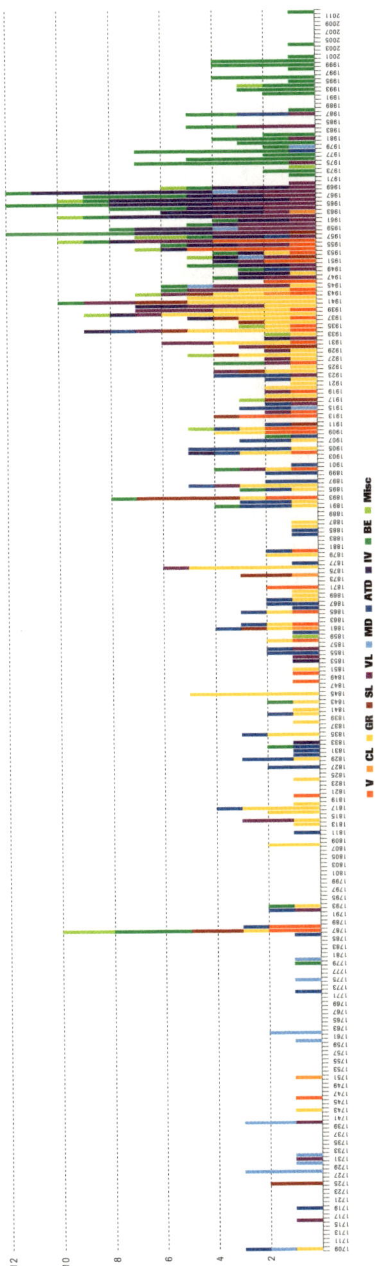

Fig. 10: Temporal distribution of musical references since 1709 (ten entries before 1709 are omitted for better legibility: 1250, 1261, 1350, 1635, 1646, and 1659).

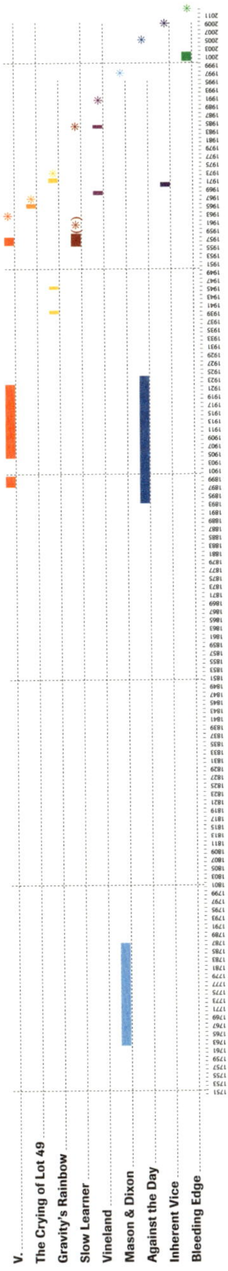

Fig. 11: Approximate time span covered by the novels; * indicates year of publication.

The earliest release or publication dates of the referenced works are 1261 ("O Salutaris Hostia" by St. Thomas Aquinas), the fourteenth-century ("In dulci jubilo" by Heinrich von Seuse), and the seventeenth century (three works). The most recent ones are 2001 ("Ulitchnyi Boyets" by Detsl [*Bleeding* 141]) and 2005 ("Piggy Bank" by 50 Cent [282]), although the latter is obviously anachronistic and only inferred from the context of Darren's rap song ("Tryin to do Tupac and Biggie thangs / with red velvet Chairman Mao piggy banks"). One allusion from 2012, the year before *Bleeding Edge* was published, may not have been intended, but I decided to include it for the beauty of multiple resonances: "Chalk Outline" by Three Days Grace (see above, note 4).

Figure 10 shows the temporal distribution of the 572 datable works of music. This distribution does not come as a surprise. Firstly, Pynchon is writing in the twentieth and twenty-first centuries so the musical references closer to his own time can be expected to be more familiar and important to him. Secondly, the distribution also mirrors the periods in which the novels take place, with most novels and episodes being set in the twentieth century. Whether the eighteenth century (*Mason & Dixon*) or the nineteenth (parts of *V.* and *Against the Day*) is more prominent in terms of narratives is open to discussion. The distribution may also mirror the availability of mass-produced music in households, first as sheet music, then additionally as recorded music, paralleled by the availability of musical instruments and the access to music education.

Broken down to decades, the 1960s have the highest number of entries (82), followed by the 1950s (68), the 1940s (53), and the 1930s (49). The most frequent years are:

Year	Entries
1958	12
1965	12
1968	12
1787	10
1941	10
1956	10
1962	10
1966	10
1934	9
1938	9

1967	9
1893	8
1959	8
1964	8
1939	7
1940	7
1943	7
1954	7
1957	7
1975	7
1978	7

Table 3: Most frequent years of release of the works of music.

Pynchon managed to have at least one reference for every year from 1913 to 1970. The major gaps in the twentieth century are in the 1980s (four years missing), 1990s, and 1900s (three years missing each).

The years 1958, 1965, and 1968 are the most frequent years. At first, it may not be unexpected to see 1968, a key year of the counterculture, appear near the top of the list. However, the actual references show a different picture. All 1968 references are part of nostalgic mainstream culture, except for two Tiny Tim songs (whose unique strangeness perhaps allows teenagers, their parents, and their grandparents alike to enjoy them); Iron Butterfly's "In-A-Gadda-Da-Vida," which, depending on the version, reaches up to seventeen minutes in length; and the Bonzo Dog Band's recording of "Bang Bang (My Baby Shot Me Down)." Much of the 'hippie' or psychedelic music (Jimi Hendrix, The Doors, The Rolling Stones, The Byrds, Jefferson Airplane, Pink Floyd, Procol Harum) comes from 1967 and 1966. This may indicate that 1967's Summer of Love (and its Monterey Pop Festival) was a turning point after which television, the commercial music industry, and petit-bourgeois sentiments started to co-opt and reterritorialize countercultural energies.[10]

10 Of course, this is a bit reductionist. In *Nation of Rebels*, Joseph Heath and Andrew Potter argue that it was precisely the counterculture which brought about the consumer society it opposed. And Thomas Frank writes: "[T]he 1967 'summer of love' was as much a product of lascivious television specials and *Life* magazine stories as it was an expression of youthful disaffection.

The prominence of 1958 is accounted for by four entries for "Volare" and two entries for "The Chipmunk Song," together making up half of that year's entries. The high number of entries for 1787 is owing to Mozart's *Don Giovanni*, the musical work most frequently referenced or alluded to by Pynchon (nine entries), and Mozart's "Ein musikalischer Spass," K. 522, from the Spike Jones liner notes (one entry).

The starting point of *Against the Day*, 1893, is also the year when Puccini's opera *Manon Lescaut* (with seven entries the runner-up among musical works) premiered. The other 1893 reference is a medley of Tchaikovsky's *Pathétique* (Symphony No. 6 in B minor, Op. 74) (*Gravity* 716). *Against the Day* itself, however, does not contain a single reference to music published in 1893.

To get an even closer look at the novels and to relate them to one another as well as to their times of narration (including analepses), one would ideally catalog every single item according to its context and draw up a diagram ranging from the thirteenth century to 2012 to locate every musical entry (and, to top it off, to note the active time in the referenced composers' and musicians' lives). Such an undertaking, however, is beyond the scope of this investigation and would exceed the possibilities of representation in a book. For an approximation, see Figures 10 and 11.

Figure 10 shows—at this point not unexpectedly—that Pynchon and his narrators and characters have a broad knowledge of music, from classical works to contemporary pop. I expected the release years of the entries to cluster sometime shortly before the time of the plot. However, except in the case of *Inherent Vice* and, to a lesser degree *V.* and *Gravity's Rainbow*, this does not seem to be the case. The majority of entries in *Inherent Vice* start with the period of Doc Sportello's adolescence. By 1970, when he turns thirty, the music he grew up with has transitioned into the music just before the time of the narration, which may account for a pronounced peak (between 1958 and 1969), which cannot be observed in any of the other novels except possibly for *Vineland*. (Of course, that period also coincides with Pynchon's own youth as he is Doc's senior by only three years.) In the case of *Bleeding Edge*, the entries peak, broadly speaking, between 1964 and

[...] So oppressive was the climate of national voyeurism that, as early as the fall of 1967, the San Francisco Diggers had held a funeral for 'Hippie, devoted son of mass media'" (7).

1981, which is probably the time between Maxine Tarnow's birth and the end of her adolescence (assuming she was born sometime between 1960 and 1965). Another, less pronounced, peak in that novel is the five years leading up to 2001. In *Gravity's Rainbow*, there is also a greater number of entries between Tyrone Slothrop's birth (c. 1920) and his early twenties but it is a less visible peak than those in *Inherent Vice*, *Vineland*, and *Bleeding Edge*. These latter peaks may indicate either that music, likely pop, worth listening to surged in the 1960s (after the somewhat bland 1950s), or that the baby boomers are less erudite than previous generations when it comes to music, or that a shift toward taking pop music seriously has occurred. As has been observed before, it may also have to do with the smaller number of main characters through which Pynchon focalizes the stories. Or, finally, it could be the more encompassing media environment featuring contemporary popular music that sets the musical tone of these novels: discotheque (1947), LP (1948), 45-rpm single (1949), color TV (1954), surge in FM radio (late 1950s), Musicassette (1962), first DJ mixers (1960s), color TV in majority of households (1965). One could argue that it does not suffice to discuss only the protagonists since Pynchon's novels are populated by a great number of characters, but it turns out that many of the supporting characters are within the same age bracket as the protagonists: the members of the Whole Sick Crew, except for Stencil, appear to be more or less within the same age bracket; the same goes for Maxine Tarnow's, Doc Sportello's, and Zoyd Wheeler's friends and for a number of characters around Tyrone Slothrop. The antagonists tend to be slightly older but they show little if any inclination toward music.

Anachronisms

These diagrams indicate some anachronisms. Many of them depend on deductions the reader may or may not make from certain allusions Pynchon has cleverly planted. This is particularly visible in *Mason & Dixon*, for instance, the "Moses supposes" line from *Singin' in the Rain* (456), Frank Sinatra's "Don't Forget Tonight, Tomorrow" (78), Ray Charles's "What'd I Say" (79), The Bellami Brothers' "You Ain't Just Whistlin' Dixie" (441), and Tammy Wynette's "Stand by Your Man" (621). Since *Mason & Dixon* dates back the farthest, it lends itself most to such playful anachronisms. These allusions are part of dialogues and not embedded in a musical context, and it appears that Pynchon is just having fun with them. The full lyrics of the songs alluded to may also comment on the plot but this usually remains at a superficial and local level. The anachronisms do not appear to comment on the story or its themes as a whole and they do not seem to comment on, for instance, the history of music. In one instance, as far as I can tell the only one in Pynchon's work, the anachronism is openly revealed. In a dream, Mason is visited by Death: "'Well Hullo, Death, what's that you're whistling?' —'Oo, little Ditters von Dittersdorf, nothing you'd recognize, hasn't happen'd yet, not even sure you'll live till it's perform'd anywhere,—have to check the 'Folio as to that, get back to you?'" (750). Since Dittersdorf (1739–1799) was already an active composer then and "scraps" of his music are played earlier on in the novel (104), the reader would not recognize the anachronism if Pynchon had not hinted at it. It might well be that Pynchon had *Doktor und Apotheker* in mind, Dittersdorf's most successful work premiered three-and-a-half months before Mason's death.

Occasionally, musical references help establish the chronology of events, especially in the more convoluted plots. Such is the case, for instance, when Umeki says that "There is a new Puccini opera. [...] Butterfly" (*Against* 636). *Madama Butterfly* was first performed in 1904 and came to the United States in 1906, which gives the reader temporal orientation. Since the reader can expect Pynchon to be very exact and informed about his references, an anachronism can be disorienting. Such an inconsistency can be frustrating when trying to keep track of the chronology but it may also open the field to novel interpretations: history may be repeating itself while its lines of conflict remain the same; an early bootleg version—perhaps a fictional one—of which only the author has knowledge may have existed; the reader should question long-held assumptions about storytelling and historiography; the author is attempting to rewrite history; the source the author consulted conflicts with that of the reader; the reference in that exact place was too tempting to resist or was a private joke; it is a reminder that the novel is, in Linda Hutcheon's terms, a work of historiographic metafiction, and that not everything dressed up as historical fact is to be taken as a "'page right out of history,' as the Flintstones might say" (*Inherent* 235). In spite of all these possible explanations, it may also be that, at times, Pynchon was simply "too lazy to find out" (*Learner* 16).

Apart from entries in the Playlist that were inferred from context, a number of anachronisms appear either inadvertent (or maybe Pynchon's sources differed from mine) or quite deliberate. In *Mason & Dixon*, George Washington's slave Gershom sings "'Havah Nagilah,' a merry Jewish Air, whilst clicking together a pair of Spoons in Syncopation" (285), likely a sign of the brother- and sisterhood of Preterites around the world. The Hebrew folk song originated only in the 1910s or 1920s. In *Vineland*, "on some stereo, Zoyd Wheeler could hear Little Charlie and the Nightcats singing 'TV Crazy'" (43). Although the band formed in 1976, it is unlikely that Zoyd could hear a recording of them in 1984, except as a bootleg, since their first album (containing "T.V. Crazy") was issued in 1987.

In 1893 or thereabouts, Lew Basnight attends an anarchist meeting where the "company began to sing, from the Workers' Own Songbook, though mostly without the aid of the text, choral selections including Hubert Parry's recent setting of Blake's 'Jerusalem,' taken not unreasonably as a great anticapitalist anthem disguised as a choir piece" (55). Although William Blake published his poem around 1808, it was only in 1916 that Hubert Parry set it to music. It may be that the "recent setting" expresses the narrator's viewpoint but that seems unlikely since the story extends to about 1922, which would stretch the notion of 'recent.' Besides, that would not explain why the anarchists sing the anthem more than twenty years before it was created. The reference to "Ausgerechnet Bananen" (803) also seems misplaced as the time of the plot at this point is somewhere around 1905–07 and the tune originated c. 1922. Maybe Pynchon's fondness for bananas (see, for instance, their prominence in *Gravity's Rainbow* and *Inherent Vice*) made this insertion irresistible. *Against the Day* appears to have more chronological inconsistencies than the other novels, especially around 1900–1903, as various contributors to the PynchonWiki have noticed and tried unsuccessfully to make sense of. Readers of *Gravity's Rainbow* are familiar with the reversal of cause and effect, which may help them contextualize the allusions to Parker tunes in the Charlie Parker passage. Along the same lines, the most readily available explanation of anachronisms in *Against the Day*—besides as mistakes or flights of fancy—is that this is the novel that introduces time travel in various forms, technological and otherwise, so a song can somehow hail from the future.

Gender Distribution

My reading experience made me suspect that female musicians were underrepresented with respect to the mark they made in pop-music history, and I was curious about the frequency of references to male and female artists. One can also investigate other categories, such as artists' ethnic background (as I have done for *Inherent Vice* in the previous chapter) or nationality, but the male/female category was of most immediate interest to me, which is why I will discuss it as an example of what else can be done with such statistical material once descriptors of interest have been added.

References that included only men or only women were coded as 'male' or 'female' respectively. References to songs co-written by men and women, songs written by men and sung by women, and mixed bands were coded as 'both' (in Pynchon's novels there are no songs written by women and performed or recorded by men). The four occurrences of "On the Good Ship Lollipop," written by two men and sung by five- or six-year-old Shirley Temple (accompanied by an airplane full of men), was coded as 'male.' This is open to debate but I felt uneasy assigning 'female' to a small girl, and, from today's perspective, one cannot help but see the men in the *Bright Eyes* movie scene as leering at the five- or six-year-old girl with a male pedophile gaze, as Graham Greene observed.[11] There are no references to artists on the trans-spectrum.

11 Allegations of pedophilia were made as early as 1937 in a film review by Graham Greene in *Night and Day* (reprinted in the *Grahame Greene Film Reader* 233–35), and it is likely that Pynchon knew of them. Greene writes: "Miss Shirley Temple's case, though, has peculiar interest: infancy is her disguise, her appeal is more secret and more adult [...]. Her admirers—middle-aged men and clergymen—respond to her dubious coquetry, to the sight of her well-shaped and desirable little body, packed with enormous vitality, only because the safety curtain of story and dialogue drops between their intelligence and their desire." 20th Century Fox subsequently sued Greene and *Night and Day*. Greene fled to Mexico and *Night and Day* shut down. With one exception (*Inherent* 360), Pynchon appears to link Shirley Temple to the topic of pedophilia and child abuse. Besides the performances of Shirley Temple songs on the orgy ship Anubis (*Gravity's Rainbow*) by the girl Bianca who will later be killed, Pynchon names a child bordello the Lollipop Lounge (*Against* 449). Jules Siegel remembered that Pynchon loved Siegel's wife's Shirley Temple impersonations of "'On the Good Ship Lollipop' sung and danced like a kid at a birthday party" (96).

The gender frequencies of the musical references reveal a quite unequal distribution:

Male	850
Female	36
Both/mixed	43
N/A	6

Table 4: Gender distribution of musical references.

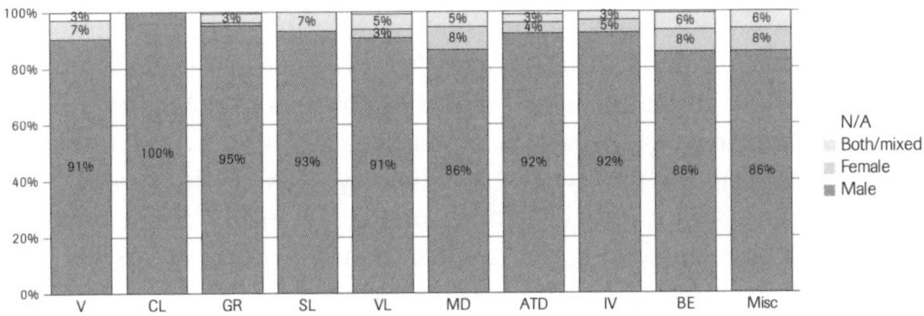

Fig. 12: Gender distribution per novel.

Four possible explanations can be offered for this distribution. First, music at a commercial level is or has been, as James Brown sez in a slightly different context, a man's world. Second, Pynchon may not try very hard to be more inclusive. Third, Pynchon himself may be more attuned to music written and recorded by men. Four, the majority of characters are men and as such they may be more attuned to music by male artists and composers.

The first explanation is supported by the more frequent occurrence of women musicians in the novels that take place after 1968, albeit still at a low level and nowhere near the frequency of male composers, songwriters, and performers. There were few well-known female composers and instrumentalists in classical European music or in jazz of the earlier twentieth century. With the rise of a large-scale music industry and women's liberation (which also brought women in as more of a target group in the mass music market), women musicians were more frequently produced. Both jazz and rock'n'roll were sexually charged genres from the start, as is evidenced by their names and by the attitudes of their male performers. First the saxophone and then the guitar as lead instruments of popular-music combos were (and still are) associated with the phallus. To this day, the aggression inherent in much of rock'n'roll music is associated with male performers. Only a few women, such as those in the Riot grrrl movement (*Bleeding* 347), have been able to reclaim some of this attitude for themselves, although never achieving as much commercial success as their male counterparts.

In the music of the West, women appear as singers much more frequently than as instrumentalists or composers. This is also the case in Pynchon's work. Of the 35 references to women, only three entries are not immediately associated with vocalists: Marianne Davies, who was the first person to publicly play Benjamin Franklin's glass armonica (*Mason* 268, 272), and Eugénie Lineff, who collected Russian and Ukrainian folk songs (*Against* 1057). Some of the other women mentioned also wrote or co-wrote songs but usually appear as vocalists.[12] Twenty-four of the female references are associated with pop music. *Bleeding Edge* with its female protagonist Maxine Tarnow has the highest number of female references (13) and references coded 'both' (10), but it still has nowhere near the number of male references. *Vineland* has slightly more female references than do most of the other books (except for *Inherent Vice* and *Bleeding Edge*). This may be due to the time in which it is set (i.e. 1968 and beyond) and to the female characters that take up more space than in his other novels.

The question remains whether Pynchon's references represent the role women play in the history of music. One way to answer this is to look at the number of fictional female musicians. Doing so reveals a similar, perhaps even more unbalanced picture. Although there is a small number of female singers, there are very few female instrumentalists. One exception is the nameless female tenor sax player traveling alone on a bus, as remembered by the black bass player Mr. McAfee in "The Secret Integration" (*Learner* 180). Another one is the "curious sort of hippie chick," the "stylish chanteuse" who plays the piano and sings Rodgers & Hart and Dietz & Schwartz torch songs in *Inherent Vice* (160). Both are minor characters viewed through male eyes. They are

12 Many of the female vocalists in Pynchon's work are also actresses: Carmen Miranda, Dolly Parton, Rocío Durcal, Irene Dunne, Marni Nixon, Tia Carrere, Shelley Fabares, and Judy Casanova.

nowhere near as interesting or well-developed as McClintic Sphere, Coy Harlingen, or the many all-male bands in Pynchon's work. The only prominent female instrumentalist is oboist Aunt Euphrenia.

As was shown in the discussion of *Inherent Vice* in the previous chapter, when it comes to pop music, Pynchon references many songs that were at the top of the *Billboard* charts at one time or another. Therefore, another way to examine the question of misrepresentation of female artists is to take a look at the *Billboard* Hot 100 number-one singles charts to see if women were underrepresented to the same extent in the history of pop music. The following figure indicates the number of weeks that female, mixed, and male acts led the charts in the respective years:

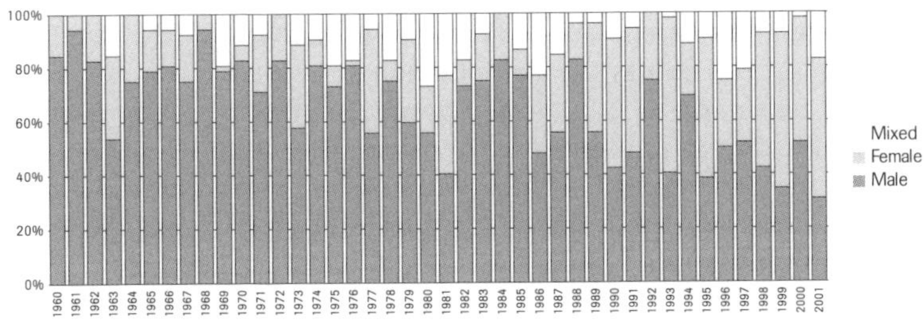

Fig. 13: Gender distribution for Billboard Hot 100 number-one singles charts, 1960–2001. Source: Wikipedia and author's own compilation.

The time span has been selected to accord roughly with the years in which *The Crying of Lot 49*, *Vineland*, *Inherent Vice*, and *Bleeding Edge* take place or in which their characters were in their youth or young adulthood. Since nearly all the #1 female acts in that time frame were vocalists (except for a handful of female bands with female instrumentalists too), Pynchon's depiction of female musicians as vocalists is close to pop-chart reality. However, it is nowhere near the singles-chart distribution of female, male, and mixed acts. A possible explanation is that many musical references are focalized through male characters whereas female artists tend to play music that is more appealing to a female audience. Still, given *Vineland*, *Bleeding Edge* or even *The Crying of Lot 49*, with their female protagonists, one would expect more references to female musicians.

Although I have not collected statistics for the distribution of references to commercially successful black (mainly African-American) artists in Pynchon's work, I have a strong feeling that black artists are underrepresented too. The difference from the misrepresenation of women is that, even though music composed and performed by black artists may be underrepresented, Pynchon partially makes up for that by having a number of black musicians as supporting characters, by introducing black surf music (Meatball Flag's "Soul Gidget" in *Inherent Vice* and *Bleeding Edge*), and by presenting ruminations on African-American music and exposing the racism inherent in its reception by white audiences (in the case of McClintic Sphere in *V.* and of Maman Tant Gras Hall in *Against the Day*). No similar gestures can be found for music written or performed by women. Some of this lack may be owing to the focalization but, in my estimation, this does not suffice to explain it away. Music in Pynchon's world remains an affair of predominantly white men.

It is not a fiction writer's obligation to include minority groups and groups that in the history of Western civilization had to fight to be granted the same rights as white men in possession of a certain fortune. Nor is it a novelist's obligation to represent his or her own demographics or social standing. However, while I do not intend to fault Pynchon for underrepresenting female artists, I cannot fail to notice that the number of female musicians in his novels is at odds with the tendency toward realism or verisimilitude that characterizes the musical references and allusions in almost every other category discussed, and it is at odds with Pynchon's track record of female protagonists and with his unwavering allegiance to the Preterite of all kinds.

Most Frequent References

The Playlist (including complementary information) was run through the Linguist extension for LibreOffice and through wordcounter.net for a word frequency count. The most frequent words were then matched manually with the Playlist to ensure that no mistakes had been made (for instance, single entries for different people with the same last name). The most frequently referenced composers and musicians are:

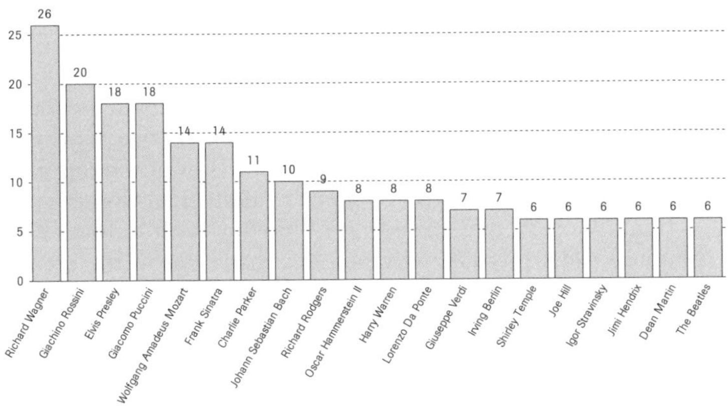

Fig. 14: Most frequently referenced composers and musicians.

Wagner, Rossini, and Puccini are no surprise.[13] Elvis Presley, however, might more easily be overlooked in the process of reading the novels, perhaps because there are no musicological discussions in Pynchon's work involving the King of Rock'n'Roll. Richard Rodgers and Oscar Hammerstein II are rarely mentioned explicitly, but as the co-authors of numerous musicals, they have made it to this Pynchon Playlist Billboard Chart. Something similar goes for Mozart's librettist Lorenzo da Ponte, Tin Pan Alley composer Harry Warren, and Irving Berlin. The Beatles, as a band, are mentioned only twice; however, each Beatle is referenced once in Pynchon's work, adding up to six entries. Dean Martin is also easily overlooked, making appearances only in *Bleeding Edge* and *Inherent Vice,* and context does not always allow distinguishing between Dean Martin the actor and Dean Martin the singer (the same is the case with Frank Sinatra). Of the twenty top-placed musicians, composers, and librettists, eight are associated with classical or new classical music, five with musicals or Tin Pan Alley, three with rock music; two are crooners, and only one—the idol of the Beat Generation—is clearly a jazz

13 One Puccini reference occurs in a paragraph in a review copy of *Bleeding Edge* that was deleted from the release edition. I included it here because relatively few other last-minute changes were made before the official release. This was a purely personal decision to honor my bookseller who procured me a review copy.

musician. Joe Hill, the hobo, union leader, and musician, makes it onto this list partly because of Pynchon's sympathy with the plight of the working class, and partly because he wrote the lyrics to "The Preacher and the Slave" (also known as "Pie in the Sky").

Eleven entries are Americans, four Italians, two Germans, one Austrian, one British, and one Russian. Half of the top-place musicians are associated with composers of musical works for the stage (mainly opera and Broadway). Starting with *V.* but less so in the more recent works, Pynchon has made use of the plots of opera to structure his own plots or to allude and foreshadow (as with Porpentine in *V.*). However, there are also other explanations for the high number of references to classical composers. One is that, unless employed anachronistically, references can be made only ex post. An explicit Beatles reference in *V.*, *Against the Day*, or *Mason & Dixon* would not work (an allusion still might), but a Bach reference can appear in any of Pynchon's books. Another explanation is that, when it comes to classical music, a limited number of canonical composers is available for reference unless one were to unearth quite obscure ones, whereas pop music, being closer to our time and possibly more diverse, offers a much greater number of recognizable artists.

Musicians and composers are not distributed equally over Pynchon's work. The many Wagner and Rossini references are due primarily to *Gravity's Rainbow*. While Mozart and Charlie Parker each appear in seven books (grouping the miscellaneous writings as one 'book'), followed by Elvis and Puccini (six books each), the Wagner and Rossini references are less evenly distributed (four and three books, respectively). Generally, Pynchon seems to have been more interested in 'serious' or 'high' European classical and new classical music in his early work (*V.*, *Gravity's Rainbow*, *Slow Learner*), where he mentions Beethoven, Wagner, Schoenberg, Stravinsky, Webern, Berg, and a number of others, sometimes discussing their work or their place in music history. After c. 1973, those composers appear less often or not at all, and the only references to opera are to romantic operas and *opera buffa*.

While Pynchon references only one Mozart opera, *Don Giovanni*, and only three Verdi operas, *Rigoletto*, *La forza del destino*, and *Il Trovatore*, he lives up to his reputation as an encyclopedic writer with Wagner, Rossini, and Puccini. Besides referencing all four operas of Wagner's *Der Ring des Nibelungen* cycle (*Das Rheingold*, *Die Walküre*, *Siegfried*, and *Götterdämmerung*) as well as the cycle itself, he also references *Tristan und Isolde*,

Die Meistersinger von Nürnberg, Tannhäuser, and *Der fliegende Holländer.* These are eight of the ten operas Wagner chose to be performed on the Grüner Hügel at Bayreuth, which makes me think I may have overlooked allusions to the remaining two, *Parsifal* and *Lohengrin.*[14] While some of these references are explicit, others are only hinted at. Such is the case of Miss Rheingold, a reference to the beauty pageant of the American Rheingold brewery, which has its fictional counterpart in Fräulein Müller-Hochleben (a word-for-word translation of "Miss Miller High Life").

For Rossini, Pynchon references *Il barbiere di Siviglia, Guillaume Tell, La gazza ladra, Tancredi,* and *L'italiana in Algeri.* Since I decided not to include musical references in the names of characters, the character Andrea Tancredi in *Against the Day* does not figure on the playlist. For Puccini, Pynchon references *Manon Lescaut, Madama Butterfly* (Pynchon prefers to write it *Madame Butterfly* in line with the title of John Luther Long's short story on which the opera is based), *La Bohème, Tosca,* and *Turandot.* Many of these works remain among the most popular and most frequently performed operas in the world, which provides a link to Pynchon's treatment of popular music.

The most frequently referenced works of music are:

	References	Books
Don Giovanni (W. A. Mozart, 1787)	9	5
Manon Lescaut (G. Puccini, 1893)	7	3
"On the Good Ship Lollipop" (R. A. Whiting/S. Clare, 1934)	5	4
"Star-Spangled Banner"/ "Anacreon in Heaven" (1760s/1814)	5	3
Tannhäuser (R. Wagner, 1845)	5	1
"Madamina, il catalogo è questo" (W. A. Mozart, 1787)	4	4
"Volare" (F. Migliacci/D. Modugno, 1958)	4	3
"Meet the Flintstones" (H. Curtin, 1960)	4	3
La gazza ladra (G. Rossini, 1817)	4	2

Table 5: Most frequently referenced works of music.

14 Cowart sees parallels to *Parsifal* but since they are at the level of plot and not musical references, this opera does not appear in the Playlist (*Allusion* 130–131).

It makes sense that longer musical works are at the top of this list since they contain more material to work with and since, for instance, the additional information in the catalog made it possible to link an aria to the opera in which it occurs. Still, Pynchon explicitly mentions only two arias each from *Don Giovanni* and *Manon Lescaut* and no particular piece from *La gazza ladra* (except for the overture of the latter, played by an organ grinder [*Gravity* 277]). "Volare," as *Bleeding Edge* has it, is "arguably among the greatest pop tunes ever written" (154). Except for the "Star-Spangled Banner" and "Anacreon in Heaven" (see the *Mason & Dixon* section of Chapter 3 for an extensive discussion), all of the above works are from either opera or TV/film, including "On the Good Ship Lollipop" discussed above. Five of the nine references are in Italian, the 'language of song,' and none of the musicals referenced are mentioned as often as the most frequent operas. Many of the explanations offered in different contexts appear to be valid here: Pynchon privileges works of music that are embedded in a narrative of sorts (opera, musical, or TV/film) because this gives him more freedom to draw parallels or contrasts with his own narratives. The list includes both classical and pop music ('high' and 'low'), but musicals may be less frequently represented because they may have had less 'high culture' appeal to the young Pynchon or because the canon of musicals is smaller than that of operas.

Songs Penned by Pynchon

In discussions of music in Pynchon's work, a number of scholars have discussed Pynchon's own songs that do not come with sheet music but more often than not come with lyrics, and sometimes even with indications of the tempo, meter, or musical style (see Chapter 1). Figure 15 shows the number of songs Pynchon has created. Naturally, the ones for which he provides lyrics are more interesting for further research, which is why songs with four or more lines (rather than only the title or a one-liner) are identified separately.

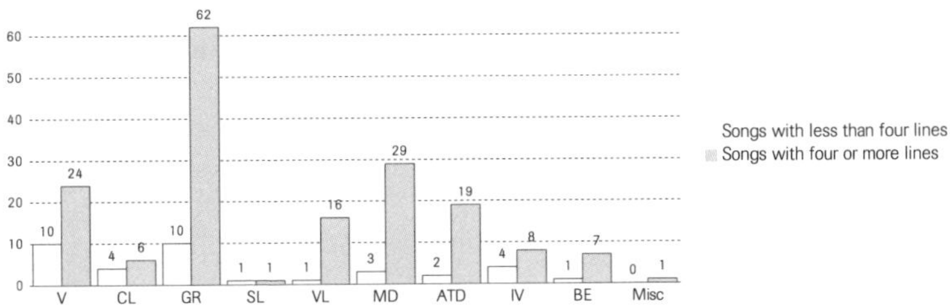

Fig. 15: Pynchon's own songs (absolute) by books.

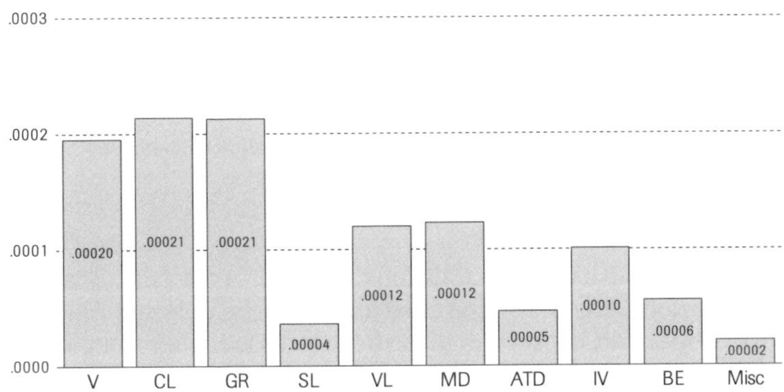

Fig. 16: Pynchon's own songs (relative to number of words).

Hess's statement that, in *Mason & Dixon*, "Pynchon's self-composed song lyrics appear [...] with roughly the same frequency that they do in his other works" (2) may be correct if we look only at the average across all the books (*Mason & Dixon* and *Vineland* are the only novels whose frequencies come within roughly 10% of the average). However, since the frequencies differ so greatly (the density of Pynchon's own lyrics in *Gravity's Rainbow* compared to in *Bleeding Edge* or *Against the Day*), it is difficult to maintain the notion of "the same frequency" across all of Pynchon's works. Looking only at an average risks failing to take into account specific differences among the books and thus not recognizing possible trends, such as the rough division into three distinct groups I discussed at the beginning of this chapter.

Comparing the density of Pynchon's own songs and the number of musical references in the Playlist yields the following:

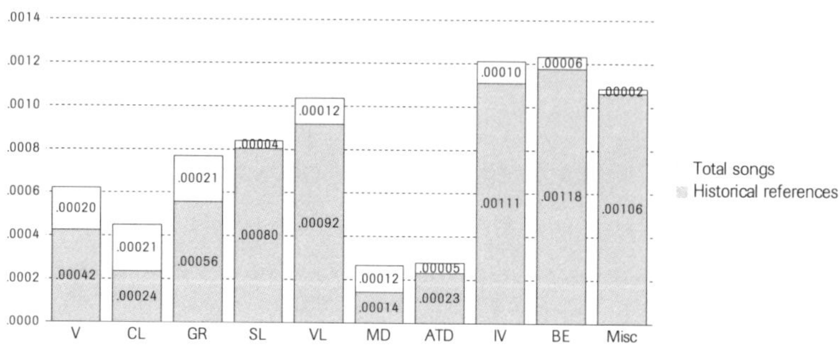

Fig. 17: Pynchon's own songs vs. number of historical references (relative to number of words).

If enough provisions and exclusions are made, patterns can always be discerned. This is also the case for the above diagram. The density of Pynchon's own songs in earlier works is higher than in later ones (except for *Vineland* whose density is considerably lower than the other pre-1998 works). The four longest novels—those I consider the more accomplished works due to their length, their global outlook, their treatment of a wide variety of subjects, and the lines of conflicts they present (*V.*, *Gravity's Rainbow*, *Mason & Dixon*, *Against the Day*)—have a higher density of Pynchon's own songs, with the exception of *Against the Day*. It is also notable that the three novels set after 1967 have by far the lowest density of Pynchon's own songs. Harking back to Attali, this relative scarcity is perhaps another comment on the imagined effects of the music industry, that it stifles creativity and that "each person listen[s] in solitude, confinement, and mutual silence" (*Inherent* 176). Or perhaps Pynchon simply became tired of writing lyrics. Only the next novel may tell. In the case of *Mason & Dixon*, which has the highest ratio of Pynchon's own songs to historical references, it is conceivable that he wanted to complement the presumably less cluttered musical soundscape in the eighteenth century by adding his own music to it.

Distribution of Media

Of great interest are the media through which music is played, and the extent to which the distribution of these media may corroborate what has been observed before about technology, mass production, and their effects on listening and playing habits. Each entry in the playlist is categorized according to whether, in the context, it is played or sung live (or referred to as a live performance), comes through the TV or the radio, is recorded music, or cannot, in fact, be categorized because no particular medium can be inferred, for instance, when characters talk about music. Initially, there was also a category 'film' (that is, cinema); but that yielded only one entry in the miscellaneous writings, so it was dropped. 'Recorded music' comprises records, CDs, tapes, music files, sound chips, and hard drives.

The following figure shows the percentages of each medium in every book:

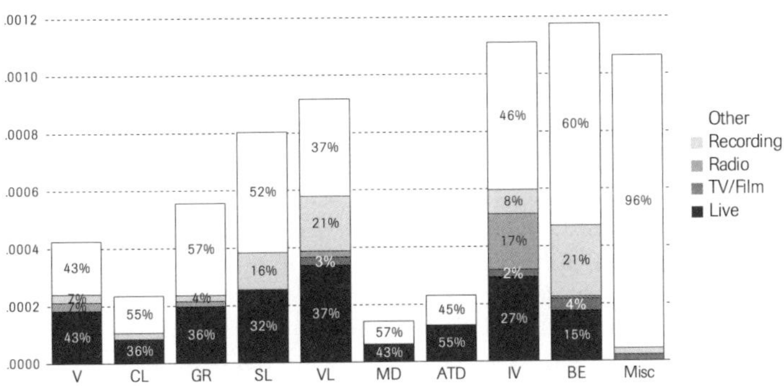

Fig. 18: Percentages of music media per book.

The first thing to notice is that there is much less overall variation than in some of the other categories that have been analyzed. Except in *Vineland* and *Against the Day*, the 'Other' category (i.e. references that could not be attributed to a particular medium, usually because music was not played but referred to by a character or the narrator) is always between 37 % and 60 % of the total number of references; in the first six books, the 'live' category is always between 32 % and 43 %.

Totaling the percentages of recorded music, radio, and TV ('schizophonic' music in R. Murray Schafer's terminology), the three novels *Vineland*, *Inherent Vice*, and *Bleeding Edge* all range between 25% and 29%, the highest in the diagram, although *Inherent Vice*'s distribution among these three media differs from the other novels' in the much higher number of tunes played on the (mainly car) radio (I suspect that *Inherent Vice* is the novel in which most car driving is done). These three novels also have the lowest percentages of live music, although *Vineland*'s number is only slightly lower than those of *V.*, *The Crying of Lot 49*, *Gravity's Rainbow*, and *Mason & Dixon*. Although music from a stereo or P.A. system is by far the most common in the category 'recorded music,' Pynchon also introduced sound chip–related music starting in *Vineland*: a police siren plays the theme from *Jeopardy*, there is a sounding business card, and a robot fridge plays "Winter Wonderland," "Let It Snow," and "Cold, Cold Heart." In *Inherent Vice*, a coffee machine plays "Volare," and in *Bleeding Edge*, there is a cell phone ring tone of "Una furtiva lagrima," a doorbell with the Westminster Chimes, a sound chip with "Baby Beluga," slippers playing the *Jaws* theme, and a car horn sounding the *Godfather* theme. Pynchon follows and reflects the development of the music industry in which, for many listeners, physical carriers of analog sound were increasingly replaced by chips, hard drives, flash drives, and other digital media. This evolution also brings to mind the development of computer games (which, for Pynchon, culminates in a 'real-life' reenactment of Tetris when the Campanile in Venice is destroyed in *Against the Day*) and speech synthesis. *Against the Day* contains two references to "Daisy Bell (Bicycle Built for Two)," the first song that was used to demonstrate speech synthesis, a song that also appears in Stanley Kubrick's *2001: A Space Odyssey*. The novel starts with the Chicago World's Fair of 1893 that boasted all the wonders of technology. With the inclusion of "Daisy Bell" (1199) a few pages before the end, Pynchon points (perhaps ironically) to the technological wonders that history still had in store.

There are a few surprises. *Vineland*, the book that most clearly broaches the issue of TV, has only 2% of musical references (i.e. three entries) that emanate from a TV: "Are You Lonesome Tonight," "One for My Baby (And One More for the Road)," and "Since I Fell for You" (all on page 36). While the novel contains many references to music themes from TV shows (*Jeopardy*, *The Flintstones*, *Hawaii Five-O*, *Alvin and the Chipmunks*, *Gilligan's*

Island) and some other music associated primarily with TV, none of them actually come from television speakers.

Another surprise is that *Against the Day*, set during a time when recording technology was invented and made available, does not contain a single song played on a phonograph or a gramophone. In fact, the words ‘phonograph’ and ‘gramophone’ do not appear in *Against the Day*, although it can be assumed that the ethno-musicologists’ “portable sound recording” (1057) and “recording device” (1061) refers to phonographs or perhaps gramophones.

Synthesizing the Findings

The Pynchon Playlist is complete to the best of my ability when it comes to direct references and more or less accessible allusions. It is, however, to be expected that some less easily recognizable allusions may have been overlooked, but this possibility should not significantly alter the outcome of the analyses. Since some of the findings may run counter to readers’ intuition, I think that the at times tedious work of indexing every single item and adding extra information has paid off.

Although Pynchon’s work offers a considerable amount of data within the field of music that allows for statistical analysis, the limits of such an undertaking are evident. First, the data collected pertains only to the identifiable musical references that can be linked to nonfictional musicians and works of music (and to Pynchon’s own songs). Also, I have not included references to musical instruments (an index of which can be found in the Appendix), to generic musical ensembles (“string orchestra,” “small band,” etc.), to fictional musicians, to unidentified pieces of possibly nonfictional music, to ruminations on music, or to musical metaphors and metonymies (for instance, the return to the tonic), even though these too are some of the ways Pynchon most frequently refers to music. Furthermore, the entries in the catalog have not been weighed according to their relative importance for the narrative or to the historical, philosophical, political, or musicological insights they offer: an entire passage discussing in depth the music of a particular composer may have the same weight as a pop song mentioned in passing. I attempted to calculate Pynchon’s ‘most musical’ novel by adding up the relative figures from the different categories (numbers of music references, of Pynchon’s own songs, of musical instruments, of occurrences of key words such as 'music' and 'singing'), but such weighing of supposed relative importance does each work an injustice because it risks leveling out significant differences and peculiarities, which is why I left out that part of the analysis. *Bleeding Edge* and *Against the Day* would have looked similar despite being very different.

Second, in some cases, the amount of data was too small (*The Crying of Lot 49*) or too scattered (*Slow Learner*, miscellaneous writings) to allow drawing sound conclusions. Some categories under analysis included so few items that the picture might have changed if another researcher had coded two or three of them differently. If Pynchon's next novel includes a great number of references to another composer or musical genre, a number comparable to the frequent references to Wagner in *Gravity's Rainbow*, the overall picture may change slightly.

Third, a statistical overview may give an overall picture, but literature thrives not on generalities but on particularities. In many instances, it was necessary to limit the significance of a particular conclusion or to explain it by looking at singular entries. For a relatively small amount of data—935 entries may be a lot for a particular writer, especially if the references are employed with as much care as Pynchon shows, but not as high as 8,000 or 80,000 or millions of items as is customary in quantitative literary analysis—there is only so much to be discovered and interpreted without having recourse to what one knows about the particular works and reading the references in context.

For a more exact overall picture it would have been necessary to add more descriptors to each entry (for instance, race, subgenre, origin of the musical material, chart ranking) and to figure out at which point in the narrative chronology a particular reference occurs. This, however, exceeded the purposes of this study and would have been overly time-consuming since many of Pynchon's intricate plots are rife with analepses, prolepses, dream sequences, and memories, not all clearly locatable on a time axis. I also leave it to future researchers to offer other interpretations of the empirical data or to find meaningful ways of cross-referencing the categories.

In spite of these limitations, some conclusions can be drawn. The intuition that *Vineland*, *Inherent Vice*, and *Bleeding Edge* are part of the same 'group' of novels is confirmed from the point of view of musical references in terms of density of references (high density), genre (more pop music, less classical music), gender (slightly more women), media (more 'schizophonic' music, less live music), and number of Pynchon's own songs (low density).

Although not detectable in the figures presented, it also seems that Pynchon is less generous with musico-philosophical passages in these three works, which may have to do with the focalization, the lower number of characters, the less intricate plots, and the historical development away from music that is played to music that is listened to, to employ a distinction Roland Barthes once made (*Image—Music—Text* 149). In some categories (jazz references, density of all references, live music, Pynchon's own songs), *Vineland* occupies an intermediate or transitional position between the earlier and the later writings although it appears to lean towards the latter. The intuition that the earlier works (*V.*, *Gravity's Rainbow, The Crying of Lot 49,* and *Slow Learner*) are part of the same group of novels is also confirmed, although to a lesser degree, particularly in the categories of modernist/high modernist music (no references after *Gravity's Rainbow*), media distribution (similar percentages of live music and 'schizophonic' music), density of Pynchon's own songs (highest densities, except in *Slow Learner*), and gender (practically no references to female artists). In some categories, *Mason & Dixon* and *Against the Day* stand out for their uniqueness and in others for sharing some characteristics both with the earlier and with the later works.

Generally, Pynchon paints an internally plausible picture of the musical landscape in the times in which the novels are set. By this I mean that within his work, some general trends in the evolution of music, the music industry, and the way people consume music can be traced. Whether this picture is historically precise is another question that would have to be answered by other means. Most of this plausibility is due to the rise of the music industry and to the means of mass-producing, mass-marketing, and mass-distributing music; some of it may be due to changing musical tastes of the characters and narrators or the author. For instance, it seems to me that the post-tonal trajectory has not yet lived (or no longer lives) up to its promise. This failure may have led to a decline in its appreciation more or less along with Pynchon's abandonment of it.

If one were to draw two lines of influence on Pynchon's choice of musical material, one would be technological and commercial developments (developments that shape a historically plausible depiction of the musical landscape), and the other would be Pynchon's own predilections and musical interests (or those of his and subsequent generations), which seem to have become less 'serious' and less experimental as his career has progressed.

Conclusion

Approaching the end of this monograph, it is hard not to think back to where I was a few years ago, with no training in literary studies to speak of, wondering, as I mention in the Preface, whether one could make a case that Pynchon played the saxophone. I have not been able to answer that particular question, and I completely lost interest in it, but during some four-and-a-half years of engagement with the way Pynchon stages music, many new questions arose and some were answered. To reiterate a point brought forth in the Introduction, I believe I have been able to show that music is the most important and most diverse cultural reference system for Pynchon (with the possible exception of his own art, literature). This is not to say that the other arts—in a very broad sense including the sciences, gastronomy, and fashion—do not play an eminent role too. It merely suggests that Pynchon has more to say, and more hopeful things to say, and more consistently so, through music than through the other arts. When it comes to other mass-mediated forms of popular entertainment, music appears to be more positively connoted and to have more emancipatory and liberatory potential than film or TV, let alone sports, a form of entertainment Pynchon barely touches upon.

Coming at the tail end of modernism with its attachment to 'high' culture and simultaneously being a child of the Beat and bebop age, Pynchon was one of the figures who took popular culture seriously as an art form. For the most part, music is no mere background noise for him but says something about its times—and about our times. The great themes particularly of lyrical music—love, death, justice—remain the same throughout the ages, and just because music may have been appropriated and commercialized by an industry does not mean it cannot bring solace, joy, or a sense of community to its preterite listeners. Music in Pynchon's worlds often acts as a force of transformation and as a karmic adjuster.

Yet it would be too simple to leave it at that. Close inspection reveals that Pynchon still speaks in the "voice of ambiguity," to quote the title of Thomas Hill Schaub's 1981 book. In the case of music, perhaps the most basic ambiguities that Pynchon develops are its occasional service to the class of the Elect and its continuous struggle between appropriation and reappropriation. Intimately tied to these is music's connection to military technology as theorized by Kittler. This topos resurfaces time and again throughout Pynchon's work and the present study, and it may not be overstating the case to say that without Pynchon, Kittler would not have been inspired to develop his media theory.

Obviously, much work remains to be done on the topic of music in Pynchon's *œuvre*. The desiderata are numerous, and only some of them have been addressed by the trajectory of this study. As Cowart has noted, the nature of the film/TV references differs from that of the music references. The former, he says, point toward a Void whereas the latter point toward extra dimensions of experience (*Allusion* 9). If this is true, one further question to address is what happens when film or TV and music intersect, as they often do, starting as early as *V.*'s references to songs of movie or TV origin such as "The Ballad of Davy Crockett," "I Only Have Eyes for You," and the Mickey Mouse theme song.

Cowart, and later Carswell ("Ukulele"), also noted that melody is Pynchon's "metaphor for the love-death theme" (*Allusion* 77). Their argument does not entirely convince me, but the claim is worth investigating further. So, more generally, is the question whether melody, rhythm, or harmony has any such consistent meaning in Pynchon's worlds.

In *Tropic of Cancer*, Henry Miller wrote: "There is one thing which interests me vitally now, and that is the recording of all that is omitted in books" (19). While this study is concerned largely with the allusions and references that can be spotted in the text, occasionally it hints at resonances with musicians or works of music that are nowhere to be found explicitly in Pynchon's writing: John Cage, Larry Adler, and Dvořák's *New World Symphony* come to mind. There are other obvious omissions. We can gather that 1960s folk music was not among Pynchon's favorite, which may explain why he does not mention a cultural force like Bob Dylan. But what to make of his omission of towering jazz figures such as John Coltrane (another rightful successor to Charlie Parker) and, earlier in history, Louis Armstrong (who is said to have asked a fan of his, a Republican senator named Richard M. Nixon, to help him carry his trumpet case through border inspection, neglecting to inform him that it contained his stash of weed)? Why is there no mention of Paul Robeson? Is he implied in the numerous allusions and references to Joe Hill? Where is the vocoder, that v-initialed encryption and decryption technology from World War II which later enabled a pre-digital form of pitch control and voice manipulation in pop and art music? Where are the American Federation of Musicians' recording ban of 1942–44 and the V-Discs, exempted from the ban, distributed to American soldiers in World War II? A theory of omissions, however impossible, speculative, or outright fantastic, could ruminate on the meanings of what is not there, particularly in writing that has been labeled encyclopaedic.

The working title of this monograph was *Pynchon's Sonic Fiction.* This suggested an acoustic turn where not just organized sound but sound, noise, and silence of all sorts would be taken into consideration. As the opening lines of *Gravity's Rainbow* and the ruminations in that novel on the sound-shadow make evident, there is indeed much more to Pynchon's acoustic layers than music. Detonations, for instance, rocket blasts in *Gravity's Rainbow,* and both the work of anarchist dynamiters and the Tunguska event in *Against the Day,* appear to have consequences for the plot and the transformation of certain characters' personalities. As with the topic of music in general, scattered investigations into different sonic dimensions of Pynchon's writing have been done, mostly in the form of articles, but the respective monographs, to the best of my knowledge, have not yet been written.

Contributions to the understanding of literature and music are often made by scholars of literature with an interest in music. Rarely do professional musicians with a trained ear and a solid knowledge of music theory and history take the time to develop sustained arguments in the field of literature. Possibly as a correlative, the sensory and sensual dimension of literature and music tends to be displaced. The question then is how, in studying the arts, to address those aspects that touch readers, listeners, and viewers, many of which are effects (or affects) of resonance and not of intellectual engagement. While digital hypertexts, and multimedia and multisensory artistic interventions offer valid workarounds, perhaps one will still have to switch back and forth between the different planes of intellectual and sensual engagement. In this spirit, I produced *"Now Everybody"—Visit Interprets Songs by Thomas Pynchon*, and I will end with the beginning of Kodwo Eshun's *More Brilliant than the Sun: Adventures in Sonic Fiction:* "Respect due. Good music speaks for itself. No Sleevenotes required. Just enjoy it. Cut the crap. Back to basics. What else is there to add?" (7).

Appendix

An early version of this book was the dissertation I submitted to the University of Basel in 2017. It included four appendices: the Pynchon Playlist, i.e. a list of all the historical musical references in Pynchon's work (at the time 927, now 935); an index of musical instruments in Pynchon's work; a list of character names in Pynchon's work likely inspired by music; and a list of musicians, albums, songs, and record labels inspired by Pynchon's work.

In the meantime, an earlier and less encompassing version of the "Pynchon Playlist" was published by *Orbit*, along with an abbreviated version of Chapter 4 of this book. It is available as an Excel database and I will update it occasionally. Since Chapter 4 is based on this playlist, I decided to include the list here, albeit without the various descriptors. The list of music inspired by Pynchon was made available as "Pynchon on Record, Vol. 4" on www.thomaspynchon.com and I will also update it periodically. The list of character names, drawing on and expanding Patrick Hurley's *Pynchon Character Names: A Dictionary*, turned out to be the weakest part of my dissertation, which is why I have left it out here.

Index of Musical Instruments

The Pynchon Playlist

This appendix lists every musician and work of music referenced or alluded to in Pynchon's writing. When an allusion may be too obscure, I have included a portion of the text or an explanation. For the Spike Jones and Lotion liner notes and the *Esquire* interview with Lotion, the musicians and songs appearing on the respective album were omitted. Credits list the composer first, followed by the lyricist. After the entries of historical musicians and works of music for the respective text, Pynchon's own works of music for the respective novel follow. Fictional musicians are not included. While this appendix is complete to the best of my abilities, there are no doubt oversights. Where no title was indicated for Pynchon's own songs, I chose a likely one, often the first or last line or a line from the chorus. All Weisenburger references are to his *Gravity's Rainbow* Companion.

Key to notes

[1] Included in The Thomas Pynchon Fake Book *Sings Songs from Gravity's Rainbow.*

[2] Recorded by Tyler Burba and available at www.haenggi.com/pynchon-songs and/or recorded by Visit on the album *"Now Everybody—" Visit Interprets Songs by Thomas Pynchon.*

[3] Included in the Amazon playlist for *Inherent Vice.*

[4] Included in the Soundtrack of the movie *Inherent Vice.*

[5] Recording of Pynchon's song exists. Refer to Chapter 1 and https://thomaspynchon.com/thomas-pynchon-inspired-music/ for details.

[6] Included in the Noriega playlist. Refer to Chapter 3 for details.

[7] Artist included in the Guantanamo playlist. Refer to Chapter 3 for details.

[8] Included in the 2001 Clear Channel memorandum. Refer to Chapter 3 for details.

V.

10 “What Shall We Do with The Drunken Sailor” (sea chanty, early 19th century). “Drunken Sailors nobody knew what to Do With.”

11 “Auld Lang Syne” (poem by Robert Burns, 1788 [possibly based on a poem by James Watson, 1711;]) set to a traditional folk song], performed by the Naval Operations Base (N.O.B.) Band.

15 “It Came Upon a Midnight Clear” (likely set to the melody of “Carol” by Richard Storrs Willis; lyrics by Edmund Sears, 1849).

18–19 “Le Déserteur” (Boris Vian and Harold Berg/Boris Vian, 1954) in the version of Marcel Mouloudji (1954). “Demain le noir matin” etc.

19 Pat Boone (*1934), American singer.

29 Richard Rodgers (1902–1979), American composer.

29 Oscar Hammerstein II (1895–1960), American librettist.

30 “Le Déserteur” (Boris Vian and Harold Berg/Boris Vian, 1954) in the version of Marcel Mouloudji (1954). “Depuis que je suis né” etc.

30 Guy Lombardo (1902–1977), Canadian-American bandleader and violinist.

30 “Auld Lang Syne” (poem by Robert Burns, 1788 [possibly based on a poem by James Watson, 1711]; set to a traditional folk song).

32 “Le Déserteur” (Boris Vian and Harold Berg/Boris Vian, 1954) in the version of Marcel Mouloudji (1954). “Algerian pacifist song.”

32 “Blue Suede Shoes” (Carl Perkins, 1955; also recorded by Elvis Presley, 1956).

32 Elvis Presley (1935–1977), American rock'n'roll singer and guitarist.

33 “Tonight You Belong to Me” (Lee David/Billy Rose, 1926).

34 “Wanderin’” (American hobo song, to an Irish tune, origin unclear, possibly late 19th or early 20th century but first reported in Carl Sandburg's *The American Songbag* in 1927 and credited to Arthur Sutherland “as learned from comrades in the American Relief Expedition to the Near East,” sometime after 1915).

41 “Tienes mi corazón” (unknown reference, possibly fictional).

57 *String Quartets No. 1 in D minor, Op. 7* (1905), *No. 2 in F sharp minor, Op. 10* (1908), *No. 3, Op. 30* (1927), and *No. 4, Op. 37* (1936) by Arnold Schoenberg.

60 Charlie “Yardbird” Parker (1920–1955), American alto saxophonist.

65 "No! No! pazzo son!" from *Manon Lescaut* (Giacomo Puccini, 1893).

87 "Hello, hello! Who's Your Lady Friend?" (Harry Fragson/ Worton David and Bert Lee, 1913).

91 *Manon Lescaut* (Giacomo Puccini, 1893).

92 Johann Sebastian Bach (1685–1750), German composer.

95 "Romeo and Juliet Overture" (Pyotr Ilyich Tchaikovsky, 1870/72).

124 "1812 Overture" (Pyotr Ilyich Tchaikovsky, 1880).

137 "Come Josephine, In My Flying Machine (Up She Goes!)" (Fred Fisher/Alfred Bryan, 1910). "This Josephine: [...] ready to come in a flying machine."

139 *Madama Butterfly* (Giacomo Puccini; libretto: Luigi Illica and Giuseppe Giacosa, 1904).

141 "T'ho voluto bene (non dimenticar)" (Gino Redi/Michele Caldieri, 1951; English lyrics by Shelley Dobbins).

144 "O Salutaris Hostia" (Eucharist hymn by St. Thomas Aquinas, probably around 1261).

158 "Deh, vieni alla finestra" from *Don Giovanni* (Wolfgang Amadeus Mozart, 1787; libretto: Lorenzo da Ponte).

184 "Madamina, il catalogo è questo" (a.k.a. "The Catalogue Aria") from *Don Giovanni* (Wolfgang Amadeus Mozart, 1787; libretto: Lorenzo Da Ponte). "That interminable Catalogue, that non picciol' libro."

189 "Onward, Christian Soldiers" (Arthur Sullivan, 1871; lyrics: Sabine Baring-Gould, 1865).

194 Possibly "My Bonnie Lies over the Ocean" (traditional Scottish folk song, likely 18th century; sheet music published in 1881). "The girl was singing now about a sailor, halfway round the world from home and his betrothed."

195 Giovanni Pierluigi da Palestrina (1552–1594), Italian composer.

198 Giovanni Pierluigi da Palestrina (1552–1594), Italian composer.

200 Wolfgang Amadeus Mozart (1756–1791), Austrian composer.

214 "Let Me Call You Sweetheart" (Leo Friedman/Beth Slater Whitson, 1910).

219 "The Ballad of Davy Crockett" (George Bruns/Thomas W. Blackburn, 1954). Recorded by The Wellingtons. "A song about Davy Crockett."

251 "Mit dem Zippel-Zappel-Zeppelin" (Otto Reuter, 1909).

280–81: "Night Train" (Oscar Washington, Lewis P. Simpkins, Jimmy Forrest, 1951; sometimes credited to Duke Ellington).

282 "The Twelve Days of Christmas" (English Christmas carol of French origin; today's version derives from an arrangement by Frederic Austin, 1909). "The Partridge in the Pear Tree."

325 "Colonel Bogey March" (Frederick Joseph Ricketts [a.k.a. Kenneth J. Alford], 1914).

325 "Hitler Has Only One Left Ball" (origin uncertain; attributed to Toby O'Brien, c. 1939), to the tune of the "Colonel Bogey March" (Frederick Joseph Ricketts [a.k.a. Kenneth J. Alford], 1914).

351 The Boston Pops, American Orchestra band.

353 "Fever" (Eddie Cooley/Otis Blackwell, 1956). Recorded by Little Willie John.

355 Joe Hill (1879–1915), Swedish-American hobo, union leader, singer, and songwriter.

357 "I Don't Hurt Anymore" (Don Robertson/Jack Rollins, 1954). Recorded by Hank Snow.

361 "Don't Be Cruel" (Otis Blackwell, 1956). Recorded by and co-credited to Elvis Presley.

362 Elvis Presley (1935–1977), American rock'n'roll singer and guitarist.

376 "Taps." Military bugle call, c. 1862.

380 Edgar Varèse (1883–1965), French-American composer.

380 "You Always Hurt the One You Love" (Doris Fisher/Allan Roberts, 1944).

387 Frédéric Chopin (1810–1849), Polish composer.

403 Possibly "Little Willow Tree" or "Old Willow Tree (Липа вековая)" (Russian folk songs). "Sentimental Russian ballads about willow trees."

404 "Adoration of the Earth" from *The Rite of Spring* (Igor Stravinsky, 1913). "Adoration of the Sun."

410 Theme from *Tristan und Isolde* (Richard Wagner, 1865).

413 "The Sacrifice" from *The Rite of Spring* (Igor Stravinsky, 1913). "Sacrifice of the Virgin."

418 Pat Boone (*1934), American singer.

418 "Be-Bop-A-Lula" (Gene Vincent, Donald Graves, Bill "Sheriff Tex" Davis, 1956).

419 Antonio Vivaldi (1678–1741), Italian composer and violinist.

420 Pat Boone (*1934), American singer.

426 "Evening Colors." Military bugle call.

427 "The Old Gray Mare" (origin unknown, possibly Stephen Foster or Ferdinand Latrobe and Thomas Francis McNulty, 19th century).

429 "People Will Say We're In Love," from *Oklahoma!* (Richard Rodgers/Oscar Hammerstein II, 1943).

433 "Route 66" (Bobby Troup, 1946).

434 "Route 66" (Bobby Troup, 1946).

V.

434 "Every Day I Have the Blues" (Aaron "Pinetop" Sparks and Milton [or Marion] Sparks, 1935).

438 "C'est magnifique" from *Can-Can* (Cole Porter, 1953).

438 Richard Ewing "Dick" Powell (1904–1963), American singer, actor, and film producer.

438 "The Song of the Marines" (Harry Warren/Al Dubin, 1937).

440 Billy Eckstine (1914–1993), American jazz and pop singer.

440 "I Only Have Eyes for You" (Harry Warren/Al Dubin, 1934).

440 "I Apologize" (Al Hoffman, Al Goodhart, Ed Nelson, 1931).

441 "Mickey Mouse March" (Jimmie Dodd, 1955).

441 Billy Eckstine (1914–1993), American jazz and pop singer.

477 "La bella Gigogin" (Paolo Giorza, 1858).

Pynchon's Songs in *V.*

1–2 "Christmas Eve on Old East Main". Performed by an old street singer with a guitar.

9–10 "Christmas Eve on Old East Main". Performed by an old street singer with a guitar.

13 "Pore Forlorn Civilian" (waltz). Performed by Dewey Gland.

51 "A Man Is No Good." Sung by Rachel Owlglass.

110 "Esther." Sung by Dr. Shale Schoenmaker.

116 "Mi corazón está tan solo" (possibly a real reference but not traceable).

124 *Volkswagens in Hi-Fi.* Album on Roony Winsome's label Outlandish Records.

124 *The Leavenworth Glee Club Sings Old Favorites.* Album on Roony Winsome's label Outlandish Records.

130 "Highway Patrol" (hillbilly song). Performed by a violin, guitar, banjo and vocalist played on an FM hillbilly station.

130 "Belinda Sue" (hillbilly song).

141 "The Eyes of a New York Woman." Sung by Benny Profane.[5]

160 "Il piove, dolor mia." Sung by Cesare.

207 "Avanti, i miei fratelli." Sung by the Gaucho.

220–21 "The Autobiography of Roony Winsome" to the tune of "The Ballad of Davy Crockett" (George Bruns/Thomas W. Blackburn, 1954).[2]

223 "Fugue Your Buddy" (McClintic Sphere). Performed by McClintic Sphere and band.

224–25 "The Rusty Spoon" (drinking song). Sung by Pig Bodine and Charisma.

238 "Love's a Lash" (tango). Played by an accordion, a fiddle, and a guitar, sung by Hedwig Vogelsang.

249 "Down by the Summertime Sea" (fox-trot). Sung by Hugh Godolphin.
254 "Dream Tonight of Peacock Tails." Sung by Kurt Mondaugen.[2]
261 "The Twilight's Just Beginning" (Charleston). Sung by Lieutenant Weissmann.
265–66 "Princess of Coquettes" (waltz). Sung by Foppl.
278 "Down by the Summertime Sea (Reprise)" (fox-trot). Sung by Hugh Godolphin. See also p. 249.
279 "Why Are You Leaving the Party?" (tango). Sung by Foppl's guests.
288–89 "Let P equal Me." Sung by Charisma and Mafia.
293 "Set/Reset." Performed by McClintic Sphere and band.
300 "Young Blood."
327 "Sylvana." Sung by Dnubietna.
351–52 "Come with Me to Lenox" (beguine). Sung by Roony Winsome.
360 "Your Teenage Romeo" (rock 'n' roll).
404 "Adoration of the Sun" (tango). Played by Vladimir Porcépic. Modeled on Igor Stravinsky's "Adoration of the Earth" from *The Rite of Spring.*
413 (and elsewhere) *L'Enlèvement des Vierges Chinoises* by Vladimir Porcépic. Modeled on Igor Stravinsky's *The Rite of Spring.*
413 "Sacrifice of the Virgin." Modeled on Igor Stravinsky's "The Sacrifice" from *The Rite of Spring.*
419 *Vivaldi Kazoo Concerto.*
427 "Let's Piss on the Forrestal." Sung by scaffold sailors to the tune of "The Old Gray Mare."
441 "Who's the Little Rodent?" Sung by Clyde, Johnny, and Pappy Hod.
465 "Fleeing the Mistral" (composed by Falconière). Recited by Mehemet.
466 "Stencil's Song." Sung by Herbert Stencil.

The Crying of Lot 49

1 *Concerto for Orchestra* (Béla Bartók, 1943).
2 Antonio Vivaldi (1678–1741), Italian composer and violinist.
16 The Beatles, British pop and rock band.
34 Karlheinz Stockhausen (1928–2007), German composer.
43 "Adeste Fideles" (origin disputed, possibly John Francis Wade, around 1751).

65 "Far Above Cayuga's Waters" (H.S. Thompson, 1857/Archibald Croswell Weeks/Wilmot Moses Smith, 1870/1874). "The tune of Cornell's alma mater."

66 "Aura Lee" (George L. Poulton/W. W. Fosdick, 1861), also known as "Love Me Tender."

114 Ringo Starr (*1940), British drummer, member of The Beatles.

114 Chubby Checker (*1941), American singer-songwriter.

114 The Righteous Brothers, American pop duo.

117 "She Loves You" (John Lennon/Paul McCartney, 1963).

Pynchon's Songs in *The Crying of Lot 49*

2 *Vivaldi Kazoo Concerto.* Performed by the Fort Wayne Settecento Ensemble; Boyd Beaver, soloist.

13 "I Want to Kiss Your Feet." Recorded by Sick Dick and the Volkswagens, likely an allusion to the Beatles' "I Want to Hold Your Hand."

16 "Miles's Song." Sung by Miles.[5]

19 "Baby Igor's Song." Sung by Baby Igor (i.e. young Metzger).

27 "Serenade." Performed by the Paranoids. [5]

43 "Hey Solid Citizen." Performed by the Paranoids to the tune of "Adeste Fideles."

65 "Hymn." Sung by the Yoyodyne shareholders and proxies to the tune of "Far Above Cayuga's Waters." [2]

66 "Glee." Sung by the Yoyodyne shareholders and proxies to the tune of "Aura Lee." [2]

96 "Tristoe, Tristoe, one, two, three." Sung by a little girl.

120–21 "Serge's Song." Sung by Serge.

Gravity's Rainbow

Dedication: Richard Fariña (1937–1966), American folk singer and songwriter; friend of Pynchon's.

14 "The Changing of the Guards" (origin unclear). Performed by Sandy MacPherson.

18 "Johnny Doughboy Found a Rose in Ireland" (Al Goodhart/Kay Twomey, 1942).

18 George Formby (a.k.a. George Hoy Booth, 1904–1961), British singer-songwriter, ukulelist and banjolelist.

20 "Silent Night" (Franz Xaver Gruber/Joseph Mohr, 1816/1818).

25 Shirley Temple (1928–2014), American (child) actress and singer.

27 "The Star-Spangled Banner" (John Stafford Smith/Francis Scott Key, 1760s/1814).

33 Falkman and His Apache Band. British light music orchestra directed by Lionel Falkman.

36 "Dancing in the Dark" (Arthur Schwartz/Howard Dietz, 1931).

60 *Variations on a Theme by Frank Bridge* (Benjamin Britten, 1937).

64 "Shawnuff" (Charlie Parker/Dizzy Gillespie, 1948). "Sho nuf."

64 "Salt Peanuts" (Dizzy Gillespie or Charlie Parker, 1942). "A pound of salted peanuts."

65 "Cherokee" (Ray Noble, 1938).

65 Charlie "Yardbird" Parker (1920–1955), American alto saxophonist.

66 "Cherokee" (Ray Noble, 1938).

69 "Red River Valley" (American folk song, origin unclear, c. 1879; alternative lyrics by Thomas Pynchon).

71 "Red River Valley" (American folk song, origin unclear, c. 1879; alternative lyrics by Thomas Pynchon).

82 "Would You Rather Be A Colonel With An Eagle On Your Shoulder Or A Private With A Chicken On Your Knee?" (Archie Gottler/Sidney Mitchell, 1918).

103 *Erwartung* (Arnold Schoenberg, 1909; libretto: Marie Pappenheim).

105 *Siegfried* (Richard Wagner, 1876).

110 "Ic heb u liever dan ên everswîn" (aka. Middle Dutch song). Lyrics possibly by Jacob Grimm, derived from the poem "Lantslot ende Sandrin," verse 374.

117 Primo Scala's Accordion Band. Primo Scala (a.k.a. Harry Bidgood, 1898–1957), English composer, band leader, and musical director for films.

119 W.S. Gilbert, 1836–1911, English dramatist and librettist.

119 Arthur Sullivan, 1842–1900, English composer

124 "There, I've Said It Again" (Redd Evans/Dave Mann, 1941). Performed by Roland Peachey and his Orchestra.

129 Nondescript Christmas music (hotly syncopated). Performed by a BBC swing band.

131 "O Have You Seen My Darlin' Lola" (unknown, possibly fictional).

131 Thomas Tallis (1505–1585), English composer.

131 Henry Purcell (1659–1695), English composer.

131 "In dulci jubilo" (attributed to Heinrich von Seuse, 14th century).

134 "Giovinezza" (Giuseppe Blanc/Salvator Gotta, 1909/1924).

134 *Rigoletto* (Giuseppe Verdi, 1851; libretto: Francesco Maria Piave).
134 *La bohème* (Giacomo Puccini, 1896; libretto: Luigi Illica and Giuseppe Giacosa).
136 "In dulci jubilo" (attributed to Heinrich von Seuse, 14th century). "Eia, eia wärn wir da!"
137 "I Left My Heart at the Stage Door Canteen" (Irving Berlin, 1942). "Just left behind with your heart, at the Stage Door Canteen." See Weisenburger 96–97.
137 Noël Coward (1899–1973), English composer, actor, singer, director, and playwright.
138 "In dulci jubilo" (attributed to Heinrich von Seuse, 14th century). "O Jesu parvule" etc.
157 *La Bohème* (Giacomo Puccini, 1896).
162 *Der Ring des Nibelungen* (Richard Wagner, 1848–1874).
166 "Knallt ab den Juden Rathenau" (unknown origin).
166 *Götterdämmerung* (Richard Wagner, 1876).
171 "Siboney" (Ernesto Lecuona, 1929).
172 "Diadem" (James Ellor/Edward Perronet, 1838/1780).
173 "Aberystwyth" (Joseph Parry, 1876).
179 "Are You Hep to the Jive" (Cab Calloway/Buck Ram, 1940). "Certain situations are just more hep to the jive than others."
180 "Hark, the Herald Angels Sing" (Felix Mendelssohn Bartholdy/Charles Wesley, 1840/1739; alternative lyrics by Iona and Peter Opie).
185 "Sur la plage" (from the Musical *The Boy Friend)* (Sandy Wilson, 1953). Anachronistic, but the lyrics resonate with the plot of the musical: "Though you may look cute / In your bathing suit / We don't know who you are // There's no knowing / Who you are going / To meet sur la plage."
186 Bing Crosby (1903–1977), American singer and actor.
194 "You Can Do a Lot of Things at the Seaside" (Charles Ridgewell/George A. Stevens, year unknown).
203 *Die Walküre* (Richard Wagner, 1870). "And your name would be Brunhilde."
206 "The Man Who Broke the Bank at Monte Carlo" (Fred Gilbert, 1891 or 1892). "Bwa-deboolong." See Weisenburger 131.
207 *Il barbiere di Siviglia ossia L'inutil precauzione* (Gioachino Rossini, 1816; libretto: Cesare Sterbini).
207 Tarantella by Gioachino Rossini, perhaps "La Danza" (1835; lyrics by Carlo Pepoli).
216 "Lady of Spain" (Tolchard Evans/Erell Reaves, 1931). According to Weisenburger (138), the version by Stanley J. Damerell and Robert Hargreaves.

225 "School Days, School Days" (Will Cobb/Gus Edwards, 1907).
225 "Come, Josephine, in My Flying Machine" (Alfred Bryan/Fred Fisher, 1910).
225 "There'll Be a Hot Time" (Theodore Metz, 1886).
228 Benny Goodman (1909–1986), American clarinetist and bandleader.
236–37 Regimental hymn, possibly "El novio de la muerte" (Fidel Prado/Juan Costa, 1921) or "La Madelon" (Camille Robert, original French lyrics by Louis Bousquet, 1914). Less likely possibilities include "Canción del Legionario" (Modesto Romero and Emilio Guillén Pedemonti, 1920) or "Tercios Heroicos" (Francisco Calles/Antonio Soler) although none of these mention a bride that is taken.
240 "Tempus es iocundum" from *Carmina Burana* (Carl Orff, 1935/1936, lyrics 11th/12th century). "O, O, O, To-tus flore-o" etc.
252 Gioachino Rossini (1792–1868), Italian composer. "Rue Rossini."
256 Gioachino Rossini (1792–1868), Italian composer. "Rue Rossini."
260 Gioachino Rossini (1792–1868), Italian composer. "Rue Rossini."
265 "Overture" to *Guillaume Tell* (Gioachino Rossini, 1829).
267 "Tangerine" (Victor Schertzinger/Johnny Mercer, 1942), from the musical movie *The Fleet's In.* Recorded by Jimmy Dorsey and His Orchestra; vocals by Bob Eberly and Helen O'Connell. "Tangerine raised in ev-ry bar across, now."
270 An old tango by Juan d'Arienzo (1900–1976).
274 *Don Giovanni* (Wolfgang Amadeus Mozart, 1787; libretto: Lorenzo da Ponte). "Don Giovanni's map of Europe."
277 "Overture" to *La gazza ladra* (Gioachino Rossini, 1817; libretto: Giovanni Gherardini).
303–04 *Tannhäuser und der Sängerkrieg auf Wartburg* (Richard Wagner, 1845). "Tannhäuserism," "minnesinger." See Weisenburger 188.
312 "For He's a Jolly Good Fellow" (traditional, melody dating back to at least 1709).
320 Richard Wagner (1813–1883), German composer.
324 Bing Crosby (1903–1977), American singer and actor. "Der Bingle."
328 Richard Wagner (1813–1883), German composer.
357 *Madama Butterfly* (Giacomo Puccini; libretto: Luigi Illica and Giuseppe Giacosa, 1904).
363 Džambul Džabajev (1846–1945), Kazakh folksinger.
367 Selections from *Die Meistersinger von Nürnberg* (Richard Wagner, 1868).
370 *Tannhäuser und der Sängerkrieg auf Wartburg* (Richard Wagner, 1845).

371 Richard Wagner (1813–1883), German composer.
378 "Berliner Luft" (Paul Lincke/Heinrich Bolten-Baeckers, 1904).
382 Gioachino Rossini (1792–1868), Italian composer.
387 *Das Rheingold* (Richard Wagner, 1869). "Miss Rheingold."
388 "Don't Sit Under the Apple Tree" (Sam H. Stept/Lew Brown/ Charles Tobias, 1939). Performed by the Andrews Sisters or sounding like it.
389 Carmen Miranda (1909–1955), Brazilian singer and actress.
393 "Aquí me pongo a cantar" from the poem *Martín Fierro* by José Hernández. Music possibly by Roberto Grela and Hector Ayala.
396 Frank Sinatra (1915–1998), American singer and actor.
399 Richard Wagner (1813–1883), German composer. "Papier-mâché Wagnerian battlements."
400 *Tannhäuser und der Sängerkrieg auf Wartburg* (Richard Wagner, 1845). "His helpless Lisaura."
419 "Ich hab mein Herz in Heidelberg verloren" (Fred Raymond/ Fritz Löhner-Beda/Ernst Neubach, 1925).
423 Richard Wagner (1813–1883), German composer.
426 Hugo Wolf (1860–1903), Austrian-Slovene composer.
428 "Lob der edlen Musika" (lyrics: Emanuel Geibel, 1840, to a traditional tune known since 1743). "Juch-heierasas-sa! o tempo-tempo-ra!"
439 "Gaudeamus igitur" (unknown, first appearance of the text in the Middle Ages, possibly 13th century).
447–49 Ludwig van Beethoven (1770–1827), German composer. See Weisenburger 247–48.
447–49 Gioachino Rossini (1792–1868), Italian composer. See Weisenburger 247–48.
447 "An die Freude" ("Ode to Joy") from the *Ninth Symphony* (Ludwig van Beethoven, 1824). See Weisenburger 247–48.
447 *La gazza ladra* (Gioachino Rossini, 1817; libretto: Giovanni Gherardini). "La Gazza Ladra," "the magpie stealing everything in sight!"
447 *L'italiana in Algeri* (Gioachino Rossini, 1813; libretto: Angelo Anelli). "The Italian girl is in Algiers."
447 *Il barbiere di Siviglia* (Gioachino Rossini, 1816; libretto: Cesare Sterbini). "The Barber's in the crockery."
448 Anton Webern (1883–1945), Austrian composer and conductor. See Weisenburger 248–49.
448 Johann Sebastian Bach (1685–1750), German composer.
448 *Götterdämmerung* (Richard Wagner, 1876).
448 Carl Orff (1895–1982), German composer and music pedagogue. See Weisenburger 250.

449 "Tarantella" from *Tancredi* (Gioachino Rossini, 1813). It could also refer to Rossini's tarantella "La Danza" (lyrics: Carlo Pepoli) from 1835. See also *Gravity's Rainbow* 207.

450 Irving Berlin (1888–1989), American composer.

450 "God Bless America" (Irving Berlin, 1918/1938)

450 "This Is the Army, Mister Jones" (Irving Berlin, 1942).

450 "Horst-Wessel-Lied" (origin of melody contested, probably 19th century; lyrics: Horst Wessel, around 1927–1929). See Weisenburger 251.

450 Anton Webern (1883–1945), Austrian composer and conductor.

458 Richard Wagner (1813–1883), German composer.

458 Hugo Wolf (1860–1903), Austrian-Slovene composer.

471 "A String of Pearls" (Jerry Gray/Eddie DeLange, 1941). Recorded by Glenn Miller. See Jonathan R. Eller and William E. McCarron 193.

473 *Wozzeck* (Alban Berg, 1922). Less likely would be *Wozzeck* by Manfred Gurlitt (1926).

473 "On the Good Ship Lollipop" (Richard A. Whiting/Sidney Clare, 1934). Sung by Shirley Temple. See Weisenburger 260–61.

473 "Animal Crackers in My Soup" (Ray Henderson/Irving Caesar, 1935). Performed by Shirley Temple. See Weisenburger 261.

474 "A String of Pearls" (Jerry Gray/Eddie DeLange, 1941). Recorded by Glenn Miller. "The string of little seed pearls." See Eller and McCarron 193.

474 "Tuxedo Junction" (Erskine Hawkins/Bill Johnson/Julian Dash/Buddy Feyne, 1938). Recorded by Glenn Miller in 1940. "Tuxedo trousers." See Eller and McCarron 193.

475 "One Dozen Roses" (Walter Donovan/Dick Jurgens/Roger Lewis/Country Washburn, c. 1940). Also recorded by Glenn Miller. "The stems of half a dozen roses."

475 "Chattanooga Choo Choo" (Harry Warren/Mack Gordon, 1941). See Eller and McCarron; Weisenburger 261–62.

478 *Tannhäuser und der Sängerkrieg auf Wartburg* (Richard Wagner, 1845). "The Pope's staff is always going to remain barren."

484 Selections from *Die lustige Witwe* (Franz Lehár, 1905).

484–85 Selections from *Il segreto di Susanna (Susanna's Secret)* (Ermanno Wolf-Ferrari, 1909; libretto: Enrico Golisciani).

501 "Oh My Goodness" from the movie *Poor Little Rich Girl* (Mack Gordon/Harry Revel, 1936). Sung by Shirley Temple. "Oh my goo'ness."

501 "On the Good Ship Lollipop" (Richard A. Whiting/Sidney Clare, 1934). Sung by Shirley Temple. "See the sugar bowl do the Tootsie Roll." See Weisenburger 260–61.

502 Anton Webern (1883–1945), Austrian composer and conductor.
506 *Der fliegende Holländer* (Richard Wagner, 1843). "I've seen the Flying Dutchman." See Weisenburger 270.
514 *Tristan und Isolde* (Richard Wagner, 1865).
521 Kurt Weill (1900–1950) medley.
521 Gene Krupa (1909–1973), American jazz drummer.
531 Howard Hoagland "Hoagy" Carmichael (1899–1981), American composer, singer, pianist, and actor.
531 Possibly "Stars and Stripes Forever" (John Philip Sousa, 1896).
532 Bing Crosby (1903–1977), American singer and actor.
538 "Running Between the Raindrops" (Carroll Gibbons/James Dyrenforth, 1931), arranged by Guy Lombardo (1931).
541 *Tannhäuser und der Sängerkrieg auf Wartburg* (Richard Wagner, 1845). "Where is the Pope whose staff will bloom for me?" See Weisenburger 280.
543 Nelson Eddy (1901–1967), American singer and actor.
547 Gilbert and Sullivan medley (Arthur Sullivan, 1842–1900; W. S. Gilbert, 1836–1911).
569 "Fifty Million Frenchmen Can't Be Wrong" (Willie Raskin/ Billy Rose/Fred Fisher, 1927). Originally performed by Sophie Tucker. "For De Mille, young fur-henchmen can't be rowing!" See Weisenburger 292.
569 *Götterdämmerung* (Richard Wagner, 1876).
569 "San Antonio Rose" (Bob Wills, 1938). "San Antonya Rose."
571 "A Needle in A Haystack" (Con Conrad/Herb Magidson, 1934). "LOOK-IN' FAWR A NEEDLE IN A HAAAAY-STACK!" etc.
571 Fred Astaire (1899–1987), American dancer, singer, and musician.
571 Ginger Rogers (1911–1995), American singer, dancer, and actress.
574 "Si me quieres escribir" (origin unknown, song from the Spanish Civil War, already sung in Africa in 1920).
577 "Laterne, Laterne, Sonne, Mond und Sterne." German's children's song, origin unknown, around 1900.
590 "Gaudeamus igitur" (unknown, first appearance of the text in the Middle Ages). "Semper sit in flores!"
594 "Galop infernal" from *Orphée aux enfers* (Jacques Offenbach, 1858), also known as "Can-Can." "Cancan girls," "some Offenbach galop."
603 Sandy MacPherson (1897–1975), Canadian organist.
605 *La forza del destino* (Giuseppe Verdi, 1862; libretto: Francesco Maria Piave).

607 "Follow the Yellow Brick Road" from the movie *The Wizard of Oz* (Harold Arlen, 1939).

609 Deanna Durbin (1921–2013), Canadian actress and singer.

610 "Love in Bloom" (Ralph Rainger/Leo Robin, 1934).

611 "The Rose of No Man's Land" (James Alexander Brennan/Jack Caddigan, 1918).

614 "San Antonio Rose" (Bob Wills, 1938).

616 "Valencia" (Lucienne Boyer/Jacques Charles/Clifford Grey/José Padilla, 1924). "Va-len-cia-a-a."

616 "Viva la quince brigada" (sung in the Spanish Civil War, origin in 1808). "Ya salimos de España" etc.

631 "Gabriel" ("Who Dat Man?") from the Marx Brothers' *A Day at the Races* (1937). Music possibly by Franz Waxman.

634 Louis Spohr (1784–1859), German composer, violinist, and conductor.

634 Gioachino Rossini (1792–1868), Italian composer.

634 Gasparo Luigi Pacifico Spontini (1774–1851), Italian composer and conductor.

635 "The Shadow Waltz" (Harry Warren/Al Dubin, 1933), performed by Dick Powell and Ruby Keeler.

666 Johann Sebastian Bach (1685–1750), German composer.

666 "Die Fahne hoch!", also known as "Horst-Wessel-Lied" (origin of melody probably 19th century; lyrics: Horst Wessel, around 1927–1929).

677 Carmen Miranda (1909–1955), Brazilian singer and actress.

688 Stephen C. Foster (1826–1864), American songwriter.

688 "Minnie the Moocher" (Cab Calloway/Irving Mills, 1929). Performed by Cab Calloway in the film *Stormy Weather* (1943). "Hi-de-hoing in the door" etc. See Weisenburger 345.

691 "Chiquita Banana" (Len MacKenzie/Garth Montgomery, c. 1944), performed by Carmen Miranda. "Bananas in the Refrigerator."

691 "Der Fuehrer's Face" (Oliver Wallace, 1943), performed by Spike Jones.

697 "Deutschlandlied" (Joseph Haydn/August Heinrich Hoffmann von Fallersleben, 1797/1841).

698 Joseph Joachim (1831–1907), Hungarian violinist, composer, and conductor.

698 *Rossini Violin Concerto* (op. posth.). Likely fictional.

698 "My Prelude to a Kiss" (Duke Ellington, 1945).

698 "Tenement Symphony" (Hal Borne/Sid Kullen/Roy Golden, 1941).

699 Elvis Presley (1935–1977), American rock'n'roll singer and guitarist. "Bodine with his guitar ambling pelvis-wiggling down the hallway."
699 *La gazza ladra* (Gioachino Rossini, 1817; libretto: Giovanni Gherardini).
699 Johann Sebastian Bach (1685–1750), German composer.
699 *Fifth Symphony* (Ludwig van Beethoven, 1808).
699 Johannes Brahms (1833–1897), German composer and pianist.
699 Harry James (1916–1983), American jazz trumpet player.
705 "Button Up Your Overcoat" (Ray Henderson/B.G. DeSylva/ Lew Brown, 1928).
709 "America the Beautiful" (Samuel A. Ward/Katherine Lee Bates, 1895) "Thine-alabaster-cities."
714 Frank Sinatra (1915–1998), American jazz singer and actor.
716 Medley from *Pathétique (Symphony No. 6 in B minor, Op. 74)* (Pyotr Ilyich Tchaikovsky, 1893).
723 Noël Coward (1899–1973), English composer, actor, singer, director, and playwright.
725 "'Kazoo' Quartet in G-Flat Minor" (Op. 74) (Joseph Haydn). Partly fictional.
726 "You Should See Me Dance The Polka" (George Grossmith, 1887).
726 Joseph Haydn (1732–1809), Austrian composer.
731 Joseph Haydn (1732–1809), Austrian composer.
731 Horst Wessel (1907–1930), NSDAP activist, known for the lyrics to the "Horst-Wessel-Lied."
757 The Rolling Stones, English rock band.
758 "Don't Sit Under the Apple Tree" (Sam H. Stept/Lew Brown/ Charles Tobias, 1939). Performed by the Andrews Sisters. "An apple tree [...]. Sitting under it, with anyone else but Slothrop."

Pynchon's Songs in *Gravity's Rainbow*

9 "Have a Banana." Sung by Osbie Feel.[1]
12 "Colder Than The Nipple on A Witch's Tit." Performed by a crew of American sappers.
12–13 "Pirate's Song." Performed by Pirate Prentice and Band (with a lotta tubas and close-harmony trombones).
15 "The Sanjak of Novi Pazar."[1]
27–28 "Adieu my friends." Inscription on Mrs. Elizabeth Slothrop's tombstone, "through bouncy Star Spangled Banner meter."
63 "Snap to, Slothrop." To the tune of "Bye Bye Blackbird." See Weisenburger 52.[2]

63	"Rhythm's Got Me" (aka "Let's Swing").
65	"Slip the Talcum to Me Malcolm."
67	"Down the Toilet." Probably performed by Tyrone Slothrop.
69	"Red Malcolm."
69	"Red River Valley" (American folk song, origin unclear, ca. 1879; alternative lyrics by Pynchon).
70	"One Little Feeb in South Dakota."
170	"Pointsman's All Alone." Possibly to the tune of the Kinks' "A Well-Respected Man" (Ray Davies, 1965).
177–78	"With a Peppermint Face in the Sky." Sung by Gretel, Roger, and the audience.
184–85	"The Englishman's Very Shy" (Fox-Trot). Sung by Teddy Bloat and Tantivy Mucker-Maffick.[1]
193–94	"The Ballad of Tantivy Mucker-Maffick".[1]
198	"Too Soon to Know" (Fox-Trot). Sung by Tyrone Slothrop.
205	"The World Over There."[1]
216	"Vulgar Song." Not to be confused with "The Vulgar Song" in *V.* (325).[1]
219	"The Penis He Thought Was His Own." Performed by Sir Stephen.[1]
232–33	"Pavlovia" (Beguine). Performed by a tropical orchestra and sung by the lab rats.[1]
234	"Wash me in the Water." Sung by Brigadier Pudding. Possibly inspired by Ms Porter and her daughter in T. S. Eliot's *The Waste Land* (lines 198–201).
247	"Mr. Debonair." Sung by Tyrone Slothrop.
248	"Julia" (Fox-Trot). Performed by a dance band and an emaciated crooner.[1]
262–63	"Loonies on Leave!" Performed by a Chorus line of Keepers and Nuts.[1]
287	"Vulgar Song." "The lovely little Queen of Transylvania."
288	"Displaced Person's Song."[1]
293	"Rocket, Sock-it Town."
294	"Love Never Goes Away" (Parisian-sounding, in 3/4). Performed by Geli Tripping.
310–12	"Rocket Limericks." Sung by the Americans.
315	"On the Mittelwerk Express."
315–16	"Rocket Limericks." Sung by the Americans.
319	"Nazis in the Woodwork."[1]
324–25	"Sold on Suicide" (possibly boogie-woogie).[1]
334	"She Headed for Rhode Island."
339–40	"Rocket Limericks". Sung by the Furies.
362	"Kazakh Singing Duel." Sung by a boy and a girl.

363–64 "The Aqyn's Song." Performed by the wandering singer.
375 "The Doper's Dream" (in 3/4 and shit-kicking style). Performed by Seaman Bodine.[1]
384 "Jubilee Jim."
421–22 "Victim in a Vacuum!" The song appears to have elements both from "Schöner Gigolo, armer Gigolo" ("Just a Gigolo") by Leonello Casucci and Julius Brammer (1929) and "Everybody Needs Somebody to Love" (Bert Berns/Solomon Burke/Jerry Wexler, 1964).
445 "A little something from Morocco" (rumba). Performed by Säure Bummer.
456–57 "Buffalo Bayou." Performed by young fellas from Schenectady.
470 "Welcome Aboard!" (up-tempo). Performed by elegantly-decked guests with band accompaniment.
504 "Bright Days" (fox-trot). By Gerhardt von Göll. Sung by Springer, Närrisch and Otto.
506 "Sea Chanty." Sung by Frau Gnahb.
531 "Desoxyephedrine Daddy" (with Hoagy Carmichael piano accompaniment).
543–44 "Doper's Greed." Improvised by Osbie Feel.[1]
547–48 "Contagious" (swing).[1]
550 "The Common Informer," Performed by Merciful Evans. Possibly inspired by or to the tune of The Rolling Stones' "Salt of the Earth" (1968), also covered by Richard Fariña's sister-in-law Joan Baez in 1971. "Say a prayer for the common foot soldier."[1]
558 "Dancing the Bad Dream Away."
584–85 "A Pig Is A Jolly Companion."[1]
595 "Bright Days (for the Black Market)" (fox-trot), reprise. By Gerhardt von Göll.
604 "Mouth-tripping Time!" Performed by a crowd of Army personnel, American sailors, NAAFI girls, and German fräuleins.
616 "Valencia" (Lucienne Boyer/Jacques Charles/Clifford Grey/José Padilla, 1924) with alternative lyrics sung by Major Marvy.
632 "The Eagle of Tooting."[1,2]
639 "The Superhighways of July." Sung by Roger Mexico.[1,2]
647 "Puke-a- hook-a-look-i Island." Performed by gorgeous girls with grass skirts playing ukuleles.
652–53 "They've Been Sleeping on Your Shoulder." Performed by everyone in Pirate's maisonette, accompanied by Thomas Gwenhidwy with a crwth.[2]
661 "Baby Bulbs." Sung by Byron the Bulb.[1]

670 "Paranoia." With tap-dancing by Andreas and Pavel.
681 "Yumsy-numsy 'n' poopsie-poo." Sung by the 175-Stadt Chorale.
684 "Just a Fool Who Never Wins."
690 "Howdy Neighbor."[1]
698 Rossini Violin Concerto (op. posth.). Probably fictional.
699 "My Doper's Cadenza." Performed by Seaman Bodine.
705 "Puke-a- hook-a-look-i Island."
725–30 "'Kazoo' Quartet in G-Flat Minor" (Op. 74) (Joseph Haydn). Performed by a quartet including André Omnopon and Gustav Schlabone.
731 "Acne à la mode." Performed by Roger Mexico, Bodine and Gustav and André's quartet.
751 "Sharper than a Mother's Tears." Performed by The Lederhoseners.
754–55 "It Don't Look like I'll See Your Face Again." By Roger Mexico and some nameless sailor. Performed by Seaman Bodine.
776 "A Hand to Turn the Time" (hymn). Composed by William Slothrop. John M. Krafft informed me that a friend of his pointed out in 1974 that this hymn fits perfectly with "The Halls of Montezuma" (see also entry in *Against* 475). [1,2]

Slow Learner: Early Stories

Introduction

8 Charlie "Yardbird" Parker (1920–1955), American alto saxophonist.
8 Clifford Brown (1930–1956), American jazz trumpeter.
8–9 Elvis Presley (1935–1977), American rock'n'roll singer and guitarist.
16 L'Histoire du soldat (Igor Stravinsky/Charles-Ferdinand Ramuz, 1917).
20 Spike Jones (1911–1965), American bandleader.
23 Frank Zappa (1940–1993), American musician.

The Small Rain

28 Lester Young (1909–1959), American tenor saxophonist.
28 Gerry Mulligan (1927–1996), American baritone saxophonist.
43 "Betty Co-ed" (Rudy Vallée, 1930).

Low-lands

56 *Sixth Concerto for Violin ("Il Piacere")* (Antonio Vivaldi, 1725).

57 "A Room with A View" from *This Year Of Grace* (Noël Coward, 1928). "We'll be as happy and contended" etc.

58 Niccolò Paganini (1782–1840), Italian violinist and composer.

60 *Sixth Concerto for Violin ("Il Piacere")* (Antonio Vivaldi, 1725). "Vivaldi discoursed on pleasure."

65 "The Golden Vanity" (a.k.a. "The Sweet Trinity," English folk song), first documented in 1635.

Entropy

81 "The Heroes' Gate at Kiev" a.k.a. "The Great Gate of Kiev" from *Pictures at an Exhibition* (Modest Mussorgsky, 1874).

82–83 "Spring will be a little late this year" (Frank Loesser, 1943), recorded by Sarah Vaughan.

83 "Lili Marlene" (Norbert Schultze, 1938/Hans Leip, 1915; first published in 1937).

83 "The Sweetheart of Sigma Chi" (F. Dudleigh Vernor/Byron D. Stokes, 1911).

83 "The Heroes' Gate at Kiev" a.k.a. "The Great Gate of Kiev" from *Pictures at an Exhibition* (Modest Mussorgsky, 1874).

86 *Don Giovanni* (Wolfgang Amadeus Mozart, 1787; libretto: Lorenzo Da Ponte).

87 "Madamina, il catalogo è questo" (a.k.a. "The Catalogue Aria") from *Don Giovanni* (Wolfgang Amadeus Mozart, 1787; libretto: Lorenzo Da Ponte). "Purche porti la gonnella" etc.

88 Earl Bostic (1912–1965), American jazz and rhythm and blues alto saxophonist.

93 "Trois Dances" (1. Tango) from *L'Histoire du soldat* (Igor Stravinsky/Charles-Ferdinand Ramuz, 1917).

94 "I Remember Clifford" (Benny Golson, 1958). "You Remember Gerry."

94 Gerry Mulligan (1927–1996), American baritone saxophonist.

94 "I'll Remember April" (Gene de Paul/Patricia Johnston and Don Raye, 1941).

94 "Love for Sale" (Cole Porter, 1930). Reference probably to The Original Chet Baker & Gerry Mulligan Quartet, but there appears to be no recording of "Love for Sale" available from that band.

94 Chet Baker (1929–1988), American jazz trumpeter.

95 Charles Mingus (1922–1979), American jazz bassist and composer.

95 John Lewis (1920–2001), American jazz pianist and composer.

95 "Happy Birthday" (Mildred J. Hill/Patty Smith Hill, 1893; today's lyrics: Robert H. Coleman, 1924).

95 Chet Baker & Gerry Mulligan Quartet, 1952/1953. "That first quartet of Mulligan's."

96 "These Foolish Things (Remind Me of You)" (Harry Link, Jack Strachey/Holt Marvell, 1936).

96 "I'll Remember April" (Gene de Paul/Patricia Johnston and Don Raye, 1941).

Under the Rose

105 "No! No! pazzo son!" from *Manon Lescaut* (Giacomo Puccini, 1893).

109 "Hello, hello! Who's Your Lady Friend?" (Harry Fragson/ Worton David and Bert Lee, 1913).

118 Giuseppe Cremonini (1866–1903), Italian tenor.

128 *Manon Lescaut* (Giacomo Puccini, 1893).

128 "Donna non vidi mai" from *Manon Lescaut* by Giacomo Puccini, 1893.

129 Johann Sebastian Bach (1685–1750), German composer.

130 Johann Sebastian Bach (1685–1750), German composer.

137 *Manon Lescaut* (Giacomo Puccini, 1893). "His Manon."

The Secret Integration

181 "Mine Eyes Have Seen the Glory", a.k.a. "The Battle Hymn of the Republic" (William Steffe, 1856/Julia Ward Howe, 1861). "Mine eyes have seen the misery of the coming draft."

Pynchon's Songs in *Slow Learner*

81 *Songs of Outer Space*. Recorded by the Duke de Angelis Quartet.

96 "Let's All Go Down and Piss on the Forrestal" performed by two girls and the sailors. In *V.*, this song appears to be sung the tune of "The Old Gray Mare" (see *V.* 427). It may well be that the alternative lyrics were not made up by Pynchon but actually sung by soldiers.

Vineland

Epigraph "Every Dog Has His Day" (Johnny Potts), recorded by Johnny Copeland (1970).

6 "I'm So Lonesome I Could Cry" (Hank Williams, 1949).

9 "Think!" ("Theme from *Jeopardy*") (likely the version by Merve Griffin, 1984).

16 "Love Is Strange" (Mickey Baker/Sylvia Vanderpool/Ethel Smith, 1956). "I know love is strange."

18 "Purple Haze" (Jimi Hendrix, 1967).

26 "Meet the Flintstones" (Hoyt Curtin, 1960).

28 "In-A-Gadda-Da-Vida", Iron Butterfly (1968).

33 "Meet the Flintstones" (Hoyt Curtin, 1960).

36 "Are You Lonesome Tonight" (Lou Handman/Roy Turk, 1926).

36 "One for My Baby (And One More for the Road)" (Harold Arlen/Johnny Mercer, 1943).

36 "Since I Fell for You" (Buddy Johnson, 1945).

37 Dick Dale (a.k.a. Richard Anthony Monsour, 1937–2019), American surf rock guitarist

38 "Pipeline" (Brian Carman/Bob Spickard, 1962/63).

39 Frank Zappa (1940–1993), American musician.

41 Elvis Presley (1935–1977), American rock'n'roll singer and guitarist.

43 "T.V. Crazy" (Little Charlie & the Nightcats, 1987).

47 "La Marseillaise" (Claude Joseph Rouget de Lisle, 1792).

50 "Stranger in Town" (David Paich/Jeff Porcaro, 1984). "I ain't the only stranger in town today."

59 "Volare (Nel blu dipinto di blu)" (Domenico Modugno/Franco Migliacci, 1958). "Those eyes of blue painted blue, as the Italian oldie goes."

64 "Do You Believe in Magic?" (John Sebastian, 1965).

65 "Tiny Bubbles" (Martin Denny/Leon Pober, 1966).

65 "Godzilla, King of the Monsters" (Akira Ifukube, 1956).

73 "In the Midnight Hour" (Wilson Pickett/Steve Cropper, 1965). "There was 'nobody else around,' as Wilson Pickett might say."

75 "Frenesí" (Alberto Domínguez Borrás, 1939; recorded by Artie Shaw in 1940).

76 "The Commonwealth of Toil" (Ralph Chaplin (1887–1961).

76 Joe Hill (1879–1915), Swedish-American hobo, union leader, singer, and songwriter.

78 The Platters, American vocal group.

78 Anson Weeks (1896–1969), American pianist and bandleader.

78 "The Star-Spangled Banner" (John Stafford Smith, c. 1773/Francis Scott Key, 1814).

78 Kate Smith (1907–1986), American singer.
78 Billie Holiday (1915–1959), American jazz singer.
78 Ramón Raquello, fictional bandleader from the 1938 radio broadcast *The War of the Worlds* by Orson Welles.
78 "La Cumparsita" (Gerardo Matos Rodríguez, 1916).
79 298th Army Band.
79 "I'll Remember April" (Gene de Paul/Patricia Johnston and Don Raye, 1941).
79 "Them There Eyes" (Maceo Pinkard/Doris Tauber/William Tracey, 1930).
85 Johnny Cash (1932–2003), American country singer and songwriter.
94 Gioachino Rossini (1792–1868), Italian composer. "Tournedos Rossini."
94 San Francisco Symphony orchestra.
96 "More (Theme from *Mondo Cane*)" (Riz Ortolani/Nino Oliviero, 1962).
96 "Senza fine" (from *Flight of the Phoenix*) (Frank De Vol, 1965).
96 "Al di là" (Carlo Donida/Mogol, 1962).
96 "C'è la luna mezzo mare." Sicilian folk song; its 1927 version credited to Paolo Citorello. This is also the first line of Gioachino Rossini's 1835 tarantella "La Danza," lyrics by Carlo Pepoli (*Gravity* 207).
96 "Way Marie" (origin unknown, possibly Perry Como).
96 "Cielo e mar" from *La Gioconda* (Amilcare Ponchielli; libretto: Arrigo Boito, 1876).
96 "Ave Maria" (most likely Charles Gounod 1853/Johann Sebastian Bach, 1716).
98 "Volare (Nel blu dipinto di blu)" (Domenico Modugno/Franco Migliacci, 1958).
99 Theme from "Hawaii Five-O." (Morton Stevens, 1968).
101 Suite from *Tosca* (Giacomo Puccini, 1900).
103 "McGarrett's Theme" from *Hawaii Five-O* (Morton Stevens, 1968).
115 "Wake Up Little Susie" (Felice and Boudleaux Bryant, 1957) performed by The Everly Brothers.
117 The Doors, American rock band.
117 Jimi Hendrix (1942–1970), American guitarist.
117 Jefferson Airplane, American acid rock band.
117 Country Joe and the Fish, American folk rock band.
133 "People Are Strange (When You're a Stranger)" (Robby Krieger/Jim Morrison, 1967), recorded by The Doors.
138 "Boulevard of Broken Dreams" (Harry Warren/Al Dubin, 1933), performed by Tony Bennett, 1950.

165 Acker Bilk (1929–2014), British jazz clarinetist.
165 Alvin and the Chipmunks, virtual band created by Ross Bagdasarian in 1958.
165 Marvin Hamlisch (1944–2012), American composer and conductor; also composed "Sunshine, Lollipops and Rainbows," performed by Alvin and the Chipmunks.
167 Andrew Lloyd Webber (*1948), British musical composer.
178 "Also sprach Zarathustra" (Op. 30) (Richard Strauss, 1896). "The tune of *2001: A Space Odyssey*."
180–81 Theme from "The Adventures of Chip 'n' Dale" (Gil George/ Oliver Wallace, 1959).
180 Alvin and the Chipmunks, virtual band created by Ross Bagdasarian in 1958.
187 Bernard Herrmann (1911–1975), American conductor and composer.
187 "Psycho" music from (Bernard Herrmann, 1960).
190 "Ghostbusters" (Ray Parker, Jr., 1984).
190 "Louie Louie" (Richard Berry, 1955), recorded by The Kingsmen, 1963. "'Me gotta go,' as the Kingsmen always used to say."
191 "Kick Out the Jams" (MC5, 1969). "Oh, kick out, the jambs, motherfuck-er."
193 "Winter Wonderland" (Felix Bernard/Richard B. Smith, 1934).
193 "Let It Snow" (Jule Styne/Sammy Cahn, 1945).
193 "Cold, Cold Heart" (Hank Williams, 1951).
193 "I'll See You Again" (Noël Coward, 1929).
193 "Drink, Drink, Drink" (Sigmund Romberg/Dorothy Donnelly, 1924).
205 The Mike Curb Congregation, American pop band (Mike Curb *1944).
209 Led Zeppelin, English rock band.
215 "There! I've Said It Again" (Redd Evans/David Mann, 1945). "There, as her mother used to sing, he said it again."
224 Jaco Pastorius (1951–1987), American bass player and composer.
225 "Who's Sorry Now" (Ted Snyder/Bert Kalmar/Harry Ruby, 1923).
225 "I Gotta Right to Sing the Blues" (Harold Arlen/Ted Koehler, 1932).
225 "Don't Get Around Much Anymore" (Duke Ellington/Bob Russell, 1940).
225 "As Time Goes By" (Herman Hupfeld, 1931).

238	"The Worms Crawl In" (a.k.a. "The Hearse Song"), unknown origin (possibly Crimean War [1853–1856] or World War I [1914–1918]). Popularized by Alvin Schwartz's children's books *Scary Stories to Tell in the Dark* in 1981. "The famous worms of song."
247	Blue Cheer, American rock band.
264	Madonna (*1958), American singer and songwriter.
265	Willie Nelson (*1933), American singer, songwriter, and guitarist.
272	"The Star-Spangled Banner" (John Stafford Smith, c. 1773/ Francis Scott Key, 1814).
279	Pink Floyd, British psychedelic rock band.
279	Jimi Hendrix (1942–1970), American rock guitarist and singer.
281	"Louie Louie" (Richard Berry, 1955).
281	"Wooly Bully" (Domingo Samudio, 1965).
281	Frank Zappa (1940–1993), American musician.
281	"Love Is Strange" (Mickey Baker/Sylvia Vanderpool/Ethel Smith, 1956), recorded by Mickey & Sylvia.
287	"Of Thee I Sing" (George and Ira Gershwin, 1931).
290	"Down Among the Sheltering Palms" (Abe Olman/James Brockman/Leo Wood, 1914).
290	"Crazeology" (Charlie Parker, year unknown).
290	"Klactoveedsedsteene" (Charlie Parker, year unknown)
290	Charlie "Yardbird" Parker (1920–1955), American alto saxophonist.
290	Miles Davis (1926–1991), American jazz trumpeter.
290	Dizzy Gillespie (1917–1993), American jazz trumpeter.
303	Augustín Lara (1897–1970), Mexican singer, actor, and songwriter.
309	Charles Manson (1934–2017), American criminal and musician.
309	Wild Man Fischer (1944–2004), American musician.
309	Tiny Tim (1932–1996), American singer and ukulelist.
312	"Do-Re-Mi" (Richard Rodgers/Oscar Hammerstein II, 1959) from *The Sound of Music*, performed by Julie Andrews.
312	The Surfaris, American surf rock band.
314	*The Best of Sam Cooke* (Sam Cooke, 1962).
319	The Osmonds, American family music group.
320	Joe Hill (1879–1915), Swedish-American hobo, union leader, singer, and songwriter.
325	"Toccata and Fugue in D minor", BWV 565, attributed to Johann Sebastian Bach (1685–1750), published 1833. "Tokkata & Fuji."

325 "Wachet auf, ruft uns die Stimme", BWV 140 (Johann Sebastian Bach, 1731).
328 "Maybellene" (Chuck Berry, 1955).
330 Elvis Presley (1935–1977), American rock 'n' roll singer and guitarist.
330 "I Fall to Pieces" (Patsy Cline, 1961).
341 "Theme from *The Smurfs*" (Hoyt Curtin, 1981).
345 "El paso" (Marty Robbins, 1959). "'Trying,' as Marty Robbins once put it in a different context, 'to stay in the saddle'."
346 Desiderio Alberto Arnaz y de Acha III (a.k.a. Desi Arnaz, 1917–1986), Cuban-American musician and actor.
346 "Babalú" (Margarita Lecuona, 1939).
346 "In Acapulco" (Harry Warren/Mack Gordon, c. 1944).
346 Likely "(I'll See You In) C-U-B-A" (Irving Berlin, c. 1919).
346 "We're Having a Baby (My Baby and Me)" (Vernon Duke/Harald Adamson, 1941).
350 Pérez Prado (1916–1989), Mexican bandleader musician, and composer.
362 "Polka Dots and Moonbeams" (Jimmy Van Heusen/Johnny Burke, 1940).
362 "In the Mood" (Wingy Manone/Andy Razaf, 1939).
362 "Moonlight Serenade" (Glenn Miller/Mitchell Parish, 1939).
368 "Theme from *Gilligan's Island*" (Sherwood Schwartz/George Wyle, 1964).
374 "Take It to the Limit" (Randy Meisner/Don Henley/Glenn Frey, 1975) from *Greatest Hits* by the Eagles.
378 Paul McCartney (*1942), English singer, bass player, and songwriter, member of The Beatles.
380 "Your Cheatin' Heart" (Hank Williams, 1952).
384 "Johnny B. Goode" (Chuck Berry, 1958).

Pynchon's Songs in *Vineland*

21 *Greatest Hits* by Fascist Toejam.
36 *Not Too Mean to Cry* (album of torch songs for male vocalists as envisioned by Zoyd Wheeler).
47 "The Marquis de Sod," to the tune of "La Marseillaise".
63 "Little Grass Skirt." Performed by Zoyd Wheeler.
66 "Wacky Coconuts." Performed by Zoyd Wheeler and Takeshi Fumimoto.[2]
91 "Digits in God's Computer" (gospel). Hummed by Frenesi.
99 "Theme from *Hawaii Five-O*" with alternative lyrics.

104–05 "A Floozy with An Uzi." Performed by DL and the Vomitones.[5]

162 "Just Like a William Powell." Performed by Takeshi Fumimoto.

164 *The All-Regimental Bagpipes Play Prime Time Favorites.*

180–81 "V & B Tow Company Theme" (based on the theme of "The Adventures of Chip 'n' Dale"). Sung by Vato and Blood.

191 "Here Comes that Stove Once Again." Sung by DL.

224 "Thanatoid World." Performed by Van Meter.

281 "Another Cheap Romance." Performed by the Surfadelics (a.k.a. the Corvairs), sung by Zoyd Wheeler.

309 "Lawrence of Arabia" (lullaby). Sung by Zoyd Wheeler.

331 "Children of the Freeway." Sung by Ché.

336–37 "The Tube."

343–44 "Es posible."

356–57 "I'm a Cop." By Billy Barf. Performed by Billy Barf and the Vomitones.[5]

363–64 "Like a Meat Loaf." Performed by Holocaust Pixels.

377 *The '83 Garage Tapes* by Billy Barf and the Vomitones.

Mason & Dixon

19 "Where the Bee Sucks" (Thomas Arne or Robert Johnson/William Shakespeare, first documented in 1659).

53 "Heart of Oak" (William Boyce/David Garrick, 1760).

53 "Rule Britannia" (Thomas Arne/James Thomson, 1740).

53 Johann Joachim Quantz (1697–1773), German flutist and composer.

78 "Don't Forget Tonight Tomorrow" (Jay Milton/Ukie Sherin), recorded by Frank Sinatra, 1945. "Don't forget to-night, Charles."

79 "What'd I Say" (Ray Charles, 1959). "Tell me, [...] what'd I say?"

104 Carl Ditters von Dittersdorf (1739–1799), Austrian composer and violinist.

104 Johann Joachim Quantz (1697–1773), German flutist and composer.

118 "For He's a Jolly Good Fellow", unknown origin, possibly 1709.

177 "Rule Britannia" (Thomas Arne/James Thomson, 1740).

213–14 William Herschel (1738–1822), British-German astronomer, composer, and organist.

229 George Frideric Handel (1685–1759), German composer.

262 "Anacreon in Heaven" (attr. to John Stafford Smith, ca. 1780; lyrics: Ralph Tomlinson).

263 "The World Turned Upside Down" (lyrics: Thomas Tracts, 1646) to the tune of "When the King Enjoys His Own Again" (Martin Parker, 1643).

268 Marianne Davies (1743/1744–c. 1818), English musician.

268 Wolfgang Amadeus Mozart (1756–1791), Austrian composer.

270 *The Beggar's Opera (*Johann Christoph Pepusch/John Gay, 1728).

272 Christoph Willibald Ritter von Gluck (1714–1787), German composer.

272 Marianne Davies (1743/1744–c. 1818), English musician.

285 "Havah Nagila" (Hebrew folk song, arranged by Abraham Zvi Idelsohn in the 1910s or 1920s).

292 *Love in a Village* (Thomas Arne/Isaac Bickerstaffe, 1762). "Mr. Arne's *Love in a Cottage.*"

317 "Yankee Doodle" (Traditional; lyrics attributed to Richard Shuckburgh, 1770s).

332 "The World Turned Upside Down" (lyrics: Thomas Tracts, 1646) to the tune of "When the King Enjoys His Own Again" (Martin Parker, 1643). "The Sky, turn'd upside down?"

377 *Margherita e Don Aldo* (Baldassare Galuppi, 1706–1785). Likely a fictional opera attributed to an actual composer.

413 Besozzi: Italian family of musicians. Composers and oboists were Alessandro Besozzi (1702–1775), Girolamo Besozzi (1745 or 1750–1788), Paolo Girolamo Besozzi (1713–1778). Composers were Antonio Besozzi (1714–1781), Carlo Besozzi (1738–1791), Gaetano Besozzi (1725–1798). Giuseppe Besozzi (1686–1760) was an oboist.

413 Johann Joachim Quantz (1697–1773), German flutist and composer.

425 "O Ruddier than the Cherry" from *Acis and Galatea* (George Frideric Handel, c. 1732).

441 "You Ain't Just Whistlin' Dixie" (David Bellamy, 1979). "He ain't just hummin' 'Love in a Cottage,' either."

441 *Love in a Village* (Thomas Arne/Isaac Bickerstaffe, 1762). "Love in a Cottage."

455 *The Beggar's Opera (*Johann Christoph Pepusch/John Gay, 1728). "Macheath."

456 "Moses Supposes" from *Singin' In the Rain* (Betty Comden/ Adolph Green, 1952).

458 *The Beggar's Opera (*Johann Christoph Pepusch/John Gay, 1728).

583 "The Black Joke" (origin unknown, England, c. 1730).

621 "Stand By Your Man" (Billy Sherrill/Tammy Wynette, 1968). "Sometimes, [...] 'tis hard, to be a Woman."

668 Catherine-Nicole Lemaure (1703/04–1786), French opera singer, or, less likely, Nicole Le Maure (1704–1783), French opera singer.

668 Besozzi. Reference unclear, see entry for page 413.

750 Carl Ditters von Dittersdorf (1739–1799), Austrian composer and violinist.

Pynchon's Songs in *Mason & Dixon*

18–19 "The Learnèd English Dog" (overture). Performed by the Learnèd English Dog, accompanied by horn, clarinet, and cello.

27–28 "Let Us Go Down to Hepsie's Tonight."[2]

34 "Sumatra." Sung by the sailors of the *Seahorse*.

40 "La France ne fait pas la guerre contre les sciences." Performed by the sailors of the *l'Grand*.

48 "Wicked Young Widows." Sung by the Rev. Wicks Cherrycoke.

50 "Off to the Indies." Sung by Charles Mason and Jeremiah Dixon.

80–81 "Cape Girl." Sung by a young gallant with a three-stringed lute.

82 "Out in the Dark."

90 "Scanderoon" (medium-tempo Cuban rhythm). Sung by Charles Mason and Jeremiah Dixon.

104 "Scamozzetta" from *I gluttoni*.

109–10 "The Brave Lord Ferrers." Sung by Florinda.

110 "Rolling out the Edgeware Road."

130 "Men in the Moon." Sung by a chorus of pleasant-looking young women.

136–37 "The Stars Will Say." Sung by Maskelyne.

143–44 "Mason on Your Mind."

168–69 "The Great Octuple." Sung by the local youths of Randwick.

177 *L'orecchio fatale* (Squivelli).

224–25 "Brothers in the S. of J." Sung by the priest.

283–84 "The Transit of Venus." Sung by George and Martha Washington.

292 *Love in a Cottage* (Thomas Arne). Spoof on *Love in a Village* (Thomas Arne/Isaac Bickerstaffe, 1762).

292 "Galop" from *The Rebel Weaver*. Hummed by Charles Mason.

311 "When Night Was Day." Sung by Charles Mason.

319–20 "Ay, Señorita." Sung by Charles Mason.

377 *Margherita e Don Aldo* (Baldassare Galuppi, 1706–1785). Likely a fictional opera attributed to an actual composer.

398 "Polecat in the Parlor." Whistled and sung by Jeremiah Dixon.

432 "Torpedo." Performed by Prof. Voam.
464–65 "Gimme That Dairy."
477–78 "Pepinazos." Played by the Vásquez Brothers' Marimba Quartet.
518–19 "Men Have the Sterling." Sung by S. Blondelle, harmonies by a couple of sisters.
552–53 "Mister Fahrenheit" (probably a blues). Performed by Ethelmer.
562–63 "The Black Hole of Calcutta" from *The Black Hole of Calcutta, or, The Peevish Wazir.* Performed by two dozen ladies and a small orchestra.
570–71 "Americans All." Sung by groups of farm girls.
670–71 "Rapture de West." Performed by Hugh Crawfford.
701 "The Chances of Night."
753 "It Was Fun While It Lasted."[2] Sung by Charles Mason and Jeremiah Dixon, accompanied by a chamber orchestra.

Against the Day

30 Medley with Hawaiian and Philippino motifs, concluding with the "Bacchanale" from *Samson and Delilah* (Camille de Saint-Saëns, 1877).
37 "Old Zip Coon" (to the tune of "Turkey in the Straw," origin disputed, probably between 1829 and 1834).
38 "It's the End of the World as We Know It (And I Feel Fine)" (Billy Berry/Peter Buck/Mike Mills/Michael Stipe, 1987). "The end of the world, not just 'as we know it'."
54 "All Coons Look Alike to Me" (Ernest Hogan, 1895). Adapted from a song entitled "All Pimps Look Alike to Me" that Hogan once heard.
55 "Jerusalem" (also known as "And Did Those Feet in Ancient Times." Hubert Parry/William Blake, 1916/ca. 1808).
88 "Hail to the Chief" (James Sanderson/Sir Walter Scott, c. 1812/1810).
182 "Bad Boys" (Ian Lewis, 1987). "Tell me, what-cha gon-na do, When they come screamin, after you?"
207 "The World Turned Upside Down" (lyrics: Thomas Tracts, 1646) to the tune of "When the King Enjoys His Own Again" (Martin Parker, 1643). "The world turned all inside out."
234 "Juanita" (attributed to Hon. Mrs. Norton, arranged by T. G. May, 1855).

243 Joe Hill (1879–1915), Swedish-American hobo, union leader, singer, and songwriter.

258 "Amán, amán." Likely "Tha spáso koúpes" (traditional song of Asia Minor). Also referred to on p. 945.

285 *Symphony No. 45 in F-sharp minor* (known as the *Farewell Symphony*, Joseph Haydn, 1772).

300 Country waltz from Österbybruk, possibly "Dunderhakens vals."

355 "Juanita" (attributed to Hon. Mrs. Norton, arranged by T. G. May, 1855).

377 *Little Nellie Kelly* (musical comedy film from 1940 or George M. Cohan's 1922 musical of the same title). "Nellie Noonan."

377 Anna Held (1872–1918), Polish-born French performer and singer.

388 Lillian Russell (1860/61–1922), American actress and singer.

391 "O'Leary's Bar" a.k.a. "Her Mother Never Told Her" (Irish, unknown origin). "Her mother never told her."

393 "Funiculì, Funiculà" (Luigi Denza/Peppino Turco, 1880).

397 Theme from *La forza del destino* (Giuseppe Verdi, 1862).

397 Luigi Denza (1842–1922), Italian composer.

407 "The Commonwealth of Toil" (Ralph Chaplin, c. 1910s; to the tune of "Nelly Grey" by Benjamin Hanby, 1856).

419 *Guillaume Tell* (Gioachino Rossini, 1829).

422 "Rock of Ages" (Thomas Hastings/Augustus Montague Toplady, 1830/1775).

424 "La Cucaracha." Spanish ballad; origin unknown. It became widely popular during the Mexican Revolution (1910–1920).

439 "La Cucaracha." Spanish ballad; origin unknown. It became widely popular during the Mexican Revolution (1910–1920).

449 "On the Good Ship Lollipop" (Richard A. Whiting/Sidney Clare, 1934). Sung by Shirley Temple. "Lollipop lounge."

471 "El Capitán" (John Philip Sousa, 1896).

471 "Whistling Rufus" (Frederick Allen "Kerry" Mills, 1899).

472 "My Country 'Tis of Thee" (also known as "America," composition unknown; same melody as "God Save the Queen," lyrics by Samuel Francis Smith, 1831).

475 "Gendarmes' Duet" from *Geneviève de Brabant* (Jacques Offenbach, 1859/1867). Here most likely in the march version known as the "The Halls of Montezuma" or the "Marines' Hymn" (copyright secured by the Marine Corps in 1919).

476 "At a Georgia Camp Meeting" (Frederick Allen "Kerry" Mills, 1897).

478 "After the Ball" (Charles K. Harris, 1892).
520 "The Preacher and the Slave" (also known as "Pie in the Sky" or "Long Haired Preachers," Joseph P. Webster/Joe Hill, 1911)
535 "Lead me Lord" (a.k.a. "For It Is Thou, Lord") (Samuel Sebastian Wesley, 1861).
558 Richard Strauss (1864–1949), German composer.
564 "The Owl and the Pussycat" (traditional, lyrics by Edward Lear, 1867).
574 Victor August Herbert (1859–1924), Irish-German composer, cellist, and conductor.
574 Ermanno Wolf-Ferrari (1876–1948), German-Italian composer.
588 Giuseppe Verdi (1813–1901), Italian composer.
588 Luigi Denza (1842–1922), Italian composer.
588 Antonio Smareglia (1854–1929), Austro-Hungarian composer.
611 "La Marseillaise" (Claude Joseph Rouget de Lisle, 1792). *"Aux armes, citoyens."*
621 "E-minor Nocturne" (Frédéric Chopin, composed 1827–1829, published 1855).
624 "E-minor Nocturne" (Frédéric Chopin, composed 1827–1829, published 1855).
636 *Madama Butterfly* (Giacomo Puccini, 1904).
636 "La Matchiche" (Charles Borel-Clerc, c. 1905).
639 Giuseppe Verdi (1813–1901), Italian composer.
703 "O Tempora, O Mores" (i.e. "Ich bin ein Musikante," German folk song, origin unknown).
703 "The Black Whale of Askalon" (i.e. "Im schwarzen Walfisch zu Askalon," German folk song with lyrics by Joseph Victor von Scheffel, 1854; melody likely from 1783 or before).
703–04 *Salome* (op. 54) (Richard Strauss, based on Hedwig Lachmann's translation of Oscar Wilde's play *Salomé*, 1905).
704 "Gaudeamus igitur" (unknown, first appearance of the text in the Middle Ages, possibly 13th century). "Judeamus igitur" etc.
728 "Daisy Bell (Bicycle Built for Two)" (Harry Dacre, 1892).
744 Richard Wagner (1813–1883), German composer.
755 "For He's a Jolly Good Fellow" (traditional, melody dating back to at least 1709).
760 "Merry Widow Waltz" (Franz Lehár, 1905/Lorenz Hart), likely in the version of the 1934 movie *The Merry Widow*. "All the world in love with love."
764 W.S. Gilbert, 1836–1911, English dramatist and librettist.
764 Arthur Sullivan, 1842–1900, English composer.
766 Perhaps *Tristan und Isolde* (Richard Wagner, 1865). "Liebestod."

786 "Ritter Georg hoch!" to the tune of "Prinz Eugen der edle Ritter" (c. 1719), which was to the tune of "Als Chursachsen das vernommen, dass der Turk vor Wien was kommen" from 1683.

789 Fiakerlieder, maybe in particular the "Fiakerlied" (Gustav Pick, 1885).

800 "Adagio" from the *Piano Concerto in A Major, K. 488* (Wolfgang Amadeus Mozart, 1786).

803 "Ausgerechnet Bananen," the German version of "Yes! We have no bananas" (Frank Silver/Irving Cohn, 1922, German lyrics by Fritz Löhner-Beda, 1923).

803 Leo Slezak (1873–1946), Moravian tenor.

804 *Schule der Geläufigkeit*, op. 299 (i.e. *School of Velocity*) (Carl Czerny, 1830s).

809 Rigó Jansci (1858–1927), Hungarian violinist.

814 "On the Banks of the Wabash, Far Away" (Paul Dresser, 1897).

833 Johann Strauss II (1825–1899), Austrian composer.

833 Luigi Denza (1842–1922), Italian composer.

833 Ermanno Wolf-Ferrari (1876–1948), German-Italian composer.

846 "Kalinka" (Ivan Larionov, 1860).

846 "Ochi Chorniya" (Florian Hermann/Evheniy Grebenka, 1884/1843).

881 "Rudolph the Red-Nosed Reindeer" (Johnny Marks, 1949).
"Reindeer [with] radiatioin into an epidermal luminescence at the red end of the spectrum, particularly around the nasal area."

914 "Variation IX (Adagio) 'Nimrod'" from *Variations on an Original Theme for Orchestra ("Enigma"), Op. 36* (Edward Elgar, 1898/1899).

914 *La gazza ladra* (Gioachino Rossini, 1817).

914 "The Song of the Volga Boatmen" (Russian folk song, collected by Mily Balakirev, 1866).

914 "Auld Lang Syne" (Scottish folk song; lyrics: Robert Burns, 1788).

945–46 "Tha spáso koúpes" (traditional song of Asia Minor, possibly composed around 1907).

948 Perhaps "You Are My Destiny" (Paul Anka, 1957), it is unclear if the Greek is a reference to a song.

948 Avraam Karakaş Kohen Efendi (sometimes transliterated Abraham Caracach Efendi), Turkish-Jewish singer (active 1890–1914).

971 "I Love You Truly" (Carrie Jacobs-Bond, 1901).

997–98 "Overture" from *Guillaume Tell* (Gioachino Rossini, 1829).

1005 Ralph Vaughan Williams (1872–1958), English composer,

conductor, and collector of English folk music.

1005–06 *Fantasia on a Theme by Thomas Tallis* (Ralph Vaughan Williams, 1910).

1018 "Constantinople" (The Residents, 1978). "Here I come, Constantinople."

1057 Béla Bartók (1881–1945), Hungarian composer and pianist.

1057 Zoltán Kodály (1882–1967), Hungarian composer and ethnomusicologist.

1057 Joseph Canteloube (1879–1957), French composer and musicologist.

1057 Ralph Vaughan Williams (1872–1958), English composer, conductor and collector of English folk music.

1057 Eugénie Lineff (Evgeniya Lineva or Linyova, 1853/4–1919), collector of Russian and Ukrainian folk songs.

1057 Hjalmar Thuren (1873–1912), Danish music historian.

1061 Johann Sebastian Bach (1685–1750), German composer.

1079 S. Cosmas of Jerusalem (eighth century), bishop and writer of hymns.

1090 "Jim Along Jo" better known as "Jim Along Josie." American folk song, possibly written by Edward Harper in 1838 or 1840 for the play *The Free Nigger of New York*.

1094 "The Man Who Broke the Bank at Monte Carlo" (Fred Gilbert, 1891 or 1892).

1099 Franz Schubert (1797–1828), Austrian composer.

1099 "I'm Going to Get Myself a Black Salome" (Ed Wynn/Stanley Murphy, 1908).

1171 Ernö Rapée (1891–1945), American composer and pianist. Author of books on music and motion pictures.

1198 "C'est pas Paris, c'est sa banlieue" from *Ciboulette* (Reynaldo Hahn, 1923).

1198 "J'ai Deux Amants" from *L'amour masqué* (André Messager/ Sacha Guitry, 1923).

1198 "Que veulent dire ces colères" (a.k.a. "Oh! Que les hommes sont bêtes") from *La Périchole* (Jacques Offenbach/Henri Meilhac/Ludovic Halévy, 1868).

1199 "Daisy Bell (Bicycle Built for Two)" (Harry Dacre, 1892). "It won't be a stylish marriage."

Pynchon's Songs in *Against the Day*

16–17 "The Chums of Chance Song." Sung by the Chums of Chance, accompanied by Miles on the ukulele.[2]

55–56	"Fierce as the Winter's Tempest" from the Workers' Own Songbook. Sung at the workers'/anarchists' congregation.
141	"The Girls of Iceland." Sung by some sailors on the Étienne-Louis Malus.
154–55	"Nansen and Johansen" (c. 1897). Sung by the Chums of Chance.
180	*Roscoe Conkling*. Operetta.
180	*Princess of the Badlands*. Operetta.
180	*Mischief in Mexico*. Operetta.
182–83	"When Those Natives Run Amuck" from *African Antics* (R. Wilshire Vibe).
204–05	"Beavers of the Brain." Performed by the inhabitants of Lew Basnight's steak.
228	"Durango Dove." Performed by Cooper with school kids singing along.
365–66	"That Göttingen Rag." Performed by Heino Vanderjuice with a ukulele.
383	*Shanghai Scampers* (R. Wilshire Vibe).
388	*African Antics* (R. Wilshire Vibe).
388	*Shanghai Scampers* (R. Wilshire Vibe).
392	"Oh, When You Talk That Talk," from *Roscoe Conkling* (R. Wilshire Vibe). Sung by Miss Oomie Vamplet.
450	"Down in Hell's Kitchen." Sung by a ten-year-old chanteuse, accompanied by the tiny jazz orchestra.
558	"Te Deum" by Filtham.
599–600	"The Quizzical, Queer Quaternioneer" (bouncy 6/8). Performed by a contralto, accompanied by a small street-ensemble.
672	"Her Idea of Banter." Sung by Günther von Quassel.
763–64	Medley from *Waltzing in Whitechapel, or, A Ripping Romance*, including "Copper Propaganda." Performed by a ukulele quartet.
770	"Singing Bird of Spitalfields" from *Waltzing in Whitechapel, or, A Ripping Romance*. Sung by Neville and Nigel, accompanied on the ukulele by Nigel.
922–23	"Idiotic." Sung by Bevis and Jacintha, accompanied by a band.
1008	*Wogs Begin at Wigan*.
1008	*Roguish Redheads*.
1026	"Machen wir einen Schaufensterbummel" (waltz) from *The Burgher King*.
1027	"Those Austro-Hungarian Blues" from *The Burgher King*.
1198	"Casse-cou" from *Fossettes l'Enflammeuse* (a.k.a. *Dimples*) (Jean-Raoul Oeuillade). Performed by Dally.

1203–04 "Dive-Bombing into The Day."
1216–17 "Vegetariano" (tango).

Inherent Vice

1 Country Joe and the Fish, American psychedelic rock band.
3 "Can't Buy Me Love" (John Lennon/Paul McCartney, 1964), recorded by The Beatles.[3]
10 "Sugar, Sugar" (Jeff Barry/Andy Kim, 1969), recorded by The Archies.[3]
11 "Runaround Sue" (Dion DiMucci/Ernie Maresca, 1961), recorded by Dion. "Sad but true, as Dion always sez."
36 Dick Dale (Richard Anthony Monsour, 1937–2019), American surf rock guitarist.
37 Jimi Hendrix (1942–1970), American rock guitarist and singer.
37 Earl Bostic (1912–1965), American jazz and rhythm and blues alto saxophonist.
37 Stan Getz (1927–1991), American jazz tenor saxophonist.
37 Lee Allen (1927–1994), American rock'n'roll tenor saxophonist.
37 The Chantays, American surf rock band.
37 The Trashmen, American rock band.
37 The Halibuts (mentioned anachronistically as they apparently started out in the 1980s).
42 Theme song from *Mighty Mouse* (Philip Scheib/Marshall Barer, c. 1955). "Here I am [...] to save the day."
43 Theme song from *The Big Valley* (George Duning, 1965).
55 "The Great Pretender" (Buck Ram, 1955), recorded by The Platters.
56 "Bang Bang (My Baby Shot Me Down)" (Sonny Bono, 1966), recorded by The Bonzo Dog Band around 1968.[3]
61 "Strangers in the Night" (Bert Kaempfert/Charles Singleton/Eddie Snyder, 1966), recorded by Frank Sinatra. "'Exchanging glances,' as Frank might put it."
69 "Oh, Pretty Woman" (Roy Orbison/Bill Dees, 1964). "If that's the way it must be, okay, as Roy Orbison always sez."
72 "Wouldn't It Be Nice" (Brian Wilson/Tony Asher/Mike Love, 1966), recorded by The Beach Boys.[3]
75 "Fly Me to the Moon" (Bart Howard, 1954), recorded by Frank Sinatra in 1964.[3]
77 "The Crystal Ship" (Jim Morrison, 1966) recorded by The Doors. "He'd slipped, as Jim Morrison might put it, 'into unconsciousness'."

77 "Blueberry Hill" (Vincent Rose/Larry Stock/Al Lewis, 1940) recorded by Fats Domino in 1950. "As Fats Domino always sez, 'never to be'."
78 The Beach Boys, American surf pop band.
81 "People Are Strange (When You're a Stranger)" (Robby Krieger/Jim Morrison, 1967), recorded by The Doors.
92 Iron Butterfly, American psychedelic rock band.
92 *Il Trovatore* (Giuseppe Verdi, 1853). "Eel Trovatore."
95 Blue Cheer (Amazon playlist: *Vincebus Eruptum* [1968]), American rock band.[3]
97 "On the Good Ship Lollipop" (Richard A. Whiting/Sidney Clare, 1934). Sung by Shirley Temple. "Get a lollipop from the Captain."
101 "Wipe Out" (Bob Berryhill/Pat Connolly/Jim Fuller/Ron Wilson, 1962), recorded by The Surfaris.[3]
103 The Electric Prunes, American psychedelic rock band.
108/9 "The Other Side" (Bill Dorsey, possibly 1966) a.k.a. "The Ice Caps are Melting," recorded by Tiny Tim in 1968.[3]
121 Pearls Before Swine, American psychedelic folk band.
124 "Pipeline" (Brian Carman/Bob Spickard). Recorded by The Chantays, 1962.[3]
124 "Surfin' Bird" (Al Frazier/Carl White/Sonny Harris/Turner Wilson Jr., 1963), recorded by The Trashmen.[3]
124 "Bam Boo" (Carl Conaster/Tom King, 1959), recorded by Johnny & The Hurricanes.[3]
124 Eddie & the Showmen, American surf rock band.
124 The Belairs, American surf rock band.
125 The Hollywood Saxons, American rhythm and blues band.
125 The Olympics, American rhythm and blues band.
125 "Tequila" (Joe Johnson, 1957), recorded by The Champs.[3]
128 Charles-Louis Hanon (1819–1900), French piano pedagogue and composer.
129 Richard William "Rick" Wright (1943–2008), British keyboardist of Pink Floyd.
130 George Formby (George Hoy Booth, 1904–1961), British singer-songwriter, ukulelist, and banjolelist.
130 "Leaning on a Lamp Post" (Noel Gay, 1937), Herman's Hermits 1966 cover of George Formby's recording.
130 Pat Boone (*1934), American singer.
131 "Donna Lee" (Miles Davis; originally attributed to Charlie Parker, 1947).
134 "Here Comes the Ho-Dads" (1962) recorded by the Marketts.[3,4]
135 "Eight Miles High" (Gene Clark/Jim McGuinn/David Crosby,

1966), recorded by The Byrds.

146 Frank Zappa (1940–1993), American musician.

148 “Runaway” (Max Crook/Del Shannon, 1961), recorded by Del Shannon.

148 Zubin Mehta (*1936), Indian conductor.

153 “Happy Trails to You” (Dale Evans, 1952), recorded by Roy Rogers.[3]

155 Wild Man Fischer (1944–2011), American musician.

156 “White Rabbit” (Grace Slick, 1966), recorded by Jefferson Airplane.

156 “This Guy’s in Love with You” (Burt Bacharach/Hal David, 1968), recorded by Herb Alpert & The Tijuana Brass.

159 Antônio Carlos Jobim (1927–1994), Brazilian songwriter and singer.

160 “Desafinado” (Antônio Carlos Jobim/Newton Mendonça, 1958; English lyrics by Jon Hendricks and Jesse Cavanagh, c. 1962).

160 “It Never Entered My Mind” (Richard Rodgers/Lorenz Hart, 1940), from the musical *Higher and Higher.*[3]

160 “Alone Together” (Arthur Schwartz/Howard Dietz, 1932).

162 “Samba Do Avião” (Antonio Carlos Jobim, 1963).

165 Tommy James and the Shondells, American rock’n’roll band.[3]

166 George Harrison (1943–2001), British guitarist and composer, member of The Beatles.

176 “Quentin’s Theme” (Theme from *Dark Shadows)* (Robert Cobert, 1968).[3]

193 “Something Happened to Me Yesterday” (Mick Jagger/Keith Richards, 1967), recorded by the Rolling Stones.[3]

198 Floyd Cramer (1933–1997), American country music pianist.

220 Władziu Valentino Liberace (1919–1987), American pianist and entertainer.

220 “Grande valse brillante in E-flat major, Op. 18” (Frédéric Chopin, 1833) or possibly Op. 34 No. 1, 2, or 3 (1834–38).

221 “There’s No Business Like Show Business” (Irving Berlin, 1946), sung by Ethel Merman, 1954.[3]

222 Mick Jagger (*1943), British rock singer.

223 L.A. Philharmonic orchestra.

223 Frank Zappa (1940–1993), American musician.

224 “One Fine Day” (Carole King/Gerry Goffin, 1963), recorded by the Chiffons.

225 Ernest Dale Tubb (1914–1984), American country music singer and songwriter.

225 James Travis “Jim” Reeves (1923–1964), American country and pop singer and songwriter.

225 Michael Webb Pierce (1921–1991), American honky tonk singer and guitarist.

227 "The Wabash Cannonball" (William Kindt, 1904), originally published as "The Great Rock Island Route" (J.A. Roff, 1882). (Amazon playlist: recorded by Roy Acuff & His Crazy Tennesseans).[3]

227 Merle Haggard (1937–2016), American country singer, songwriter, and guitarist.

229 Les Paul (Lester William Polsfuss, 1915–2009), American jazz, country and blues guitarist and songwriter.

232 The Monkees, American pop and rock band.

232 Elvis Presley (1935–1977), American rock'n'roll singer and guitarist.

233 "Wunderbar" (Cole Porter, 1948) from *Kiss Me Kate.*

233 Frank Sinatra (1915–1998), American jazz singer and actor.

233 Dean Martin (1917–1995), American singer and actor.

233 Sammy Davis, Jr. (1925–1990), American singer and actor.

233 "Haunted Heart" (Howard Dietz/Arthur Schwartz, 1948) from *Inside U.S.A.*

234 "Viva Las Vegas" (Doc Pomus/Mort Shuman, 1963), recorded by Elvis Presley.

235 "Meet the Flintstones" (Hoyt Curtin, 1960). "'Page right out of history,' as the Flintstones might say."

235 Kismet, possibly named after "Kismet" (Sid Tepper/Roy C. Bennet), recorded by Elvis Presley, 1965.

239 Frank Sinatra (1915–1998), American jazz singer and actor.

239 Dean Martin (1917–1995), American singer and actor.

239 Sammy Davis, Jr. (1925–1990), American singer and actor.

239 "El Paso" (Marty Robbins, 1959). "What Marty Robbins'd call *foul evil deeds.*"

240 Pat Boone (*1934), American singer.

242 Ella Fitzgerald (1917–1996), American jazz singer, possibly a reference to "How High the Moon." "My girlfriend Ella / She's got the werewolf blues."

243 Elvis Presley (1935–1977), American rock'n'roll singer and guitarist.

244 Dolly Parton (*1946), American singer, songwriter, and actress.

244 Roy Acuff (1903–1992), American country music singer and fiddler.

245 Dean Martin (1917–1995), American singer and actor.

247 "(You're not Sick) You're Just in Love" (Irving Berlin, 1950), from

Call Me Madam, recorded by Ethel Merman and Russel Nype.

247 "Tiptoe Through the Tulips" (Joe Burke/Al Dubin, 1929), recorded by Tiny Tim in 1968. "Ain't exactly been tip-toein through no tulips."

247 "Everything's Coming Up Roses" (Stephen Sondheim/ Jule Styne, 1959), from *Gypsy*, recorded by Ethel Merman. "Everything's comin up roses, as Ethel always sez."

248 "A Puzzlement" (Richard Rodgers/Oscar Hammerstein II, 1951), from *The King and I*. "Forever, et cetera et cetera, and so forth as the King of Siam always sez."

249 Roza Eskenazi (mid-1890s–1980), Greek folk music singer. Exact song reference unclear.[3]

249 Bessie Smith (1894–1937), American blues singer.

257 Lawrence Welk (1903–1992), American musician, accordionist, bandleader, and TV personality.

257 Norma Zimmer (1923–2011), American singer.

261 Country Joe and the Fish, American psychedelic rock band.

271 "All Shook Up" (Otis Blackwell/Elvis Presley, 1957), recorded by Elvis Presley. "Uh who do you thank, as Elvis always sez, when you have such luck."

276 Antonio Vivaldi (1678–1741), Italian baroque composer and violinist.

277 Frank Sinatra (1915–1998), American jazz singer and actor, and the Rat Pack. "Hanging with Frank and the gang."

278 "That's Amore" (Harry Warren/Jack Brooks, 1953), recorded by Dean Martin.

289 Bonzo Dog Band, British pop band.

298 Clifford Everett "Bud" Shank, Jr. (1926–2009), American alto saxophonist and flute player.

299 "Interstellar Overdrive" (Syd Barrett/Roger Waters/Rick Wright/Nick Mason, 1967), recorded by Pink Floyd.[3]

300 "Tears on My Pillow" (Sylvester Bradford/Al Lewis, 1958), recorded by Little Anthony & The Imperials. "What Little Anthony & the Imperials call 'tempt the hand of fate'."

304 "Que Sera, Sera (Whatever Will Be, Will Be)" (Jay Livingston/ Ray Evans, 1956).

318 Mike Curb's score for *The Big Bounce* (1969).

330 "Elusive Butterfly" (Bob Lind, 1965).[3]

331 Glen Campbell (1936–2017), American country music singer, songwriter, and guitarist.

332 "Yummy Yummy Yummy" (Arthur Resnick/Joey Levine, 1968), recorded by Ohio Express (in the novel played as a—

probably fictional—Herb Alpert arrangement).[3]

337	Frank Sinatra (1915–1998), American jazz singer and actor.
338	Rocío Durcal (María de los Ángeles de las Heras Ortiz, 1944–2006), Spanish singer and actress.
356	"Something in the Air" (Speedy Keen, 1969), recorded by Thunderclap Newman.[3]
360	"We Should Be Together" (Harold Spina/Walter Bullock, 1938) from *Little Miss Broadway*, recorded by Shirley Temple and George Murphy.
363	Dick Dale (Richard Anthony Monsour, 1937–2019), American surf rock guitarist.
364	"Help Me Rhonda" (Brian Wilson/Mike Love, 1965), recorded by the Beach Boys.[3]
365	"Volare" ("Nel blu dipinto di blu") (Franco Migliacci/ Domenico Modugno, 1958), recorded by Domenico Modugno.[3]
365	"Java Jive" (Ben Oakland/Milton Drake, 1940).
368	"Super Market" (Fapardokly, 1966).[3]
368	Elephant's Memory, American rock band.[3]
368	"A Stranger in Love" (J. Hudson, possibly 1958), recorded by The Spaniels in 1958.[3]
368	"God Only Knows" (Brian Wilson/Tony Asher, 1966), recorded by The Beach Boys.[3]

Pynchon's Songs in *Inherent Vice*

43–44	Theme Song from Big Valley. Performed by Beer.[3]
51	"The Repossess Man" by Droolin' Floyd Womack.[3]
78–79	"Leo Carillo" by the Boards (on the Amazon playlist as "Motion by the Ocean").[3]
155	"Soul Gidget" by Meatball Flag.[3]
198–99	"Long Trip Out" by Spotted Dick.[2,3]
216	"Serenade for Peterbilt Rig and VW Bus.[3]
223	Symphonic Poem for Surf Band and Orchestra. Performed by the L.A. Philharmonic and The Boards.
229–30	"Just the Lasagna" by Carmine & the Cal-Zones.[3]
241–42	"Full Moon in Pisces" by Lark. [2,3]
337–38	"A Skyful of Hearts." Performed by Larry "Doc" Sportello.[3]
363	"Steamer Lane."
363	"Hair Ball."

Bleeding Edge

7 “Oops!... I Did It Again” (Max Martin/Rami Yakoub, 2000), recorded by Britney Spears.

12 “Landslide” (Stevie Nicks, 1975).

13 “Borderline” (Madonna, 1984).

16 “The Love Boat” (Charles Fox, Paul Williams, 1979). “Love, exciting and new, as they used to sing on *The Love Boat*.”

21 “Purple Haze” (Jimi Hendrix, 1967). “Figures, it’s that white food y’all eat, white bread and that,’ paraphrasing Jimi Hendrix.”

21 “Life Is A Party” (The Michael Zager Band, 1978). “Life is a party isn’t it Daytona.”

27 *West Side Story* (Leonard Bernstein/Steven Sondheim, 1957; here in the movie version from 1961).

43 “Korobeiniki” (a.k.a. “Korobushka,” Russian folk song based on a poem by Nikolay Nekrasov, 1861). “Nintendo’s Tetris theme.”

47 Britney Spears (*1981), American pop singer.

47 Jay-Z (a.k.a. Shawn Corey Carter, *1969), American rapper.

47 “1999” (Prince, 1982). “Even if hashslingrz is hirin like it’s 1999.” [7]

47–48 “Time Is on My Side” (Jerry Ragovoy, 1963), here in the version by The Rolling Stones, 1964.[6]

48 *Evil Empire* (Rage Against the Machine, 1996). “The next Evil Empire.” [7,8]

50 Elvis Presley (1935–1977), American rock ’n’ roll singer and guitarist.

52 John Lennon (1940–1980), British guitarist, singer and songwriter, member of The Beatles.

55–56 *West Side Story* (Leonard Bernstein/Steven Sondheim, 1957).

58 “It’s the End of the World as We Know It (And I Feel Fine)” (Billy Berry/Peter Buck/Mike Mills/Michael Stipe, 1987), recorded by R.E.M. “Anything short of the end of the world” etc. [8]

59 “Run Like Hell” (Roger Waters/David Gilmour, 1980), recorded by Pink Floyd. “Maybe I should be telling him to run like hell.” [6,8]

61 “Don’t Stop Believing” (Jonathan Cain, Steve Perry, Neal Schon, 1981).

65 “That’s Amore” (Harry Warren/Jack Brooks, 1952), recorded by Dean Martin in 1953). “When the stars make-a you droli” etc.

66 “Una furtiva lagrima” from *L’elisir d’amore* (Gaetano Donizzetti/Felice Romani, 1832).

69 “It’s Cool at the Mall” (Melanie’s Mall commercial, 1996).

92 “Won’t You Be My Neighbor?” (a.k.a. “It’s a Beautiful Day in the Neighborhood”, Mr. Rogers’ theme song) (Fred Rogers, 1967).

92 *Guys and Dolls* (Frank Loesser, 1950).

96 *Guys and Dolls* (Frank Loesser, 1950).
97 Frank Loesser (1910–1969) American composer.
97 Jussi Björling (1911–1960), Swedish opera tenor.
97 Deanna Durbin (1921–2013), Canadian singer and actress.
97 "Nessun dorma" from *Turandot* (Giacomo Puccini/Giuseppe Adami and Renato Simoni, 1926).
98 Giuseppe Verdi (1813–1901), Italian composer.
98 Giacomo Puccini (1858–1924), Italian composer.
98 Richard Wagner (1813–1883), German composer.
98 Aretha Franklin (1942–2018), American soul singer.
98 Luciano Pavarotti (1935–2007), Italian opera tenor.
100 *Tosca* (Giacomo Puccini/Giuseppe Giacosa and Luigi Illica, 1900).
100 Plácido Domingo (*1941), Spanish opera tenor.
100 Hildegard Behrens (1937–2009), German opera soprano.
102 "Strangers in the Night" (Avo Uvezian, Charles Singleton, Eddie Snyder, 1966), popularized by Frank Sinatra.
106 Big Ben theme (a.k.a. "Westminster Quarters" or "Westminster Chimes", origin disputed).
107 *The Flying Dutchman* (Richard Wagner, 1843).
112 "Billie's Bounce" (Charlie Parker, 1945).
121 Elvis Presley (1935–1977), American rock 'n' roll singer and guitarist.
124 John Kander (*1927), American composer.
124 Fred Ebb (1928–2004), American musical theater lyricist.
124 Richard Rodgers (1902–1979), American composer.
124 Oscar Hammerstein II (1895–1960), American librettist.
124 Andrew Lloyd Webber (*1948), British musical composer.
125 "The Chipmunk Song (Christmas Don't Be Late)" (Ross Bagdasarian Sr., 1958). "Me, I want a hula hoop."
127 "The Chipmunk Song (Christmas Don't Be Late)" (Ross Bagdasarian Sr., 1958). "Al-vinnn?"
141 Detsl (a.k.a. Kirill Aleksandrovich Tolmatskiy, a.k.a. Le Truk, *1983), Russian hip hop artist.
141 "Вечеринка у Децла" ("Vetcherinka U Detsla"; "Party at Detsl's") from Кто ты? (*Who Are You?*) (Detsl, 2000).
141 "Уличный боец" ("Ulitchnyi Boyets"; "Street Fighter") (Detsl, 2001).
149 "Don't Stop Believin'" (Jonathan Cain, Steve Perry and Neal Schon, 1981), recorded by Journey.
151 "More Than a Feeling" (Tom Scholz, 1976), recorded by Boston.
151 "Bohemian Rhapsody" (Freddie Mercury, 1975), recorded by

Queen.[7]

151 "Dancing Queen" (Björn Ulvaeus, Benny Andersson, Stig Anderson, 1976), recorded by ABBA.

153 *Oklahoma!* (Richard Rodgers/Oscar Hammerstein II, 1943), here in the movie version of 1955 with Gloria Grahame in the role of Ado Annie Carnes.

153 Irene Dunne (1898–1990), American film actress and singer.

154 "Volare (Nel blu dipinto di blu)" (Domenico Modugno/Franco Migliacci, 1958).

154 "Africa" (David Paich/Jeff Porcaro, 1981), recorded by Toto. "I left my brains down in Africa."

155–56 "September" (Maurice White, Al McKay and Allee Willis, 1978), recorded by Earth, Wind & Fire.

156 "What a Fool Believes" (Michael McDonald/Kenny Loggins, 1978), recorded by The Doobie Brothers.

158 "Doctor Wu" (Walter Becker/Donald Fagen, 1975), recorded by Steely Dan.

164 Celia Cruz (1925–2003), Cuban singer.

164 "Cuando Volverás" (Anthony "Romeo" Santos, 1999), recorded by Aventura.

166 "This Land Is Your Land" (Woody Guthrie, 1944). "This Land Is My Land, This Land Also Is My Land."

177 "Green Haze" (Elvis Hitler, 1988), a mashup of the next two entries. "Elvis Hitler [...] singing the *Green Acres* theme to the tune of 'Purple Haze'."

177 *Green Acres* theme (unknown, c. 1965).

177 "Purple Haze" (Jimi Hendrix, 1967).

187 Meat Loaf (*1947), American rock musician.

189 "Lyin' Eyes" (Don Henley/Glenn Frey, 1975), recorded by the Eagles. "Cheatin side of town, as the Eagles like to say."

189 "Kick Out the Jams" (MC5, 1969). "Where a man can kick out the jambs."

190 Shania Twain (*1965), Canadian singer-songwriter.

204 "Whoomp! (There It Is)" (Steven Gibson/Cecil Glen [Tag Team], 1993). "And whoop there it is."

209 "Nowhere to Run" (Lamont Dozier/Brian Holland/Eddie Holland, 1965), recorded by Martha and the Vandellas. "Nowhere to run to, nowhere to hide."[6, 8]

217 Henry "Henny" Youngman (1906–1998), American comedian and violinist.

217 *The Sound of Music* (Richard Rodgers/Oscar Hammerstein II, 1959), here in the movie version of 1965.

221 U2, Irish rock band.

221 Guns N' Roses, American hard rock band.

221 Journey, American rock band.

221 Moby (*1965), American singer, songwriter, and DJ.

221 "That's When I Reach for My Revolver" (Clint Conley, 1981), here in the version by Moby.

222 "Canned Heat" (Jay Kay/Sola Akingbola/Wallis Buchanan/Simon Katz/Derrick McKenzie/Tony Smith, 1999), recorded by Jamiroquai.

222 "Cosmic Girl" (Jay Kay/Derrick McKenzie, 1996), recorded by Jamiroquai.

231 "Baby Beluga" (Raffi, Ken Whiteley, 1980).

232 Les Paul (Lester William Polsfuss, 1915–2009), American jazz, country and blues guitarist and songwriter.

235 "Bird Dog" (Boudleaux Bryant, 1958,) recorded by The Everly Brothers.

239 "The Imperial March" (a.k.a. "Darth Vader Theme") (John Williams, 1980).

241 "Ride the Wild Surf" (Jan Berry/Brian Wilson/Roger Christian, 1964).

251 "Tzena, Tzena, Tzena" (Issachar Miron/Jehiel Hagges, 1941).

253 "Shall We Dance?" from *The King and I* (Richard Rodgers/Oscar Hammerstein II, 1951), here also referring to the movie version of 1956. "On the clear understanding, [...] as Deborah Kerr, or Marni Nixon, might say, or actually sing" etc.

253 Marni Nixon (1930–2016), American soprano and actress.

254 Tiny Desk Unit, American psychedelic dance band.

254 Bad Brains, American punk band.

263 Al Jolson (1886–1950), American singer and actor.

263 "Nessun dorma" from *Turandot* (Giacomo Puccini/Giuseppe Adami and Renato Simoni, 1926). "Talk about *nessun' dorma.*" [4]

267 *Jaws* theme (John Williams, 1975).

273 "Meet the Flintstones" (Hoyt Curtin, 1960).

279 "Donna non vidi mai" from *Manon Lescaut* (Giacomo Puccini, 1893).

282 Jay-Z (a.k.a. Shawn Corey Carter, *1969), American rap musician.

282 "The World Is Yours" (Nasir Jones/Peter Phillips, 1992), recorded by Nas.

282 Tupac Shakur (1971–1996), American rap musician and actor.[7]

282 The Notorious B.I.G. (a.k.a. Biggie or Biggie Smalls; Christopher George Latore Wallace) (1972–1997), American rap musician.

282 "Piggy Bank" (50 Cent, 2004). "Chairman Mao piggy banks."

283 "Hong Kong" (Jalacy Hawkins/I. Nahan, 1958), recorded by Screamin' Jay Hawkins.

289 Hy-Vee commercial (Annie Beacham/James Poulsen, 1990s).

295 "It's the End of the World as We Know It (And I Feel Fine)" (Bill Berry, Peter Buck, Mike Mills, Michael Stipe, 1987), recorded by R.E.M. "Something like this particular End of the World As We Know It." [8]

296 Johnny Pacheco (*1935), Dominican musician.

300 "Copacabana" (Barry Manilow, Jack Feldman, Bruce Sussman, 1978), recorded by Barry Manilow.

302 "1999" (Prince, 1982). "Party like it's 1999." [7]

302 Blink-182, American rock band.

302 Echo & The Bunnymen, British rock band.

302 Barenaked Ladies, Canadian rock band.

302 Bone Thugs-N-Harmony, American hip hop band.

302–03 "Erica Kane" (John Rowan, Edward Roeser, Nathan Kaatrud), recorded by Urge Overkill, 1993.

308 "Copacabana" (Barry Manilow, Jack Feldman, Bruce Sussman, 1978), recorded by Barry Manilow.

308 "What a Fool Believes" (Michael McDonald/Kenny Loggins, 1978), recorded by The Doobie Brothers.

311 "Closing Time" (Dan Wilson, 1998), recorded by Semisonic.

328 "America the Beautiful" (Samuel A. Ward/Katherine Lee Bates, 1895).

328 "Amazing Grace" (Christian hymn; lyrics: John Newton, 1779).

332 "Time After Time" (Sammy Cahn/Jule Styne, 1947), recorded by Frank Sinatra.

333 Sarcófago, Brazilian metal band.

333 Burzum, Norwegian metal band project.

333 Mayhem, Norwegian metal band.

344 Andrew Lloyd Webber (*1948), British musical composer.

347 "Macarena" (Rafael Ruiz Perdigones, Antonio Romero Monge, 1993), recorded by Los del Río.

351 "Dancing in the Street" (Marvin Gaye, William "Mickey" Stevenson, Ivy Jo Hunter, 1964), recorded by Martha and the Vandellas. "So he's working in 'D.C. now,' as Martha and the Vandellas might say." [6,8]

355 Tia Carrere (*1967), American actress, model, and singer.

355–56 "Regulate" (Nate Dogg/Warren G, 1994), recorded by Warren G and Nate Dogg.

356 "Don't Fear the Reaper" (Buck Dharma, 1976). "More Cowbell." [6]

356 Theme from *Deus Ex* (Alexander Brandon, 2000).

358 “Chalk Outline” (Adam Gontier/Neil Sanderson/Brad Walst/Barry Stock/Craig Wiseman, 2012), recorded by Three Days Grace on the album *Transit of Venus*. “The dead can't speak.”

362 “A Whiter Shade of Pale” (Gary Brooker/Keith Reid/Matthew Fisher, 1967), recorded by Procol Harum.

366 “Take Me Out to the Ballgame” (Albert Von Tilzer/Jack Norworth, 1908). “Buy me some peanuts and Cracker Jack?.”

369 “The Fez” (Walter Becker/Donald Fagan/Paul Griffin), recorded by Steely Dan, 1976.

369 “My Way” (Claude François/Jacques Revaux, 1967; lyrics by Paul Anka, 1968), likely the 1969 recording by Frank Sinatra.

382 “Beyond the Sea” (Jack Lawrence/Charles Trenet, 1946), here in the version of Bobby Darin, 1959.

382 Dean Martin (1917–1995), American singer and actor.

387 “Movin' on Up” (Theme from The Jeffersons) (Jeff Barry/Ja'net Dubois, 1975).

387 “Theme from *New York, New York*” (Fred Ebb/John Kander, 1977), popularized by Frank Sinatra. “The City That Doesn't Sleep.” [8]

392 “Already Gone” (Jack Tempchin/Robb Strandlund, 1973), recorded by The Eagles.

396 “Rudolph the Red-Nosed Reindeer” (Johnny Marks, 1949).

417 Theme from *The Godfather* (Nino Rota, 1972).

417 Wolfgang Amadeus Mozart (1756–1791), Austrian composer.

418 *Don Giovanni* (Wolfgang Amadeus Mozart, 1787), here in the fictional version by the Marx Brothers.

418 “Madamina, il catalogo è questo” (a.k.a. “The Catalogue Aria”) from *Don Giovanni* (Wolfgang Amadeus Mozart; libretto: Lorenzo Da Ponte, 1787).

418 “Deh, vieni alla finestra” from *Don Giovanni* (Wolfgang Amadeus Mozart; libretto: Lorenzo Da Ponte, 1787).

418 Nelson Eddy (1901–1967), American singer and actor.

422 Joe Hill (1879–1915), Swedish-American hobo, union leader, singer, and songwriter.

429 Eddie Fisher (1928–2010), American entertainer and singer.

433–34 “At Long Last Love” (Cole Porter, 1938; recorded by Frank Sinatra in 1957 and 1962). “It's just the strangest feeling [...] And Frank, I believe, was singing about love.”

434 Richard Wagner (1813–1883), German composer.

451 “Candle in the Wind” (Elton John/Bernie Taupin, 1973).

456 “Ты не один” (“Ty Nye Odin”) (recorded by DDT, 1992).

456 “Ветер” (“Veter”) (recorded by DDT, 1994).

457 “Marching to Astoria.” Unknown. Probably a pun on “Marching to Pretoria” (unknown origin, likely during the Boer Wars, 1880–1902).

457 “Zum Gali Gali” (Israeli children’s song, origin unknown).

457 “Ride wit Me” (Nelly, El DeBarge, William DeBarge, Jason Epperson, Steven Bojovich, Eugene Webb, Joe Islardo, 2000), recorded by Nelly.

464 Music from *Girl Happy* (George E. Stoll, 1965). “Elvis-movie music [...] I’M EVIL.”

464 Elvis Presley (1935–1977), American rock’n’roll singer and guitarist.

464 Michele Ann Marie “Shelley” Fabares (*1944), American actress and singer.

464 “Love Will Find A Way.” Likely a song reference, for instance to a song recorded either by Pablo Cruise (1978), Lionel Richie (1983), Yes (1987), or Christina Aguilera (1999).[7]

466 Elvis Presley (1935–1977), American rock’n’roll singer and guitarist.

467 “Can’t Smile Without You” (Christian Arnold/Geoff Morrow/David Martin, 1976).

467 “Reunited” (Dino Fekaris/Freddie Perren, 1977), recorded by Peaches & Herb.

474 *Mamma Mia!* (Björn Ulvaeus/Benny Andersson/Stig Anderson/Catherine Johnson, 1999).

474 Tammy Wynette (1942–1998), American country music singer and songwriter.

Pynchon’s Songs in *Bleeding Edge*

55–56 “Throw Those Puerto Ricans Out” (allegedly by Leonard Bernstein). Performed by Robert Moses.

151–53 “Massapequa” from *Amy & Joey* (1994). Sung by Cornelia.

185 “Middletown New York.” Recorded by Slade May Goodnight.[2]

195 “Throbbin’ Brain.” Recorded by Droolin Floyd Womack.

232–34 “Remember the Alley.” Performed by Driscoll Padgett.

282 “Tupac and Biggie Thangs.” Performed by Darren.

307–08 “In the Toilet” (hustle tempo). Recorded by Nazi Vegetable.

311 *The Attractive Schoolgirl of Zazhopinsk*.

362 “Soul Gidget” by Meatball Flag.

Miscellaneous Writings

Mortality and Mercy in Vienna

201 "Trio-Finale" from *Faust* (Charles Gounod, 1859).

207 "Madamina, il catalogo è questo" (a.k.a. "The Catalogue Aria") from *Don Giovanni* (Wolfgang Amadeus Mozart; libretto: Lorenzo Da Ponte, 1787).

210 *Concerto for Orchestra, Sz. 116, BB 123* (Béla Bartók, 1943).

Voice of the Hamster

157 Eddie Condon (1905–1973), American banjoist, guitarist, and bandleader.

161 "The Ballad of High Noon" (a.k.a. "Do Not Forsake Me Darlin'") (Dimitri Tiompkin/Ned Washington, 1952).

Pynchon's Song for "Voice of the Hamster"

159–160 "I Don't Care Anymore." Sung by Mr. Faggiaducci.

161 "Do Not Forsake Me, Faggiaducci." Sung by Mr. Faggiaducci's class.

The Heart's Eternal Vow (Review of Gabriel García Márquez's Love in the Time of Cholera)

1 "Love Is Strange" (Mickey Baker/Sylvia Vanderpool/Ethel Smith, 1956).

Introduction to Richard Fariña's Been Down So Long It Looks Like Up to Me

viii Peter Yarrow (*1938), American singer and songwriter.

viii Peter, Paul and Mary, American folk band.

ix "Peggy Sue" (Buddy Holly/Jerry Allison/Norman Petty, 1957), recorded by Buddy Holly.

ix *Back Country Suite* (Mose Allison, 1957).

ix *The Threepenny Opera* (Kurt Weill/Bertold Brecht/Elisabeth Hauptmann, 1928; adapted into English by Gifford Cochran and Jerrold Krimsky, 1933).

x Mimi Baez (1945–2001), American singer and songwriter, wife of Richard Fariña.

Introduction to Donald Barthelme's The Teachings of Don B.

xviii Howard Dietz (1893–1983), American lyricist and librettist.

xviii Arthur Schwartz (1900–1984), American composer.

xviii Fred Astaire (1899–1987), American dancer, singer, and musician.

xix Sir John Barbirolli (né Giovanni Battista Barbirolli, 1899–1970), British conductor and cellist.

xxi Dame Kiri Te Kanawa (*1944), New Zealand opera soprano.

xxi Willie Nelson (*1933), American singer, songwriter, and guitarist.

xxi "Baby Please Don't Go" (unknown origin), recorded by Lightnin' Hopkins (1912–1982).

Introduction to Jim Dodge's Stone Junction

xi "Mi Vida Loca (My Crazy Life)" (Jess Leary/Pam Tillis, 1994), recorded by Pam Tillis. "As Pam Tillis […] reminds us, Destiny turns on a dime."

Liner Notes for Spike Jones' Spiked! The Music of Spike Jones

6 Billy Eckstine (1914–1993), American jazz and pop singer.

8 Igor Stravinsky (1882–1971), Russian-French-American composer, pianist, and conductor.

8 Arnold Schoenberg (1874–1951), Austrian-American composer.

8 Charlie "Yardbird" Parker (1920–1955), American alto saxophonist.

8 Miles Davis (1926–1991), American trumpet player.

9 *The Firebird* (Igor Stravinsky, 1910).

10 Percy Faith (1908–1967), Canadian bandleader, composer, and conductor.

10 Hugo Winterthaler (1909–1973), American arranger and composer.

10 Guy Lombardo (1902–1977), Canadian-American bandleader and violinist.

10 Robin "Bob" Burns (1890–1956), American musical comedian.

10 Judy Canova (1913–1983), American actress, singer, and radio personality.

10 Dorothy Shay (1921–1978), American musical comedian.

11 The Nilsson Twins, American vocal act.

12 Paul Whiteman (1890–1967), American bandleader, composer, director, and violinist.

12 Leopold Anthony Stokowski (1882–1977), British conductor.

13 "Over There" (George M. Cohan, 1917).

13 *Ein musikalischer Spass K. 522* ("A Musical Joke") (Wolfgang Amadeus Mozart, 1787).

13 "Begin the Beguin" (Cole Porter, 1935).

13 "Stardust" (Hoagy Carmichael/Mitchell Parish, 1927/1929).

13 "San Antonio Rose" (Bob Wills, 1938).

15 Freddie "Schnickelfritz" Fisher (1904–1967), American musician and bandleader.

15 Tommy Dorsey (1905–1956), American trombonist, trumpeter, bandleader, and composer.

Liner Notes for Lotion's Nobody's Cool

n.pag. "Monster Mash" (Bobby Pickett/Leonard Capizzi, 1962), recorded by Bobby "Boris" Pickett & the Crypt-Kickers.

n.pag. "Love Boat Theme" (Charles Fox/Paul Williams, 1977), released by Jack Jones in 1979.

Lunch with Lotion

86 R.E.M. American rock band.

86 Hüsker Dü. American Rock band.

86 Burt Bacharach (*1928). American composer and singer.

87 "Fly Me to the Moon" (Bart Howard, 1954), recorded by Frank Sinatra in 1964.

87 "Walk Away Renée" (Michael Brown/Bob Calilli/Tony Sansone, 1966).

87 Reference ambiguous, probably "Feelings" (Louis "Loulou" Gasté 1957/Morris Albert 1974).

Bibliography

Aaron, Sam. "A5. Acid Bass." *Electronic manual of Sonic Pi—The Live Coding Synth for Everyone, v.2.9*. Cambridge. Software.

Adler, Renata. "Letter from Selma." *The New Yorker*, April 10, 1965. Web. October 1, 2018. <www.newyorker.com/magazine/1965/04/10/letter-from-selma>.

Agamben, Giorgio. *Homo Sacer. Sovereign Power and Bare Life*. Stanford: Stanford University Press, 1998. Print.

———, et al. *Democracy in what State?* New York: Columbia University Press, 2011. Print.

"American Music. Dr. Antonin Dvorak Expresses Some Radical Opinions." *Boston Herald*, May 28, 1893, n.p. Web. February 17, 2017. <www.artsinteractive.org/DT/Pages/67.html>.

Attali, Jacques. *Bruits: essai sur l'économie politique de la musique*. Paris: Presses Universitaires de France, 1977. Print.

———. *Noise: The Political Economy of Music*. 1985. Trans. Brian Massumi. Minneapolis: University of Minnesota Press, 1987. Print.

Badiou, Alain. "A Musical Variant of the Metaphysics of the Subject". Trans. Justin Clemens. *Parrhesia* 2 (2007): 29–36. Print.

———. *Plato's Republic*. Cambridge: Polity Press, 2012. Print.

———. *Saint Paul: The Foundation of Universalism*. Stanford CA: Stanford University Press. Print.

———. *The Meaning of Sarkozy*. London/New York: Verso, 2008. Print.

Baker, Bill. "Alan Moore on the forthcoming *The League of Extraordinary Gentlemen: The Black Dossier*." Baker's Dozen. January 3, 2007. Web. February 17, 2017. <www.worldfamouscomics.com/bakersdozen/back20070103.shtml>.

Banksy. *Wall and Piece*. London: Random House, 2005. Print.

Barry, Sam. *How to Play the Harmonica and Other Life Lessons*. Leyton: Gibbs Smith, 2009. Print.

Barthes, Roland. *Image—Music—Text*. New York: Hill and Wang, 1977. Print.

———. "The Death of the Author." *Image—Music—Text*. New York: Hill and Wang, 1977. 142–48. Print.

Bass, Thomas A. "*Gravity's Rainbow* as Orphic Text." *Pynchon Notes* 13 (October 1983): 25–46. Print.

Baudrillard, Jean. *The Spirit of Terrorism and Other Essays*. London/New York: Verso, 2002. Print.

Bauer, Christian. *Sacrificium intellectus: Das Opfer des Verstandes in der Kunst von Karlheinz Stockhausen, Botho Strauß und Anselm Kiefer.* Munich: Wilhelm Fink Verlag, 2008. Print.

Beloff, Jim. *The Ukulele—A Visual History.* San Francisco: Miller Freeman Books, 1997. Print.

Benjamin, Walter. *Über Haschisch.* 1972. Frankfurt am Main: Suhrkamp, 1977. Print.

Blesh, Rudy. *Shining Trumpets: A History of Jazz.* London: Cassell & Company Ltd., 1949. Print.

Boucourechliev, André. *Stravinsky.* London: Victor Gollancz, 1987. Print.

Boyer, Paul S., et al. *The Enduring Vision: A History of the American People.* 8th edition. Boston: Wadsworth Publishing, 2013. Print.

Bramlage, Larry R. "Castration: Creation of a gelding from a colt or stallion." American Association of Equine Practitioners. Web. February 17, 2017. <www.aaep.org/info/horse-health?publication=702>.

Brockhaus Musik: Personen, Epochen, Sachbegriffe. Mannheim: Brockhaus, 2001. Print.

Brown, Richard D., ed. *Major Problems in the Era of the American Revolution, 1760–1791.* 2nd Edition. Boston: Wadsworth, 2000. Print.

Bumas, E. Shaskan. "The Utopian States of America: The People, The Republic, and Rock and Roll in Thomas Pynchon's *Vineland.*" *Arizona Quarterly* Vol. 52, N° 3 (Autumn 1995): 149–75. Print.

Burba, Tyler. "The Ecstasy of Difference: The Phenomenology of Repetition and Variation in Music." *On Becoming-Music: Between Boredom and Ecstasy.* By Peter Price and Tyler Burba. New York/Dresden: Atropos Press, 2010. 67–148. Print.

Burroughs, William S. *Letters to Allen Ginsberg 1953–1957.* New York: Full Court Press, 1982. Print.

Caesar, Terry P. "A Note on Pynchon's Naming." *Pynchon Notes* 5 (February 1981): 5–10. Print.

Cage, John. *Empty Words.* 1973. Middletown CT: Wesleyan University Press, 1979. Print.

———. *Silence.* 1961. 50th Anniversary Edition. Middletown CT: Wesleyan University Press, 2011. Print.

Carswell, Sean. *Occupy Pynchon: Politics after Gravity's Rainbow.* Athens: University of Georgia Press, 2017. Print.

———. "Thomas Pynchon's Ukulele." *The Journal of American Culture* 38:3 (2015): 205–17. Print.

Casell, Chuck. Liner notes. Various artists. *The First Great Rock*

Festivals of the Seventies: Isle of Wight and Atlanta Pop Festival. Columbia, 1971. LP.

Charters, Ann, ed. *The Portable Beat Reader.* New York: Penguin Books, 1992. Print.

Chomsky, Noam. *What Uncle Sam Really Wants.* Berkeley CA: Odonian Press, 1993. Print.

Chorier-Fryd, Bénédicte. "'A Beat Late'—Rhythmical Oddities in Thomas Pynchon's *Mason & Dixon.*" *Thomas Pynchon.* Ed. Gilles Chamerois and Bénédicte Chorier-Fryd. Montpellier: Presses universitaires de la Méditerranée, 2014. 259–70. Print.

———. *Le Badass et autres excentriques: de la subversion chez Thomas Pynchon.* Dissertation, Université Paul Valéry, Montpellier III, 1987.

———. "Mason & Dixon, 'a Novel in Musick'—syncopes de la Révolution chez Thomas Pynchon." Mélanges offerts à Bernard Vincent. *Source,* 2008 (automne). Orléans: Editions Paradigme, 2008. 205–15. Print.

Clemons, Clarence and Don Reo. *Big Man: Real Life & Tall Tales.* New York/Boston: Grand Central Publishing, 2009. Print.

Clerc, Charles. *Mason & Dixon & Pynchon.* Lanham/New York/Oxford: University Press of America, 2000. Print.

Collins, Nick, and Julio d'Escriván, Eds. *The Cambridge Companion to Electronic Music.* Cambridge: Cambridge University Press, 2007. Print.

Cowart, David. "'Down on the Barroom Floor of History': Pynchon's *Bleeding Edge.*" *Postmodern Culture* 24.1 (September 2013). Web. http://www.pomoculture.org/2016/09/25/down-on-the-barroom-floor-of-history-pynchons-bleeding-edge/

———. "Pynchon and the Sixties." *Critique* 41.1 (Fall 1999): 3–12. Print.

———. *Thomas Pynchon & The Dark Passages of History.* Athens & London: The University of Georgia Press, 2011. Print.

———. *Thomas Pynchon: The Art of Allusion.* Carbondale and Edwardsville: Southern Illinois University Press, 1980. Print.

Crouch, Stanley. *Kansas City Lightning: The Rise and Times of Charlie Parker.* New York: HarperCollins, 2013. Print.

Daw, Laurence. "More on Pynchon on Record." *Pynchon Notes* 12 (June 1983): 46–47. Print.

Deleuze, Gilles. "Postscript on the Society of Control." *October,* Vol. 59: (Winter 1992). 3–7. Print.

Deleuze, Gilles and Félix Guattari. *A Thousand Plateaus: Capitalism and Schizophrenia.* Minneapolis: University of Minnesota Press, 1987. Print.

Derrida, Jacques. "A Certain Impossible Possibility of Saying the Event." Trans. Gila Walker. *Critical Inquiry* 33 (Winter 2007): 441–61. Print.

Dewey, Joseph. "The Sound of One Man Mapping: Wicks Cherrycoke and the Eastern (Re)solution." *Pynchon and* Mason & Dixon. Ed. Brooke Horvath and Irving Malin. Newark: University of Delaware Press, 2000. 112–31. Print.

Dollar, Steve. "Hummable Genius: Jazz Pianist Thelonius Monk." *Duke Magazine* (November–December 2007): 38–44. Print.

Downey, Dennis B. *A Season of Renewal: The Columbian Exposition and Victorian America.* Westport CT: Praeger, 2002. Print.

Dvořák American Heritage Association. Web. February 17, 2017. <www.dvoraknyc.org/dvorak-in-america/>.

"Dvorak on his New Work." *New York Herald,* December 15, 1893, 11. Web. February 17, 2017. <http://fultonhistory.com/Newspaper%2014/New%20York%20NY%20Herald/New%20York%20NY%20Herald%201893/New%20York%20NY%20Herald%201893%20-%205826.pdf>.

Eckstaedt, Aaron. *Beitrag zu einer Soziologie der Handharmonikainstrumente.* 1991/2003. Web. February 17, 2017. <www.aaroneckstaedt.de/soziologie.pdf>.

Eco, Umberto et al. *Interpretation and Overinterpretation.* Ed. Stefan Collini. Cambridge: Cambridge University Press, 1992. Print.

Eickhoff, Thomas. *Kultur-Geschichte der Harmonika.* Kamen: Schmülling, 1991. Print.

Eller, Jonathan R. and William E. McCarron. "Pynchon and Glenn Miller." *Pynchon Notes* 32–33 (spring–fall 1993): 193–95. Print.

Erbe, Marcus. "The Transcription of Electronic Music in *The Crying of Lot 49.*" *Pynchon Notes* 54–55 (spring–fall 2008): 99–107. Print.

Eshun, Kodwo. *More Brilliant Than The Sun: Adventures in Sonic Fiction.* 1998. London: Quartet Books, 1999.

Essex, Andrew. "Godzilla Meets Indie Rockers." *The New Yorker:* June 24 & July 1, 1996: 44. Print.

Evens, Aden. *Sound Ideas: Music, Machines, and Experience.* Minneapolis: University of Minnesota Press, 2005. Print.

Fariña, Mimi and Richard Fariña. *Celebrations For A Grey Day.* 1965. Vanguard Records, 1995. CD.

Fariña, Richard. *Been Down So Long It Looks Like Up to Me.* 1966. New York: Penguin, 1996. Print.

Field, Kim. *Harmonicas, Harps, and Heavy Breathers.* New York: Simon & Schuster, 1993. Print.

Fink, Robert. *Repeating Ourselves: American Minimal Music as Cultural Practice.* Berkeley: University of California Press, 2005. Print.

Flusser, Vilém. *Medienkultur.* Frankfurt am Main: Fischer, 1997. Print.

Foucault, Michel. "What Is an Author?" 1970. *The Essential Foucault: Selections from the Essential Works of Foucault, 1954–1984.* Ed. Paul Rabinow and Nikolas Rose. New York: The New Press, 2003. 377–91. Print.

Fowler, Douglas. *A Reader's Guide to* Gravity's Rainbow. Ann Arbor MI: Ardis Press, 1980. Print.

Frank, Thomas. *The Conquest of Cool: Business Culture, Counterculture, and the Rise of Hip Consumerism.* Chicago and London: The University of Chicago Press, 1997. Print.

Freedland, Michael. "Larry Adler: The man who gave mouth organs their dignity." *The Guardian,* 7 August 2001. Web. February 17, 2017. <www.theguardian.com/news/2001/aug/07/guardianobituaries>.

Fröhlich, Werner D. *Wörterbuch Psychologie.* München: Deutscher Taschenbuch Verlag, 1998. Print.

García Iborra, Juan and Oscar de Jódar Bonilla. "Cultural Confrontation in Pynchon's 'Entropy' and *Vineland.*" *REDEN: revista española de estudios norteamericanos,* 17–18 (1999): 35–50. Print.

Gazi, Jeeshan. "On Deleuze and Guattari's *Italian Wedding Fake Book*: Pynchon, Improvisation, Social Organisation, and Assemblage". *Orbit: A Journal of American Literature.* Vol. 4 issue 2 (2016). Web. December 29, 2019. <doi: https://doi.org/10.16995/orbit.192>.

Ginsberg, Allen. *Howl and Other Poems.* 1956. San Francisco: City Lights Books, 1997. Print.

Glazek, Christopher. "The Pynchon Hoax." *The New Yorker,* August 10, 2009. Web. February 17, 2017. <www.newyorker.com/news/news-desk/the-pynchon-hoax>.

Goldberg, Joe. "Charlie Parker with Strings: The Master Takes. Liner Notes." *Charlie Parker with Strings: The Master Takes. Volume 1.* Verve 314 523 987-2. 1995. CD.

Goodman, Steve. *Sonic Warfare: Sound, Affect, and the Ecology of Fear.* Cambridge MA: The MIT Press, 2012. Print.

Gordon, Andrew. "Smoking Dope with Thomas Pynchon: A Sixties Memoir." *The Vineland Papers: Critical Takes on Pynchon's Novel.* Eds. Geoffrey Green, Donald J. Greiner, and Larry McCaffery. Normal IL: Dalkey Archive Press, 1994. 167–78. Print. Online version: http://users.clas.ufl.edu/agordon/pynchon.htm.

Grant, J. Kerry. *A Companion to* The Crying of Lot 49. 1994. 2nd edition. Athens and London: University of Georgia Press, 2008. Print.

Greenaway, Peter, director. *Four American Composers.* Les films du paradoxe, 1983. DVD.

Greene, Graham. *The Graham Greene Film Reader: Reviews, Essays, Interviews & Film Stories.* Ed. David Parkinson. New York: Applause Books, 1995. Print.

Greve, Julius and Sascha Pöhlmann, eds. *America and the Musical Unconscious.* New York/Dresden: Atropos Press, 2015. Print.

Große, Günter. *Von der Edisonwalze zur Stereoplatte.* Berlin: Lied der Zeit, 1989. Print.

Häffner, Martin. *Harmonicas: Die Geschichte der Branche in Bildern und Texten.* Trossingen: Hohner-Verlag, 1991. Print.

Hajdu, David. *Positively 4th Street: The Lives and Times of Joan Baez, Bob Dylan, Mimi Baez Fariña and Richard Fariña.* New York: Farrar, Straus and Giroux, 2001. Print.

Handley, Gen. "Tiger Army's Nick 13 Talks About 'V •••–,' the Band's First Album in Nearly a Decade." *Noisey/Vice.* March 14, 2016. Web. February 17, 2017. <https://noisey.vice.com/en_us/article/tiger-army-nick-13-interview-prisoner-of-the-night>.

Hänggi, Christian. "From Vivaldi to 'Volare': Pynchon's Love for Italian Music." Unpublished paper presented at the 2019 International Pynchon Week in Rome, Italy.

———. "'Harmonica, kazoo—a friend.' Pynchon's Lessons in Organology." *America and the Musical Unconscious.* Eds. Julius Greve and Sascha Pöhlmann. New York/Dresden: Atropos Press, 2015. 289–327. Print.

———. *Hospitality in the Age of Media Representation.* New York/Dresden: Atropos Press, 2009. Print.

———. "Pynchon on Record, Vol. 4." September 28, 2017. Web. June 12, 2018. <https://thomaspynchon.com/thomas-pynchon-inspired-music>.

———. "The Pynchon Playlist: A Catalog and Its Analysis" (including the Pynchon Playlist as an Excel file). *Orbit: A Journal of American Literature* Vol. 6 issue 1 (2018). Web. June 12, 2018. <https://doi.org/10.16995/orbit.487>.

———. "Stockhausen at Ground Zero". *Fillip* No. 15 (2011): 89–109. Print.

Hanson, Josef. "German National Songs in the Third Reich: A Tale of Two Anthems." *Music & Politics* 7, No. 1 (Winter 2013): 1–12. Web. February 16, 2017. <http://quod.lib.umich.edu/cgi/p/pod/dod-idx/german-national-song-in-the-third-reich-a-tale-of-two.pdf?c=mp;idno=9460447.0007.104>.

Hardt, Michael, and Antonio Negri. *Empire.* Cambridge and London: Harvard University Press, 2000.

Hayles, N. Katherine, and Mary B. Eiser. “Coloring Gravity’s Rainbow.” *Pynchon Notes* 16 (Spring 1985): 3–24. Print.

Heath, Joseph and Andrew Potter. *Nation of Rebels: Why Counter-culture Became Consumer Culture.* New York: HarperCollins, 2004. Print.

Heidegger, Martin. *Basic Writings.* Ed. David Farrell Krell. San Francisco: HarperCollins, 1977. Print.

Herman, Luc and John M. Krafft. “Fast Learner: The Typescript of Pynchon’s *V.* at the Harry Ransom Center in Austin.” *Texas Studies in Literature and Language* Vol. 49, No. 1 (Spring 2007): 1–20. Print.

———. “Race in Early Pynchon: Rewriting Sphere in *V.*” *Critique* Vol. 52, No. 1 (2011): 17–29. Print.

Hess, John Joseph. “Music in Thomas Pynchon’s *Mason & Dixon.*” *Orbit: Writing Around Pynchon* Vol. 2, issue 2 (2014). Web. February 16, 2017. <https://doi.org/10.7766/orbit.v2.2.75>.

Hock, Stephen. “The Black Box of Genre in Colson Whitehead and Charles Yu.” *The Poetics of Genre in the Contemporary Novel.* Ed. Tim Lanzendörfer. Lanham, Maryland: Lexington Books, 2016. Print.

Hollander, Charles. “Does McClintic Sphere in *V.* stand for Thelonius Monk?” 1999. Web. February 17, 2017. <www.vheissu.net/articles/hollander_V.php>.

Horowitz, Hal. Tiger Army: “V • • • –.” *American Songwriter,* May 19, 2016. Web. February 17, 2017. <http://americansongwriter.com/2016/05/tiger-army-v-•••>.

Hoskyns, Barney. *Waiting for the Sun: Strange Days, Weird Scenes, and The Sound of Los Angeles.* New York: St. Martin’s Press, 1996. Print.

Hume, Kathryn and Thomas J. Knight. “Orpheus and the Orphic Voice in *Gravity’s Rainbow.*” *Philological Quarterly* 64 (1985): 299–315. Print.

———. “Pynchon’s Orchestration of *Gravity’s Rainbow.*” *Journal of English and Germanic Philology* 85 (July 1986): 366–85. Print.

Hurley, Patrick. *Pynchon Character Names: A Dictionary.* Jefferson NC: McFarland & Company, 2008. Print.

Hutcheon, Linda. *A Poetics of Postmodernism: History, Theory, Fiction.* New York and London: Routledge, 1988. Print.

Huxley, Aldous. *Point Counter Point.* 1928. London: Grafton, 1988. Print.

Ingham, Richard, ed. *The Cambridge Companion to the Saxophone.* Cambridge: Cambridge University Press, 1998. Print.

Ishiguro, Maho A. "The Affective Properties of Keys in Instrumental Music from the Late Nineteenth and Early Twentieth Centuries." Master's thesis, Graduate School of the University of Massachusetts Amherst, 2010.

Itkowitz, Colby. "This '80s pop star is miffed that Majority Whip Steve Scalise uses his song." *The Washington Post*, March 25, 2015. Web. February 17, 2017. <www.washingtonpost.com/blogs/in-the-loop/wp/2015/03/25/this-80s-pop-star-is-miffed-that-majority-whip-steve-scalise-uses-his-song/>.

"Jackson Pynchon's Rock 'n Roll Dreams." *Adweek/GalleyCat*, October 10, 2006, n.p. Web. February 17, 2017. <www.adweek.com/galleycat/jackson-pynchons-rock-n-roll-dreams/4026>.

Jahn, Janheinz. *Blues und Work Songs*. Frankfurt am Main: Fischer Bücherei, 1964. Print.

Jameson, Fredric. "Postmodernism and Consumer Society." *Modernism/Postmodernism*. Ed. Peter Brooker. New York: Longman, 1992. 163–79. Print.

Jansen, Will. *The bassoon: its history, construction, makers, players and music*. Buren: Frits Knuf, 1978. Print.

Jarrett, Michael. *Drifting on a Read: Jazz as a Model for Writing*. Albany: State University of New York Press, 1999. Print.

"Jeru: In the Words of Gerry Mulligan: An Oral Autobiography." The Library of Congress. Web. February 17, 2017. <http://lcweb2.loc.gov/diglib/ihas/html/mulligan/gm-addiction.html>.

Jones, LeRoi (Amiri Baraka). *Black Music*. 1968. New York: Akashi Books, 2010. Print.

———. *Blues People: Negro Music in White America*. 1963. New York: Harper Perennial, 1999. Print.

Jones, Spike. *Spiked! The Music of Spike Jones*. Catalyst, 1994. CD.

Jost, Ekkehard. *Free Jazz*. n.p.: New York: Da Capo Press, 1994. Print.

———. *Sozialgeschichte des Jazz in den USA*. Frankfurt am Main.: Fischer Verlag, 1982. Print.

Joyce, James. *Finnegans Wake*. London: Faber and Faber, 1939. Print.

———. *Ulysses*. 1922. London: Penguin Classics, 2000. Print.

Juliani, Richard N. *Building Little Italy: Philadelphia's Italians Before Mass Migration*. University Park: The Pennsylvania State University Press, 1998. Print.

Kachka, Boris. "On the Thomas Pynchon Trail: From the Long Island of His Boyhood to the 'Yupper West Side' of His New Novel." *Vulture*, Aug 25, 2013. Web. February 17, 2017. <www.vulture.com/2013/08/thomas-pynchon-bleeding-edge.html>.

Kahn, Douglas. *Noise Water Meat: A History of Sound in the Arts.* Cambridge MA: The MIT Press, 1999. Print.

Kennelly, Arthur E. "Biographical Memoir of George Owen Squier." National Academy of Sciences, 1938. Web. February 16, 2017. <www.nasonline.org/publications/biographical-memoirs/memoir-pdfs/squier-george-o.pdf>.

Kerouac, Jack. *On the Road.* 1957. London: Penguin, 1972. Print.

———. *The Subterraneans.* 1958. London: Penguin, 2001. Print.

Kittler, Friedrich. "Der Gott der Ohren." *Die Wahrheit der technischen Welt.* Ed. Hans Ulrich Gumbrecht. Frankfurt am Main: Suhrkamp, 2013. 198–213. Print.

———. *Gramophone Film Typewriter.* Stanford: Stanford University Press, 1999. Print.

———. "Medien und Drogen in Pynchons Zweitem Weltkrieg". *Die Wahrheit der technischen Welt.* Ed. Hans Ulrich Gumbrecht. Frankfurt am Main: Suhrkamp, 2013. 113–31. Print.

———. "Pynchon and Electro-Mysticism." *Pynchon Notes* 54–55 (spring–fall 2008): 108–21. Print.

———. "Rock Musik – Ein Mißbrauch von Heeresgerät". *Die Wahrheit der technischen Welt.* Ed. Hans Ulrich Gumbrecht. Frankfurt am Main: Suhrkamp, 2013. 198–213. Print.

———. "Romantik – Psychoanalyse – Film: eine Doppelgängergeschichte" *Draculas Vermächtnis: Technische Schriften.* Leipzig: Reclam, 1993. 81–104. Print.

———. "Wenn das Bit Fleisch wird." *Hyperkultur: Zur Fiktion des Computerzeitalters.* Ed. Martin Klepper, Ruth Mayer, and Ernst-Peter Schneck. Berlin/New York: Walter de Gruyter, 1996. Print.

Lacey, Robert J. "Thomas Pynchon on Totalitarianism: Power, Paranoia, and Preterition in *Gravity's Rainbow.*" *Americana: E-Journal of American Studies in Hungary.* Vol. VI, No. 2 (Fall 2010). Web. March 21, 2017. <http://americanaejournal.hu/vol6no2/lacey>.

Langwill, Lyndesay G. *The Bassoon and Double Bassoon. A short illustrated history of their origin, development, and makers.* Hinrichsen Edition Limited, n.d. Print.

Lessig, Lawrence. *Free Culture: How Big Media Uses Technology and the Law to Lock Down Culture and Control Creativity.* New York: The Penguin Press, 2004. Print.

Levey, Nick. "Mindless Pleasures: Playlists, Unemployment, and Thomas Pynchon's *Inherent Vice.*" *Journal of Modern Literature* Vol. 39, No. 3 (Spring 2016): 41–56. Print.

Levin, Michael and John S. Wilson. "No Bop Roots In Jazz: Parker." *Down Beat* (September 9, 1949): 26. Print.

Levine, Yasha. "Almost Everyone Involved in Developing Tor was (or is) Funded by the US Government." *Pando*, July 16, 2014. Web. February 17, 2017. <https://pando.com/2014/07/16/tor-spooks/>.

Liley, Thomas. "Invention and development." *The Cambridge Companion to the Saxophone.* Ed. Richard Ingham. Cambridge: Cambridge University Press, 1998. Print.

Logan, William. "Pynchon in the Poetic." *Southwest Review*, Vol. 83, No. 4 (1998): 424–37. Print.

Mac Kay, Mw. "Mindless Pleasures." *Pynchon Notes* 24–25 (spring–fall 1989): 105–08. Print.

Maconie, Robin. *Experiencing Stravinsky: A Listener's Companion.* Lanham: The Scarecrow Press, 2013. Print.

———. *Musicologia: Musical Knowledge from Plato to John Cage.* Lanham: The Scarecrow Press, 2010. Print.

Mailer, Norman. "The White Negro." *Dissent* (fall 1957). Reprinted in, ed., Ann Charters. *The Portable Beat Reader.* New York: Penguin Books, 1992. 581–605. Print.

Marcus, Greil, and Werner Sollors, eds. *A New Literary History of America.* Cambridge MA/London: The Belknap Press of Harvard University Press, 2009. Print.

Mattheson, Johann. *Das Neu-Eröffnete Orchester.* 1713. Hildesheim/Zürich/NewYork: Georg Olms Verlag, 1997. Print.

McClintock, Scott, and John Miller. "Introduction: Surveying Pynchon's California." *Pynchon's California.* Iowa City: University of Iowa Press, 2014. Print.

McGowan, David. *Weird Scenes Inside The Canyon: Laurel Canyon, Covert Ops & The Dark Heart of the Hippie Dream.* London: Headpress, 2014. Print.

McHale, Brian. "Gravity's Angels in America, or, Pynchon's Angelology Revisited." *Pynchon Notes* 42–43 (spring–fall 1998): 303–16. Print.

McLaughlin, Robert L. "Movie Music in Gravity's Rainbow." *Pynchon Notes* 28–29 (spring–fall 1991): 143–45. Print.

McLuhan, Marshall. *Understanding Media: The Extensions of Man.* 1964. Cambridge MA: The MIT Press, 2002. Print.

Mead, Clifford. *Thomas Pynchon: A Bibliography of Primary and Secondary Materials.* Chicago: Dalkey Archive Press, 1992. Print.

Melley, Timothy. *Empire of Conspiracy: The Culture of Paranoia in Postwar America.* Ithaca and London: Cornell University Press, 2000. Print.

Metzger, Heinz-Klaus. "Gescheiterte Begriffe in Theorie und Kritik der Musik." *Kommentare zur Neuen Musik 1*. Cologne: Verlag M. DuMont, n.d. 197–213. Print.

———. "Webern und Schönberg." *Kommentare zur Neuen Musik 1*. Cologne: Verlag M. DuMont, n.d. 25–31. Print.

Miller, Paul D. a.k.a. DJ Spooky That Subliminal Kid. *Rhythm Science*. Cambridge MA: The MIT Press, 2004. Print.

Miller, Henry. *Tropic of Cancer*. 1934. St Albans, Herts: Panther Books, 1965. Print.

Mingus, Charles. *Beneath the Underdog: His World as Composed by Mingus*. Ed. Nel King. New York: Vintage: 1991. Print.

———. *Oh Yeah*. 1962. Atlantic Recording Corp., 1999. CD.

Monk, Thelonius. *Criss-Cross*. 1963. Columbia Records, 2003. CD.

Montagu, Jeremy. *Origins and Development of Musical Instruments*. Lanham: The Scarecrow Press, 2007. Print.

Moore, Steven. "Pynchon on Record." *Pynchon Notes* 10 (1982): 56–57. Print.

Moretti, Franco. *Distant Reading*. London/New York: Verso, 2013. Print

———. *Graphs, Maps, Trees: Abstract Models for a Literary History*. London/New York: Verso, 2005.

Mouffe, Chantal. *Hegemony, radical democracy, and the political*. Ed. James Martin. New York: Routledge, 2013. Print.

Nancy, Jean-Luc. *Being Singular Plural*. Stanford: Stanford University Press, 2000. Print.

———. *The Truth of Democracy*. Bronx: Fordham University Press, 2010. Print.

Nietzsche, Friedrich. "Nietzsche contra Wagner." *The Works of Friedrich Nietzsche*. Trans. Thomas Common. London: T. Fisher Unwin, 1899. 61–94. Print.

———. "The Case of Wagner." *The Works of Friedrich Nietzsche*. Trans. Thomas Common. London: T. Fisher Unwin, 1899. 1–60. Print.

———. *The Gay Science. With a Prelude in German Rhymes and an Appendix of Songs*. Trans. Josephine Nauckhoff. Cambridge: Cambridge University Press, 2001. Print.

Nyman, Michael. *Experimental Music: Cage and Beyond*. 1974. Second Edition. Cambridge: Cambridge University Press, 2003. Print.

O'Shaughnessy, Andrew Jackson. *The Men Who Lost America: British Leadership, the American Revolution, and the Fate of the Empire*. New Haven & London: Yale University Press, 2013. Print.

Ocker, David. "Eight Facts About Thomas Pynchon, His Pavane and Galliard, A Piece for Cello and Piano." *Pynchon Notes*, 28–29 (spring–fall 1991). 147–50. Print.

———. "Spike Jones and Lotion: Connected by a Fragile Pynchon Thread." *Pynchon Notes*, 36–39 (1995–1996). 184–88. Print.

Olson, Charles. "Projective Verse." *Selected Writings of Charles Olson*. Ed. Robert Creeley. New York: New Directions, 1966. 15–26. Print.

Oxford English Dictionary Online. Ed. J.A. Simpson and E.S.C. Weiner. Second Edition. Oxford: Clarendon Press, 2009. Web. November 8, 2014. <www.oed.com/>.

Parker, Charlie. *Charlie Parker Omnibook*. Transcriptions by Jamie Aebersold. n.p. Atlantic Music Corp., 1978. Print.

Parry, Sally E. "Who Broke the Bank at Monte Carlo?: Musical Moods in the Casino Hermann Goering." *Pynchon Notes* 40–41 (spring–fall 1997): 176–79. Print.

Pascale, Amy. "PG Interview: David Lowery of Cracker and Camper Van Beethoven." *PopGurls*, June 4, 2006. Web. February 17, 2017. <www.popgurls.com/2006/06/04/popgurls-interview-david-lowery-of-cracker-and-camper-van-beethoven>.

Pérez-Llantada Auría, Carmen. "Beyond Linguistic Barriers: The Musical Fugue Structure of Thomas Pynchon's 'Entropy'." *Cuadernos de Investigación Filológica*, 17, no. 1–2 (1991): 127–40. Print.

Pieslak, Jonathan. *Sound Targets: American Soldiers and Music in the Iraq War*. Bloomington IN: Indiana University Press, 2009. Print.

Plato. *The Republic*. Trans. C.D.C. Reeve. Indianapolis/Cambridge: Hacket Publishing Company, 2004. Print.

———. *The Republic*. Trans. Chris Emlyn-Jones and William Preddy. Cambridge: Harvard University Press, 2014. Print.

———. *The Republic*. Trans. Paul Shorey. New York: Putnam's, 1930, 1968. Print.

Pöhlmann, Sascha. "The Complex Text." *Against the Grain: Reading Pynchon's Counternarratives*. Ed. Sascha Pöhlmann. Amsterdam/New York: Rodopi, 2010. 9–34. Print.

———. *Pynchon's Postnational Imagination*. Heidelberg: Universitätsverlag Winter, 2010. Print.

Price, Peter. "Sound as Art in the Age of Global Entertainment." *On Becoming-Music: Between Boredom and Ecstasy*. By Peter Price and Tyler Burba. New York/Dresden: Atropos Press, 2010. 15–66. Print.

———. *Resonance: Philosophy for Sonic Art*. New York/Dresden: Atropos Press, 2011. Print.

Pynchon, Jackson. "Breaking: Sam Sparro." *Rolling Stone*, October 6, 2008. Web. February 17, 2017. <www.rollingstone.com/music/news/breaking-sam-sparro-20081006>.

Pynchon, Thomas. *Against the Day*. 2006. London: Vintage, 2007. Print.

———. *Bleeding Edge*. New York: The Penguin Press, 2013. Print.

———. *Gravity's Rainbow*. 1973. New York: Penguin, 2006. Print.

———. *Inherent Vice*. New York: Penguin, 2009. Print.

———. "Introduction." *Been Down So Long It Looks Like Up to Me*. By Richard Fariña. 1966, 1983. New York: Penguin Books, 1996. v–xiv. Print.

———. Introduction to *Stone Junction*, by Jim Dodge. New York: Grove, 1998. Print.

———. Introduction to *The Teachings of Don B.: Satires, Parodies, Fables, Illustrated Stories, and Plays of Donald Barthelme*. Ed. Kim Herzinger. New York: Turtle Bay, 1992. xv–xxii. Print.

———. "Journey into the Mind of Watts". *The New York Times*, June 12, 1966. Print. Electronic version: https://archive.nytimes.com/www.nytimes.com/books/97/05/18/reviews/pynchon-watts.html. Web.

———. "Letter to the Ford Foundation." 1959. Copy in author's personal collection.

———. Liner Notes. *Spiked! The Music of Spike Jones*. Catalyst, 1994. CD.

———. Liner Notes. *Nobody's Cool*, by Lotion. spinART Records/Shock Records, 1995. CD.

———. "Lunch with Lotion." *Esquire* Vol. 125, No. 6 (June 1996): 86–90. Print.

———. *Mason & Dixon*. 1997. London: Vintage, 1998. Print.

———. "Mortality and Mercy in Vienna." *Epoch* 9, no. 4 (Spring 1959): 195–213. Print. Also available as: *Stories from Epoch: The First Fifty Issues*. Ed. Baxter Hathaway. Ithaca: Cornell University Press, 1966. 181–201. Print.

———. *Slow Learner: Early Stories*. 1984. London: Vintage, 2000. Print.

———. "The Boys." *Purple and Gold* 9, no. 6 (March 19, 1953): 8. Print. Reproduced in Mead, 166–67.

———. *The Crying of Lot 49*. 1965. New York: HarperPerennial, 1999. Print.

———. "The Heart's Eternal Vow." Review of *Love in the Time of Cholera*, by Gabriel García Márquez. *The New York Times Book Review*, April 10, 1988: 1, 47, 49. Print

———. "Togetherness." *Aerospace Safety*, 16: 12 (1960): 6–8. Print.

———. *V*. 1963. London: Picador, 1975. Print.

———. *Vineland*. Boston: Little, Brown and Company, 1990. Print.

———. "Voice of the Hamster." *Purple and Gold* 9, no. 2 (November 13, 1952): 2; no. 3 (December 18, 1952): 3; no. 4 (January 22, 1953): 2, 4; and no. 5 (February 19, 1953): 8. Print. Page numbers refer to the reprint in Mead, 156–63.

———. "Words for Ian McEwan." *The Daily Telegraph*, December 6, 2006. Web. October 10, 2019. <https://www.telegraph.co.uk/news/uknews/1536152/Recluse-speaks-out-to-defend-McEwan.html>.

———. "Ye Legend of Sir Stupid and the Purple Knight." *Purple and Gold* 9, no. 6 (March 19, 1953): 2. Print. Page numbers refer to the reprint in Mead, 163–66.

"Radiohead's Secret Influences, From Fleetwood Mac to Thomas Pynchon." *Rolling Stone*, August 28, 2012. Web. February 17, 2017. <www.rollingstone.com/music/news/radioheads-secret-influences-from-fleetwood-mac-to-thomas-pynchon-19691231>.

Rancière, Jacques. *Chronicles of Consensual Times*. London/New York: Continuum, 2010. Print.

———. *Hatred of Democracy*. London/New York: Verso, 2006. Print.

"Recent Acquisitions." *Summer 2002 Newsletter*. Harry Ransom Center at the University of Texas at Austin. Web. February 17, 2017. <www.hrc.utexas.edu/ransomedition/2002/summer/recent_acquisitions.html>.

Redfield, Robert, and Peter L. Hays. "Fugue as a Structure in Pynchon's 'Entropy'." *Pacific Coast Philology*, Vol. 12 (Oct. 1997): 50–55. Print.

Redmond, Shana L. *Anthem: Social Movements and the Sound of Solidarity in the African Diaspora*. New York: New York University Press, 2014. Print.

Rickels, Lawrence A. *The Case of California*. Baltimore and London: The Johns Hopkins University Press, 1991. Print.

Rizzo, Mary. "South Philadelphia." *The Encyclopedia of Greater Philadelphia*, 2013. Web. February 17, 2017. <http://philadelphiaencyclopedia.org/archive/south-philadelphia-essay>.

Rodger, N.A.M. *The Insatiable Earl: A Life of John Montagu, 4th Earl of Sandwich*. London: HarperCollins, 1993. Print.

Ronell, Avital. *Crack Wars: Literature, Addiction, Mania*. Lincoln & London: University of Nebraska Press, 1992. Print.

———. *Stupidity*. Urbana and Chicago: University of Illinois Press, 2002. Print.

———. *The Test Drive*. Urbana and Chicago: University of Illinois Press, 2005. Print.

Rorive, Jean-Pierre. *Adolphe Sax, 1814–1894, Inventeur de génie*. Brussels: Éditions Racine, 2004. Print.

Rothkopf, Joshua. "Sex, Drugs, and the Postal Service: Thomas Pynchon, A Beginner's Guide." *Rolling Stone*, December 16, 2014. Web. February 17, 2017. <www.rollingstone.com/culture/features/pynchon-for-beginners-20141216>.

Rouyan, Anahita. "Singing Thomas Pynchon's Gravity's Rainbow: Interfaces of Song, Narrative, and Sonic Performance." *Partial Answers: Journal of Literature and the History of Ideas*, Vol. 15, No. 1 (January 2017): 117–33. Print.

Russell, Ross. *Bird Lives*. 1973. Boston: Da Capo Press, 1996. Print.

Sacks, Oliver. *Musicophilia: Tales of Music and the Brain*. New York and Toronto: Alfred A. Knopf, 2008. Print.

Sales, Nancy Jo. "Meet Your Neighbor, Thomas Pynchon." *New York* Magazine. November 11, 1996. Web. February 17, 2017. <http://nymag.com/arts/books/features/48268/>.

Schafer, R. Murray. *The Soundscape: Our Sonic Environment and the Tuning of the World*. 1977. Rochester: Destiny Books, 1994. Print.

Schaub, Thomas Hill. "Atonalism, Nietzsche and *Gravity's Rainbow:* Pynchon's Use of German Music History and Culture." *Pynchon Notes* 54–55 (spring–fall 2008): 26–38. Print.

———. "*The Crying of Lot 49* and other California novels." *The Cambridge Companion to Thomas Pynchon*. Ed. Inger H. Dalsgaard, Luc Herman and Brian McHale. Cambridge: Cambridge University Press, 2012. Print.

———. *Pynchon: The Voice of Ambiguity*. Urbana and Chicago: University of Illinois Press, 1981. Print.

Schirmacher, Wolfgang. *Ereignis Technik*. Vienna: Passagen-Verlag, 1990. Print.

———. "Homo Generator in Artificial Life: From a Conversation with Jean-François Lyotard." *Poiesis*. Vol. 7 (2005): 86–99. Print.

———. "Homo Generator: Media and Postmodern Technology." *Culture on the Brink: Ideologies of Technology*. Ed. Gretchen Bender and Timothy Druckrey. New York: The New Press, 1994/1999. Print.

Schmidt, Michael, ed. *Philosophy of Media Sounds*. New York/Dresden: Atropos Press, 2009. Print.

Schubart, Christian Friedrich David. *Ideen zu einer Ästhetik der Tonkunst*. Ed. Ludwig Schubart. Vienna: Bey J. V. Degen, 1806. Print.

Schumann, Otto. *Meyers Opernbuch*. Leipzig: Bibliographisches Institut, 1937. Print.

Schwartz, Steve. "Ralph Vaughan Williams: Fantasia on a Theme by Thomas Tallis (1910)". *ClassicalNet*. Web. 12 January 2017. <www.classical.net/music/comp.lst/works/v-w/tallisfantasia.php>.

Schweighauser, Philipp. "Literary Acoustics." *Handbook of Intermediality: Literature—Image—Sound—Music*. Ed. Gabriele Rippl. Berlin/Boston: Walter DeGruyter, 2015. 475–493. Print.

———. "Some Reflections on the Place of Aesthetics and Politics in American Studies." *ranam – recherches anglaises et nord-américaines*, n° 49 (2016): 43–53. Print.

———. *The Noises of American Literature, 1890–1985*. Gainesville: University Press of Florida, 2006. Print.

Segell, Michael. *The Devil's Horn: The Story of the Saxophone from Noisy Novelty to King of Cool*. New York: Picador, 2005. Print.

Serrà, Joan, et al. "Measuring the Evolution of Contemporary Western Popular Music." *Scientific Reports 2* (26 July 2012): n.p. Web. February 17, 2017. <www.nature.com/articles/srep00521>.

Shelden, Michael. "How the world caught up with Pynchon." *The Telegraph*, 7 December 2006. Web. 16 February 2017. <www.telegraph.co.uk/culture/books/3656962/How-the-world-caught-up-with-Pynchon.html>.

Siegel, Jules, et al. *Lineland: Mortality and Mercy on the Internet's Pynchon-L@Waste.Org Discussion List*. Philadelphia: Intangible Assets Manufacturing, 1997. Print.

Škvorecký, Josef. *The Bass Saxophone*. 1977. London: Picador, 1980. Print.

Smith, Frances Grace and Ezra Barker. "The American Revolution Hits Church Music." Reproduced in *The New England Quarterly* Vol. 4, No. 4 (October 1931): 783–88. Print.

Southern, Eileen. *The Music of Black Americans: A History*. New York: W. W. Norton & Company, 1971. Print.

St. Clair, Justin. "Music and Sound." *Pynchon in Context*. Ed. Inger H. Dalsgaard. Cambridge: Cambridge University Press, 2019. Print.

———. "The *Inherent Vice* Soundtrack." Unpublished paper presented at the 2015 International Pynchon Week in Athens, Greece.

Stearns, David Patrick. "Muzak's Vivaldi puts on muscle." *Philly.com*. Web. 15 January 2015. <http://articles.philly.com/2008-03-09/entertainment/25260901_1_antonio-vivaldi-nisi-dominus-disc>. Article no longer available online.

Stewart, Barbara. *The Complete How To Kazoo*. 1983. New York: Workman Publishing, 2006. Print.

Stockhausen, Karlheinz. "I. Elektronische und Instrumentale Musik." *Kommentare zur Neuen Musik 1*. Cologne: Verlag M. DuMont, n.d. 98–112. Print.

Sublette, Ned and Constance. *The American Slave Coast: A History of the Slave-Breeding Industry.* Chicago: Lawrence Hill Books, 2016. Print.

Taibbi, Matt. "Greed and Debt: The True Story of Mitt Romney and Bain Capital." *Rolling Stone*, 29 August 2012. Web. February 17, 2017. <www.rollingstone.com/politics/news/greed-and-debt-the-true-story-of-mitt-romney-and-bain-capital-20120829>.

Tanner, Tony. *Thomas Pynchon.* London: Methuen, 1982. Print.

Taruskin, Richard. *The Danger of Music and Other Anti-Utopian Essays.* Berkeley/Los Angeles/London: University of California Press, 2009. Print.

Tate, J.O. "*Gravity's Rainbow*: The Original Soundtrack." *Pynchon Notes* 13 (1983): 3–24. Print.

The Beatles Anthology. San Francisco: Chronicle Books, 2000. Print.

The Godfather. Directed by Francis Ford Coppola. Paramount, 1972. DVD.

Theremin—An Electronic Odyssey. Directed by Steven M. Martin. MGM, 1993. DVD.

Theweleit, Klaus, and Rainer Höltschl. *Jimi Hendrix: Eine Biographie.* Berlin: Rowohlt, 2008. Print.

Thomas, Samuel. "Blood on the Tracks: Pynchon, *Bleeding Edge*, and (Un)popular Music from Britney to Black Metal", *Orbit: A Journal of American Literature.* Vol. 7, issue 1 (2019): 3, 1–55. Web. 19 September, 2019. doi: https://doi.org/10.16995/orbit.788

Tibbets, John C., ed. *Dvořák in America, 1892–1895.* Portland OR: Amadeus Press, 1993. Print.

Tiffou, Augustin. *Le basson en France au XIXe siècle: Facture, théorie et répertoire.* Paris: L'Harmattan, 2010. Print.

Tompkins, Dave. *How to Wreck a Nice Beach: The Vocoder from World War II to Hip-Hop.* Brooklyn: Melville House, 2010. Print.

Tranquada, Jim, and John King. *The 'Ukulele: A History.* Honolulu: University of Hawai'i Press, 2012. Print.

"Transcript of the Laurie Anderson Interview." *Silicon Valley Radio*, n.d. Web. February 17, 2017. <www.transmitmedia.com/svr/vault/anderson/ander_transcript.html>.

Twigg, George William. "'Sell Out With Me Tonight': Popular Music, Commercialization and Commodification in *Vineland* , *The Crying of Lot 49*, and *V.*" *Orbit: Writing Around Pynchon* Vol. 2, issue 2 (2014): n.pag. Web. February 16, 2017. <https://www.pynchon.net/articles/10.7766/orbit.v2.2.55/>.

Usher, Shaun, ed. *Lists of Note: An Eclectic Collection Deserving of a Wider Audience.* Canongate: Unbound, 2014. Print.

Vesterman, William. "Pynchon's Poetry." *Mindful Pleasures: Essays on Thomas Pynchon*. Eds. George Levine and David Leverenz. Boston/Toronto: Little, Brown and Company, 1976. 101–12. Print.

Virilio, Paul. *Ground Zero*. London/New York: Verso, 2002. Print.

Vonnegut, Kurt. *Player Piano*. 1952. New York: Avon, 1970. Print.

———. *The Last Interview and Other Conversations*. Ed. Tom McCartan. Brooklyn: Melville House, 2011.

Waldo, Terry. *This Is Ragtime*. Foreword by Eubie Blake. New York: Da Capo, 1991. Print.

"Wallichs' 'New Look' Spurs Music City Chain's Profits." *Billboard Newspaper*. Issue 18 (December 1971):3,66. Print.

Watts, Cedric. "Introduction." *Heart of Darkness and Other Tales*. By Joseph Conrad. Oxford: Oxford University Press, 2008. Print.

Weisenburger, Steven C. *A* Gravity's Rainbow *Companion*. Second edition. Athens and London: The University of Georgia Press, 2006. Print.

———. "Thomas Pynchon at Twenty-Two: A Recovered Autobiographical Sketch." *American Literature* Vol. 62, No. 4 (Dec. 1990): 692–97. Print.

Wenzel, Haik, and Martin Häffner. *Legende Hohner Harmonika —Hohner: The Living Legend*. Bergkirchen: PPVMEDIEN, Edition Bochinsky, 2006. Print.

Werner-Jensen, Arnold, in collaboration with Franz Josef Ratte and Manfred Ernst. *Das Reclam Buch der Musik*. Stuttgart: Philipp Reclam jun., 2001. Print.

Westerath, Gerhard. "Pynchon's Parker Passage: A Source and Sound Analysis." *Pynchon Notes* 20–21 (1987): 109–14. Print.

Wild, David. "The Thomas Pynchon Connection." *Wildmusic. 1997*. Web. February 17, 2017. <http://wildmusic-jazz.com/oc_pynchon.htm>.

Williams, Martin. *The Jazz Tradition*. New York: Oxford University Press, 1970. Print.

Wilson, Rob. "On the Pacific Edge of Catastrophe, or Redemption: California Dreaming in Thomas Pynchon's *Inherent Vice*." *Boundary* 2 (Summer 2010): 217–25. Print.

Wimsatt, W.K., and Monroe C. Beardsley. "The Intentional Fallacy." *The Verbal Icon: Studies in the Meaning of Poetry*. By W.K. Wimsatt. Lexington: University of Kentucky Press, 1954. 3–18. Print.

Winston, Mathew. "The Quest for Pynchon." *Mindful Pleasures: Essays on Thomas Pynchon*. Ed. George Levine and David Leverenz. Boston/Toronto: Little, Brown and Company, 1976. 251–64. Print.

Winthrop-Young, Geoffrey. "Drill and Distraction in the Yellow Submarine: On the Dominance of War in Friedrich Kittler's Media Theory." *Critical Inquiry*, Vol. 28, No. 4 (Summer 2002): 825–54. Print.

———. *Friedrich Kittler zur Einführung*. Hamburg: Junius Verlag, 2005. Print.

Winthrop-Young, Geoffrey and Michael Wutz. "Translators' Introduction." *Gramophone Film Typewriter*. By Friedrich A. Kittler. Stanford: Stanford University Press, 1999. xi–xxxviii. Print.

Witen, Michelle. *James Joyce and Absolute Music*. London: Bloomsbury Academic, 2018. Print.

Witzling, David. *Everybody's America: Thomas Pynchon, Race, and the Cultures of Postmodernism*. New York: Routledge, 2008. Print.

———. "The Sensibility of Postmodern Whiteness in *V.*, or Thomas Pynchon's Identity Problem." *Contemporary Literature* Vol. 47, No. 3 (Fall 2006): 381–415. Print.

Wolf, Werner. "Literature and Music: Theory." *Handbook of Intermediality: Literature—Image—Sound—Music*. Ed. Gabriele Rippl. Berlin/Boston: Walter DeGruyter, 2015. 459–73. Print.

———. *The Musicalization of Fiction: A Study in the Theory and History of Intermediality*. Amsterdam/Atlanta, GA: Editions Rodopi, 1999. Print.

Wordsworth, William. "From the Preface to Lyrical Ballads." *The Arnold Anthology of British and Irish Literature*. Ed. R. Clark and T. Healy. London: Arnold, 1997. 673–77. Print.

WW2 People's War: An Archive of World War Two Memories—written by the public, gathered by the BBC. Web. February 17, 2017. <www.bbc.co.uk/history/ww2peopleswar>.

Zappa, Frank, and Peter Occhiogrosso. *The Real Frank Zappa Book*. London: Picador, 1989. Print.

Žižek, Slavoj. *Welcome to the Desert of the Real*. London–New York: Verso, 2002. Print.

Index of Musicians

This index lists all historical musicians, librettists, instrument makers, and ethnomusicologists mentioned in the main text of this book. References in the Pynchon Playlist are only included when the respective name is mentioned in the main text.

Acknowledgments

Writing a book may be a solitary activity but it is rare that one can accomplish it entirely on one's own. My boundless gratitude extends first of all to my readers Philipp Schweighauser, Peter Price, and Sascha Pöhlmann. Without their support and ideas, I would not have been able to write this book. Period.

Then, to other people and institutions who supported the publication of the book. Avital Ronell, Steven Shaviro, and John M. Krafft for writing blurbs, and John in particular for his helpful comments and corrections; the good people at Diaphanes, particularly Michael Heitz, and my copy-editor Catherine Lupton; and the Swiss National Science Foundation whose significant financial support made it possible to publish this book both in print and open-access.

Then, to the musicians who accompanied my public lectures and events on the topic (in order of appearance): Tyler Burba (vocal, guitar, ukulele, harmonica, kazoo in New York City, Philadelphia, and Zürich), Peter Price (kazoos and electronics in Philadelphia), Caleb Herron (kazoo) and Reese Burgan (saxes) in Atlanta, and Michelle Witen with a wall-shaking rendition of "Nessun' dorma" at Cabaret Voltaire.

Then, to an assortment of Pynchon scholars (in counter-alphabetical first-name order), including Yorgos Maragos, Umberto Rossi, Terry Reilly, Tore Rye Andersen, Tim Ware, Thoren Opitz, Sergej Macura, Sean Carswell, Nina Engelhardt, Michel Ryckx, Martin Paul Eve, Luc Herman, Kostas Kaltsas, Gilles Chamerois, Inger H. Dalsgaard, David Cowart, Bénédicte Chorier-Fryd, and Ali Chetwynd. Apologies, as always, for undue omissions. The entire scholarly Pynchon community has been nothing but kind and helpful.

Then, to many friends who took an interest in my undertaking, who hosted me on my peregrinations metaphorical and otherwise, and who contributed with their wisdom. In alphabetical order, not claiming to be complete, let alone exhaustive: Alejo Duque, Andreas Hägler, Ania Mauruschat, Berit Soli-Holt, Christopher Peckham, David Procuniar, Freya Price, Heidi Klose, Heidi Walter, Jacob Miller, Jake McNeill, Jamie Allen, Jenn McCranie, Jennifer Davy, Jeremy Fernando, Jess Holl, Joshua Taylor, Julia Hölzl, Karin Schraner, Kristian Marti, Martin Heinrich, Mathis

Füssler, McManus Woodend, Megan Bridge, Michael Koller, Michelle Miller, Michelle Witen, Paul Boshears, Paul D. Miller, Ridvan Askin, Ryan Kopaitich, Sandra Lang, Stephen Reyna, Tristan Price, Viola Marchi, and Will Sims. And, of course, my family and the countless, nameless contributors to the Pynchon Wikis. Sincere apologies for undue omissions.

I also want to honor my teachers who, more or less unwittingly, shaped my thinking and in various ways left their marks in this book. To name but a few, in no particular order: Michael Schmidt, Wolfgang Schirmacher, Avital Ronell, Siegfried Zielinski, Sylvère Lotringer, Alain Badiou, Hubert Thüring, Manuel Delanda, Chris Kraus, Patrick Henderson, Dave Sisler, Marcel Danesi, David Cook, Alexander Honold, Nicola Gess, Paul Virilio, Slavoj Žižek, Column McCann, Jean-Luc Nancy, Larry Rickels, and Martin Hielscher.

I would like to acknowledge the financial support I received from the Freiwillige Akademische Gesellschaft Basel (for my dissertation), the James Fenimore Cooper fund of the English Department at the University of Basel (for a research and lecture tour of the USA in 2015), and the English Department at the University of Basel (for another, shorter research and lecture trip to Philadelphia and New York City in 2016).

Finally, many thanks to all the venues and organizers that allowed me to present my work in progress: thefidget space, Philadelphia PA; the Plotting Poetry/Machiner la poésie conference and the EUCOR conference at the University of Basel; the America and the Musical Unconscious conference at Ludwig-Maximilians-Universität in Munich; the International Pynchon Week in La Rochelle, France; Eyedrum Art & Music Gallery in Atlanta GA; The Bookshop in Phoenix AZ; Marlene Tavern & Wine Bar in Sunnyside NY; Whitebox Gallery in Manhattan NY; Cabaret Voltaire and Rote Fabrik in Zurich; and the Breitzeit broadcast on Radio Stadtfilter in Winterthur, Switzerland.

Basel/Zurich, March 2020